False Dawn

Markets and Governments in Economic History

A SERIES EDITED BY PRICE FISHBACK

Also in the series:

The Young Fed: The Banking Crises of the 1920s and the Making of a Lender of Last Resort
by Mark Carlson

The Continental Dollar: How the American Revolution Was Financed with Paper Money
by Farley Grubb

Law and the Economy in a Young Democracy: India 1947 and Beyond
by Tirthankar Roy and Anand V. Swamy

From Old Regime to Industrial State: A History of German Industrialization from the Eighteenth Century to World War I
by Richard H. Tilly and Michel Kopsidis

Bankrupt in America: A History of Debtors, Their Creditors, and the Laws in the Twentieth Century
by Mary Eschelbach Hansen and Bradley A. Hansen

Hawai'i: Eight Hundred Years of Political and Economic Change
by Sumner La Croix

A Land of Milk and Butter: How Elites Created the Modern Danish Dairy Industry
by Markus Lampe and Paul Sharp

Deconstructing the Monolith: The Microeconomics of the National Industrial Recovery Act
by Jason E. Taylor

The Public Good and the Brazilian State: Municipal Finance and Public Services in São Paulo 1822–1930
by Anne G. Hanley

Selling Power: Economics, Policy, and Electric Utilities Before 1940
by John L. Neufeld

Law and the Economy in Colonial India
by Tirthankar Roy and Anand V. Swamy

Golden Rules: The Origins of California Water Law in the Gold Rush
by Mark Kanazawa

The Pox of Liberty: How the Constitution Left Americans Rich, Free, and Prone to Infection
by Werner Troesken

Well Worth Saving: How the New Deal Safeguarded Home Ownership
by Price Fishback, Jonathan Rose, and Kenneth Snowden

The Charleston Orphan House: Children's Lives in the First Public Orphanage in America
by John Murray

The Institutional Revolution: Measurement and the Economic Emergence of the Modern World
by Douglas W. Allen

FALSE DAWN

The New Deal and the Promise of Recovery, 1933–1947

GEORGE SELGIN

The University of Chicago Press
Chicago and London

The University of Chicago Press, Chicago 60637
The University of Chicago Press, Ltd., London
© 2025 by The University of Chicago
Published 2025
Printed in the United States of America

34 33 32 31 30 29 28 27 26 25   1 2 3 4 5

ISBN-13: 978-0-226-83293-7 (cloth)
ISBN-13: 978-0-226-83899-1 (e-book)
DOI: https://doi.org/10.7208/chicago/9780226838991.001.0001

Library of Congress Cataloging-in-Publication Data

Names: Selgin, George A., 1957– author.
Title: False dawn : the New Deal and the promise of recovery, 1933–1947 /
    George Selgin.
Other titles: Markets and governments in economic history.
Description: Chicago : The University of Chicago Press, 2025. |
    Series: Markets and governments in economic history |
    Includes bibliographical references and index.
Identifiers: LCCN 2024035543 | ISBN 9780226832937 (cloth) |
    ISBN 9780226838991 (ebook)
Subjects: LCSH: New Deal, 1933–1939. | United States—Economic
    conditions—1918–1945.
Classification: LCC HC106.3 .S364 2025 | DDC 330.973—dc23/eng/20240904
LC record available at https://lccn.loc.gov/2024035543

♾ This paper meets the requirements of ANSI/NISO Z39.48-1992 (Permanence of Paper).

A Lara

Hope is a good breakfast, but it is a bad supper.

FRANCIS BACON

A Lara

Hope is a good breakfast, but it is a bad supper.

FRANCIS BACON

Contents

Illustrations

Figures

Tables

Preface

Anyone who dares to add another book to the vast heap of writings on the Great Depression and the New Deal had better have a good excuse for doing so. Having plowed through no small part of that heap, I think I have one. There is no book specifically aimed at answering these questions: How did the United States recover from the Great Depression? And what was the New Deal's contribution to that recovery?

Yet it is largely thanks to disagreements concerning the answers to these questions that the New Deal is still a hot topic. Every severe downturn has one set of pundits taking the New Deal's success at combating the Depression for granted and calling for a new one, and another replying that far from helping, the original only made things worse.

Such blunt commentaries are better at bolstering preconceived opinions than they are at shedding light on the New Deal's actual role in the recovery. Of course the New Deal didn't end the Depression: despite the occasional op-ed or blog post saying otherwise, no competent economic historian thinks so. Nor could any American adult alive in 1939, when the New Deal had ended and Europe was about to go to war, have thought so. But there were times, such as the summer of 1933 and the first months of 1937, when the New Deal seemed to be doing the trick. The hopes it raised on those occasions were dashed. But it doesn't follow that New Deal policies dashed them.

The New Deal's critics, on the other hand, hardly enlighten us by crediting World War II, instead of the New Deal, with ending the Depression. Even if it were true, the claim wouldn't supply useful advice for dealing with the next downturn. But the shortcomings of the hypothesis that World War II ended the Great Depression run deeper. Although it's certainly true that massive wartime spending on military matériel got factories running again, while the armed forces' drafting or recruitment of over 16 million persons replaced a labor surplus with a labor shortage, they could only do these things while the war lasted. The real key to recovery consisted not of temporary wartime changes but of whatever it was that kept the Depression from cropping up again after 1945, when military spending shrank as dramatically as it had risen and millions of troops were thrust back into civilian life. If the war can't account for the Depression's permanent end, perhaps slow-working New Deal policies did the job after all.

It should go without saying that it's hardly likely that *every* New Deal policy helped bring about recovery or that *all* New Deal policies stood in recovery's way. The question therefore isn't whether we should ever consider reviving the New Deal lock, stock, and barrel but whether we should ever resort again to specific parts of it and, if so, which. That means taking a close look at *particular* New Deal policies to see how each influenced the course of production and employment. This will tell us which ones to consider reviving. It will also tell us which ones to avoid like the plague.

Although I've written *False Dawn* to fit this bill and I believe that its overall portrayal of the New Deal's contribution to economic recovery is distinct from that found in most other works on the topic, the portrayal is nonetheless a synthesis of findings of numerous other scholars. Economists and economic historians, in particular, have had plenty to say about the consequences of various New Deal policies, why the Great Depression lasted as long as it did, and how the United States finally got out of it. But while their findings have occasionally been gathered into books aimed at general readers, there's still room for a fresh effort. Concerning previous works, Lester Chandler's *The Great Depression* (1970), though superb in its day, is now very long in the tooth. Elliot Rosen's *Roosevelt, The Great Depression, and the Economics of Recovery* (2005) is more recent, and its title suggests a work with the same purpose as mine. But Rosen's book is more concerned with the origins and evolution of New Deal economic policies than with assessing those policies' consequences. As its title suggests, Jim Powell's otherwise excellent survey *FDR's Folly: How Roosevelt and His New Deal Prolonged the Great Depression* (2003) is only concerned with the debit side of the New Deal balance sheet. Finally, parts of Gene Smiley's *Rethinking the Great Depression* (2002) might serve as a digest of my own effort. But like Powell's book, Smiley's book is now over two decades old.

Two decades may not seem a long time. Yet a glance at *False Dawn*'s list of references will show that the literature on the economic consequences of the New Deal, mostly consisting of articles in academic journals and working papers intended for other experts, has grown immensely since 2004. Nor is the reference list's significance merely a matter of quantity. Collectively these works substantially modify, when they don't radically alter, our understanding of the New Deal's consequences, including its bearing on recovery. The time is overdue for the findings of these journal articles and working papers to be reconciled with earlier research, with the whole served up as a meal nonexpert readers can digest.

Having said what *False Dawn* is, I had better say what it isn't. It isn't—and I hope no one will take it to be—a polemic. None of us can entirely escape our prejudices, and I don't pretend to have escaped mine. Of political partisanship in its usually understood sense I can safely declare myself quite free. But I have other prejudices that, as far as this topic is concerned, are those of a neoclassical economist with a libertarian bent. Knowing this, I've striven to base my arguments on academic studies and to steer clear of polemical works. While I don't hesitate to point out what I consider to be the New Deal's failures, I've also tried to recognize its successes. If strident critics of the New Deal find grist for their mills here, they will also encounter arguments and evidence contradicting some of their cherished beliefs, including the belief that the New Deal was a failed exercise in Keynesian economics.

I should also make clear that *False Dawn* is a critique of the New Deal as a recovery program only, not a critique of the New Deal tout court. Franklin Delano Roosevelt famously identified his administration's goals as those of relief, recovery, and reform. My concern is with recovery. If I discuss New Deal programs with other aims, I do so only because those programs also either contributed to or discouraged recovery. It follows that I have little to say concerning the New Deal's longer-term legacy. Whether that legacy would make the New Deal worth it even if it lengthened the Depression instead of shortening it is for others to decide.[1]

False Dawn also steers clear of bold counterfactuals. It says nothing—and isn't meant to imply anything—about what Herbert Hoover or any other politician might have done in FDR's place. This book's concern is policies, not politicians. Just what course the Depression would have taken had Hoover been reelected in 1932, or had Alf Landon—or Huey Long!—been elected in 1936, is for more venturesome minds than mine to pronounce upon.

Finally, *False Dawn* isn't meant just for academics and other experts. Its intended audience includes anyone interested in the Great Depression or the New Deal or anyone who just wants to learn more about how governments can and cannot fight recessions and depressions. For those readers' sakes, I've left out the more technical details of statistical and theoretical works to which I refer. I've also tried my best to avoid both economics jargon and the stilted mannerisms and bombast characteristic of so much academic prose.

* * *

Many people made it possible for me to write this book. Foremost are my colleagues at the Cato Institute, including its president, Peter Goettler, and Norbert Michel, my immediate boss and head of Cato's Center for Monetary and Financial Alternatives (CMFA), who allowed me to devote myself almost exclusively to this project for more than a year. In doing so, they took a gamble on this book and on me, for which I very much hope my efforts will reward them.

I also owe thanks to my other CMFA colleagues for their encouragement and help, and especially to Nick Anthony, who helped me prepare the original series of online essays that served as this book's foundation, and to Nick Thielman, whose help in turning that foundation into a finished work has been absolutely indispensable.

Writing a book is one thing; giving it a fighting chance of being noticed and read is another. For doing that, I thank my publisher, the University of Chicago Press; Chad Zimmerman, the executive editor of its book division; and Price Fishback, who edits the Markets and Governments in Economic History series to which this book belongs. They also took a chance on me and my ambitious book proposal, and I very much hope they will think I pulled that proposal off. I'm also grateful to Yvonne Ramsey for her expert copyediting and for letting me have my way with commas.

As must be the case for the author of any work of synthesis, I've relied very heavily on the work of other experts, including feedback from several who were kind enough to read parts of my work in progress. I hope I'm remembering them all in naming Don Boudreaux, Mark Carlson, Charles Calomiris, Sebastian Edwards, Price Fishback, Claudia Goldin, Joshua Hausman, David Henderson, Doug Irwin, Deirdre McCloskey, Joseph Mason, Gabriel Mathy, Chris Meissner, Valerie Ramey, Gary Richardson, Gene Smiley, Scott Sumner, Nathan Tankus, Jason Taylor, David Wheelock, and Lawrence White.

My brother, Peter Selgin, has always encouraged me in all my projects, and this one is no exception. Among his many talents, Peter is a professional cover designer and is responsible for this book's lovely cover.

Finally, I wish to thank all the *granadinos* who have befriended me since I moved to their lovely city, where I proceeded to finish this book, in October 2022. They've been like a second family to me, and anyone who writes a book is bound to try his family's patience if only by often secluding himself from them. My Spanish friends have borne it well; beyond that, they made it possible for me to complete this project without undue strain by occasionally helping me to forget all about it.

Granada, Spain
January 2024

PART I

Groundwork

The Record

If you are reading this book not long after its appearance, have been living in the United States, and are at least two decades old, you've lived through two of your country's worst business downturns.

Although the COVID-19 recession officially lasted only two months, from February until April 2020, and was followed by a quick recovery, it involved an almost complete shutdown of the US economy, the deepest plunge of real gross domestic product (GDP) since the 1930s, and a peak unemployment rate of almost 15 percent.

The downturn of 2007–2009, though less sharp, was no less awful: during that period the US housing market collapsed, taking some of the country's largest financial institutions down with it. By the time the economy bottomed out in the summer of 2009, experts were already calling it the "Great Recession" (Rampell 2019). Yet that was just the beginning: the unemployment rolls kept swelling until October 2009, when over a tenth of the nation's workers were unemployed. And in what economists dubbed the "jobless recovery," many stayed unemployed long afterward. The recovery of medium household earnings was even more sluggish: it took until 2016, nine years after the recession started, for them to return to their prerecession level.

So, assuming you're one of those readers, you've seen your share of hard times. And yet, relatively speaking, you haven't seen anything. You haven't seen a Great *Depression*. And, God willing, you never will.

The Great Depression remains *the big one*, the mother of all downturns. It was both much deeper than the COVID-19 recession, with a quarter of the labor force out of work at one point, and much longer lasting than the Great Recession. Yet the Great Depression was also the first downturn the federal government made a concerted effort to end, using what it considered to be all the resources at its disposal and what many of its critics considered to be more resources than it could safely dispose of. The government was Franklin Roosevelt's, and the effort to end the Depression was part of the Roosevelt administration's package of reforms known as the New Deal.

Why did the US economy take so long to recover from the Great Depression? How did it finally manage to do so? And how does the New Deal figure in the answers to both questions?

Asking these questions is, admittedly, asking for trouble. Responses to them tend to be passionate, partisan, and extreme. A search for the combination "New Deal" and "Great Depression" on X.com (formerly Twitter.com) quickly yields two sets of opposite replies. One has the New Deal resulting in "a resounding recovery from the Great Depression" or words to that effect. The other says that instead of helping, the New Deal delayed recovery from the Depression "for a decade." Such opinions are often based on nothing beyond their utterers' political leanings. But the topic is just as capable of putting professional economists and historians, who have a lot more than their politics to go by, at loggerheads.

Coming to Terms

If prejudices tend to grow "firm as weeds among stone,"[1] so that we can never quite rid ourselves of them, we can at least try to avoid disputes having no basis other than confusion about terms' meanings. So, by the "New Deal" I mean the various projects and regulations supported and carried out by the Roosevelt administration between early March 1933 and the end of 1939. By the "Great Depression" I mean the collapse of economic activity and its subsequent, incomplete recovery in the United States between 1929 and sometime after the start of World War II.

Although these meanings shouldn't be controversial, one occasionally sees different ones. For example, although almost all authorities have the New Deal lasting until 1939, the New Deal is sometimes used to refer to the Roosevelt administration's pre-1935 program only, a particularly "recovery minded" program now often called the "First New Deal" (Keller 1999, 657; see also Wilson 1966). Still other sources recognize not just a "Second New Deal" running from 1935 until 1939 but also a "Third New Deal," said to have continued through if not beyond World War II (Jeffries 1996).

The Great Depression, on the other hand, is often said to have ended by 1939 rather than later. But while it had ended by then in many countries, in the United States it dragged on. Some economists even claim that the US Great Depression only lasted until March 1933, because the economy started to recover then. But what ended that March is what Milton Friedman and Anna Schwartz (1963, 299) dub the "Great *Contraction*." The Great *Depression* is usually understood to have consisted of both that contraction and the protracted recovery that followed.

The Three Rs

During its famous first hundred days, the Roosevelt administration passed fifteen major pieces of legislation, creating roughly as many new federal agencies. These early efforts were followed by many others, and although several early Roosevelt administration interventions had Hoover administration roots, the scale and overall scope of New Deal undertakings was such that they constitute a fundamental change in the federal government's role, including its role in combating recessions, that has endured ever since.

But not all New Deal undertakings were aimed at promoting economic recovery. Instead, the New Deal had three distinct aims, famously summarized by Roosevelt during his fifth fireside chat as relief, recovery, and reform, and known ever since as the New Deal's "three R's" (Roosevelt 1938, 3:312–18). This doesn't mean that every New Deal effort can be neatly assigned to just one "R." A deficit-financed relief program, for example, might promote recovery simply by boosting demand. Relief and recovery are nonetheless different things. Roosevelt himself insisted on the difference. "Emergency relief under way and planned," he wrote in *Looking Forward*, "will succeed only in the vital work of maintaining life. But it corrects nothing" (Roosevelt 1933, 224). Reform was also, and more obviously, distinct from recovery. As we'll see, some New Deal reforms actually got in recovery's way.

Measuring Unemployment

Did New Deal programs on the whole hinder or promote recovery? Answering that question requires that we also define "recovery" and identify reliable measures of its progress. The definition is simple enough: by "recovery" I mean the return of real economic activity not just to its level before the Depression began but to a level consistent with full employment of the US labor force.

One often hears of the rapid pace of the US recovery after Roosevelt took office. But that speedy start was only the first brief chapter of a long and less happy story, one of a recovery that, in the words of economic historian Lester Chandler (1970, 1), was "tragically slow, halting, and incomplete." Consider the progress of employment. The solid line in figure 1.1 is the long-standing Bureau of Labor Statistics (BLS) unemployment measure developed by Stanley

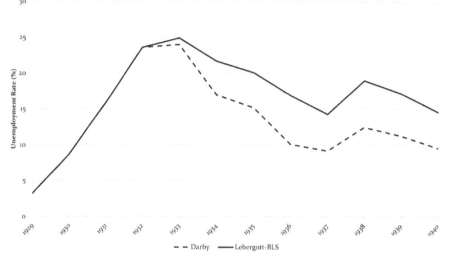

FIGURE 1.1. Lebergott-BLS and Darby unemployment rates, 1929–1940. (Data from Darby 1976, Table 2.)

Lebergott. This measure suggests that progress toward full employment was both far from steady and ultimately quite limited. From 3.2 percent in 1929 the BLS unemployment rate rose to just under 25 percent in 1933. By 1936 the rate had fallen to a little less than 17 percent. But it rose again, to 19 percent, in 1938 and was still 14.6 percent at decade's end. To put the last figure in perspective, the *peak* unemployment rate during the Great Recession, reached in October 2009, was less than 11 percent, while the peak for the short-lived 1920–1921 recession, which was then the highest rate since the 1890s, was 11.7 percent.

As for the dashed line, it shows a different measure of unemployment proposed some years ago in a highly influential article by Michael Darby (1976). It is different because Darby doesn't consider participants in New Deal work relief programs unemployed. Although his numbers still don't show unemployment dropping much below double digits (the lowest level, for 1937, is 9.1 percent), they paint a considerably less gloomy picture than the standard numbers do of the extent of unemployment during the New Deal.

Simple justice seems to favor Darby's alternative. Calling people "unemployed" just because theirs were "emergency" jobs, as if that meant doing nothing but leaning on shovels, is both misleading and uncharitable. Were the question simply whether, and to what extent, the New Deal kept people working, Darby's numbers would supply the better answer.

But our concern is with the progress of *recovery*, meaning the extent to which the gap separating actual from potential output has closed. And closing that gap meant not just keeping workers working but also getting them "real" (nonemergency) jobs (Smiley 1983, 493). The New Dealers themselves understood this. "What we had to do," Rexford Tugwell (1968, 304), one of the New Deal's principal architects, explains, referring to a discussion he had with Roosevelt during the 1932 campaign, "was to get the unemployed into those empty factories and mines, and back to running the railroads, rather than on to jobs provided by public agencies. This might not be easy or quick, but it was what was meant by recovery."[2] Henry Wallace's reckoning of the gap between actual and full employment during the 1930s was likewise consistent with Lebergott's numbers, not Darby's (Wallace 1945, 11; Santoni 1986).

It would be wrong, however, to view Darby's lumping together of emergency and ordinary workers as a mere matter of definitions. Instead, it reflects his belief that relief work served not to give employment to workers who would otherwise be unemployed but instead to give better-paying or otherwise more attractive jobs to workers who could have found ordinary jobs had they really tried. In short, like other New Classical economists, Darby questions the very notion that "involuntary" unemployment can persist for long, New Deal or no New Deal.

A Work-Relief Trap?

If Darby's understanding is correct, his unemployment series is, after all, a better guide to the progress of recovery than Lebergott's. This isn't necessarily good news for fans of the New Deal, because it means that instead of helping to get workers "into those empty factories and mines, and back to running the railroads," New Deal work relief programs were the only thing keeping them out!

But Darby's thesis isn't an easy one to swallow. Although relief workers were often accused of refusing outside job offers, when work relief agents looked into these complaints they often found that the accused workers weren't on their payrolls at all, that they'd only been offered seasonal work, or that the jobs they were offered paid "sweat shop" wages (Clague and Schwartz 1935, 295). Concerning New Haven's experience, E. Wight Bakke (1940, 369), director of Unemployment Studies at Yale University's Institute of Human Relations from 1934 to 1939, says that after "six years of attempts to find genuine cases of refusal of jobs with any claim to minimum standards, we have developed a thorough conviction that this state of affairs is so unusual as to be of no real concern to public administration."

Nor is it true, as some suppose, that relief work was more attractive than other work. The Roosevelt administration, for its part, had always intended relief work to be less so. The idea, Roosevelt (1938, 4:21) explained in his January 4, 1935 address to Congress, was to avoid encouraging "the rejection of opportunities for private employment or the leaving of private employment to engage in Government work." Roosevelt was then anticipating the creation of the Works Progress Administration (WPA), which would later replace—and vastly overshadow—previous New Deal work relief programs. At its peak during November 1938, the WPA employed more than 3.2 million workers.[3]

The wage policy Roosevelt referred to, with hourly wages set deliberately below those paid by private employers, was actually followed by the WPA at first. In 1936, however, under pressure from organized labor that policy gave way to one of paying workers "prevailing market rates" for their assigned job categories. But this change still left WPA workers with plenty of reasons for preferring to work elsewhere. Between 75 and 80 percent of them were, first of all, classified as "unskilled" and paid the lowest rate (Bremer 1975, 648). Furthermore, until 1939 their *monthly* earnings were capped at a "security wage" considered adequate for their families' subsistence, but no better. Consequently, many ended up earning less than what other work paid despite getting the same *hourly* pay. As William Bremer (648) points out, WPA workers' *monthly* earnings tended to be no greater than what they might have earned on general relief.

Finally, because relief workers were also "subjected to tests, investigations, and supervision traditionally applied to paupers and other unemployables," they could hardly escape the demoralizing effects of "perceiving themselves as 'charity' cases" (Bremer 1975, 646). "Try as Hopkins and his aides might to make the work vital and prideworthy," Frederick Lewis Allen (1940, 178) writes in *Since Yesterday,* his acute glance back at the depression decade, "the fact remained that it was made work, ill-paid, uncertain, undemanding of real quality of workmanship; and that the reliefers became perforce, by degrees, a sort of pariah class, unwelcome by private industry, dwelling in an economic twilight."

Harry Hopkins, who ran most of the large New Deal work relief programs, understood relief workers' plight as well as anyone. "Is it reasonable," he asked rhetorically, "to suppose that an American worker [on work relief] will reject private employment to remain in such a situation?" (quoted in Bremer 1975, 645).

Whether one considers Darby's claims reasonable or not, there is plenty of evidence that instead of rejecting private employment, relief workers simply couldn't find it. That evidence starts, Jonathan Kesselman and N. E. Savin (1978) note in response to Darby, with the millions of workers Darby himself considers unemployed, many of whom were no less employable than those on work relief. If there were plenty of private jobs to be had, why didn't those poor souls snap them up? The fact that they didn't, together with the results of a painstaking econometric test of Darby's hypothesis, led Kesselman and Savin to conclude that had workers employed by New Deal programs been thrown into the labor market, few if any would actually have found gainful employment there.

Plenty of direct evidence supports Kesselman and Savin's conjecture. "Even at the depths of the depression," Richard Jensen (1989, 564) points out, factories were hiring a million workers every three to four months." But they were also reviewing "several applicants . . . for every vacancy," so that "millions of applicants . . . were turned away at the hiring gate" (560). The applicants chosen tended to be not the cheapest but rather those who seemed likely to be most productive or at least without "obvious faults." That many job openings were for skilled rather than unskilled workers itself put most relief workers at a disadvantage. But that wasn't all. When it came to choosing among unskilled applicants, many employers considered being on work relief itself an "obvious fault." Nor was there any shortage of non-WPA unskilled workers. On the contrary, a 1937 *Fortune* magazine study found that if employers wanted unskilled workers, instead of turning to the WPA they could have them "merely by wagging a come-hither finger at the factory gates" (quoted in Freidel 1964, 119). Consequently, roughly half of all WPA workers dismissed during its history ended up either "relegated to the good offices of friends, relatives, and [other] relief agencies" or without any source of support at all (Howard 1943, 628–33).

Employers' tendency to spurn WPA workers wasn't entirely a matter of blind prejudice. The Depression's least employable workers—the "hard-core" unemployed—were especially likely to end up in work relief programs, some of which, including the WPA, were created with them specifically in mind (Jensen 1989, 580). "The cream of the crop who were on WPA in 1935," the above-mentioned *Fortune* study found, "have been absorbed by private employment. . . . Naturally, the men who are left on WPA tend to be older and slower workers. Where they have skills, these skills are negatived by age or physical disability. . . . [T]he private contractor would rather have had the benefit of younger, faster laborers" (quoted in Freidel 1964, 120).

Some (admittedly crude) estimates have such hard-core cases making up more than half and as much as 75 percent of all WPA workers at various times. Such workers' odds of finding other jobs were slim even by Great Depression standards. This point was driven home to those regional WPA administrators who either encouraged or required their workers to register with local unemployment offices. Many discovered to their chagrin that the employment offices made no attempt to place their workers because, when they first tried doing so, employers told them that they'd rather quit posting jobs with them than end up saddled with WPA workers (Howard 1943, 482–83).

Relief workers' odds of getting "real jobs" also shrank over time. In response (once again) to pressure from organized labor, the government refrained from offering those workers any sort of job training. The work they got also made little use of whatever skills they already possessed, causing those skills to "rust" (Jensen 1989, 577). According to a 1937 study of unemployed workers in Philadelphia, a male who'd been working for the WPA for less than a year had a 70 percent chance of getting a job within twelve months, whereas one who'd been there three or four years had only a 41 percent chance of doing so (Woytinsky 1942, 103). Gabriel Mathy (2018, 148) finds that there was "a strong relationship between the unemployment rate and unemployment duration" during the Depression and a correspondingly substantial unemployment "hysteresis effect."

The WPA supplies yet another sort of evidence against Darby's view. As Nancy Rose (1994, 80) reports, its "workers were required to accept private sector employment if it became available." Until 1937 they had to accept such employment even if it paid lower wages. Although this last requirement was dropped in 1937 due to pressure from labor unions, it was restored in 1939 when the so-called eighteen-month provision was adopted. That provision, Rose explains, "mandated that people who had been working on a WPA project for eighteen consecutive months had to be removed from the rolls and wait thirty days, during which they weren't eligible for general relief, before they could be reassigned to another project" (100).

The WPA's new rule set the stage for what economists call a "natural experiment," one that in this case served to test whether workers forced out of work relief were able to get jobs elsewhere. The results of that experiment seem conclusive: of 775,000 WPA workers dismissed under the eighteen-month provision during July and August 1939, fewer than 18 percent were able to find private-sector work, and about half of those could only find it at wages even lower than the WPA's measly "security wage" (US Department of Labor 1940; "Federal Agencies under New Set-up" 1939).

More recent attempts to determine, by statistical means, whether New Deal work relief programs crowded-out private employment have instead yielded mixed results. While the findings of an initial study by John Wallis and Daniel Benjamin (1981) are "strikingly at odds" with the crowding out hypothesis, a later study by Wallis and Benjamin (1981) finds some evidence of crowding out. Price Fishback, Shawn Kantor, and Todd Neumann (2004) also find indirect evidence of crowding out in the shape of a positive relation between relief spending and private-sector real wages. Finally, Robert Fleck (1999) concludes that while work relief programs may have resulted in inflated conventional unemployment statistics, they did so not by causing workers to forgo private-sector jobs but by causing workers to be classified as (BLS) unemployed who would otherwise have left the labor force. Because a good case can be made for including discouraged workers with unemployed ones in gauging the progress of recovery, Fleck's findings go against Darby's thesis.

To sum up, all things considered, although the long-standing BLS unemployment series may somewhat overstate the numbers of involuntarily unemployed workers during the New Deal, between that series and Darby's, with the latter's implicit assumption that anyone on work relief could have had a nonemergency job for the asking, the first probably paints the less distorted picture of the progress of recovery. Moreover, as we shall see, because nonrelief job growth during the first phase of the New Deal was mostly a consequence of job sharing, meaning the division of existing full-time jobs among larger numbers of workers, even the BLS numbers exaggerate that progress.

The Course of Output

Turning to the progress of real output, the picture here seems at first glance to put the New Deal in a much more favorable light. "Under the New Deal," Eric Rauchway (2015, 100) observes, "the US economy grew at rapid rates, even for an economy in recovery." Real GDP returned to its pre-Depression level by 1936 and, despite a serious setback in 1937–1938, ultimately surpassed it.

Here again, the statistics must be handled with care. Healthy economies tend to grow, so a mere return of output to its starting level or slightly above it after a decade is not much to brag about. A better measure of progress is the proximity of output to its precrisis trend path, usually estimated using a constant compound growth rate starting from a time, such as mid-1929, of full employment. The gap between actual US output and its pre-Depression trend remained substantial until the start of World War II, when the New Deal was set aside for the sake of rearming first Europe and then the United States itself. According to Lester Chandler (1970, 4), until the war the US gross national product (GNP) was never less than 20 percent and was sometimes more than 30 percent below its pre-Depression trend. Using a different method than Chandler's to estimate the path of full-employment or "potential" output during the 1930s, Robert J. Gordon and Robert Krenn (2010) arrive at very similar "output gap" estimates.

That unemployment was persistently high throughout the 1930s itself tells us that output could have been considerably higher than it was. Factories and equipment were correspondingly underutilized if not entirely idle. "The Depression years," Alexander Field (2013, 359) reports, "were disastrous from the standpoint of capacity utilization. . . . Double digit unemployment for more than a decade represented a terrible waste of human and other resources."

These observations raise a question: How could actual output have grown even as much as it did during the 1930s? The answer, Field says, is that despite the Depression, the decade witnessed remarkable improvements in total factor productivity (TFP), that is, the amount of real output the US economy was able to squeeze out of any given amount of land, labor, and capital. "Since private sector input growth was effectively absent, all of the growth in output was on account of TFP advance. And since there was virtually no capital deepening, almost all of the growth in output per hour (labour productivity) can also be attributed to TFP growth" (Field 2013, 367).

As for *why* productivity itself grew so rapidly during the 1930s, although the New Deal contributed to that growth, according to Field its contribution, mainly through the Public Works Administration's construction of streets and highways, was quite limited: the fruits of New Deal public works, though substantial, were mainly harvested after World War II. Instead, Field says, the coincidence of depression and TFP gains was fortuitous. Instead of being due to steps taken in the 1930s, the technology harvest of that decade was mostly due to seeds sown by inventors and investors during the previous two decades.

What about private business investment during the 1930s? In brief, despite the presence of many new investment opportunities, not to mention the investment needed to simply maintain the nation's pre-Depression capital stock, there wasn't much. Not until 1941 did *gross* private domestic investment approach its 1929 level. The closest it got during the 1930s was 74 percent in 1937. "In most of the other years," Chandler (1970, 132) says, "it was at least 40 percent below." Bad as that was, *net* fixed domestic investment for the 1930s as a whole was a much worse *minus* $3.1 billion. As Chandler notes, given prevailing levels of net foreign investment and government expenditure, the lack of private investment ruled out a full and sustainable recovery. Such a recovery called for a sum of private investment, net foreign investment, and government expenditures sufficient to offset "the large amounts that households and business would have saved out of a full-employment level of income" (132).

To summarize, if one wants to properly gauge the progress of economic recovery after any collapse, one can't simply look at the number of persons doing any sort of work or the amount of stuff being produced. One must ask how close the economy is to making full use of its valuable resources, including its labor force. How close, in other words, is it to achieving its full potential? If we ask that question of the US economy in 1939, when the New Deal had ceased to be an active legislative program, the answer is not close at all. On the contrary, as Frederick Lewis Allen (1940, 334) says, despite all the programs and promises, after a decade "the prosperity which had vanished in 1929" still seemed "as unattainable as a rainbow."

The International Picture

Another way to judge the progress of the US recovery is by comparing it with those of other nations. As figure 1.2, from a study by Barry Eichengreen, shows, despite rapid productivity growth, by 1937 the US index of industrial production was still below its 1929 level, having grown relatively slowly, in spurts, since 1932. In contrast, the indexes of most other European nations had increased steadily, surpassing their pre-Depression levels. France alone made even less progress than the United States.

Eichengreen's chart considers only seven countries and stops at 1937. But extending the chart to 1939 while adding data for Italy and other major economies hard hit by the Depression makes little difference. According to a chart so modified, the United States and France were still the big losers in the Great Depression recovery race. Only instead of at least beating France, the United States ends the decade neck and neck with it.[4]

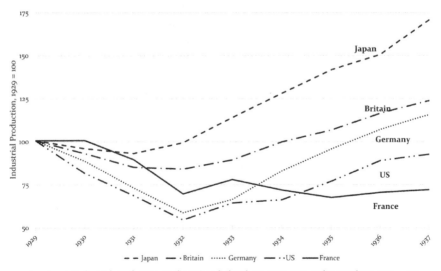

FIGURE 1.2. Industrial production in the US and elsewhere, 1929–1937, index numbers, 1929 = 100. (Source: Eichengreen 1992b, 233, Figure 5. Reproduced by permission of John Wiley and Sons.)

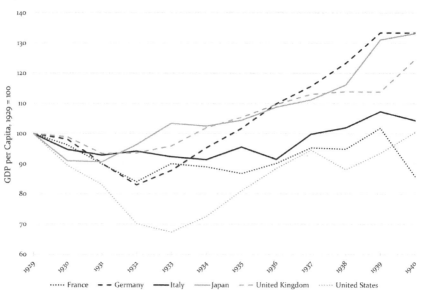

FIGURE 1.3. Per capita GDP in six countries, 1929–1940, index numbers, 1929 = 100. (Data courtesy of the Maddison Project Database, version 2020.)

Figure 1.3 shows how living standards in the United States and elsewhere, represented by Angus Maddison's per capita GDP estimates, evolved during the 1930s. It took until 1940 for the average US citizen to once again enjoy the same standard of living as in 1929. Until the war began, even France managed to do somewhat better. The average citizens of Germany, the United Kingdom, and Japan all ended the decade *much* better off than at its start, although it's only fair to note that Japan only had to recover from a relatively mild depression. The average Italian did better than the average American or Frenchman although not as well as the average German, Japanese, or Briton.

Returning to unemployment, according to the League of Nations (1939, 124–27), out of eighteen industrial countries for which data could be secured only two—the United States and France—had fewer persons working fewer overall hours in 1938 than in 1929.[5] All the rest experienced gains, and many experienced substantial gains, in at least one of those two measures of employment.

Because the size of a nation's labor force can change substantially over a decade, neither changes in total persons employed nor changes in total hours worked can serve as a reliable indicator of progress toward "full" employment. For that, unemployment rates must be considered. But comparing different nations' overall unemployment rates is tricky, because many lack reliable overall unemployment statistics. Statistics for *industrial* unemployment

TABLE 1.1. Industrial unemployment rates in eleven countries, 1920–1939 (Data from Grossman and Meissner 2010, table 1, 319)

Country Year	Australia	Belgium	Canada	Denmark	France	Germany	Netherlands	Norway	Sweden	UK	US
1920	5.5		4.6	6.1		3.8	5.8	2.3	5.4	3.2	8.6
1921	10.4	9.7	8.9	19.7	5.0	2.8	9.0	17.7	26.6	17.0	19.5
1922	8.5	3.1	7.1	19.3	2.9	1.5	11.0	17.1	22.9	14.3	11.4
1923	6.2	1.0	4.9	12.7	2.0	10.2	11.2	10.7	12.5	11.7	4.1
1924	7.8	1.0	7.1	10.7	3.0	13.1	8.8	8.5	10.1	10.3	8.3
1925	7.8	1.5	7.0	14.7	3.0	6.8	8.1	13.2	11.0	11.3	5.4
1926	6.3	1.4	4.7	20.7	3.0	18.0	7.3	24.3	12.2	12.5	2.9
1927	6.2	1.8	2.9	22.5	11.0	8.8	7.5	25.4	12.0	9.7	5.4
1928	10.0	0.9	2.6	18.5	4.0	8.6	5.6	19.2	10.6	10.8	6.9
1929	10.2	1.3	4.2	15.5	1.0	13.3	2.9	15.4	10.2	10.4	5.3
1930	18.4	3.6	12.9	13.7	2.0	22.7	7.8	16.6	11.9	16.1	14.2
1931	26.5	10.9	17.4	17.9	6.5	34.3	14.8	22.5	16.8	21.3	25.2
1932	28.1	19.0	26.0	31.7	15.4	43.8	25.3	30.8	22.4	22.1	36.3
1933	24.2	16.9	26.6	28.8	14.1	36.2	26.9	33.4	23.2	19.9	37.6
1934	19.6	18.9	20.6	22.2	13.8	20.5	28.0	30.7	18.0	16.7	32.6
1935	15.6	17.8	19.1	19.7	14.5	16.2	31.7	25.3	15.0	15.5	30.2
1936	11.3	13.5	16.7	19.3	10.4	12.0	32.7	18.8	12.7	13.1	25.4
1937	7.4	11.5	12.5	21.9	7.4	6.9	26.9	20.0	10.8	10.8	21.3
1938	7.8	14.0	15.1	21.5	7.8	3.2	25.0	22.0	10.9	12.9	27.9
1939	8.8	15.9	14.1	18.4	8.1	0.9	19.9	18.3	9.2	10.5	25.2

compiled by Walter Galenson and Arnold Zellner (1957) are, on the other hand, "reasonably reliable" as a basis for cross-country comparisons (Eichengreen and Hatton 1988, 8). Those statistics, shown in table 1.1, make the difference between the progress of recovery in the United States and its progress in most other industrialized countries appear especially glaring. Although the US industrial unemployment rate, having risen from 5.3 percent in 1929 to a peak of 37.6 percent in 1933, declined afterward, in 1939 more than a quarter of all US industrial workers were still either unemployed or on work relief. Only the Netherlands and Belgium had similarly poor records based on their pre-Depression unemployment rates. In contrast, the industrial unemployment rates of Australia, France, Germany, Sweden, and the United Kingdom had all fallen to 10.5 percent or less, with those of Australia, Germany, Sweden, and the United Kingdom close to or below their 1929 levels. Yet thanks largely to New Deal "work sharing" legislation, the United States also witnessed a more substantial reduction in daily and weekly full-time industrial work hours than elsewhere (Eichengreen and Hatton 1988, 18).[6]

As Eichengreen and Hatton (1988, 10) point out, "it would be a mistake to dismiss" the comparisons made here "as uninformative." But it would also be a mistake to conclude from them that the New Deal, in whole or in part, was to blame for the vacillating and incomplete US recovery. Both the severity of different nations' Great Depressions and the time it took for them to recover depended on all sorts of things, including whether they endured banking crises, how long they took to devalue their currencies, and how dependent they were on exports (Grossman and Meissner 2010). The only way to properly assess the New Deal's influence is by separately and carefully evaluating each New Deal policy, or at least each policy that is generally supposed to have mattered, whether by slowing the recovery or by hastening it.

Most of the chapters to come try to do this. But before we get to them, it is necessary to say more about what the New Deal was, and what it wasn't.

Inventing the New Deal

In *Winter War*, his account of the tense months between Roosevelt's election and his inauguration, Eric Rauchway (2015, 7) says that Franklin Roosevelt "campaigned on a clear and specific New Deal Program." "It is difficult," Rauchway says, "to think of an important aspect of the New Deal to which Roosevelt had not plainly pledged himself before taking office" (15). Other historians instead maintain that far from carrying out a coherent plan prepared and revealed well in advance, the New Deal was mostly cobbled together *after* Roosevelt took office.

Which perspective is closest to the truth? The answer matters not simply as a footnote to the history of the New Deal but because the different perspectives inform equally distinct portrayals of the New Deal's success at combating the Great Depression. Whereas the "coherent plan" view informs portrayals of the New Deal as a well-oiled economic recovery machine, the "cobbled together" alternative is easier to reconcile with its having occasionally bucked and stalled like an ill-tuned jalopy. For this reason, the merits of each perspective deserve close attention.

New Deal Revisionism

As Rauchway himself recognizes, the coherent plan view goes against most New Deal historiography, including works written by Roosevelt's intimates. These works bristle with claims to the effect that if Roosevelt did know what steps he planned to take once in office, he kept most of them to himself.

Although journalist Robert Wright (2001) indulges in poetic license when he writes that "FDR threw a bunch of policies against the wall, and the ones that stuck became the New Deal," his opinion isn't all that far removed from what most New Deal scholarship maintains. "Considered as an economic movement," Richard Hofstadter (1960) writes, the New Deal "was a chaos of experimentation." Alan Brinkley (2002, 2) describes the New Deal as a "blizzard of experiments that coexisted, and sometimes clashed, within the Roosevelt administration." According to Chandler (1970, 133), "neither at the time of his inauguration nor soon thereafter did [Roosevelt] have either a well-defined, ordered set of objectives or a set of strategies and tactics for promoting those objectives." Alberto Romasco (1983, 14, 27–28) says that although Roosevelt came to the White House equipped with "an imposing baggage of ideas from which he might pick and choose," because he let the decision on which to use "depend primarily upon events he had yet to confront . . . [t]he New Deal evolved, and its evolution was the product of a protracted process." By William Leuchtenburg's (1963, 11) reckoning, the results of that evolutionary process that Roosevelt's campaign failed to anticipate included "deficit spending, a gigantic federal works program, federal housing and slum clearance, massive and imaginative relief programs, [and] a national labor relations board with federal sanctions to enforce collective bargaining." Finally, the late Roosevelt biographer Roger Daniels (2015) turns Rauchway's opinion on its head. "The notion," Daniels says, "that when Franklin Roosevelt became president he had a plan in his head called the New Deal is a myth no serious scholar has ever believed" (131).

Rauchway is certainly a serious scholar. So how does he arrive at his contrarian opinion? In brief, he argues that (1) the New Deal *must* have been a coherent and well-advertised program as well as a radical one, for otherwise Herbert Hoover could not have made opposition to it the cornerstone of his 1932 campaign; (2) the memories and motives of Roosevelt's own colleagues and advisers who insist there was no plan can't be trusted; (3) other historians haven't examined the right documents; and (4) opinions such as Roger Daniels's can't be correct because they imply that Roosevelt misled voters, depriving his program of "democratic legitimacy," when in fact democratic legitimacy "was the New Deal's ultimate goal" (Rauchway 2018, 17).

To each of these arguments there's a straightforward answer. Concerning democratic legitimacy, that Roosevelt didn't tell voters just "what he was going to do" (Rauchway 2018, 17) needn't mean that he hoodwinked them. It could have meant nothing more than that Roosevelt himself hadn't decided on or couldn't otherwise anticipate many of the steps he'd take once in office. Concerning Hoover, although he did accuse the Democrats of "proposing changes and so-called new deals which would destroy the very foundations of our American system" (Hoover 1932a), it is of course common for candidates to accuse their opponents of harboring sinister intentions. If Hoover's frightening portrayal of Roosevelt's plans was unusual, it wasn't because it was based on things Roosevelt actually said, plainly or otherwise, but instead because Hoover seems to have sincerely believed it.[1] Concerning other historians' inability to consider crucial evidence, although Rauchway (2018, 17n27) refers to various manuscript collections that supposedly inform his position, he never points to any smoking guns.

On the other hand, Rauchway ignores or summarily dismisses the first-hand testimony of Raymond Moley, Frances Perkins, and Rexford Tugwell, three of Roosevelt's closest associates, to the effect that there was no coherent New Deal plan in 1932 or even in the first two months of 1933. According to Moley (1939, 370), the founding member of Roosevelt's so-called Brain Trust and, by November 1932, his main policy adviser, believing that New Deal policies were "the result of a unified plan" is like believing "that the accumulation of stuffed snakes, baseball pictures, school flags, old tennis shoes, carpenter's tools, and chemistry sets in a boys bedroom could have been put there by an interior decorator." Although Rauchway refers to Moley frequently, he doesn't mention this statement.

Dissing Frances Perkins

Because Moley parted company with Roosevelt in 1936 and then became both a conservative Republican and one of Roosevelt's more severe critics, Rauchway dismisses Moley's testimony as that of a disenchanted ex-acolyte. Such a dismissal hardly seems justified. Allowing that some of Moley's opinions must be taken with a grain of salt, the testimony of Roosevelt's key policy adviser during his campaign can hardly be said to have no probative value at all. Furthermore, Moley's eventual break with Roosevelt had to do with much later disagreements. Moley had no reason at all to misrepresent the nature and origins of the earliest and most famous phase of the New Deal, with which he was happy to be associated (Cohen 2009, 62). He also held fast to his 1939 view of the New Deal long after any old wounds must have healed, declaring as late as 1966 that instead of being "the product of a single integrated plan," it was "a loose collection of many ideas—some new, some borrowed from the past—with plenty of improvisations and compromises" (Moley 1966, xvii).

The charge of personal animus can by no means be leveled at Frances Perkins, who first served with Roosevelt in Albany, was his secretary of labor for all four of his terms in Washington, and was fiercely loyal to him. Yet Perkins's testimony entirely agrees with Moley's. In *The Roosevelt I Knew* (1946, 167), Perkins calls the idea that the New Deal was worked out before the 1932 election "ridiculous." "The pattern it was to assume," she says, "was not clear or specific in Roosevelt's mind, in the mind of the Democratic party, or in the mind of anyone else taking part in the 1932 campaign."

"*Not* clear or specific." Although Rauchway (2018, 15) refers to Perkins's claims, he avoids quoting these words that flatly contradict his own. Instead he says, condescendingly, that while "Perkins may have been a great secretary of labor, . . . she was a poor historian: not a word of her remarks is true."

Dismissing a firsthand witness for not also being a historian is odd, to say the least. And Rauchway's suggestion that Perkins wasn't capable of understanding and accurately reporting on the policies of an administration in which she played a key part is far from compelling. "In reminiscing," Rauchway (2018, 16) says, "she may merely have forgotten how things stood thirteen years before." But "ridiculous" isn't the sort of adjective one uses to describe something one recalls only vaguely; and Howard Taubman, who helped Perkins write *The Roosevelt I Knew,* considered her memory "extraordinarily good, particularly for detail" (Martin 1976, 473). Nor is it likely that Perkins's supposedly foggy memory inspired not only the passage in question but others to the very same effect. Thus, "when Franklin Roosevelt and his administration began their work in Washington in March 1933, the New Deal was not a plan with form and content. It was a happy phrase he had coined during the campaign, and its value was psychological. It made people feel better, and in that terrible period of depression they needed to feel better" (Perkins 1946, 166), and "it is important to repeat, the New Deal was not a plan, not even an agreement, and it was certainly not a plot, as was later charged" (173). The last statement reads almost as if Perkins wanted to make sure no future historian would attribute her other statements to mere forgetfulness!

Still other passages in Perkins's memoir illuminate her general claim by pointing to specific New Deal programs. For example, she says that as late as April 1933, Roosevelt's "mind was as innocent as a child's of any such program as the NRA [National Recovery Administration]" (Perkins 1946, 197). In short, far from being confined to scattered obiter dicta, Perkins's claim that the New Deal wasn't planned in advance forms one of her memoir's central themes.

Recognizing perhaps that questioning Perkins's memory won't do, Rauchway goes on to impugn her motives. "In reminiscing," Rauchway says (2018, 16), "Perkins may have wanted to minimize Roosevelt's own role in the New Deal so she could maximize her own." To label as "ungenerous" this accusation against someone elsewhere described as "a modest woman" with a "passion for veracity" who "didn't care if other people took credit" (Baker 2017; Tugwell 1968, 78) is itself being generous. As George Martin (1976, 474), Perkins's biographer, remarks, one of the "extraordinary qualities" of her memoir "is that it is so entirely about Roosevelt and so little about Perkins."

Although Moley and Perkins were especially adamant in claiming that the New Deal hadn't been worked out in 1932, they weren't the only New Dealers to say so. Looking back many years later at the New Deal's first year, Rexford Tugwell (1968), who also advised Roosevelt during the 1932 campaign before becoming his assistant secretary of agriculture, makes it clear that he himself wasn't sure what Roosevelt would do once in office. While Roosevelt sometimes gave Tugwell and others of his inner circle the impression that he planned to "emerge[] from the orthodox progressive chrysalis and [lead] us into a new world," instead he ultimately "chose rather rickety repairs for an old one" (xxi). "If now an observer brings himself to look beyond the year of action and through the haze of hope that so fortunately hid the facts of failure, he must see that the Roosevelt measures were really patches on agencies he ought to have abandoned forthwith when leadership was conferred on him in such unstinted measure" (xxii).

"Concerning what might be done about the depression," Tugwell (1968, xxv) adds, "there was no agreement." Pressed during the campaign by Tugwell and other members of his "Privy Council" to take up concrete ideas for ending the Depression, Roosevelt, who already tended "to evade all questions of substance" when speaking publicly, became "evasive even with us" (172–74). Months later, as election day approached, instead of having committed himself at last to one or a few of the many often incompatible plans that different Brain Trust factions had been urging on him, Roosevelt was "falling into absurd inconsistencies" (512). Nor did Roosevelt make up his mind during the interregnum. Instead, Tugwell says, when March 4 finally arrived, the new administration had to resort to "emergency makeshifts" (571).

So much for what Roosevelt made clear to his own advisers. Concerning what he told the public during his campaign, Tugwell (1957, 185) is still more blunt: "He said what would attract votes, not what he believed or even what he felt would have to be done. Thus he wound up without commitments."

Campaign Clues

To turn from the opinions of Roosevelt's associates to the facts of the case, they are, in brief, that while during the 1932 campaign many facets of what the New Deal came to mean had been recommended to Roosevelt by one or more of his many advisers, and Roosevelt was glad to consider them, he studiously avoided committing himself to most, either privately or publicly. In contrast, he *did* publicly pledge to uphold the Democratic platform expressly disavowing many of the policies he eventually put into practice.

Concerning what Roosevelt did make explicit, until his nomination his most revealing remarks, meaning ones that most accurately described the actual New Deal, came during his May 22, 1932, speech at Oglethorpe University (Roosevelt 1938, 1:639–47). Although he spoke then of "the vital necessity of planning for definite objectives," if he had some actual blueprint in mind, he said little about it. Instead, he famously declared that "the country demands bold, persistent experimentation. It is common sense to take a method and try it: If it fails, admit it frankly and try another. But above all, try something."

"Bold, persistent experimentation" was an accurate description of what the New Deal would entail. But this describes something much more like a plan to throw policies against a wall to see which ones stick than a "clear and specific . . . program" (Rauchway 2018, 7). The closest Roosevelt came in his Oglethorpe speech to revealing even part of such a program was when he declared it "self-evident that we must . . . restore commodities to a level approximating their dollar value of several years ago or else see more defaults or loan write-downs" (Roosevelt 1938, 1:644). Even then he didn't say *how* he planned to get "commodities" up again.

From the opening of the Democratic National Convention on June 27, 1932, the Democratic platform became the most complete official statement of its candidate's intentions. "We believe," the platform states, "that a party platform is a covenant with the people to have faithfully kept by the party when entrusted with power, and that the people are entitled to know in plain words the terms of the contract to which they are asked to subscribe" (Democratic National Convention 1932). Far from disavowing the platform, Roosevelt expressly endorsed it in his acceptance speech. "I have many things," he said, "on which I want to make my position clear at the earliest possible moment in this campaign. That admirable document, the platform which you have adopted, is clear. I accept it 100 percent. . . . And you can accept my pledge that I will leave no doubt or ambiguity on where I stand on any question of moment in this campaign" (Roosevelt 1932a).

In fact, Roosevelt's pledge to uphold the Democratic platform was one of the least ambiguous parts of his speech. "He promised to make his position clear," journalist Elmer Davis wrote, "and he did—upon the Prohibition plank. . . . For the rest, you could not quarrel with a single one of his generalities. But what they mean (if anything) is known only to Franklin D. Roosevelt and God" (quoted in Allen 1940, 81–82). Davis exaggerated, for Roosevelt also made clear his intent to have the government lighten the burden of mortgages that millions of farmers and home owners were then struggling to pay. But

Roosevelt's speech divulged little else in the way of details concerning his recovery program.

As for the Democratic platform itself, Frederick Lewis Allen (1940, 82) notes that while it listed several measures that would form part of the New Deal, far from giving any "hint of any intention to expand enormously the Federal power," it "represented in the main an old-fashioned liberalism—a return to the days of small and simple business units and modest and frugal government units." By way of promoting economic recovery, the platform promised (1) "an immediate and drastic reduction of governmental expenditures . . . to accomplish a saving of not less than twenty-five per cent in the cost of the Federal Government"; (2) "a federal budget annually balanced on the basis of accurate executive estimates within revenues, raised by a system of taxation levied on the principle of ability to pay"; (3) "a sound currency to be preserved at all hazards"; (4) "an international monetary conference called on the invitation of our government" for the purpose of preserving it; and (5) "a strengthening and impartial enforcement of the anti-trust laws, to prevent monopoly and unfair trade practices, and revision thereof for the better protection of labor and the small producer and distributor" (Democratic National Convention 1932). The platform also "condemn[ed] the extravagance of the [Hoover administration's] Farm Board," including its "unsound policy of restricting agricultural products to the demands of domestic markets." Reviewing these disparate commitments, Roosevelt's closest advisers found it "hard to believe that they were seriously meant to be taken as a whole" (Tugwell 1968, 379). Yet Roosevelt swore to take them all seriously.

As we'll see, Roosevelt did strive to cut spending and balance the federal budget, or that part of it not consisting of "emergency" spending. But he was ultimately unsuccessful on both scores, and today it is his failure to do either that's often wrongly considered a deliberate if not crucial part of the New Deal's recovery strategy. As for "strengthening and impartial enforcement of the anti-trust laws," the National Recovery Administration, one of the New Deal's centerpieces, of which Perkins says Roosevelt had no inkling before he was elected, was notorious for doing just the opposite (Hawley 1966). Another New Deal centerpiece, the Agricultural Adjustment Administration, would, through its "domestic allotment plan," implement the very "policy of restricting agricultural products to the demands of domestic markets" that the Democratic platform renounced.

To sustain the claim that the New Deal's agricultural recovery plan was announced in advance, Rauchway has to overlook Roosevelt's very public pledge to uphold the Democratic platform, including its rejection of any domestic allotment plan. He also has to argue that Roosevelt made his *support* for such a plan "clear" merely by "ruling out other production-controlling policies" (Rauchway 2018, 97).[2] The truth is that although Roosevelt hadn't ruled out the domestic allotment option when he spoke at Chicago, both there and in his public utterances throughout his campaign he "appeared almost merrily flexible on agriculture as compared to Hoover" (Fausold 1977, 374). Instead of committing himself to domestic allotment, Roosevelt "walk[ed] a thin line between advocating some ambiguous program to control crop surpluses and delineating any program that might alienate him from an established constituency" (Goldstein 1989, 44). "As the presidential campaign took shape," Gertrude Slichter (1956, 245) writes, "Roosevelt, having previously dodged any specific pledge to stabilize farm prices, was even more wary of any such commitment. Encouraging all suggestions, he gave a sympathetic ear, but no promises."

Nor was Roosevelt more forthcoming with farmers. During his Topeka, Kansas, address on the farm problem that September (Roosevelt 1932b), for example, he never mentioned "domestic allotment" and otherwise summarized his plan "so delicately," according to Ray Moley (1939, 45), as to "win the Midwest without waking up the dogs of the East." Among other omissions, Roosevelt's speech made no mention of "production control, reduced acreage, and a processing tax," referring only to "a tariff benefit which would raise farm income 'with-out stimulating further production'" (Slichter 1956, 254). Even once in office, despite having been encouraged to embrace the domestic allotment plan by Moley and Rex Tugwell and despite ultimately tapping Henry Wallace, a forthright advocate of that plan, for his secretary of agriculture, Roosevelt hedged his bets by appointing George Peek, an equally steadfast opponent of the domestic allotment plan who had also been in the running for the cabinet post (Tugwell 1965, 164), to head the Agricultural Adjustment Administration.

Turning to monetary policy, that the bank holiday and the Emergency Banking Act were adventitious measures rather than ones Roosevelt had been planning all along should go without saying. As we shall see, Roosevelt also remained adamantly opposed to deposit insurance—his position throughout his campaign—until the very eve of the passage of the Banking Act of 1933. His contribution to the "international monetary conference" promised by the Democratic platform ultimately consisted of little beyond a series of talks held in May and June of 1933 as preliminaries to the World Economic Conference scheduled to take place that summer in London. (The London Economic Conference itself, aimed at securing agreements that would both limit deflation and stabilize exchange rates, had been Hoover's idea.) According to Lewis Douglas, Roosevelt's director of the budget at the time, "the upshot" of those preliminary talks was "that if the London Economic Conference was not successful . . . Hitler would doubtless move his frontiers out by force" (Sargent 1973, 101). In fact, the London event ended up being torpedoed by Roosevelt, who surprised all concerned in it with a peevish telegram announcing the US decision to not take part in any exchange rate agreement. "There has never been a case," Neville Chamberlain (then Britain's chancellor of the exchequer) wrote afterward, "of a conference being so completely smashed by one of its participants." This doesn't mean that Roosevelt lacked reasons for doing what he did (see Eichengreen and Uzan 1993) or that other conference participants deserve no blame for its failure (see Clavin 2002). But far from having been anticipated by or consistent with Roosevelt's campaign pledges, his decision shocked even his own delegates to the London event.

As for the most controversial New Deal monetary measures, including the suspension of gold payments and the confiscation of all monetary gold, the abrogation of gold clauses in both private and government contracts, the gold purchase plan, and the dollar's formal devaluation, the Democratic platform's commitment to preserving a "sound currency . . . at all hazards" can hardly be said to have prepared anyone for them.

According to Ernest Lindley (1937, 61), the Democrats intentionally left the word "gold" out of their platform because "silverites and other advocates of price-lifting by monetary action were strong enough to keep it out." The fact remains, however, that "sound currency" is a variant of "sound money," from the French *monnaie sonnante et trébuchante*. Although that literally means "money that rings and stumbles," it has always stood for undiluted—as opposed to debased—precious metal coins, which do in fact sound unlike their debased counterparts when tossed onto and allowed to "stumble" on a hard surface. And ever since the great silver agitation of the 1890s, "sound money" stood specifically for *gold*. Certainly it would have surprised Republicans, whose own 1932 party platform included a passage promising "to defend and preserve a sound currency" without specifying gold, to have been told that "sound currency" could mean something else (Republican Party Platforms, 1932).

In fact, to practically everyone who read it in 1932, including James Warburg, a financially savvy banker who was yet another Roosevelt adviser and later felt bitterly betrayed by Roosevelt's decision to go off gold, the Democrats' promise to preserve "sound currency" could mean nothing other than that Roosevelt was also not planning to mess with the gold standard (Warburg 1935, 19–23).[3] On the very eve of Roosevelt's decision to go off gold, Warburg attests, "No one, so far as I know, in the Administration circles, unless it was the President himself, had any idea at that time of embarking upon the course which we subsequently followed" (Warburg 1934, 97). If members of Roosevelt's inner circle didn't anticipated his decision, it's hardly surprising that the business community was caught off guard. "When Roosevelt promised in his inaugural address to give the country a currency 'adequate but sound,'" the editor of the *Journal of Commerce* wrote two days after the United States indefinitely suspended gold payments, "it was taken for granted that he meant to maintain the gold standard and pursue fiscal policies that would put an end to deficit financiering" (Romasco 1983, 69).

The Democratic platform did anticipate, if only vaguely, some actual New Deal measures, including federal public works programs, the Glass-Steagall Act's separation of investment from commercial banking, the Tennessee Valley Authority, unemployment insurance, and social security. But the anticipated bits mostly had to do with relief and reform rather than recovery. So far as the voting public was concerned, the New Deal's overall *recovery* plan, if one existed at all, was a black box. According to Roosevelt's first authorized biographer (Lindley 1934, 37), Roosevelt's September 23, 1932, address at San Francisco's Commonwealth Club (Roosevelt 1932c) was "probably the fullest presentation of his economic philosophy." But "philosophy" was all: the address offered little in the way of concrete plans. According to Lindley (1934, 38, emphasis added), "The desirability of a more specific speech on the 'economic constitutional order' was discussed by Mr. Roosevelt and his brains trust. *At that time they had not chosen from among the many plans proposed or formulated a plan of their own.* For the purposes of the campaign, the development of a specific plan was superfluous; in fact, it was not to Mr. Roosevelt's political advantage to disturb his comparatively smooth course toward victory by raising a contentious issue to prominence with too much emphasis and detail."

A Secret New Deal?

Whatever specific promises the Democratic platform made, the public believed. Reporting just after the election, *The Economist* (October 29, 1932, quoted in Jamil and Rua 2016, 30) spoke for many when it said that it didn't "anticipate that any very radical experiments will be made." One might suppose that any remaining doubts concerning Roosevelt's intentions would have been dispelled during the interregnum, that is, the months separating his election from his inauguration. But as James MacGregor Burns (1956, 147) notes, "Despite the pleadings of reporters, despite the strictures of editorial writers, [Roosevelt] refused to issue statements on the sharpening economic crisis or to announce his plans. He merely waited."

So, instead of diminishing, doubts multiplied. A few weeks before the inauguration, *The Economist* noticed the change. "The market," it said, "has tacitly suspended action and judgment until the new Roosevelt administration has assumed office and *declared its policy on major questions*" (November 12, 1933; quoted in Burns 1956, 30, emphasis added). It would, of course, have been perfectly unnecessary for the incoming administration to "declare its policy on major questions" had Roosevelt "campaigned on a clear and specific New Deal Program."

That Roosevelt didn't clarify his plans, and that the specifics of the actual New Deal often ran counter to his less vague campaign pledges, raises two possibilities. One is that there really was no well worked out New Deal plan, as Raymond Moley, Frances Perkins, Rex Tugwell, and most historians have insisted. The other, which we must also consider, is that there *was* such a plan, blueprinting more or less what took place, but that Roosevelt kept it under his hat. This last possibility appears especially plausible with respect to his plans for the dollar. After all, if Roosevelt intended all along to suspend the gold standard and eventually devalue the dollar, he could hardly have afforded to put the word out in advance! That didn't stop Hoover from charging him with planning to abandon the gold standard in favor of "fiat money," and by early 1933 many had begun to suspect that Hoover was on to something. But did this mean that Roosevelt really had planned to dismantle the gold standard all along, or did it simply mean that the public had finally fallen for Hoover's FDR bogeyman?

The most plausible answer is neither. Roosevelt wanted to keep his options open. "I do not want to commit to the gold standard," he told Brain Trust member Adolf Berle a few days before the election (S. Edwards 2018, 19). "I haven't the faintest idea whether we will be on the gold standard on March 4th or not; nobody can foresee where we shall be." This was an astute position, but it spoke not of a definite plan for gold but of the folly of any such plan.

And it seems to have been Roosevelt's position all along. Having carefully looked into the matter, Sebastian Edwards (2017, abstract and 2) concludes "that during the primary and presidential campaigns, neither Roosevelt nor his inner circle had a strong view on gold or the dollar. . . . Tinkering with the value of the currency was a possible area for experimentation; but it was an option with a relatively low priority. . . . Until inauguration day FDR's views on the gold standard were ambivalent and noncommittal; he was neither a diehard fan of the system, nor . . . a severe critic."

In short, while Roosevelt certainly contemplated abandoning the gold standard during his campaign, he wasn't counting on it. What's more, nothing changed during the interregnum. "To put it simply," Edwards (2017, 30) says, "on March 4th . . . there was no concrete or definitive plan for taking the U.S. off gold and devaluing the dollar."

What was true of Roosevelt's secret plans for the dollar was almost certainly true of his other secret New Deal plans, namely, that he didn't have any. That is, there is no reason to disbelieve what Perkins, Moley, Tugwell, and most historians have had to say on this subject.

A Bright Thread

To insist that Roosevelt began his presidency with few specific plans for ending the Depression isn't to say that he lacked convictions, much less that he had no good reasons, if often only political ones, for the steps he eventually took. Rex Tugwell (1956, quoted in Sternshen 1964, 123) put the matter nicely by noting how "a bright thread of intention ran through the confusions and contradictions" of Roosevelt's election campaign. Among other things, Roosevelt, who had no patience with laissez-faire conservatism, intended to see the federal government—and the executive branch especially—assume responsibilities and wield powers never assumed or wielded by any previous administration. As Alan Brinkley (2002, 2) observes, this intention was of a piece with the "bold experimentation" Roosevelt promised, both having been products "of inherited ideologies that he and other New Dealers had derived from the reform battles of the first third of the century from which they felt at liberty to pick and choose."

In other words, despite what Hoover and some other New Deal opponents claimed, the "bright thread" that ran through Roosevelt's campaign wasn't red. But it also wasn't strong enough to keep the New Deal recovery program that eventually took shape from unraveling. The thing about bold experiments is that they often fail.

3

The Banking Crisis

When at noon on March 4, 1933—a drizzly Saturday—Franklin Roosevelt stood before the Capitol's East Portico to deliver his first inaugural address, the US economy had reached its nadir. Assuming that the tens of millions of Americans who listened to him were representative of the US population as a whole, more than a quarter of them were unemployed. Hundreds of thousands had lost their homes and their farms, and many more were haunted by the specter of foreclosure. Many who didn't hear Roosevelt that day couldn't because they were roaming the country in freight cars, looking for work, or living in Hoovervilles with neither radios nor electricity. Although the long downward slide of the US economy had begun almost four years earlier, at the start of 1933 no one realized that it had yet to reach bottom.

What brought the US economy to its nadir was a banking crisis—the last and worst of several—that culminated in a nationwide run not just on commercial banks but on the Federal Reserve System itself. By Friday, March 3, banks in thirty-seven states had either closed or placed severe limits on their depositors' withdrawals. Finally, on the very morning of the inauguration the Federal Reserve banks themselves shut their doors, with the intent of keeping them shut for some time (Jabaily 2013).

In short, when Roosevelt was sworn in, the US economy, or a large part of it, was closed for business.

Small Wasn't Beautiful

To understand how the world's largest economy ended up shutting down, one must appreciate the peculiar nature of its banking system and the laws that shaped it. Those laws led to the proliferation of small and underdiversified banks and, eventually, to waves of bank failures.

The existence of so many fragile banks during the decades leading to the Great Depression was largely a result of unit banking. A unit bank is a bank that conducts all its business at one location only instead of having, besides its headquarters, branches set up elsewhere. Although branch banking is now the rule, for most of US history it was the exception because laws made it so. In 1920, branching was altogether prohibited in eighteen states. Elsewhere it was allowed on a very limited basis only. In some cases, banks could only set up branches in the same town as their headquarters, while in a few they might have them elsewhere in the same state. Until as late as the 1980s, branching across state boundaries was almost unheard of (Neely 1994).

By the eve of World War I, or a few months before the Federal Reserve System opened for business, the combination of unit banking laws and low regulatory capital requirements of many state banking laws (national banks' minimum capital requirements tended to be higher) had led to the establishment of more than ten thousand tiny banks. Because the United States was then a predominantly rural nation—not until 1920 would more Americans live in cities than in the countryside—with farm output making up about a quarter of US private GDP, most of these banks served rural farm communities. Their fortunes were therefore necessarily bound up with those of the farmers they served, where those farmers' earnings in turn depended on the success of a small number of crops if not of a single crop. Unit banking laws also made it difficult for most banks in larger towns and cities to diversify their assets and liabilities, though not quite so severely.

Unit banks were extremely vulnerable to local economic shocks. So it's hardly surprising that economy-wide shocks, including panics such as those of 1884, 1893, and 1907, witnessed big clusters of bank failures including, though not necessarily limited to, failures of rural banks. Paradoxically, the Panic of 1907 ended up making matters worse by inspiring laws that led to the creation of even more weak banks. World War I would cause the number of such banks to grow still further.

The change brought by the Panic of 1907 consisted of deposit insurance schemes set up in eight states (Kansas, Mississippi, Nebraska, North Dakota, Oklahoma, Texas, South Dakota, and Washington) between then and 1917. According to David Wheelock (1995), the premiums that banks paid in these systems were small in comparison with, but otherwise unrelated to, the riskiness of their loans and other investments. Insurance therefore subsidized risky banks in states that adopted it.

The Great Farm Boom and Bust

But it was World War I that did the most to set the stage for the banking crises to follow. Because the war shut down many European farms and because troops needed to be fed, crop and livestock prices rose sharply, encouraging US farmers and ranchers to extend their acreage (Bryan 2012). When the United States entered the war, the Agricultural Cooperative Service egged farmers on further through a vigorous campaign aimed at getting them to farm more intensively using tractors and new methods of pest and weed control (Kosmerick 2017). New banks popped up in turn to finance farmers' purchases of land and tractors and other inputs using credit secured by mortgages. Between them, subsidized deposit insurance and the World War I farm boom caused the number of banks to more than double, from 12,427 to 30,291, between 1900 and 1920. Bank lending to farmers itself doubled between the start of the war and 1920.

After the war, both crop prices and US farm exports fell as sharply as they'd risen during it, triggering a farm crisis that was to ruin many farmers over the course of the next decade, often bringing their banks down with them (Belongia and Gilbert 1985).

In 1921 alone more than 500 banks failed, topping the previous record established during the Panic of 1893. The 1921 failures coincided with the general economic depression of that year. But while most other industries recovered quickly from the downturn, and did so with little help from either the Federal Reserve or the Treasury, agriculture and banking didn't. Instead, bank failures mounted. Almost twice as many banks failed in 1926 as had failed in 1921. By the end of the decade 5,411 banks had failed, over 80 percent of them rural and four-fifths in states that altogether prohibited branch banking (Alston, Grove, and Wheelock 1994). As Eugene Nelson White (1984, 131–32) observes, although Canada's farmers were also hard hit by the postwar agricultural slump, only one of Canada's 18 banks, all of which had extensive branch networks, failed during the 1920s, and none failed during the Great Depression itself.[1]

US bank failure rates were also higher, other things being equal, in states with deposit guarantees than in those without them. Nor did state deposit guarantee schemes spare depositors from losses: every one of those schemes failed during the 1920s, and except for Texas's guarantee fund, all proved unable, upon being liquidated, to make the depositors they'd insured whole (Thies and Gerlowski 1989).

Panic, within Limits

Although thousands of US banks managed to survive the 1920s, many were in no condition to withstand any further shocks. So when commodity and security prices sagged after the onset of the Depression, bank failures became even more frequent.

Rural banks were still the main casualties, although now instead of being concentrated in the western grain-growing states, bank failures were especially frequent in the South and the Midwest, where collapsing cotton, tobacco, and livestock prices combined with reduced cotton and wheat yields—a result of what the Weather Bureau described as "the most severe drought in the climatological history of the United States"—proved to be the last straw (Hamilton 1985, 602).

So far, panic wasn't a factor in bank failures. Banks failed because they were insolvent and not simply because their depositors all asked for their money back. But the last months of 1930 witnessed a disconcerting change: the failures now included a number of urban banks, and they occurred in a cluster big enough to qualify as a banking panic. This was the first bank panic since 1907 and the first of three that were to strike the US banking system before Roosevelt took office.

Until the last of these panics, in February and early March 1933, fundamentals—namely poorly performing bank loans and investments as well as some remarkably bad bank management—continued to account for most bank closings, including two spectacular ones (Wicker 1980). But now it wasn't just depressed prices of farm commodities but also a more general decline in asset values that chipped away at banks' net worth.[2]

The first spectacular failure was the November 1930 collapse of Caldwell and Company, a Nashville municipal bond house founded by Rogers Caldwell in 1917. "The Caldwell crash," David Hamilton (1985, 593) writes, "was as stunning a blow to the mid-South as the stock market crash was to Wall Street." Between its founding and 1929, Caldwell and Company served as the foundation stone of a vast financial complex involving either outright ownership of or a controlling interest in various hotels, newspapers, real estate ventures, insurance companies, department stores, and . . . banks, including the South's largest banking chain and some big banks in Nashville, Memphis, Knoxville, and Little Rock.

Like many rural banks, Caldwell and Company was already "in no condition to absorb even a minor shock" on the eve of the Depression (Wicker 1980, 574). But the roots of Caldwell and Company's weakness lay not in the prior decade's agricultural slump but rather in all sorts of risky investments it undertook during the last two years of its existence. These investments, which doubled its size, were mostly financed with borrowed money, including funds borrowed from Caldwell and Company's own bank affiliates (576).

The immediate cause of Caldwell and Company's collapse was state examiners' discovery, on November 7, that the biggest of those affiliates, the Bank of Tennessee, was insolvent. Caldwell and Company went into receivership several days later. Before long every bank having any substantial connection to it—dozens all told—had gone under (Wicker 1980, 573). Just how poor Caldwell and Company's investments were only came to light when, upon its liquidation many months later, its creditors ended up settling for about thirty cents on the dollar.

What was more disturbing than the failure of so many banks actually connected to Caldwell and Company was the spread of what Milton Friedman and Anna Schwartz (1963, 308) call a "contagion of fear" to depositors at banks that had nothing to do with Caldwell and Company. In all, within the space of just two weeks more than 120 banks in Tennessee, Arkansas, Kentucky, North Carolina, and several other states gave up the ghost.

A Long Way from Kansas

No sooner had the Caldwell and Company crisis subsided than another banking crisis broke out. The trigger this time was the failure of a bank that couldn't have been more unlike most of the banks that failed during the 1920s. Despite its official-sounding name, the Manhattan-based Bank of United States (note the missing "the") was a state-chartered commercial bank, albeit New York City's third largest and the twenty-eighth largest bank in the country, with sixty-two branches and 450,000 depositors to whom it owed $268 million.

In the lead-up to the 1929 crash, the Bank of United States grew like a weed. But it did so, according to Benjamin Anderson (1949, 205), who was then Chase National Bank's chief economist, only by having "departed to an incredible degree from sound commercial bank practices." By the autumn of 1930 the Bank of United States was in desperate straits. In late November three other large New York banks tentatively agreed to save the Bank of the United States by merging with it. But they gave themselves two weeks to find out just what the Bank of United States had been up to. On December 8, having seen enough, they pulled out. Two days later several thousand depositors showed up at the Bank of United States' Bronx branch asking for their money. Before long lines started forming at the bank's other branches, and by the end of the day the quickest depositors had withdrawn almost $2 million. The rest went away empty-handed. To avoid further runs, the bank stayed closed the next day while its directors scrambled around for help. They got some, but it wasn't enough. On December 11 the Bank of United States entered the record books as the nation's biggest bank failure.

Both the causes and the consequences of the failure of the Bank of United States have been objects of sometimes heated controversy, with Friedman and Schwartz (1963, 308–11) claiming both that the bank was actually solvent, though illiquid, when it was allowed to fail and that its failure gave new vigor to the "contagion of fear" that had already broken out. But subsequent research casts doubt on both claims and, incidentally, on Friedman and Schwartz's claim that anti-Semitism may have played a part in the Jewish-owned bank's failure.

Concerning the claim that the Bank of United States was solvent when it failed, although its creditors ultimately received more than eighty cents on the dollar, it took *fourteen years* for this to happen (O'Brien and Trescott 1992, 378), mainly because 45 percent of the bank's loans—some $90 million worth—consisted of mortgages, including many second and third mortgages, on New York real estate, the value of which plummeted after 1929.

Nor was the Bank of United States the victim of a wave of depositor worries that rolled in from elsewhere. As Kris Mitchener and Gary Richardson (2020, 11) report, far from victimizing New York banks by confronting them with a "contagion of fear," the Caldwell and Company panic led to a substantial *increase* in their deposits, a result of the public's (generally correct) belief that New York remained a "safe haven" for their savings. Total deposits at New York banks actually "remained elevated even after the Bank of United States suspended operations."

The last-mentioned fact contradicts Friedman and Schwartz's (1963, 308) claim that "a contagion of fear . . . knows no geographical limits." It also challenges their view that the failure of the Bank of United States itself undermined the public's general confidence in banks, thereby contributing to the overall decline in bank deposits that turned what might have been a mere recession into a "Great Contraction." That New York banks as a whole didn't lose deposits after the Bank of United States failed means that its failure didn't even lead to a general distrust of banks in New York City itself.

In fact, although December saw a sharp increase in bank failures, only one other New York bank—the Chelsea Bank and Trust Company—failed that month, succumbing to a run on December 23. But instead of being a delayed reaction to the closing of the Bank of United States, the run on the Chelsea Bank and Trust appears to have been provoked by rumors deliberately spread the night before by Communist Party agitators (Fuller 2014, 70).

Unlike either the Chelsea Bank and Trust or the Bank of United States, most of the banks that failed that December were rural banks located far from New York City, and they failed not because their depositors panicked but because, like many other rural banks that managed to get through the 1920s, they'd been hanging by threads that finally snapped. They were, in other words, yet more victims of the postwar agricultural boom and bust and US banking laws that made them so vulnerable to it (Wicker 1980, 581).

Going for Gold

If the failure of Caldwell and Company caused a regional panic only, while that of the Bank of United States doesn't seem to have caused a panic of any sort except among its own depositors, something closer to a general panic did occur when, on September 18, 1931, the Bank of England suspended gold payments (Titcomb 2015). That decision, which took both British depositors themselves and others utterly by surprise, caused other European central banks and those of Belgium and France especially to bolster their own gold reserves by withdrawing their US deposits. By the end of October, the US gold stock had shrunk by $320 million, or roughly 10 percent of its level before Britain's unexpected move. According to Susan Kennedy (1973, 30), "the rush from abroad to convert dollar balances into gold frightened American depositors," causing them to start cramming gold coins into safety deposit boxes and stuffing mattresses with gold certificates (Allen 1940, 50). By November 7 they'd withdrawn another $500 million in gold, putting that much more pressure on an already badly strained banking system. During October 1932 alone, another 522 banks, with almost half a billion dollars in deposits, failed.

This was a "contagion of fear," all right. But unlike the sort of contagion Friedman and Schwartz had in mind, it had people everywhere worrying not that their banks might be insolvent but that the US dollar might be devalued. "England's abandonment of the gold standard," Chase National Bank's CEO recalled some months later, "caused a great scare regarding the standard itself" that gave depositors a reason to run on banks they knew to be perfectly solid (Richardson and Van Horn 2018, 90). As we'll see, the same worry played a major part in the final and most severe Depression-era banking panic.

President Herbert Hoover responded to the fall 1931 banking crisis by launching an antihoarding campaign and by establishing the National Credit Corporation, a voluntary banker funded and operated credit pool. When these steps proved inadequate, Hoover encouraged Congress to pass the Reconstruction Finance Corporation (RFC) Act, which he signed on January 22, 1932.[3] By

March the RFC had made a thousand loans, mostly to banks and trust companies, and these seemed to help: only 46 banks failed that month, compared to 342 in January. (Elsewhere I'll say more about the RFC's undertakings.)

In the meantime, however, domestic and foreign gold withdrawals reached the point of causing Treasury Secretary Ogden Mills to inform Hoover, on February 7, 1932, that the country was within two weeks of having to either default on its foreign obligations or violate the Fed's gold reserve requirements. It was this close call that inspired the passage on February 27 of the first Glass-Steagall Act, allowing Federal Reserve notes to be backed by Treasury securities instead of either gold or commercial paper. As we'll see, this change paved the way for the Federal Reserve's first—and alas only—Depression-era monetary stimulus program. Unfortunately, badly needed structural reforms, including a plan to ease barriers to branch banking, tenaciously fought for by Virginia senator Carter Glass but doggedly opposed by Alabama congressman and House Banking Committee chair Henry Steagall, failed to make it into law (Gutwillig 2014).

Despite the lack of fundamental reform, and thanks in part to the RFC's emergency loans, the banking situation calmed down that spring. By May it seemed to some that the worst might be over. In New England especially, economic conditions were improving. Commodity prices, stock prices, and output were heading up again, and gold was finding its way back into banks' coffers. Hoover even dared to believe that his policies were working and that their vindication would cinch his reelection.

But things didn't turn out that way, in part because Hoover himself inadvertently rekindled depositors' fears.

Campaign of Fear

Despite Hoover's hopes, New England's example wasn't followed elsewhere. Instead, conditions worsened, particularly when Chicago and surrounding towns suffered another wave of bank failures that June (Calomiris and Mason 1997). Late summer brought another respite, but that also proved short-lived. By the fall, banks everywhere, including metropolitan ones, were finding it necessary to rein in their lending to protect themselves from runs (Kennedy 1973, 131).

For all his efforts, to be considered later, to shore up ailing banks and despite all his preaching about the importance of confidence, Herbert Hoover unwittingly contributed to banks' troubles. He did so, first of all, by revealing during his October 4, 1932, campaign speech in Des Moines how close the government had come, according to Ogden Mills, to defaulting on its gold payments. As Scott Sumner (2015, 141–42) explains, although Hoover hoped to gain kudos for having saved the situation, he only managed to raise new doubts concerning the state of the US gold stock. After Hoover's speech the dollar fell sharply against other gold standard currencies, becoming, according to the *New York Times,* as "feeble and delicate" as ever (Sumner 2015, 141; Sumner 2010). Having been repeatedly assured until then that the dollar was rock solid, depositors now had reason to distrust such assurances. Because of this, Paul Einzig (1933, 64) observes, when another run on the dollar started some months later, "no official reassuring statement was able to restore confidence."

If in Des Moines Hoover unintentionally undermined voter's confidence in his own government, both there and elsewhere he very deliberately tried to undermine their confidence in his opponent, telling them, among other things, that Roosevelt planned to devalue the dollar, if not to ditch the gold standard altogether. As we'll see, when Roosevelt finally resorted to it, devaluation would help to bring gold rushing back into the US monetary system. But devaluation is one thing; the *prospect* of devaluation is quite another. If people at home or abroad anticipate the reduction of a currency's gold content, to avoid a capital loss they'll want to trade their paper notes, deposits, and securities denominated in that currency for gold itself. So, the more people believed Hoover's lurid account of Roosevelt's plans, the more banks and the dollar suffered.

Yet Roosevelt himself did little to assuage their fears. In fact, as he told his own staff, he had no idea whether the country could stay on the gold standard, and he therefore wished to avoid committing himself to that standard. But Roosevelt could hardly declare that he was *not* committed to the gold dollar—not without guaranteeing a crisis. He therefore left it largely to others, including Carter Glass, to deny Hoover's charges. When Roosevelt did finally refer to those charges during a November 4 speech at the Brooklyn Academy of Music, he still avoided committing himself to the gold standard, if only barely. Instead, he accused Hoover of conjuring up a "rubber dollars" bogeyman while referring to Carter Glass's "devastating challenge that no responsible government would have sold to the country securities payable in gold if it knew that the promise, yes, the covenant embodied in these securities, was as dubious as the President of the United States claims it was" (Hoover 1951, 286). Otherwise, the more Roosevelt was pressed during the interregnum regarding his specific plans for gold, the less he said, and the more the exchanges turned against the dollar (Sumner 2015, 181).

Nevada Takes a Holiday

Faith in the dollar could only weaken so much before it broke, and several other developments in late 1932 and early 1933 hastened that breaking point's arrival. One happened in a mostly deserted state with fewer than 100,000 citizens, the other in the nation's fourth-largest city of roughly 1.6 million.

Although banking troubles had ceased to be a uniquely rural problem, falling crop and livestock prices were still taking their toll on banks, and the official response to another spate of such failures was about to join forces with concerns about the dollar in setting the stage for a truly nationwide crisis. In October 1932, thanks mainly to fallen cattle and sheep prices, a dozen Nevada banks found themselves in hot water. All were owned by one person, a high-rolling miner and cattleman named George Wingfield, and together they supplied more than 75 percent of Nevada's bank loans (Olson 1975).

Having failed to secure credit elsewhere, Wingfield's banks turned to the RFC, borrowing more than $5 million from it (Olson 1975, 153). But the RFC's assistance, which it offered only on very strict banker's terms, proved insufficient. When, on October 31, Wingfield told the state banking authorities that his banks were about to shut down, freezing the state government's deposits along with the rest, Nevada governor Fred Balzar chose to buy time for them by declaring a twelve-day bank holiday that was eventually extended to December 14. Although Wingfield's own banks never reopened, the remains of his former banking empire were ultimately consolidated, with the help of supporting loans, to form the Bank of Nevada. But Wingfield himself was ruined, and Balzar's holiday set a precedent that was to spread like wildfire, eventually engulfing the entire US banking system.

Panic in Detroit

As if the RFC's tight-fistedness weren't enough to discourage banks from counting on it, developments in Washington made them hesitate to even ask for its help. On July 21, 1932, Congress passed the Emergency Relief and Construction Act, which among other things called for the RFC to submit monthly reports to Congress listing specific loans it made. Congress could in turn make the list public.

The House clerk and the Senate secretary were supposed to hold on to the first RFC reports until Congress convened that December.[4] But on August 22 the clerk, having misunderstood what was intended, shared the first of the reports with the *New York Times*, which published it. The mistake wasn't repeated, but during December and January Congress received, and the *New York Times* published, six more RFC reports, including one divulging all RFC loans made *before* the Emergency Relief and Construction Act was passed. By making the RFC's loans public, Congress gave banks a powerful incentive to avoid turning to the RFC: word that it was helping them could expose even solvent banks fully worthy of that help to "heavy withdrawals by frightened depositors" (Kennedy 1973, 132).

The publication of RFC loans proved all the more unfortunate because it began just as another crisis, this one entirely urban, was about to put more banks in dire straits. Detroit was a one-industry town, whose banks were mostly owned by just two companies: the Guardian Detroit Union Group, comprising thirty-one banks, and the forty-bank Detroit Bankers Company. By the start of 1933 several of them, including the Guardian Group's Union Guardian Trust Company, were in trouble because automobile sales had collapsed and also because their holding companies had been squeezing fat dividends from them.

Come mid-January, it was clear that Union Guardian Trust couldn't survive without help, which it tried to get from the RFC. But the RFC wasn't able to lend it enough on the collateral it had to offer. The only hope then was local support, including having Henry Ford agree to "freeze" his $7.5 million deposit with the Union Guardian Trust, in effect reducing its current liabilities by that amount. Alas for Detroit, Ford not only refused but also threatened to cash in his firm's deposit at Detroit's First National Bank, the Detroit Banking Group's flagship. When failed pleas from the RFC, other regulatory authorities and ultimately Herbert Hoover himself made it clear that Ford meant what he said, only two options remained: either Michigan could declare a bank holiday, as Nevada had done, or upon reopening for business the next day most of its banks would fail. At last, in the small hours of Valentine's Day, Michigan's recently elected governor, William Comstock, declared a holiday.

Although it gave Michigan's own bankers a breathing spell, Comstock's declaration was bad news for surviving banks elsewhere. Fearing that their own governors might follow Comstock's example, depositors at banks elsewhere, including bankers themselves who until then kept substantial balances with their correspondents, rushed to withdraw their money. Their prophecies proved to be self-fulfilling. State banking systems started shutting down one after another, like so many dominoes toppling: New Jersey on February 20, Maryland and Ohio on February 25, and a dozen other states before March 2. By March 3, another two dozen states had shut their banks down.

The Run on the Dollar

State bank holidays weren't quite the last straw, for there was another important cause of bank runs during the first months of 1933: the growing conviction, both at home and overseas, that the gold standard's days were numbered.

Several developments informed that conviction, including Congress's attempt in January to provide for devaluation in the (ultimately doomed)

Glass-Steagall bill then being considered. But the most disturbing development occurred during the second week of February, when Carter Glass definitively refused to serve as Roosevelt's secretary of the treasury. It was generally understood that Glass did so because Roosevelt would not promise to preserve the gold standard (Lindley 1934, 53–54; Crawford 1940, 24; Wigmore 1987, 744). That understanding, together with Michigan's declaration of a bank holiday just days before, sparked another run on the dollar worse even than the one triggered by Britain's abandonment of the gold standard.[5] By its end, $1.8 billion in paper currency had been withdrawn from the banks, of which almost a third—$563 million—was afterward presented to the Fed for payment in gold. Soon the Federal Reserve Bank of New York, where most of the nation's gold was kept, had lost so much gold that it had to suspend its gold reserve requirement (Wigmore 1987). According to the *Commercial and Financial Chronicle* (1933, 2287), foreigners' fear that the United States would be forced off the gold standard was the proximate cause of the New York Fed's heavy gold losses. But as those losses mounted they helped deepen the domestic distrust that "greatly added to the home propensity to hoard."[6]

Even so, it was the leaders of the New York Fed rather than New York's commercial bankers who first pleaded for a national bank holiday, and it was those Fed leaders who had the greatest reason to be relieved when New York state governor Herbert Lehman finally closed New York's banks on inauguration day. Fearing that a holiday would damage their banks' reputations, officials from several of New York's big commercial banks actually argued *against* it, telling Lehman that they'd "rather stay open and take their beating'" (Jabaily 2013). Those banks could well have withstood a beating. If they ultimately joined the New York Fed in asking Lehman to declare a holiday, it wasn't because they needed one. Instead, they did it as a favor to George Harrison, the New York Fed's governor, who didn't want the public to realize that the New York Fed's own back was against the wall. When Lehman agreed, officials at the other Federal Reserve banks began urging the governors of states in their districts that hadn't yet declared holidays to do so.

Gold, Gold, Almost Everywhere

Remarkably, although a shortage of gold at the New York Fed was the proximate cause of the national bank holiday, the Federal Reserve System was never short of gold. The Federal Reserve Act called for the twelve Federal Reserve banks to have gold reserves equal to at least 40 percent of their outstanding Federal Reserve notes plus a reserve of either gold or greenbacks equal to at least 35 percent of their member bank deposits. At its nadir, the

Federal Reserve System's gold stock was worth almost $3 billion, or almost 55 percent of reserve banks' note and member bank deposit liabilities. When the New York Fed pled for the holiday that eventually shut the entire US banking system down, the Federal Reserve System had $1 billion in gold to spare.

"It is difficult," Scott Sumner (2015, 145) says, "to imagine a more shocking indictment of U.S. monetary policy than the fact that on the day FDR took the United States off the gold standard it still held over 37 percent of the world's gold stock." It is indeed. So why did it happen? The bare-bones answer, well-put by Michael Bordo and David Wheelock (2013, 86–87), is that instead of providing for "effective leadership," the Federal Reserve System's decentralized organization "enabled parochial interests and petty jealousies to hamstring policy."

Part of the problem was the faintheartedness of both individual Federal Reserve Bank governors (as they were then called) and the Federal Reserve Board in Washington. The Federal Reserve Act's 40 percent gold backing requirement applied to each of the twelve Federal Reserve banks. But it also allowed the Federal Reserve Board to suspend that requirement for 30 days and again for another 15 if that seemed necessary. During a crisis, in other words, "*all* Fed-held gold was on the table" (Timberlake 2007, 326). The idea, long practiced by ordinary banks facing runs, was to fork out enough gold to convince everyone that there was no shortage of the stuff.

Yet the Fed Board didn't seriously consider the option of suspending the requirement until March 1, when the New York Fed's gold reserves actually fell below the 40 percent requirement. Even then, it did so only reluctantly. But by that late date its decision hardly mattered, for the state of panic was such that the New York Fed might have shown the public a mountain of gold bullion without stopping the stampede. For that reason, New York Fed governor Harrison himself told the board not to bother (Jabaily 2013). When on March 3 the board finally did suspend the Fed's gold reserve requirement, the step was but a futile gesture.

A question remains whether the crisis might have been averted had the Fed responded to it sooner, that is, when the 40 percent gold reserve constraint wasn't binding anywhere and sheer panic hadn't set in. In fact, the Fed had acted relatively aggressively between September 18, when Great Britain went off gold the gold standard, and August 1932, when, to counter deflation, the Federal Reserve banks purchased $1.124 billion in Treasury securities on the open market. As a later chapter will show, although those purchases initially caused more gold to flow out of the Fed, they ultimately had the opposite effect, leading several experts to conclude that had the purchases continued, the 1933 crisis might have been avoided.

The other problem with the Fed's makeup in those days was that getting the twelve Federal Reserve Banks to cooperate was like herding cats. For example, on March 3, with the New York Fed in violation of its gold reserve limit, the Chicago Fed pointedly refused to swap some of its own surplus gold for the New York bank's Treasury securities (Meltzer 2003, 387n136; Epstein and Ferguson 1984). When the Chicago Fed also refused, along with the Boston Fed, to participate in another round of Federal Reserve System open market purchases, the Fed Board, instead of insisting that the two Federal Reserve banks cooperate, "watched passively while its staff prepared for a final collapse" (Meltzer 2003, 379).

Although Franklin Roosevelt was not yet president as the nationwide banking crisis unfolded, he couldn't help playing a part, however inadvertently, in allowing the banking system to slip into a coma. As president he would play a very different and much bigger part as the man who promised to breathe new life into that system and into the whole US economy.

The Bank Holiday

During the days leading to the inauguration, the US economy resembled a body slowly bleeding out, its organs failing one by one. The Federal Reserve System at its heart was hemorrhaging gold, and state banking systems were shutting down one after another. It was up to Franklin Roosevelt to first stanch the bleeding and then arrange for a transfusion.

Panic at the Fed

Recall again how that crisis came about. It began with the official closing of Michigan's banks in mid-February 1933. Michigan's decision led other states to start declaring holidays as well. In the meantime, fear of an impending devaluation led to both foreign and domestic runs on the dollar. Together these events set the stage for Roosevelt's declaration of a nationwide bank holiday on March 6, two days after taking office.

So much for the barest facts. In *Drifting Toward Mayhem*, his superb but underappreciated history of the Depression-era banking crises, historian Robert Lynn Fuller (2009) supplies many crucial details. Perhaps the most striking of these is that "hysteria" didn't take hold of bank depositors until after state governments everywhere began shutting down or limiting withdrawals from banks. Until then it was mainly commercial bankers and (most importantly) Federal Reserve officials who took to fright.

During the "wave of fear" set in motion by Michigan's crisis, Fuller (2009, 364) says, "the public remained mostly calm," and "depositors did not rush to their banks to withdraw their funds." Instead, the fear was mostly that of bankers and state politicians, who reacted less to actual depositor runs than they did to "each other's anxiety about what *might* happen" (Fuller 2014, 157).

The governors of Tennessee and Maryland immediately followed Michigan's example by declaring their own bank holidays, while those of seventeen other states allowed their banks to limit depositors' cash withdrawals. Unfortunately, such responses only gave bankers elsewhere more reason to panic, denying them access to correspondent balances that often made up a substantial share of their liquid reserves or making them worry that they might lose access to those balances at any moment. The ensuing scramble for funds upped the pressure on governors who hadn't yet decided to close their banks.

As holidays and restrictions multiplied, even bank depositors who weren't concerned about devaluation had reason to join the fray, not because they distrusted their banks but because they worried that a statewide holiday would deny them access to their deposits. For example, when on March 2 crowds lined up at the Howard Savings Institution in Newark to withdraw their savings, they did so because they suspected that New Jersey's governor was about to declare a holiday that would put those savings out of reach.[1] Fear of local holidays thus joined the growing fear that Roosevelt would suspend gold payments to inspire people to get their money out of banks they considered solvent.

Once one allows for depositors' perfectly rational fear of both state bank holidays and devaluation, there isn't much need for any appeal to blind panic. This doesn't mean that depositors *never* mistook sound banks for unsound ones, and it certainly doesn't mean that there were no unsound banks left after those around Detroit went belly-up. But awareness of the role of devaluation fears and bank holidays does cast doubt on the notion that depositors had come to suspect every bank in the country of being broke.

No Holiday for Hoover

As we've seen, it was the run on the dollar—and especially foreigners' part in it—that ultimately led the federal government to shut down the entire US banking system. Although the February–March run harmed commercial banks, it posed less of an immediate threat to many of them than it posed to the Federal Reserve Bank of New York, for it was a run out of dollars of all kinds and into gold, which was mostly kept there. The final, fatal blow to the nation's banks came when the "wave of fear" engulfed New York Fed officials who, Fuller says, "reacted against future expectations of actions by European central bankers, who acted on their own worries about the future of the dollar under President Roosevelt" (Fuller 2014, 297).

Those New York Fed officials first tried to get President Hoover to declare a nationwide bank holiday. It was only when that attempt failed that they asked Governor Lehman to declare a state holiday instead. Because state governments lacked the authority to act on the Fed's behalf rather than on behalf of commercial banks operating under their authority, the New York Fed asked the New York Clearing House Association to take part in its request, which the clearing house ultimately did, albeit with considerable reluctance. Once New York's banks had shut down, it was clear that still-open commercial banks elsewhere would also have to close. Fed officials informed other state governors accordingly. By the time of Roosevelt's inauguration, state bank holidays had been declared almost everywhere, and the few banks that stayed open mostly did so in defiance of state officials' orders (Fuller 2014, chap. 11).

Yet the crisis still wasn't over. While widespread state bank holidays stopped runs on ordinary banks, so far as the Fed was concerned those holidays were a mere stopgap: although they ended the drain of gold from the Fed to US banks and their customers, the holidays couldn't stop foreign central banks from cashing their dollars in for gold. Only a national bank holiday declared by federal authorities could do that. This point deserves emphasis: a national bank holiday was declared not to keep ordinary banks from failing but to keep the Fed from doing so.

Why, then, hadn't Hoover declared such a holiday when the New York Fed first approached him? Why did he leave it to Roosevelt, allowing the Fed to lose that much more gold and also exposing sound commercial banks to runs until state holidays shut them down? The answer isn't that Hoover was a cold-blooded social Darwinist who "wanted to keep banks open and failing from panic until the weak banks had all collapsed," as Eric Rauchway (2018, 199) claims. Hoover may have been pusillanimous, but he was by no means "inhumane."[2] The thirty-first president's problem wasn't a lack of compassion, let alone a morbid desire to see more banks fail; it was legal and political scruples. Nor were those scruples groundless, for while it was clear that no state governor could legally shut down the Fed, it was far from certain that Hoover himself could do it.

Not that Hoover didn't consider it. With his approval, sometime during the first half of 1932 Treasury and Fed officials looked into the possibility of invoking the 1917 Trading with the Enemy Act (as amended in 1918) to suspend or restrict the Fed's gold payments (Raymond Moley says June; another source says January) (Moley 1966, 158; Ackerman 1996, 7). Walter Wyatt, the Fed Board's general counsel, even went so far as to prepare a resolution to that end for Hoover's signature. But Hoover chose not to use it. When Michigan closed its banks in mid-February 1933, Wyatt and others again urged Hoover to make use of the plan. Hoover then agreed to consult both Carter Glass and William Mitchell, his attorney general, concerning the resolution. But both—Mitchell in particular—doubted that it could withstand a legal challenge unless the Democratic-controlled Congress gave the plan its ex post facto concurrence.

Just what the consequences would have been of Congress's refusal to go along with the proposed resolution is far from clear. Ogden Mills thought it would be "fatal" (Awalt 1969). But Raymond Moley (1966) may be right in suggesting that there was no good reason for Hoover to anticipate such a refusal. "In a matter of this sort," Moley says, "the strong men were [John Nance] Garner as Speaker of the House and [Joseph T.] Robinson and Glass in the Senate. I cannot believe that these men would have invited a catastrophe by refusing to approve the proclamation of a holiday already established by Presidential action. Nor could Roosevelt have dared to rescind the order after he took office without also inviting chaos" (212).

Whatever might have happened, Hoover vacillated. Over the coming days as the monetary system crumbled around him, he made various attempts to persuade Roosevelt to publicly support Wyatt's resolution and to otherwise secure Congress's backing. To shorten a long story that flatters neither of its main protagonists, Hoover's haughtily ham-fisted approaches to Roosevelt on one hand and the fact that Roosevelt on the other hand had little politically to gain by cooperating with Hoover ruled out any hope that Hoover's effort would succeed. Hoover accused Roosevelt of wanting to blacken his reputation at the nation's expense; Roosevelt wondered why Hoover couldn't muster up the pluck to close the banks without his help. Each had a point, and each therefore deserves some blame for the fact that a national bank holiday wasn't declared until the early morning of March 6, when the banking system had already been shut down.

Yet both men also deserve some leniency, for as Frederick Lewis Allen (1940, 98) observes, "the real villain of the piece was the antiquated political arrangement by which an administration had to remain in nominal power for nearly four months after it had been rejected at the polls."

His Finest Week

Regardless of why it fell to Roosevelt to declare it, the national bank holiday that began on March 6 and ultimately ended on March 13 was to be among the greatest achievements, if not the greatest single achievement, of his first term. Yet the holiday was much less a New Deal achievement and much more one for which the Hoover administration deserves credit than is generally appreciated. Although Roosevelt took the lead and played his part brilliantly, his performance was based on a playbook prepared while Hoover was still president. Hoover Treasury officials also stuck around to help Roosevelt's still very green team orchestrate the closing and reopening of the nation's banks. "If it had not been for help from the outgoing Treasury group," Raymond Moley (1948, 100) wrote later, "the storm could never have been weathered."

To appreciate just how much Hoover's men did, it helps to first review the timing of the holiday and public events surrounding it. Roosevelt was sworn in on the afternoon of March 4, a Saturday. Thirty-six hours later, at 1 a.m. on Monday, March 6, citing the authority granted him by the 1917 Trading with the Enemy Act, he issued his proclamation closing the banks and prohibiting any export or sale of gold until March 9. On the evening of March 9, at the end of an emergency joint session, Congress passed the Emergency Banking Act, retroactively amending the Trading with the Enemy Act so it could be used not just during a war but also "during any other period of national emergency declared by the President."[3] Later that same evening Roosevelt signed an executive order dated Friday, March 10, extending the bank holiday until March 13 but continuing the moratorium on gold exports indefinitely. Finally, on March 12, he gave his first and most famous fireside chat, explaining what had taken place and how sound banks would begin reopening in stages starting the next day.

As already noted, the idea of using the Trading with the Enemy Act to suspend gold payments was first considered by Hoover well before Roosevelt took office. Roosevelt's proclamation of March 9 was one of two versions that William Mitchell, Hoover's attorney general, had prepared for Roosevelt's signature, with help once again from Walter Wyatt (Awalt 1969, 358). Much of what became the Emergency Banking Act, including the plan for gradually reopening banks, was itself conceived in advance by Ogden Mills, Hoover's treasury secretary, while the final legislation was drafted by Arthur Ballentine, Hoover's treasury undersecretary, Wyatt, and some of Wyatt's staff (363). Ballantine also sketched the famous first fireside chat that Roosevelt delivered so brilliantly after giving it his own "homelike" touch (Moley 1966, 194).

To say that the incoming administration was unlikely to have managed without all this help is putting things mildly. The truth is that Roosevelt's own team, including William Woodin—whom journalist Arthur Krock (1965, 225) later described as "the most surprised man who ever became Secretary of the Treasury"—came to Washington with no ideas or plans of their own for resolving the crisis (Moley 1966, 169). The new officials were accordingly grateful for any help Hoover's men gave them. When in June 1933 Arthur Ballantine finally left DC after turning down Roosevelt's offer to stay on as his own undersecretary of the treasury, Woodin tried to convey his gratitude in a letter to Ballantine, only to end up explaining that "all dictionaries in the English language that I possess do not some way or other seem to have the proper words to express my thoughts" (quoted in Moley 1966, 216).

Given these facts, it seems only fair to conclude that while from a strictly chronological perspective the national bank holiday and the various steps taken during it, including passing the Emergency Banking Act, were part of the New Deal, in a more fundamental sense they were the Hoover administration's swan song.[4]

Confidence Tricks

Whoever deserves credit for it, the fact remains that the nationwide banking holiday marked the turning point of the Great Depression. With it the Great Contraction that began in 1929 came to an end. Afterward, as banks reopened, a recovery began that was to continue, with fits and starts, until the summer of 1937. That recovery wouldn't have been possible had the public not been convinced to not only quit withdrawing money from their banks but also start putting it back into them.

Conventional wisdom attributes this amazing revival of trust in the banking system to Roosevelt's confidence-inspiring fireside chat and especially to the public's willingness to take him at his word when he promised that banks would reopen only once they were determined to be sound. According to this view, depositors no longer had to judge for themselves whether an open bank might fail and so had no need to hesitate to place their life savings with it.

It's a pleasant story. But it isn't the whole story. Although Roosevelt's words were certainly encouraging and may have allayed some depositors' concerns, they could hardly have won over the many sophisticated bank customers who knew perfectly well that there weren't enough bank examiners around to thoroughly go through thousands of banks' books, with less than a week at their disposal, to determine which ones were solvent. Nor did it help matters that thousands of bankers were "converging upon an emergency office set up in the Washington Building by the Acting Comptroller of the Currency—an office in which four men found themselves the bottleneck between the banking system and the government"—to plead their banks' cases (Allen 1940, 112).

As Barrie Wigmore (1987, 752) reports, bank examiners in the New York Fed district complained that it wasn't "humanly possible . . . to appraise with accuracy" the banks they'd been asked to appraise. Their opinion was presumably shared by examiners elsewhere, including those charged with certifying state banks that weren't Federal Reserve System members, which tended to be the weakest, for reopening. Consequently, the initial classification of banks relied heavily on information from pre–bank holiday exam-inations and "quick value judgments, almost in the nature of speculation" (Moley 1966, 191).

Furthermore, neither Roosevelt's remarks nor any proof of commercial banks' soundness could quell the fears of devaluation that lay behind the biggest run of all, namely that by foreigners—and foreign central banks especially—to con-vert dollars into gold.

Yet within three days from the end of the national banking holiday, more than three-quarters of the 5,916 national banks that had been closed by proc-lamation were licensed to reopen. And as the *New York Times* reported on the first day after the holiday, far from rushing to withdraw the money still left in them, "the public plainly showed that it recovered from the fear and hysteria which characterized the last few days before the banking holiday was proclaimed" ("135 Banks Reopen Here" 1933; see also Patch 1939). By March 29, more than two-thirds of the roughly 18,000 banks that had been operating before the holiday were back in business.

What, then, was the real key to the reopening's success? William Silber (2009) says that it consisted of steps that amounted to a full, if only implicit, guarantee of deposits in reopened banks. First, among its other provisions, the Emergency Banking Act allowed Federal Reserve Notes to be backed by not only gold, commercial paper, and US government securities but also any "notes, drafts, bills of exchange, or bankers' acceptances," that is, by just about any Federal Reserve bank assets.[5] Second, in his fireside chat, Roosevelt promised that new currency was "being sent out by the Bureau of Engraving and Printing to every part of the country" so that "banks that reopen will be able to meet every legitimate call" (Roosevelt 1938, 2:62–63). Finally, William Woodin promised to have the Treasury indemnify the twelve Federal Reserve banks for any losses they incurred in fulfilling his commitment to the public. This arrangement, Silber says, amounted to a 100 percent deposit guarantee, that is, a guarantee more complete than the one that took effect when the Federal Deposit Insurance Corporation began insuring deposits the follow-ing January.

Silber's argument is compelling. But it overlooks a more mundane expla-nation for the fact that so many reopened banks were trusted, namely, that many depositors had never distrusted their banks in the first place: if they took their money out, it was because they feared either that the dollar would soon be devalued or that state authorities were about to make their accounts inaccessible. For banks that weren't suspected of being unsound before the national holiday, no guarantees were needed. Nor did examiners have to scrutinize these banks with great care in order to declare them fit to reopen.

For the most part they simply relied on the clean bills of health those banks received after their last pre–bank holiday exams.[6]

The nine large banks of the New York Clearing House Association were a case in point. With one notable exception, they were, despite everything, in remarkably solid condition when Governor Lehman closed them. For this reason—and despite all their carping about lacking time for proper audits—New York's bank examiners didn't hesitate to certify all except one for reopening on March 13, the day the nationwide holiday ended.[7]

Nor were New York's banks unique: more than half of the some fifteen thousand national, state, and private banks closed en masse by state authorities, representing 90 percent of closed banks' deposits, were judged perfectly safe and ready to open that week on the basis of perfunctory assessments that mainly reflected the general understanding among depositors and regulators alike that the banks in question were never in danger of being insolvent. Even so, according to Jesse Jones (1951, 21), who was a director of the Reconstruction Finance Corporation (RFC) at the time and would soon become its chairman, "a great many unsound banks were allowed to resume business" as soon as the bank holiday ended. Most of these shaky banks were eventually shorn up by RFC capital injections. RFC support also allowed many banks still closed on March 16 to reopen before the end of the year.[8]

But what about gold? So long as devaluation fears persisted, how could people be convinced to hold either bank deposits or paper dollars instead of gold? First of all, they had to be prevented from withdrawing any more gold from their banks. This much was largely accomplished by Roosevelt's March 6 bank holiday proclamation, which among other things provided that no "banking institution or branch shall pay out, export, earmark, or permit the withdrawal or transfer in any manner or by any device whatsoever, of any gold or silver coin or bullion or currency or take any other action which might facilitate the hoarding thereof" (Roosevelt 1938, 2:25). Roosevelt's subsequent proclamation of March 10 announcing that the banks would begin reopening on March 13 extended the suspension of gold dealings indefinitely. The domestic run on gold that had played so large a part in the banking troubles of the last several weeks would never trouble US banks or the Federal Reserve again.

This leaves but a single conundrum. People didn't just quit exchanging paper dollars for gold. Many also hastened to *return* gold they'd been hoarding and did so well before the notorious April 5, 1933, Executive Order No. 6102 prohibiting gold ownership outright. By May the Federal Reserve System had recovered more gold than it had lost since the start of February. Yet devaluation, far from having become less likely, was daily becoming more likely than ever.

Why, then, were Americans seen literally lining up to hand their gold back to the Fed on March 9 before their banks had even reopened? Eric Rauchway (2015, 52) claims that they were glad to take advantage of the governments' offer to take "a great burden from them . . . by accepting their gold for safe paper money," as if the public hadn't always had the option of holding paper dollars instead of gold, and as if gold were not safer than nominal paper equivalents everyone expected to see devalued!

In fact, there's a much more obvious reason why gold started flowing back into the Fed. On Wednesday, March 8, just before all those long lines formed, the Federal Reserve Board let it be known, first, that the Fed banks had compiled lists of those "unpatriotic" persons who had withdrawn gold from the system during the preceding weeks and, second, that it planned to have the press publish their names if they didn't bring the gold back at once. At least one Fed bank—Philadelphia's—even threatened to refuse to supply currency to member banks that failed to help identify such unpatriotic citizens. According to Fuller (2009, 465), "this tack served its purpose." That Friday alone, $200 million in gold coin and bullion came back. Soon Fed officials were able to report that they now had all the gold backing they needed for their notes so that the Fed's gold backing requirement no longer had to be suspended. Whatever Roosevelt's fireside chat accomplished, it can't be credited with this gold inflow, most obviously because gold had already started coming back before the chat but also because Roosevelt offered no assurance against devaluation, fear of which had prompted gold hoarding in the first place.

Intimidation was all well and good for getting Americans to bring their gold back to the Fed. But it couldn't do a thing about any of the gold that had escaped abroad. Getting that gold, or at least some of it, back called for very different policies, including some for which the Roosevelt administration bore no responsibility. We'll come to that later. But first we must consider steps taken during the bank holiday that eventually allowed not only undoubtedly strong banks but many weaker ones to reopen.

Deposit Insurance

"Your Government," Franklin Roosevelt (1938, 2:63) told the American people during his first fireside chat, "does not intend that the history of the past few years shall be repeated. We do not want and will not have another epidemic of bank failures."

Keeping that promise wasn't easy. It meant somehow convincing bank depositors not only that their banks were solvent for the moment but also that they didn't have to worry about them failing in the foreseeable future. And depositors had to be convinced of this despite the US banking system's now all-too-obvious fragility. Of the steps taken to convince them and thereby clear the way toward economic recovery, none was more significant than the establishment, by the Banking Act of June 16, 1933, of the Federal Deposit Insurance Corporation (FDIC).

No step was more significant. And none has been more misunderstood. To delve into that misunderstanding is to realize, among other things, just how difficult it can be to decide how much credit Franklin Roosevelt and his New Deal deserve for ending the Great Depression.

Deposit Insurance Myths

The Banking Act of 1933 was the most sweeping reform of the US banking system since the passage of the Federal Reserve Act.[1] Also known as the Glass-Steagall Act, the Banking Act was in fact the second measure to be so named, the first having been the 1932 Glass-Steagall Act allowing the Federal Reserve to back its currency with US government securities in lieu of gold or "eligible paper." The newer legislation subjected commercial banks to three new sorts of regulation. It prohibited them from underwriting or otherwise dealing in corporate securities, imposed limits on the interest rates they could pay on deposits, and established the FDIC. All Fed member banks had to take part in the FDIC's deposit guarantee ("insurance") scheme. Nonmember state banks could also take part on the condition (from which smaller ones were eventually exempted) that they were or became Fed members. While all three reforms had important consequences, either at once or in the long run, deposit insurance had the most obvious bearing on the course of economic recovery.

Because banks needed time both to qualify for insurance and to contribute to the FDIC's funding by purchasing shares in it, the FDIC's opening was scheduled for January 1, 1934. Starting then, under a temporary plan, all deposits would be insured up to $2,500. The temporary plan was supposed to give way to a permanent one, with much higher coverage limits, on July 1, 1934. But in mid-June Congress put off that change until July 1, 1935, while raising the temporary plan's coverage to $5,000 for all accounts. The start of the permanent plan was postponed yet again, by a congressional resolution, until August 31, 1935. Finally, just days before that deadline, the 1935 Banking Act introduced a new permanent plan, preserving the $5,000 coverage limit. In the meantime, the National Housing Act, passed on June 17, 1934, provided for the establishment of the Federal Savings and Loan Insurance Corporation (FSLIC), to guarantee deposits at savings and loans much as the FDIC guaranteed those kept at banks.

So much for the settled facts. The misunderstandings have mainly to do with the novelty of the deposit insurance plan, the purpose it was meant to serve, and the part that the Roosevelt administration played in its adoption. In 1960 Carter Golembe, a highly regarded bank consultant then working at the FDIC, tried to set the record straight. "Deposit insurance," Golembe (1960, 181–82) wrote, "was not a novel idea; protection of the small depositor, while important, was not its primary purpose; and, finally, it was the only important piece of legislation during the New Deal's famous 'one hundred days' which was neither requested nor supported by the new administration."[2]

Relief or Recovery?

Golembe's second point has to do with the role deposit insurance played in enabling economic recovery. Instead of merely being aimed at protecting depositors, as many suppose, its more crucial purpose was, Golembe (1960, 189) says, to "restore to the community, as quickly as possible, circulating medium destroyed or made unavailable as a consequence of bank failures." Insurance was, in other words, no less an element of macroeconomic policy than of welfare policy. Its ambitious macroeconomic goals were those of getting people to put their paper money back into banks, preventing further bank runs, and reviving bank lending.

To appreciate the necessity for some such reform, one need only realize that the banking system that emerged from the national bank holiday was essentially the same one that led to it. Of course, many closed banks would never be licensed to reopen, but thousands would be, including many rural banks of the sort that accounted for most preholiday bank failures. In the short run, the Fed's agreement to cover all cash withdrawals from such banks, together with Reconstruction Finance Corporation's capital injections, would bolster confidence in the reopened banks. But those measures were mere stopgaps that could neither rule out future runs nor convince people to redeposit all the paper currency they'd hoarded. If confidence in banks was to be fully restored and to never melt away again, something more had to be done.

In defending its insurance plan on May 19, 1933, the House Banking and Currency Committee made the macroeconomic case for it clear. "The public," the committee's report says, "was still afraid to deposit their money in the banks, and the banks are afraid to employ their deposits in the extension of bank credit for the support of trade and commerce. Businessmen and investors are victimized by the same fear. The result is curtailment of business, decline in values, idleness, unemployment, breadlines, national depression, and distress. We must resume the use of bank credit if we are to find our way out of our present difficulties" (US House 1933, 6).

Although the FDIC's limited insurance coverage couldn't alone assuage the fears of larger bank depositors, upon whom large urban banks were especially dependent (Calomiris and Wilson 2004), at a time when the average bank account balance was less than $250, the $5,000 coverage of the FDIC's permanent plan was enough to fully insure 98.5 percent of all bank depositors (Federal Deposit Insurance Corporation 1934, 60), including practically all depositors at otherwise vulnerable rural banks. The plan was therefore fully capable of shoring up much of the nation's otherwise notoriously feeble unit banking system. Had deposit insurance not served this macroeconomic purpose, Congress would almost certainly have spurned it, just as it had spurned scores of similar plans introduced to it over the course of several decades before the Great Depression struck.

And it would have done so for perfectly good reasons.

History Lessons

The FDIC wasn't the world's first nationwide deposit insurance arrangement. Czechoslovakia beat the United States to that punch by a decade. Nor was the FDIC the first US experiment with government-sponsored deposit insurance. Various state governments tried guaranteeing both banknotes and bank deposits. The first to do so was New York, which established a bank Safety Fund in 1829. The permanent FDIC plan shared many features in common with New York's Safety Fund, including (ultimately) the latter's provision exempting the owners of contributing banks from double liability, a once-common arrangement that required shareholders of a failed bank to fork up as much as their shares' par value if that proved necessary to make the bank's creditors whole.[3]

Begun with high hopes, the Safety Fund ended up a fiasco: by the early 1840s it was broke, so the government had to lend it the money by which it met its outstanding commitments. What Howard Bodenhorn (2002, 157, 182) refers to as a "combustible" mixture of inadequate supervision, "mispriced insurance premia, a limited ability to impose emergency assessments, and fraud," caused the fund to quickly fall victim to "the standard insurance problems of moral hazard and adverse selection."[4]

The Safety Fund's undoing came too late to stop Vermont and Michigan from resorting to similar schemes, with similar results. Michigan's fund, established in 1836, went bust just five years later, having failed to pay a nickel to any of the creditors it was supposed to insure (Golembe 1960, 185). Vermont's version, set up in 1831, survived longer but ultimately went awry by letting its members quit whenever they pleased. By 1859 none were left, so the fund could only cover 72 percent of its obligations, leaving Vermont taxpayers holding the bag for the rest (Golembe and Warburton 1958, 108).

Three other antebellum insurance schemes, in Indiana, Ohio, and Iowa, did much better. But unlike the New York, Vermont, and Michigan arrangements, and also unlike the FDIC's plan, they depended on the *unlimited* mutual liability of their members. Mutual liability gave participating banks a powerful incentive to police one another and to close down suspect banks before they became deeply insolvent. All three systems had good records, and all were still solvent when in 1866 a federal tax on state banknotes, aimed at compelling state banks to join the then-new national banking system, shut them down (Calomiris 1990, 288; Selgin 2000).

Because the tax on state banknotes nearly did away with state banks altogether, for a while it looked as though the United States had seen the last of its experiments with state-sponsored deposit insurance. But over time, as checks came to be more widely used in payments, non–note-issuing banks became increasingly viable. Before long, states were chartering hundreds of such banks every year. The result was a dual banking system, consisting of a mix of banks with federal ("national") and state charters, that survives to this day.

As we've seen, until the last decades of the twentieth century most US banks were unit banks, with a single office only and correspondingly heavy exposure to local shocks. Because state banks tended to be smaller than national banks, they were especially fragile. Not surprisingly, such banks failed relatively often, putting pressure on their sponsoring governments to come up with ways to protect their creditors. So, what first looked like state deposit insurance schemes' last curtain call turned out to be a mere intermission between two acts, with eight new schemes coming onstage between 1917 and 1927.

Alas, these later schemes merely "repeated and compounded the earlier errors of New York, Vermont, and Michigan" (Calomiris 1990, 288), and so ended up faring no better. Thanks mainly to the agricultural bust of the 1920s, by the spring of 1930 every one of them had gone belly-up.

Insurance or Branches?

Those early twentieth-century deposit insurance schemes were all established in states—Oklahoma, Kansas, Nebraska, Texas, Mississippi, South Dakota, North Dakota, and Washington—where there was strong opposition to branch banking, where laws either prohibited branching altogether or put very strict limits on its scope, and where "business prosperity in general depended on one or two commodities" (White 1983, 191).[5] This was no coincidence. Not letting prospective bank depositors choose between unit and branch banks was one way to keep poorly diversified unit banks in business. But it didn't spare them from runs once they got into hot water.

That's where insurance came in. Here again Golembe zeroes in on the truth. "It is not reading too much into history," he says, to regard deposit insurance schemes as "attempts to maintain a banking system composed of thousands of independent banks by alleviating one serious shortcoming of such a system: its proneness to bank suspensions, in good times and bad" (Golembe 1960, 195). Henry Steagall, who was second to none in his determination to save the small US unit banks, made no bones about this. "This bill," he said, referring to his May 1933 effort, "will preserve independent dual banking in the United States. . . . This is what the bill is intended to do" (198).

Insurance and branching were, in short, rival reform options. One sought to preserve the unit banking status quo, particularly state-chartered unit banks, despite their inherent weaknesses; the other would instead have allowed banks to branch statewide, if not nationwide, creating a system consisting of numerous large and well-diversified banks with branches and many fewer unit banks. Alabama representative Henry Steagall, the House Banking Committee Chair, favored the insurance option, having long opposed branch banking tooth and nail. Virginia's Carter Glass, who chaired the Senate Appropriations Committee, upheld the opposite view just as adamantly.

Until the Great Depression began, despite scores of attempts on behalf of federal deposit insurance and branch banking, neither seemed capable of gaining political traction. But as the Depression took its toll, and the number of bank failures mounted, so did the pressure to do *something* to stop runs, limit bank depositors' losses, and otherwise overhaul the US banking system. That pressure, plus some adept horse trading, finally broke the logjam. But it did so only after one of the more determined opponents of deposit insurance blinked.

That determined opponent was none other than Franklin Delano Roosevelt.

Outliving a Cat

"In June 1933," Council of Economic Advisers chair Christina Romer (2009) testified in 2009, "President Roosevelt worked with Congress to establish the Federal Deposit Insurance Corporation." The occasion was a hearing on lessons from the Great Depression being conducted by the Subcommittee on Economic Policy of the Senate Banking Committee.

It's true, of course, that Roosevelt helped establish the FDIC, since it was his signature that turned the 1933 Glass-Steagall bill into a law. What Romer didn't say is that Roosevelt *opposed* the Glass-Steagall bill's deposit insurance provision until the eleventh hour, even threatening to torpedo the whole banking bill unless it was taken out.

Roosevelt's opposition to deposit insurance was sincere, earnest, and perfectly conventional. In October 1932, while campaigning for the presidency, he responded—privately—to a letter from a supporter urging him to declare his support for federal deposit insurance so as to reassure the public and gain more votes. Roosevelt demurred. Although it might be popular, he said in reply, insurance was also "dangerous." In time it "would lead to laxity in bank management and carelessness on the part of both banker and depositor," one result of which would be "an impossible drain on the Treasury" (Gates 2017, 310).

Once in office, Roosevelt continued to oppose deposit insurance, causing what Frank Freidel, one of his preeminent biographers (1973, 441–42), calls Roosevelt's "major quarrel" on banking legislation with Congress. Asked his opinion of deposit insurance on March 8, during his very first press conference, Roosevelt repeated, off the record, the argument he made privately in his letter of the previous October. He added a nice numerical example of what he had in mind and finished by saying that he opposed "having the United States government liable for the mistakes and errors of individual banks" as well as "putting a premium on unsound banking" (The White House 1933, 13–14). When a reporter pressed harder, Roosevelt replied emphatically:

Q: You do have in mind guaranteeing deposits of banks on the new basis?
FDR: No; no government guarantee.
Q: You would have to have that guarantee under the new banking system.
FDR: There would have to be a guarantee? Oh, no. The government isn't going to guarantee any banks (The White House 1933, 15–16).

In this exchange Roosevelt wasn't entirely candid, for as we saw earlier, by various provisions of the 1933 Emergency Banking Act the government and the Federal Reserve were in effect planning to guarantee the deposits of reopened banks, if only briefly (Silber 2009). Roosevelt apparently saw no inconsistency between his acceptance of those emergency provisions and his opposition to more explicit and permanent deposit insurance. In any event, the emergency provisions, being stopgaps only, did not end the legislative battle for fundamental reform of the banking system that raged through ninety-nine of the Roosevelt administration's first hundred days.

By mid-May, however, the tide of that battle was turning decidedly in favor of insurance. A new Steagall bill had made it to the Senate Committee, and Carter Glass, who had already gone so far as to include an optional deposit insurance plan in his own bill, was persuaded to amend it further to provide for temporary but mandatory and immediate insurance of all Fed member bank deposits. Arthur Vandenberg, the Republican senator from Michigan who did that persuading, rose in the Senate to explain why. "There is no remote possibility," he said, "of adequate and competent economic recooperation [recuperation] in the United States in the next twelve months . . . until confidence in normal banking is restored; and in the face of the existing circumstances, I am perfectly sure that the insurance of bank deposits immediately is the paramount and fundamental necessity of the moment" (Gates 2017, 315). Glass accepted Vanderberg's amendment on the understanding that Steagall would in turn support Glass's plan for separating investment and commercial banking. The amendment passed handily, allowing Glass's bill to join Steagall's in conference.

When Roosevelt learned what had happened, he was anything but pleased. Instead, on June 1 he called both Glass and Steagall to a meeting at the White House whose other attendees were a motley assortment of administration critics of deposit insurance (Gates 2017, 316). Roosevelt also wrote to both Glass and Steagall individually and to the conference committee, threatening to veto any compromise that included deposit insurance. But Roosevelt's bluff was called, first by Huey Long, who announced that Congress had votes enough to override the veto, and then by Carter Glass, who told the president that Congress was determined to have insurance one way or another. At last Roosevelt, seeing discretion as the better part of valor, and perhaps thinking that bitter as its insurance provisions made the reconciled bill, its other provisions, which he supported, made it a pill worth swallowing, agreed to endorse it. Chatting with reporters after finally signing the Banking Act, he remarked that its insurance provision had "more lives than a cat" ("The Presidency: Signings" 1933).

Role Reversal

How is it that Roosevelt so often gets credit for deposit insurance despite having opposed it so relentlessly? Part of the explanation is that, once he'd signed off on it, he also took credit for it. His doing so merely amused his professional contemporaries. But it has confused later generations, who have taken Roosevelt's politic display of self-satisfaction at face value. Another is that Roosevelt's criticisms of deposit insurance were often made either privately or off the record, while his efforts to kill it in Congress took place behind closed doors. Finally, Roosevelt did after all sign the Glass-Steagall Act, thereby making it possible, if somewhat misleading, for historians to consider deposit insurance part of his New Deal.

If the popular view of Roosevelt as a champion of deposit insurance is more fiction than fact, the equally common view that Herbert Hoover opposed insurance isn't much better. It's true that for most of his career Hoover's views on deposit insurance and on banking reform more generally differed little from Roosevelt's, just as Roosevelt suggested in his March 8 press conference. Instead of favoring insurance, both men preferred Carter Glass's original reform program. So, on December 8, 1931, when Hoover (1951, 122) asked Congress to look into various possible banking reforms, including "the need for separation between the different kinds of banking; an enlargement of branch banking [and] the methods by which enlarged membership in the Federal Reserve System may be brought on," he didn't mention insurance, which he, like Roosevelt and Glass, considered a bad idea.

But while Roosevelt continued to oppose insurance after the February–March banking crisis, that debacle changed Hoover's mind. On February 28, 1933, he wrote to the Federal Reserve Board on February 28, 1933, asking whether the board considered it desirable

(a) To establish some form of Federal guarantee of banking deposits; or

(b) To establish clearing house systems in the affected areas; or

(c) To allow the situation to drift along under the sporadic State and community solutions now in progress. (Myers and Newton 1936, 359)

Despite his reputation as a do-nothing president, Hoover considered the third option unacceptable, including it only to compel the Board to choose between the others. On March 2, with the banking system in free fall, the Board replied that it wasn't prepared to recommend deposit insurance given its "inherent dangers" and the history of states' experiments with it (Myers and Newton 1936, 362). To this Hoover replied at once. He was, he said, "familiar with the inherent dangers in any form of federal guarantee of banking deposits." Even so, he wondered "whether or not the situation has reached the time when the Board should give further consideration to this possibility" (364). Hoover even included a "rough outline" of an insurance plan, asking the Board for its opinion. But the Board replied that it preferred a nationwide bank holiday to any sort of guarantee.

Two days later Hoover handed the reins to Roosevelt, who announced the bank holiday a day later.

FDR's Last Laugh

If Roosevelt has gotten too much credit for the FDIC's establishment, he deserves more credit than he's gotten for having recognized the dangers it posed and for having preferred other options for that reason.

That deposit insurance wasn't the *only* way to keep a banking system from collapsing was evident enough in 1933 from other countries' experiences. Hoover, for one, was well aware of this. "That it was possible," he said, "by proper organization and inspection, to have a banking system in which depositors were safe was demonstrated by Britain, Canada, Australia, and South Africa, where no consequential bank failure took place in the depression. Their governments gave no guarantee to depositors. Their economic shocks were as great as ours" (Hoover 1951, 24). Hoover might also have mentioned Bulgaria, Denmark, Finland, Greece, Lithuania, the Netherlands, Portugal, Spain, and Sweden, for these countries also had neither deposit insurance nor a banking crisis during the 1930s. Although the examples of France and Belgium showed that nationwide branching was no guarantee against a crisis, nations that allowed it tended to be less vulnerable than others (Grossman 1994).[6]

That uninsured banking systems could be stable explains the fact that, apart from the United States and Czechoslovakia, no other nation chose to guarantee its banks' deposits until the 1960s, and only a score had done so as late as 1980. Furthermore, those that opted for insurance didn't necessarily do so because their banking systems had proven unstable without it. Canada, for example, decided to establish the Canadian Deposit Insurance Corporation in 1967 even though no Canadian commercial bank had failed since 1923 and none were in danger of failing (Selgin 2021).

Nor does the spread of deposit insurance since the 1960s appear to have occurred in response to evidence that uninsured banking systems were at risk of collapsing without it. Instead, many nations appear to have jumped on the deposit insurance bandwagon either because (mostly US-trained) economists at the World Bank and the International Monetary Fund pressured them to do so (Demirgüç-Kunt, Kane, and Laeven 2008) or simply because doing so had become fashionable (Demirgüç-Kunt and Detaigiache 2002, 1394).[7]

What about Roosevelt's claim that deposit insurance was "dangerous," that once insured, "the weak banks would pull down the strong ones" (Freidel 1973, 442)? That, after all, was what had happened in states that tried insuring banks before the Great Depression.[8] But so far as FDIC insurance was concerned, for many years it looked as though Roosevelt had been mistaken. "Despite initial concerns to the contrary," Eugenie Short and Gerald O'Driscoll (1983, 1) observed in the early 1980s that "the federal deposit insurance system has worked remarkably well in reducing the number of bank failures and in eliminating depositor loss. The total number of insured bank failures since 1933 has not greatly exceeded the average number of bank failures in any single year during the 1920s. . . . Moreover, between 1933 and 1982, nearly 99 percent of *all* deposits in insured banks that failed were recovered by depositors."[9]

But just as Short and O'Driscoll were saying this, great fissures started appearing in the once-solid insurance arrangement. Before long, the former banking arcadia looked more like a house of cards. Short and O'Driscoll were themselves aware of what was happening. The FDIC, they recalled, was part of a package of regulations. Other parts of the package—including laws that prohibited banks from underwriting securities, limited the interest rates they could pay on deposits, prevented them from branching, and otherwise insulated them from competition—served to reduce banks' incentives and ability to attract insured deposits by taking on greater risks (Short and O'Driscoll 1983, 1–2).

The fissures started out as hairline cracks formed during the mid 1960s, when inflation began taking its toll on financial intermediaries' bottom line. From then on rising inflation and interest rates, international competition, and the rise of money market mutual funds put more and more banks in hot water. Regulators responded by peeling back risk-constraining regulations and boosting insurance coverage. The most important changes came with the Depository Institutions Deregulation and Monetary Control Act of 1980 and the Garn–St. Germain Act of 1982. Those reforms phased out deposit interest rate limits while raising both FDIC and FSLIC insurance coverage from the $40,000 (per account) limit set in 1974 to $100,000 (Keeton 1984; Bundt, Cosimano, and Halloran 1992).

The combination of relaxed regulations and increased explicit insurance coverage, coupled with the implicit insurance of banks regarded as "too big to fail," created just the sort of dynamics Roosevelt and other critics of deposit insurance had feared. The ironic twist was that reforms once seen as ways to strengthen the US banking system, such as allowing banks greater freedom to branch, now allowed them to compete more aggressively for underpriced insured funds to invest in risky assets. Soon enough weak banks, including some very big ones, were pulling down not just stronger ones but also their insurers.

For the FDIC, the reckoning took the form of what one of its publications describes as "an extraordinary upsurge in the number of bank failures" between 1980 and 1994. Those failures put extraordinary strains on its resources, eventually costing it $36.6 billion (Federal Deposit Insurance Corporation 1997, 3). But that was nothing compared to what happened in the $617 billion savings and loan industry. There, after breaking yet another batch of state-run insurance schemes, moral hazard problems also visited the FSLIC. Its fate was ultimately sealed by regulators' willingness to allow insolvent institutions to keep trying their luck while using accounting gimmicks to boost their reported net worth (Kane 1992). The result was scads of high-risk gambles by savings and loan associations whose owners had nothing to lose. These left the industry even deeper in the red. Eventually the losses finished off the FSLIC, making it necessary for taxpayers to cover $132.1 billion of failed savings and loan associations' $160.1 billion in insured deposits. Although it wasn't "impossible" for the Treasury to pay that bill, the tab was certainly big enough to show that Roosevelt hadn't just been crying wolf.

Ironically, just as these events were unfolding in the United States, national deposit insurance schemes started sprouting everywhere. By the summer of 2018, 107 countries had joined the deposit insurance craze. Most have since struggled with moral hazard problems, with depositors losing their incentive to look out for risky banks and banks in turn taking greater risks. In dozens of cases where insurance coverage has been high and supervision has been lax, instead of enhancing banking-system stability, insurance has done just the opposite, "increas[ing] the likelihood of bank crises significantly" (McCoy 2008, 423; see also Demirgüç-Kunt and Detragiache 2002; Anginer and Demirgüç-Kunt 2018). This too must be accounted as part of the 1933 Glass-Steagall Act's legacy and as evidence of Roosevelt's prescience.

∗ ∗ ∗

How much credit do Roosevelt and the New Deal deserve for ending the Great Depression? Answering that question means answering a similar question about every important component of the Roosevelt administration's recovery program. So far as the decision to insure bank deposits is concerned, the best answer, I think, is that Roosevelt and the New Deal deserve a lot less credit than they're usually given. A lot less credit; and very little blame.

Appendix: The Rest of the Banking Act

Deposit insurance was only one of several reforms provided for by the Banking Act of 1933. Two others have also been credited with helping to end the Great Depression. Regulation Q altogether outlawed the payment of interest on checking accounts while limiting interest payments on other sorts of deposits. Several other Banking Act provisions—routinely but confusingly referred to as "the Glass-Steagall Act," as if they made up a separate statute—prohibited banks from dealing in most kinds of private securities and severely restricted their ability to affiliate themselves with other firms that dealt in them. While the FDIC was supposed to help restore confidence in the nation's banks and thereby promote recovery by limiting depositors' exposure to the risks banks took, these other reforms were supposed to achieve the same goals by preventing banks from taking big risks in the first place.

But while there is no reason to doubt that the FDIC achieved its intended purpose, there's a compelling reason for doubting that these other measures helped the US economy to recover, namely the lack of evidence that the practices they prevented were to blame for the Depression or any significant part of it.

Although several arguments were made during the early 1930s and before for limiting banks' ability to pay interest on deposits (Board of Governors of the Federal Reserve System 1977, 9–10), the most relevant for our purposes held that doing so would discourage banks from making risky loans and investments. When banks competed by bidding for deposits, the popular if controversial theory went, they also tended to take on riskier assets with higher promised returns to cover the cost of doing so. Riskier bank portfolios meant more bank failures, other things being equal. So, keeping bankers from bidding for deposits wouldn't just make life easier for the bankers themselves. It would also boost confidence in the banking system by making banks safer.

While the theory that allowing banks to pay interest on deposits makes them riskier isn't entirely groundless, research since the 1930s suggests that it holds up only with the help of some heroic assumptions, including the assumption that, instead of caring about their banks' anticipated lifetime profitability or net worth, bankers are inclined to maximize the expected return on their investment portfolios even when doing so is likely to prove unprofitable (Gambs 1975; Caperaa and Eeckhoudt 1977).[10]

Nor was any evidence supporting the theory offered during the hearings that led to the Banking Act's passage. Although there was, naturally enough, plenty of talk concerning the causes of bank failures, "not a single witness stressed interest on deposits and, indeed, few even mentioned the practice" (Cox 1967, 276). Subsequent studies of the years leading to the Banking Act's passage, when "frenzied bidding for deposits" is supposed to have "led many banks into eventual failure" (279), have also failed to uncover any evidence consistent with that belief. On the contrary, despite considering different sets of banks and measures of bank risk, including the probability that a bank would fail, these studies either found that the riskiness of banks' investments—or their odds of failing—was unrelated to the rates they paid on bank deposits or uncovered a *negative* relationship (Benston 1964; Cox 1966). In light of such research, a 1977 study by Federal Reserve Board staff concluded that "the arguments for prohibition of interest on deposits in the 1930's appear to have had little validity at the time the prohibition was enacted" (Board of Governors of the Federal Reserve System 1977, 14). It follows that prohibiting or limiting interest payments on deposits is unlikely to have contributed to economic recovery by making banks any safer.

The story concerning the Banking Act's "Glass-Steagall" provisions is much the same. It was claimed during the Banking Act hearings and also during the concurrent Pecora Commission hearings that the securities dealings of commercial banks and their affiliates were, as the Senate's Banking Act Report put it, "a very fruitful source of bank failures" and, consequently, an important cause of the Depression (Benston 1990, 12).[11] According to Carter Glass, who led the effort to separate commercial from investment banking, by "fill[ing] the bank portfolios of this country with these [risky] investment securities," banks' securities affiliates made "one of the greatest contributions to the unprecedented disaster which has caused this uncurable depression" (35). Banks' securities dealings were also blamed for the stock market boom and bust that, in the opinion of many, would have led to the subsequent downturn even if banks themselves hadn't loaded up on risky securities.

Yet no actual evidence supporting these claims was offered during the hearings (Benston 1990; Ang and Richardson 1994). Instead, in a process that brings to mind the children's game of Chinese Whispers, what were mere accusations during the hearings came to be remembered later on first as evidence and eventually as proof of guilt.[12] Although the Glass subcommittee offered the Bank of United States as an example—indeed, its *only* important example—of a bank that failed owing to dealings with its many affiliates, the Bank of United States dealt in real estate, not securities. "There is nothing in the record," economist George Benston (1990, 31) concludes, "to indicate that the failure of the Bank of United States or its use of affiliates was related to securities operations or could have been prevented had the separation of commercial and investment banking the Glass-Steagall Act mandated been in effect."

Nor have investigations since 1933 discovered evidence linking Depression-era bank failures to banks' securities dealings. Instead, they find that if those dealings made any difference at all, they did so by making banks *less* likely to fail.[13] "The evidence from the pre–Glass-Steagall period," Benston (1990, 41) says in summing up several of these studies, including his own, "is totally inconsistent with the belief that banks' securities activities or investments caused them to fail or caused the financial system to collapse. Those who claim otherwise . . . either misread the record, did not look at any actual data, or simply uncritically believed unsupported assertions made by senators and their staff."[14]

As for the claim that even if they weren't to blame for bank failures banks' security dealings helped bring about the Depression by sponsoring the stock market boom and bust, it too won't stand scrutiny. Although it's true that interior banks' deposits with New York correspondents were used to finance brokers' loans, that had been going on for many decades before the crash. Nor was it the case, as some have alleged, that margin requirements on brokers' loans were lower in the 1920s than they'd been in previous decades: instead, as the boom approached its peak, those requirements were raised to exceptionally *high* levels (Smiley and Keehn 1988). If the volume of brokers' loans increased substantially during the 1920s, it wasn't because lenders were *pushing* money into the stock market. It was because growth in the demand for stocks was *pulling* money into it (White 1990, 76).

What changed in the 1920s was small investors' appetite for common stocks, which until then were mainly purchased by bankers and businessmen

(Rutterford and Sotiropoulos 2017). That increased appetite itself had many causes unrelated to banks' involvement in the securities business, which it anticipated: according to one estimate, the number of US shareholders quadrupled between 1900 and 1920 (495). In fact, causation ran mainly from growth in the public's appetite for stocks to the proliferation of bank security affiliates, not the other way around. By the start of the 1920s, companies were issuing stocks instead of taking out bank loans, while people were buying stocks instead of depositing money in banks. For that reason bank deposits rose only modestly, from $8.7 billion in 1921 to $10.5 billion in 1929, while commercial loans, which made up 58 percent of national banks' assets in 1920, made up only 37 percent in 1929 (Lowenstein 2011, 40; White 1990, 70n4). Banks responded to these shifts by increasing their own involvement in the securities business—hence the tenfold increase in the number of bank security affiliates during the same period (Peach 1941). In short, instead of banks enticing the public to mess around with stocks, the public enticed banks to do so!

What's more, even if banks' securities affiliates convinced people to invest more in stocks than they would have otherwise, it doesn't follow that their doing so caused stock prices to rise beyond levels consistent with market fundamentals. And even if stocks *did* rise above that level, it doesn't follow that the ensuing crash itself made a depression inevitable.

Whether there was actually a stock "bubble" during the 1920s, meaning a rise in stock prices beyond levels consistent with fundamentals, remains controversial.[15] But allowing that there was, it is doubtful that the crash that followed caused or contributed significantly to the Depression. Back in 1968, financial historian Robert Sobel (1968, 147) could declare, truthfully, that "no causal relationship between the events of late October 1929 and the Great Depression has ever been shown through the use of empirical evidence." While some subsequent research (e.g., Romer 1990) has rendered that sweeping claim obsolete, the causal links later research points to at most explain a modest postcrash recession, not a depression and certainly not the Great Depression. "Scholars," a 2001 survey of this literature concludes, "have produced no more consensus on the question of links between the crash and the onset of the depression than on the causes of the crash itself" (Klein 2001, 348).

If there is little reason for blaming banks' securities activities for the Depression, there is equally little reason to suppose that by putting a stop to those activities, the Glass-Steagall provisions of the 1933 Banking Act contributed to the recovery. Nor is there any evidence that they did so. "More than two decades after the 1929 Crash," Janice Traflet (2013, 4) observes in her history of the postwar securities market, "the shadow of 1929 remained dark." Although by the early 1950s Americans had plenty of cash available to invest in stocks, "they overwhelmingly chose to place whatever savings they had into other vehicles," including good-old savings accounts. In 1952, less than 10 percent of US households owned any common stock, as compared to up to 20 percent during the 1920s (4–5). Securities underwriting and trading were then only just returning to their pre-Depression levels (Benston 1990, 125).

To sum up, while there is every reason to suppose that deposit insurance played an important part in the post-1933 recovery, there is none for thinking that the rest of the 1933 Banking Act did so.

The RFC, Part 1

Everybody knows that after the bank holiday deposit insurance helped stabilize the US banking system. Relatively few realize that it couldn't have done so, or could have done so only at the cost of having many more banks stay closed forever, without lots of help from the Reconstruction Finance Corporation (RFC). Although the RFC was not a New Deal innovation—it was established a year and six weeks before Franklin Roosevelt took office—the Roosevelt administration took far more advantage of it than the Hoover administration ever did, eventually turning it into the largest New Deal agency of all.

This chapter deals with the RFC's efforts to prevent and then help resolve the banking crisis. Chapter 12 takes up its subsequent activities.

Hoover's New Deal

There have been few more successful examples in history of the propaganda technique known as the "big lie" than the charge that Herbert Hoover was a do-nothing president. In fact, Hoover was being perfectly truthful when, during the 1932 campaign, he said, "We might have done nothing. . . . Instead, we met the situation with . . . the most gigantic programs of economic defense and counterattack ever evolved in the history of the Republic." For that matter Hoover's Democratic opponent, who accused Hoover's administration "of being the greatest spending administration in all our history" (Lyons 1948, 287), was also being truthful. On public works alone, the Hoover administration spent more than the previous *nine* administrations combined, notwithstanding that their undertakings included the Panama Canal (269). No previous administration, David Kennedy (1999, 48) observes, ever "moved so purposefully and so creatively in the face of an economic downturn." And "no man in the White House ever struggled harder," Frederick Lewis Allen (1940, 93) adds, only to see "his efforts so scantily rewarded."[1]

Although the RFC started out as the centerpiece of the "Hoover New Deal," it went on to play an even larger role in the Roosevelt version. Under the leadership of Texas entrepreneur Jesse Jones, it became nothing less than "America's largest corporation and the world's biggest and most varied banking organization" (Jones 1951, 3).

But did it help the US economy recover from the Great Depression?

A Shadow Fed

Although Hoover eventually supported the RFC, credit for its establishment is mostly due to Eugene Meyer, a staunch Republican Hoover put in charge of the Federal Reserve Board in 1930. Between 1918 and 1925 Meyer served as managing director of the War Finance Corporation (WFC), the original goals of which were making cheap credit available to firms producing war materials and propping up the price of Liberty Bonds. After the war, Meyer kept the WFC alive by converting it into an agricultural credit agency. But in 1925 he stepped down, and the WFC quit extending credit, although it didn't officially close until it finished collecting on its loans fourteen years later.

As bank failures mounted after 1930, Meyer, in his new post as head of the Federal Reserve Board, pushed hard for the WFC's revival. But Hoover favored a private and voluntary alternative, so Meyer instead tried to get bankers to cooperate toward that end. Thanks to Great Britain's suspension of the gold standard on September 18, 1931, and the large-scale gold drain and numerous bank failures it inspired, he finally succeeded.[2]

The result, announced by Hoover in the wee hours of October 7, 1931, was the National Credit Corporation (NCC), a half billion–dollar private credit pool established and run by bankers and insurance executives (Olson 1972). Because the NCC was prepared to rediscount bank assets the Federal Reserve wouldn't accept and could do so for financial institutions that weren't Fed members, Hoover and the bankers hoped that together with the Fed the NCC could keep the nation's banks liquid enough to avoid widespread suspensions. But Meyer was far from sanguine, and it was owing to his importuning, rather than to any enthusiasm for the idea on Hoover's part, that Hoover promised in announcing the NCC that "if necessity requires, I will recommend the creation of a finance corporation similar in character and purpose to the WFC, with available funds sufficient for any legitimate call in support of credit" (Hoover 1931b).

It didn't take long, in fact, for the NCC's inadequacy to show itself: the new corporation took a month just to open for business and still longer to start making loans. By December it had lent only $10 million.[3] By then Meyer had a bill ready calling for a revived WFC, to be known as the Reconstruction Finance Corporation. Congress pushed the legislation through as quickly as it could, allowing for the holiday recess, and Hoover made it law on January 22, 1932. The new executive agency thus established had a capital stock of $500 million, subscribed to by the Treasury, and was authorized to borrow three times that amount. Serving as its head was Chicago banker and former vice president Charles G. Dawes.

Thrown for a Loop

While Dawes oversaw the RFC, its lending was limited to financial institutions and railroads. Its precise remit, according to Hoover's remarks upon signing the RFC Act, was narrower still. "It is not created for the aid of big industries and big banks," Hoover said. "Such institutions are amply able to take care of themselves. It is created for the support of smaller banks and financial institutions, through rendering their resources liquid, to give renewed support to business and agriculture" (Hoover 1932c).

But just which banks the RFC helped during its first five months remained a mystery for some time: the corporation's quarterly reports only revealed the aggregate sums it lent to various broad categories of borrowers, with nothing about particular loan recipients. In other words, as journalist John T. Flynn (1933) later complained, the RFC "passed round hundreds of millions of dollars of public money to banks and railroads without affording either to the public, or even to Congress itself, a grain of information about the identity of the objects of its bounty."

Chicago's banking crisis changed things. In early June 1932, Dawes abruptly resigned; days later as he boarded a train to the Windy City, he explained that he was heading there to take charge of the Central Republic Bank, of which he was still nominal chairman. Just over a week after he arrived, with the Democratic National Convention about to convene, Dawes coolly informed a group including Chicago's leading bankers and RFC board member Jesse Jones that Central Republic, one of several Loop banks that had been hemorrhaging money for weeks, wouldn't open the next morning. Fearing a general collapse, Jones quickly arranged, with Hoover's approval, to have the RFC lend Central Republic $90 million—by far its biggest loan yet—to keep it and the other Loop banks from closing.

When word of this other "Dawes Loan" got out, accusations of favoritism flew ("Dawes Bank Loan by RFC Attacked" 1932).[4] Congress's response became part of the Emergency Relief and Construction Act, signed by Hoover on July 27, 1932 (Hoover 1932c). On the plus side, this amendment to the RFC Act increased the RFC's borrowing authority to $3.3 billion, for use in supporting state and local relief agencies, public works programs, and various agricultural credit agencies, among other things. But the amendment also placed new limits on the RFC's lending. The amendment forbade loans to financial institutions whose officers or board members included anyone who sat on the RFC's board or had done so within a year prior to the date on which a loan was granted. The new law also made the corporation submit monthly reports on its activities, including borrowers' names, to the Senate and House or, if Congress wasn't in session, to the Senate secretary and the House clerk.

Bigger Isn't Better

Although the public disclosure clause wasn't retroactive, Congress eventually asked the RFC to supply it with details concerning the loans it made during its first five months, which it did on January 25, 1933. At last Congress and the public would see just how well the RFC had lived up to President Hoover's claim that it wasn't there to help big banks.

What they discovered was that during the RFC's first five months, Central Republic was far from being the only big bank to receive its help. Although the corporation's officers and its champions, including Hoover, had technically been telling the truth when they insisted that "most of its loans" went to small banks, the claim glossed over the fact that most of the RFC's *money* went to large ones. For example, after the corporation had been in business for five weeks, the White House declared that it lent the greater part of $61 million to 255 "mostly small country banks." What the White House failed to say was that more than two-thirds of the total went to just three banks, all of which were located in fair-sized cities. During the whole of the RFC's first five months, before its loan recipients' names were shared with Congress, more than 40 percent of the $642 million of loans it authorized went to banks in just seven good-sized cities, with Chicago and San Francisco banks alone receiving $136 million (Flynn 1933). In many instances, the RFC's loans to smaller banks were themselves aimed at indirectly helping larger ones that were among the smaller banks' creditors.

There were actually good reasons for the RFC's record. The extent of RFC lending to large banks mostly reflected the distribution of US banks by size and the fact that bigger banks tended to suffer larger deposit losses than small ones. And contrary to Hoover's claim, some big banks, such as Central Republic, were quite unable to "take care of themselves." Finally, the failure of a big bank was more likely to cause other banks to fail. Contemporary complaints notwithstanding, economic historians have not found much evidence that politics or favoritism, as opposed to a desire to limit bank failures, informed the pattern of the RFC's loans to banks (Mason 2003).

Even so, once it had to submit detailed monthly reports, the RFC quit making very large loans to very big banks. In fact, it made fewer loans to banks of all sorts. Jesse Jones (1951, 83), who sat on the RFC's board at this time and later became its most famous chairman, believed that fear of public disclosure of their loans "prevented many bankers from applying for help that was sorely needed," owing either to pride or to fear of having their banks stigmatized. Whatever the reason, it didn't make the RFC's job any easier.

Lent to Death

Needless to say, the Hoover RFC didn't keep the US financial system safe from "unexpected shocks." Nor did it otherwise arrest the US economy's downward spiral. "Perhaps it is too much," Harvard's Franklin Ebersole (1933, 484) observed in reviewing the RFC's one-year record, "to expect [that] the Corporation should have effected a cure for the crisis and depression. But the label 'Reconstruction' offered more than hope and mere salvage." Although the RFC had authorized $951 million in loans to open banks and trust companies and another $200 million to closed banks' receivers for distribution to their depositors, these amounts simply weren't enough to either keep open banks liquid or fully pay off deposits at closed ones.

Did the RFC's loans at least help? "To criticize the Corporation for not keeping banks open or stimulating business recovery," Ebersole (1933, 486) says, "assumes a large objective—the maximum achievement." But, he allows, it was only supposed to tide banks, railroads, state relief agencies, and farmers over until other steps could be taken. Alas, he concludes, "even for such a limited objective, it must be said . . . that [Hoover's RFC] was a gamble that failed." Charles Calomiris and his coauthors (2013, 528) go still further: they find not only that the RFC's loans were generally unhelpful but also that they seem to have made banks that took advantage of them worse off. Besides disqualifying many banks, the RFC's strict collateral requirements stripped those that secured loans from it of their best collateral. The fact that the RFC had priority over banks' other creditors gave better-informed depositors a reason to avoid banks that borrowed from it. This in turn gave bankers yet another reason to think twice before asking for the RFC's help. According to Joseph Mason (2001, 90), their reluctance was especially important before July 1932, when (owing largely to Eugene Meyer's influence) the RFC's collateral requirements were especially strict.

Some other economists' verdicts are less severe. Ernest Klemme (1939, 366) and Beryl Sprinkel (1952, 218) maintain that until the Michigan banking crisis struck, the RFC's loans reduced bank suspensions and bolstered depositor confidence. James Butkiewicz (1995) in turn finds that the RFC's loans cut bank suspensions "almost in half" until the RFC was compelled to publicize them, after which its loans made little difference. Joseph Mason (2001, 89), on the other hand, finds "a *positive* significant relation between loan publicity and bank survival." One explanation for such apparently contradictory findings is that the most vulnerable banks were also the ones that chose not to seek the RFC's help, since they could no longer have it confidentially.

Standing back from all these findings, the picture one takes in shows an RFC persistently hampered in its efforts to keep the banking system liquid, but not always for the same reason. The corporation's strict collateral requirements limited its success through July 1932, while banks' fear of adverse publicity did so afterward. The result, either way, was that the RFC's bank lending program failed to deliver the goods.

Six Thousand Bailouts

Five days after Roosevelt took office, with the nation's banks on vacation and economic activity almost at a standstill, no one doubted that the RFC, considered as a recovery device, had been a flop. "Despite unprecedented efforts on behalf of the private economy," James Stuart Olson (1982, 17) writes, "the RFC had not revived commercial credit, business investment, production, or employment." The Roosevelt administration "was not even sure the RFC was really strengthening the banking system."

So far as the nation's banks were concerned, the fundamental problem, which became all too evident in the course of the national bank holiday, was no longer a lack of liquidity. On mark-to-market terms, the US banking system was broke (Kimmel 1939, 9). What banks needed was capital, and plenty of it. And the RFC was about to start giving it to them by buying their preferred stock shares, notes, and debentures. Although the RFC would still lend to banks after its share purchase program began, its loans would no longer have as their primary aim keeping struggling banks alive. Instead, they would mostly be used to assist in the liquidation of banks that died.[5] As for banks that were fundamentally sound, after the holiday they had access to other sources of funds by which to remain liquid, including foreigners who were increasingly inclined to send capital their way (Chandler 1970, 150).

Although the share purchase program was the first major New Deal addition to the RFC's powers, Fed officials first proposed it in the wake of the

Chicago banking crisis.[6] Hoover resisted the idea at first, but in late January 1933, having at last been won over, he asked for legislation to be drawn up. But like some other Hoover administration ideas for dealing with the then unfolding banking crisis, this one could get nowhere without Democratic support, which Hoover was unable to secure. Instead, a modified version of the plan became Title III of the New Deal's Emergency Banking Act (Olson 1982, 38–39).[7]

Two sorts of banks and trusts benefited from the RFC's "capital correction plan." First, of the 4,215 banks that couldn't be licensed to reopen immediately after the holiday, 3,100 were considered salvageable with the help of RFC-supplied capital. The RFC would also inject capital into several thousand other banks that, although licensed to reopen, lacked enough capital to qualify for Federal Deposit Insurance Cooperation (FDIC) insurance when that became available. Regulators were determined to see most if not all banks enrolled in the new insurance scheme once it was running, whether they were legally required to join it or not. The FDIC was willing to help by insuring still-undercapitalized banks provided the RFC pledged to recapitalize them within six months of its doing so.

Despite its ultimately impressive scale, as figure 6.1 shows, the RFC's share purchase program got off to a slow start. One reason for this was Jesse Jones's personal dislike of the plan. According to Walter Wyatt, "it took [Fed governor] Eugene Black and White House pressure several months to get him going on the program," for which he later took credit (Moley 1966, 175). But the same stigma problem that limited banks' willingness to borrow from the RFC once its loans were publicized also made them hesitate to sell their shares to it. So, for that matter, did their fear that the RFC would end up interfering with their management, as it eventually did in some instances.

So it happened that during its first months the RFC only purchased shares from a few dozen banks and trusts. But as Jones became more cooperative and banks' deadline for qualifying for deposit insurance approached, the trickle of purchases became a torrent. When the temporary deposit insurance program went into effect on January 1, 1934, 90 percent of the nation's commercial banks and 36 percent of its savings banks were able to take part in it. By March the RFC had purchased stock from more than half of the nation's banks (Moley 1966, 23). Yet it had to inject even more capital into many banks before they could meet the FDIC's stricter capital requirements when those kicked in the following July.

Not surprisingly, the RFC's share purchase program proved more capable of nursing banks back to profitability than its lending had been (Calomiris et al. 2013, 543). The program thus became a crucial part of the government's

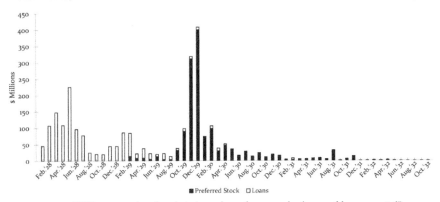

FIGURE 6.1. RFC loans to and preferred stock purchases from open banks, monthly, 1932–1936. (Reproduced from Mason 2000, Figure 2. Data courtesy of Joseph R. Mason.)

solution to the banking crisis and also rescued untold numbers of bank depositors who might have lost their savings otherwise or endured lengthy delays in recovering them.

But important as the RFC's contributions to financial stability and relief were, they fell short of achieving its ultimate objective, which was the revival of bank lending (Olson 1982, 128; Mason 2000, 24). Disappointed by the lack of any such revival, and observing that bankers were sitting on substantial excess reserves, officials at the RFC and elsewhere blamed them for not living up to their end of the bargain. Some of those officials then decided that if the bankers wouldn't do their part, the government would do it for them.

Big Engines That Couldn't

Although Hoover's RFC was "more largely a banker's loan bank than anything else" (Ebersole 1933, 477), financial institutions were never the only firms eligible for its support. Railroads were an important exception from the start, although they were so mainly because financial institutions—commercial banks and insurance companies especially—were railroads' main investors. Thanks to New York and other state regulatory authorities' inclusion of many railroad bonds among permissible investments for the banks and insurance companies they regulated, by 1932 those bonds made up 16 percent and 23 percent, respectively, of bank and insurance company assets (Mason and Schiffman 2002, 3).

Until 1929, railroad bonds had a good reputation: some had paid dividends without fail for generations, hence their triple-A ratings. But the Depression hit railroads hard. Between 1929 and 1933 their operating revenues were cut in half, while their fixed charges, including the interest they owed on their debts, stayed roughly the same. Even railroads that had been paying dividends continuously for decades had to quit doing so, causing their bonds to be downgraded. The RFC's loans to railroads were supposed to help the financial industry by keeping railroads from defaulting. Some of its loans also helped them to pay for repairs and new constructions and otherwise keep their workers employed.

By the end of 1932, when financial institutions held 45 percent of the RFC's outstanding loans, railroads were next in line with 21 percent (Ebersole 1933, 477). Unlike the RFC's loans to banks, its railroad loans were made public from the start: the Interstate Commerce Commission had to sign off on them, and the commission's policy was to report every loan it approved. Because it was mainly Class I railroads, with annual operating revenues of over $1 million, whose securities were on state regulators' approved lists, most RFC railroad support went to them, with $280 million of a total of $350 million going to just fifteen large lines. Over the course of its entire life, the RFC authorized 248 loans, totaling more than $1 billion, to eighty-nine different railroads.

Whether they went to big railroads or smaller ones, the RFC's railroad loans were generally earmarked for paying those railroads' other creditors, with just a fifth being designated for upkeep and new construction. The fact that large investment houses were among the railroad creditors whose loans the RFC helped repay gave it still more bad publicity. One of its very first railroad loans, for example, helped Missouri Pacific repay a $5.75 million loan to J. P. Morgan and Company. The fact that the Missouri Pacific went bankrupt just over a year later didn't make the loan smell any better ("Missouri Pacific Put in Bankruptcy" 1933).

Yet apart from the Morgan connection, the Missouri Pacific case was to prove typical: during the Hoover years, two-thirds of the fifteen Class I railroads that received most of the RFC's help ended up either going under or surviving only after courts intervened to adjust their debts (Olson 1982, 23, 97). Between Hoover's departure and 1939, when the RFC wound up its railroad lending program after having lent a grand total of $802 million, twenty-five more Class I railroads it had helped suffered the same fate (Schiffman 2003, 806). Evidently, however much it may have helped their creditors, the RFC's largess alone wasn't generally enough to save the railroads themselves.

The unvarnished truth was that railroads' woes weren't just cyclical. Their losses also reflected the growing importance of newer forms of transportation. In October 1932 a group of major universities and insurance companies, all saddled with lots of railroad debt, established the National Transportation Committee, with former president Calvin Coolidge as its head, to investigate the railroad situation. The committee's February 1933 report, *The American Transportation Problem,* concluded that instead of just being victims of the Depression, the railroads were facing "stiff, permanent competition from the airlines, automobiles, and trucks," from which nothing short of "massive consolidation" could rescue them (National Transportation Committee 1933; see also Olson 1982, 99–100).

So, more credit was no real solution. But that's not all. A recent and careful study (Daglish and Moore 2018) finds that word of a railroad's first RFC loan tended to raise the spread between the yield on its bonds and that of Treasury securities by about 55 basis points, presumably because the public considered such loans evidence that their recipients were in trouble. In the long run, RFC assistance tended to lower railroads' bond prices even more. So instead of helping financial institutions with substantial railroad investments stay solvent, RFC support for railroads may have done just the opposite, shifting losses to them and other creditors from railroads' shareholders. Garet Garrett—never one to mince words when it came to pointing out the New Deal's missteps—made the point scathingly:

> Suppose every other railroad that was insolvent had been let go into receivership. Where would the losses have fallen? Not upon the savings banks and the insurance companies and the private investors who owned the bonds; they were the creditors, they had been receiving interest, not profit, and in the end should all have been not only safe but better off, because the railroads were easily worth their bonds. The loss would have fallen were it belonged—that is, upon the stockholders, who were the owners. . . . They had had their profit, and having had the profit, they were obliged by the first implicit law of capitalism to take the loss. (Garrett 2023 [1938], 230)

Nor does RFC support appear to have done the railroads themselves much good. On the contrary, most experts believe that RFC loans harmed railroads by allowing them to put off both their bankruptcy and the reorganization they desperately needed (Olson 1982, 98–99; Spero 1939). Because avoiding bankruptcy meant having to continue paying all their creditors, fallen revenues notwithstanding, railroads that received RFC loans also tended to skimp on repairs and maintenance (Ebersole 1933, 486–87). For brief downturns, this strategy made sense. During the Great Depression, it became a recipe for railroad suicide. And because they allowed railroads to stave off bankruptcy longer, RFC loans tended to make them that much less viable when they eventually did file.

Bankruptcy, on the other hand, did not itself force railroads to shut down. Instead of liquidating them, receivers usually kept bankrupt railroads running while their owners drew up plans for their reorganization. Those plans typically emphasized rehabilitating a railroad's neglected rights of way and equipment (Spero 1939; Mason and Schiffman 2002, 7). Jesse Jones (1951, 107) put it pithily: "A bankrupt railroad cannot cut bait; it has to keep on fishing." And because they're relieved of the obligation to pay the fixed charges on their securities, bankrupt railroads "are often able to keep their properties in better shape than those which remain out of receivership" (108). Eventually, Garrett observed, "a great deal of old and profitless capital would have been rubbed out, new capital would have come in[,] . . . and the railroad situation today would not be the nightmare that it is" (Garrett 2023 [1938], 230). One ought therefore to take Jones's claim that RFC railroad loans "created tens of thousands of jobs" (106) with a pinch of salt: even according to Jones's own understanding, those loans more likely ended up reducing overall railroad employment.

And that, according to several studies, is just what the loans did. Surveying the whole 1929–1940 period, Daniel Schiffman (2003) finds that once they went bankrupt, large railroads (which received 96.7 percent of the RFC's railroad credits) tended to devote considerably more resources to maintaining their equipment and rights of way and to keeping their workers employed than they did while avoiding bankruptcy by taking RFC loans. This was especially so, Schiffman says, during the crucial years 1930 through 1933. "Had all large firms been bankrupt over that period," he writes (820), "the additional maintenance spending would have boosted GDP by an average of 0.199 percent a year, and employment would have increased by an average of 0.125 percent per year." He adds that his findings leave out multiplier effects. The lesson, Schiffman concludes, is "that governments should allow distressed firms to go bankrupt, instead of providing bailouts that merely postpone the inevitable" (822). It is, alas, a lesson many governments have yet to learn.

FDR and Gold

Getting people to trust their banks was a crucial step along the road to recovery. But that step couldn't quell fears that the dollar would be devalued, fears that triggered the bank holiday by depleting the US monetary gold stock. Suspending gold payments could prevent further gold withdrawals. But that wouldn't get the lost gold back. And as long as the gold standard's future remained uncertain, the quantity of bank reserves as well as banks' ability to lend and thereby help replenish the nation's shrunken money stock would go on being severely constrained.

In fact, Americans did end up returning most of the gold they'd hoarded. But that was a drop in the bucket compared to what happened after Franklin Roosevelt finally made up his mind about the dollar by officially devaluing it in January 1934. The "golden avalanche" that followed this decision turned out to be the most important driver of economic recovery for the rest of the decade.

Yet as we shall see, although Roosevelt made that avalanche possible by settling the dollar's fate, the avalanche was mostly triggered by a different world leader who wasn't the least bit concerned about Americans' well-being.

Unto Caesar

Before we come to the dollar's devaluation and its aftermath, let's revisit the steps that got gold flowing into the Fed not from overseas but from American hoards. As we've seen, one of these steps consisted of telegrams the Federal Reserve Board sent to each of the twelve Federal Reserve banks on March 8, asking them to "prepare and forward to the Board as soon as possible after

Mar. 13 1933, as complete a list as can be made from information you are able to obtain, of the names and addresses of all persons who have withdrawn gold from your bank or a member bank in your district since Feb. 1 1933, and who have not redeposited in a bank on or before Mar. 13 1933."[1] The Fed banks in turn went a step further, asking their members to supply not only the information requested by the Fed Board but also "a separate list containing similar information, so far as available, regarding withdrawals of gold coin and gold certificates from your bank prior to Feb. 1, 1933."

These requests anticipated a clause in the Emergency Banking Act, details of which were then being hashed out (Krock 1933), granting Roosevelt the authority to prohibit the "export, hoarding, melting, or ear-marking of gold or silver coin or bullion . . . by any person within the United States or any place subject to the jurisdiction thereof." The same act would also stipulate that anyone who violated the prohibition might "be fined not more than $10,000, or, if a natural person, may be imprisoned for not more than ten years, or both; and any officer, director, or agent of any corporation who knowingly participates in such violation may be punished by a like fine, imprisonment, or both."[2]

Under the circumstances, it's hardly surprising that bankers complied with the Fed's request and that many hoarders whose names they divulged rushed to redeposit coin and bullion. According to the *New York Times* ("Hoarders in Fright Turn In $30,000,000" 1933, 1), "repentant hoarders displayed a good deal of agitation, but they were received courteously by the guards of the reserve bank, and came out with an evident air of relief when they had disposed of their dangerous treasure."

When this *New York Times* report came out, $65 million in gold had already been handed in to the Fed. By the end of the month, after the deadline for preparing and forwarding lists of gold hoarders had been extended to March 27, the Fed's gold reserves were up to $625 million, as compared to just $365 million on inauguration day.

But the government wasn't through raking in hoarded gold. On April 5, Roosevelt issued Executive Order No. 6102, "forbidding the hoarding of gold coin, gold bullion, and gold certificates." What was a mere threat until then now became hard reality: those who still hadn't surrendered hoarded gold and gold certificates were given until May 1 to return all but $100 worth of coins (excepting collectible coins and gold for nonmonetary uses) to the Fed or face the stiff penalties provided for by the Emergency Banking Act. On April 28, Roosevelt issued Executive Order No. 6260, calling for anyone who still possessed gold coin, gold bullion, or gold certificates to file a return within forty-five days with the Internal Revenue Bureau, documenting what they possessed and for whom, where, and what for. Finally, in a step that brings Ebenezer Scrooge to mind, the government revoked the $100 gold coin exemption three days after Christmas, obliging even children who found shiny coins in their Christmas stockings to trade them for the Treasury's paper slips. Thanks to such draconian measures, and despite the fact that gold Americans had spirited away in European banks was beyond US authorities' reach, by May 10 $770 million worth of gold—a sum roughly equal to what they'd hoarded between the start of the year and the start of the bank holiday—was back in the Fed's coffers.

While he rounded up what remained of the nation's gold, Roosevelt also made sure it could no longer escape abroad. On April 20 in Executive Order No. 6111, he formally suspended the gold standard, indefinitely extending the restrictions on gold exports that he had temporarily imposed in Executive Order No. 6073 on March 10, and otherwise prohibiting "the earmarking for foreign account and the export of gold coin, gold bullion or gold certificates from the United States or any place subject to the jurisdiction thereof" except when licensed to do so by the treasury secretary (Roosevelt 1938, 2:142). The April 28 executive order calling for those possessing gold to report their holdings to the Internal Revenue Bureau also spelled out the few circumstances under which gold export licenses might be granted.

The Thomas Amendment

With most American gold back in the Fed's vaults, strict limits placed on gold exports, and deposit insurance shoring up people's faith in the banking system, the specter of another monetary collapse was at last laid to rest. But if the collapse that had already occurred was to be reversed, further action was needed.

Roosevelt's options for such action were greatly enlarged by the passage, on May 12, 1933, of the Agricultural Adjustment Act, and specifically by that act's so-called Thomas Amendment. This highly controversial provision, named after Oklahoma senator Elmer Thomas, who introduced it on April 17, allowed Roosevelt to ask the Fed to buy up to $3 billion in Treasury securities directly from the Treasury or (if the Fed demurred) to have the Treasury itself issue up to $3 billion in its own "greenbacks." The amendment also gave Roosevelt the option of reviving bimetallism by authorizing the minting of full-bodied (as opposed to token or subsidiary) silver coins and the tendering of silver certificates for silver received by the Treasury for that purpose. Finally, the amendment paved the way toward formal devaluation by allowing Roosevelt to cut the dollar's gold content by as much as one-half.

These were sweeping powers and, so far as many were concerned, exceedingly dangerous ones. Testifying in 1941 before the Senate Banking Committee, Edwin Kemmerer, the famous international "Money Doctor" and gold standard champion (Drake 1989), said that the Thomas Amendment gave "the President and his appointees a legal authority over the nation's currency that is almost complete. A Stalin or a Hitler could hardly have more. The things that the President has legal authority to do to the currency directly and their necessary implications could give us a gold standard, a silver standard, a bimetallic standard, a paper money standard or a commodity dollar standard. They could give us serious deflation or a runaway inflation" (US Senate 1941a, 35).

Roosevelt accepted the Thomas Amendment on April 18. He probably understood at the time that by encouraging renewed speculation against the dollar, his doing so sealed the fate of the old gold standard, which he officially suspended two days later. He may also have looked forward to substantially reducing the dollar's official gold content. But he never intended to take full advantage of the other powers the amendment gave him. Roosevelt was neither a Greenbacker nor a Silverite. In fact, he was not an "inflationist" at all in the then-current sense of that term, which meant someone who favored steps directly aimed at boosting the money supply. As Elmus Wicker (1971, 864) explains, despite wishing to see prices, especially farm commodity prices, restored to their pre-Depression levels, Roosevelt "did not view with favor the expedient of simply adding to the stock of money to achieve the desired price level. He objected to outright money creation as 'inflationary' because [it] had historical connotations of reckless spending by government, extreme difficulty in funding the public debt, and a general wage and price spiral." According to Wicker and most historians, Roosevelt went along with the Thomas Amendment's "inflationary" provisions in order to kill another amendment, proposed by Montana senator Burton Wheeler, that would have authorized additions to the money stock whether Roosevelt approved of them or not. Rather than risk having Congress override his veto of a Wheeler-amended farm bill, Roosevelt supported Thomas's alternative, which merely gave him the *option* of calling for outright money creation.

No matter why Roosevelt supported it, the Thomas Amendment made it possible for him to compel the Fed to create more of its own money by threatening to have the Treasury issue greenbacks or silver money instead. Yet he wielded that threat only once when, in September 1933, he said he'd issue greenbacks if the Fed didn't roll over $50 million in maturing securities. Roosevelt also went on to authorize Treasury silver purchase. But he did so not because he favored monetary expansion but to placate the powerful silver lobby and senators and representatives beholden to it. For that reason, it made no difference to him that the Treasury retired enough national banknotes to offset most of the new silver currency it issued.[3] In short, despite the Thomas Amendment, Roosevelt ended up doing little to encourage any monetary expansion beyond whatever devaluation itself would promote.

The Rocky Road to Devaluation

Neither did Roosevelt rush to reduce the dollar's official gold value. Instead, after officially suspending the gold standard on April 20, he let the dollar float, whereupon it began depreciating on its own, as he hoped it would, relative to both gold and other commodities. By scuttling the World Economic Conference that July, Roosevelt saw to it that no agreement made there got in the way of the dollar's value falling considerably more. But just three weeks after he sent his "bombshell" telegram to London, when stock and commodity prices started sagging again, Roosevelt decided to have the government deliberately boost gold's market price.

The result of Roosevelt's decision, revealed by him on October 22 during his fourth fireside chat, was the controversial gold purchase program. Proposed by Cornell University agricultural economist George Warren, based on a theory developed by him and his colleague Frank Pearson (Warren and Pearson 1935) to the effect that rising commodity prices were the flip side of a depreciating dollar (Sumner 2001; Richardson, Komai, and Gou 2013; S. Edwards 2018, chap. 10), that program called for the Reconstruction Finance Corporation to purchase gold at prices determined daily by Roosevelt and Henry Morgenthau, Roosevelt's second treasury secretary.[4] Once the program began, instead of depending on market forces alone, the extent of the dollar's depreciation relative to gold became a matter of official policy. Having been persuaded by Morgenthau to try out Warren's plan, Roosevelt hoped that by reducing the dollar's gold value sufficiently he would fulfill his campaign promise to get farm commodity prices back to their level in the mid-1920s.

So, the dollar fell. Yet until January 31, 1934, when its gold content was officially and permanently reduced from 25.8 to 15 5/21 grains of gold, nine-tenths fine, the dollar's depreciation did little to spur growth in either the US gold stock or broader money measures. Instead, despite increased world gold output, between March 1933 and the end of January 1934 the US monetary gold stock *shrank* slightly, while the money stock (M2) grew by little more than 2 percent—hardly enough to sustain a recovery. Real GNP, having risen considerably for some weeks following the bank holiday, itself started to decline again after July.[5] After the dollar's official devaluation, in contrast, all three measures grew steadily, with the gold stock rising especially rapidly and the money stock and real GNP growing at more modest (and almost identical) rates. These trends continued through 1935, 1936, and the first quarter of 1937.

Why was the dollar's de facto devaluation between April 1933 and January 1934 ineffective in luring gold back to the United States and in promoting money growth and recovery? And how did the de jure devaluation that followed help?

Letting the dollar depreciate could promote recovery in several ways. By raising the price of US imports and cheapening US exports, dollar depreciation can by itself boost spending on domestic goods while attracting gold from abroad. Since unilateral depreciation also *reduces* both the demand for the goods of other gold standard nations and those nations' gold reserves, deliberate reliance on it has come to be known as beggar-thy-neighbor policy. Beggar-thy-neighbor strategy can backfire, however, by inspiring nations it harms to counter by devaluing their own currencies so that both the nation that first resorts to it and the world as a whole end up worse off than before.

But a nation that allows its currency to depreciate relative to gold also increases the nominal value of its existing gold reserves, thereby enhancing its ability to pursue expansionary monetary policies whether it attracts gold from elsewhere or not. If the authorities take advantage of the increase, their doing so will itself boost demand, domestic prices, and output. To the extent that it raises domestic prices, monetary expansion undertaken along with unilateral currency depreciation limits beggar-thy-neighbor effects and can even avoid them altogether. In that case, the stimulus to domestic demand, instead of coming at other nations' expense, can help to boost spending worldwide (Eichengreen and Sachs 1985, 935).

As we'll see in subsequent chapters, between them the US government and the Federal Reserve failed to take full advantage of the dollar's depreciation after April 1933 to pursue more expansionary monetary policies. Partly for that reason, the decision to allow the US dollar to depreciate is usually understood to have been a particularly "clear instance of beggar-thy-neighbor policy" (Eichengreen and Sachs 1985, 930). The policy's effectiveness therefore depended in part on whether, when, and to what extent other nations chose to retaliate. In fact, several South American nations, South Africa, and Japan retaliated quickly, letting their own currencies depreciate. This retaliation alone limited the gains from the dollar's depreciation. But until the dollar was formally and permanently devalued, there was a more important reason for the gold purchase program's failure to lead to any substantial increase in domestic demand: doubts concerning just where the dollar was headed. Uncertainty about the dollar's future value tended to discourage both exports and foreign investment in long-term dollar-denominated securities. "Although the decline in dollar exchange lowered American commodities in price to foreign buyers," a Commerce Department official remarked, "there was some tendency for buyers to withhold purchases in the expectation of still lower dollar prices, and some reluctance to sell on the part of American exporters in view of exchange uncertainties" (quoted in Boeckel 1934).

What was true of exports went for investment as well, as Jacob Viner, the University of Chicago economist who was then serving as Henry Morgenthau's assistant, complained to his boss in a November 27 letter. "I do not believe," Viner wrote, that "Americans will freely invest their funds at home as long as the dollar is sinking on the exchange markets, and I do not believe recovery in American prices or economic activity is possible on a substantial scale until a resumption of internal investment on a large scale takes place. I believe . . . that expectation of further depreciation will operate as a check against recovery instead of a stimulus" (quoted in Nerozzi 2011, 65). In line with Viner's fears, the London *Times* reported on November 17 that Roosevelt's gold policy was having "less effect in raising prices in America than in depressing prices and checking recovery in the rest of the world. It must moreover, continue to exert a deflationary influence until there is some plain indication of the level to which President Roosevelt intends to drive the dollar" (quoted in Sumner 2015, 251).

In his famous first open letter to the *New York Times*, John Maynard Keynes (1933a) offered a diagnosis complementing Viner's of the gold purchase program's failure to promote recovery. "The recent gyrations of the dollar," he said, "have looked to me more like a gold standard on the booze than the ideal managed currency of my dreams." The dollar's gyrations presumably looked that way to others as well. By breeding uncertainty, Keynes argued, a drunken gold standard discouraged both foreign trade and foreign investment. "In the field of gold-devaluation and exchange policy," he said, "the time has come when uncertainty should be ended. This game of blind man's bluff with exchange speculators serves no useful purpose and is extremely undignified. It upsets confidence, hinders business decisions, occupies the public attention in a measure far exceeding its real importance, and is responsible both for the irritation and for a certain lack of respect which exists abroad." One consequence of the lack of respect Keynes referred to was a renewed flight from the dollar. On November 18, the *New York Times* reported that $1 billion in American capital had fled via sterling into gold, including some purchased on the open market "for private American accounts" (Sumner 2015, 252n28). Clearly, if devaluation was going to aid recovery, it would have to be devaluation of the sober sort.

Yet even the drunken dollar may have accomplished something. Whatever

Keynes and Frenchmen might think of it, the bulls of Chicago and Wall Street were at first keen on the dollar's wobbly descent, and for a time, as gold rose and the dollar fell, stocks and commodities responded much as George Warren said they would. According to Sumner (2015, 197–98), who himself refers to research by Peter Temin and Barrie Wigmore (1990) and Gauti Eggertsson (2008), instead of rising in response to money growth, those exceptionally sensitive prices rose *in anticipation* of such growth, because the gold purchase program led traders to expect "a dramatic change [in] the future path of monetary policy." Like the bank holiday, which started the process of recovery by quelling expectations of further deflation, and the April 19 prohibition of gold ownership, which succeeded in raising inflation expectations above zero, the gold purchase program did some good by further boosting inflation expectations (Jalil and Rua 2016).

Later we'll take up these arguments at greater length. For now, it's sufficient to note that the Reconstruction Finance Corporation's gold purchases were of too small a scale to have mattered much in themselves, and that the government's daily gold *price settings* must instead have convinced traders that it was testing the devaluation waters. But the longer the government put actual devaluation off, the more traders' devaluation expectations faded. Consequently, when the dollar was finally devalued, commodity prices were once again well below their 1925 level.

All things considered, it's hard to resist the conclusion that the gold purchase program was a costly waste of time. It accomplished nothing that Roosevelt couldn't have accomplished much sooner, with a lot less turmoil, by not waiting until 1934 to throw the devaluation switch.

The Gold Reserve Act

That switch was thrown, at last, by the passage of the Gold Reserve Act of January 30, 1934, which Fed economists Gary Richardson, Alejandro Komai, and Michael Gou (2013) call "the culmination of Roosevelt's controversial gold program." The new law called for a reduction of the dollar's gold content by *at least* 40 percent. By raising gold's official price from $20.67 per ounce to $35 per ounce by proclamation the next day, Roosevelt settled for a reduction of 41 percent.

The Gold Reserve Act also called for the Fed to transfer its gold holdings to the US Treasury in exchange for Treasury gold certificates. Although Richardson, Komai, and Gou (2013) suggest that the government compensated the Federal Reserve "at a rate of $35 per ounce," that's not so. As a different

Fed publication points out, because the Treasury took possession of the Fed's gold before Roosevelt announced gold's new price, it paid for the gold at the old statutory price of $20.67 per ounce (Board of Governors of the Federal Reserve System 2014). The Fed's nominal "gold" reserves, now represented by Treasury gold "certificates," therefore stayed unchanged. Because the nominal profit from devaluation went not to the Fed but to the Treasury, devaluation didn't result in any immediate increase in the Fed's assets, bank reserves, or the money stock. The way in which devaluation was handled thus demonstrated, in an especially neat fashion, Roosevelt's willingness to try to raise prices generally by raising the price of gold but *not* by encouraging growth in the money stock.

As for what the Treasury did with its gold profit, $2 billion of it went to establish the Exchange Stabilization Fund. According to Roosevelt's proclamation announcing the dollar's devaluation, that fund would serve "to stabilize domestic prices and to protect the foreign commerce against the adverse effect of depreciated foreign currencies" (Roosevelt 1938, 3:69). But Fed officials saw it rather differently: according to an internal Fed memo sent to Fed Board governor Eugene Black, the Exchange Stabilization Fund would allow the treasury secretary "to assume complete control of general credit conditions and to negate any credit policies that the Federal Reserve might adopt" (quoted in Meltzer 2003, 457). As we'll see later, the use the Treasury made of this newly acquired control was anything but conducive to economic recovery.

Gold Rush

As Sumner (2015, 34) points out, once the dollar was formally devalued, "gold flows continued to influence U.S. monetary policy, perhaps even more so than prior to 1933." So far as the United States was concerned, those flows were positive, persistent, and prodigious: between January 31, 1934, and May 1, 1939, the US gold stock rose from $6,829 million to $15,795 million. The money stock rose with it, as did bank lending and investment. But these rose less than the nation's gold reserves, in part because banks' reserve ratios also rose substantially.

Why did the US gold stock grow so rapidly after 1933? There were several reasons, the most obvious of which was devaluation's immediate effect on the dollar value of existing US gold holdings, which rose at once by $2.8 billion. As we've seen, that increase didn't itself add to the Federal Reserve's resources because the Treasury pocketed the full $2.8 billion profit from devaluation,

$2 billion of which went to establish the Treasury's Exchange Stabilization Fund, while the rest went into the Treasury's general Fed account (Schwartz 1997). Until the Treasury started spending it, its windfall did nothing to promote growth in the US money stock. But as the Treasury disbursed funds from its Fed account, member banks' reserve balances increased by the same amount.

Devaluation also altered the terms of trade in a way that temporarily favored US exports while discouraging imports. Those changed terms of trade are said to have accounted for over a third of the $1.217 billion in gold imports during 1934. But this effect wore out after some months. As Christina Romer (1999, 174–75) explains, devaluation resembles "a one-time supply shock" because it leads to a jump in tradable goods' dollar prices, but since exchange rates must eventually reflect that increase, it ultimately leaves prices expressed in terms of gold—and the terms of trade—unchanged.

More aggressive gold mining, spurred by the devaluation of the dollar and other gold bloc currencies and also by Joseph Stalin's successful attempt to dramatically boost the output of Siberia's gold mines (Grebenyuk 2019), also increased US gold reserves for several years to come, to the tune of about $1 billion per year.

Hot Money

But it was inflows of foreign *capital* that accounted for most of gold that came to the United States after the dollar was devalued. Between 1934 and 1937 alone, those inflows contributed almost $5.5 trillion to the US gold stock (Feinstein and Watson 1995, 103), or about four times the amount contributed by the same period's positive trade balance.

Thanks to the unprecedented currency arbitrage opportunities that the dollar's initial postdevaluation overvaluation offered speculators, short-term capital inflows held sway at first, leaving little space for anything else. As William Adams Brown Jr. (1940, 1306) relates, no sooner had Roosevelt made his announcement than "substantial shipments were arranged by the next available steamers leaving Europe for New York. . . . Never before has such a huge movement of gold taken place in so short a time. Accommodation on all mail steamers was booked well ahead and many other vessels other than the regular liners were pressed into service as bullion carriers."

However, as Brown also observes, by February that part of the flood of gold that could be attributed to arbitrage was already slackening off. Although foreign capital kept pouring into the United States after that, it did so mainly because keeping gold in Europe was getting riskier. This was so in part because the dollar's devaluation threatened to inspire further European devaluations. But it was also because war clouds, which had been gathering ever since Adolf Hitler became Germany's chancellor in January 1933, thickened rapidly after he proclaimed himself führer in August 1934.

From Hitler's rise to power onward a steady stream of capital flowed in from Europe, with larger waves set off by every new European crisis. The first big wave followed Hitler's March 16, 1935, announcement that he planned to rearm Germany. By May the French were "changing a billion francs a day into gold" to ship overseas, and "all the steamers scheduled to depart France were loaded with the stuff" (Rauchway 2015, 121). As if the Nazi threat weren't reason enough to send gold to the United States, the French also worried that their government might "devalue the franc, embargo gold, or institute exchange controls" at any moment (121). And the French weren't the only ones sending gold to the United States. Many continental Europeans did so, with the French, Germans, and Belgians leading the pack (Feinstein and Watson 1995, 104).

And more gold was still to come. Italy's invasion of Ethiopia (then Abyssinia) that October triggered a second wave of gold exports. Other waves followed the foreign exchange crisis brought about by Germany's rearmament (August and September 1936), the Munich crisis (September 1938), Germany's occupation of Prague (April 1939), the Nazi-Soviet pact (August 1939), Germany's invasion of Poland (September 1939), and the first rumors of an impending invasion of France (November 1939). Perhaps surprisingly, European capital didn't fly to the United States following the *Anschluss* of March 12, 1938. But that was only so because Germany's annexation of Austria coincided with a US crisis: the severe recession of 1937–1938, also known as the Roosevelt Recession.

These huge European capital exports weren't just unconnected to the dollar's devaluation: no New Deal policy was responsible for them. Far from seeking to attract capital from abroad or welcoming it as it flew in, Roosevelt and his Treasury team became increasingly alarmed that what they disapprovingly dubbed "hot money" would sponsor unwanted inflation. In the late summer of 1936, they decided to do something about it. As we'll see, it was mainly owing to the steps they took that the promising recovery of 1937 gave way to another downturn that undid many of the preceding years' gains.

* * *

To sum up, if one world leader deserves the lion's share of credit for the post-1933 US monetary boom, it was someone who, despite having once expressed admiration for Roosevelt's New Deal,[6] had a very different and for most of the world much rawer deal in mind. Frank Steindl (2007, 186) puts it starkly. "Without Adolf Hitler to spawn a capital flight to the United States," he says, "virtually no U.S. recovery would have occurred before 1941." Of course, Americans owed Hitler no thanks for this help. But they couldn't thank the New Deal for it, either.

PART II

The New Deal

The AAA

Because Franklin Roosevelt came into office in the midst of this country's worst-ever banking crisis, he was bound to devote most of his earliest actions to addressing that crisis. Only once he'd done so could he begin to implement the New Deal properly understood, meaning his ideas for "relief, recovery, and reform" apart from those the banking crisis itself inspired.

The Agricultural Adjustment Administration (AAA) and the National Recovery Administration (NRA) were the twin pillars of Roosevelt's recovery program. The NRA was supposed to boost manufacturers' revenues by ending cutthroat competition, while enhancing workers' purchasing power by raising their wage rates. The AAA, in the meantime, was supposed to raise farm product prices, and thereby boost farmers' purchasing power, by getting farmers to cut their output. Despite the programs' names, if Roosevelt considered one more crucial to recovery than the other, it was the AAA, the one pillar he and his Brain Trust had long been contemplating.

In fact, almost all assessments of the NRA conclude that, despite its name, it ended up hampering national recovery instead of promoting it. In contrast, as Frederick Lewis Allen (1940, 203) observed in 1939, "just how successful the AAA program could be considered was . . . a subject of ferocious controversy." Far less controversial is the view that, whatever its contribution to economic recovery in the 1930s, the AAA's longer-run consequences have been anything but benign.

US Agriculture in War and Peace

To understand why Roosevelt and others attached so much importance to helping farmers, one must realize, first of all, that farming played a much larger role in the US economy then than it does now. In 1930, farm families made up a quarter of the total US population, with farm employment accounting for almost as large a share (22 percent) of total employment, and farm output making up about 8 percent of GDP. These figures are roughly ten times their current counterparts. Apart from their direct importance, farms supported larger rural populations comprising 44 percent of all Americans and a large food processing industry. So, it wasn't just farmers who suffered when crop and livestock prices fell. Two recent studies suggest that falling farm incomes in 1930 may have accounted for as much as 30 percent of the overall decline in US output that year (Hausman, Rhode, and Wieland 2019; Hausman, Rhode, and Wieland 2021).[1]

Although the 1930 decline in farm earnings was exceptionally severe, by then farmers had been struggling for a decade. As we saw in discussing the banking crisis, during and immediately after World War I prices of crops and livestock rose dramatically. At its peak in May 1920, the farm products price index stood at almost 2.5 times its average between 1910 and the war's outbreak. Then, in the brief span from May to December, it fell to half that level. The rise and decline in crop prices were especially severe. In contrast, although the general price level also rose sharply during the war and the immediate postwar period, it remained well above its prewar level after the 1920–1921 bust. In short, while the 1920s may have "roared" for some, for American farmers they whimpered.

During the boom, however, the same farmers, encouraged by high farm product prices, including a government-guaranteed wheat price, and other wartime government policies, did all they could to boost their output, including investing heavily in new farmland. As Robert Sobel (1998, 247) notes in his biography of Calvin Coolidge, "wheat acreage rose from forty-eight million acres to more than seventy-five million between 1914 and 1919. Iowa farmland that sold for $82 an acre in 1910 went for $200 in 1920."

Farmers typically paid for new land and for the resources they needed to cultivate it by arranging mortgages with the sellers, joint stock land banks, and commercial banks, the last of which supplied a bit more than half of all farm mortgage credit in 1920. Mortgage debt per farm acre rose 135 percent between 1910 and 1920, or at roughly the same pace as the per-acre value of crops (Rajan and Ramcharan 2015, 1444). After farm product prices collapsed, farm foreclosure rates rose to record levels. From an average of just 3.2 foreclosures per one thousand farms for 1913–1920, they climbed to 17.4 by 1926 and ultimately to a 1933 peak of 38.8 foreclosures per thousand farms.

As we've seen, the souring of farm mortgages was a major cause of bank failures during both the 1920s and the first years of the Great Depression. Rising crop prices encouraged not just more borrowing but also the formation of many new banks to administer it (Jaremski and Wheelock 2020). Because they tended to be especially aggressive lenders, the newer banks failed in disproportionate numbers when farm prices tumbled. Lee Alston (1983, 886) suggests that the overall damage done by farmers' defaults was such that, had it not been for them, "the country at large would have been far less receptive to a New Deal."

Hoover's Farm Problem

Long before the New Deal, while he was still President Warren Harding's secretary of commerce, Herbert Hoover recognized the farm problem as one of overproduction. "The fundamental need," he told a gathering of dairy farmers then, "is the balancing of our home production to our home demand" (Wilson 1977, 341). Although he encouraged voluntary cutbacks, Hoover opposed any government scheme that would compel farmers to produce less. The key role he favored for government was that of encouraging the formation of national farm marketing cooperatives. He hoped that resorting to such cooperatives, together with generally rising prosperity, would eventually raise farmers' profits enough to end their plight.

But farmers were keen on neither national cooperatives nor voluntarily reducing their harvests. Instead, they wanted higher prices for the harvests they were already generating, and they wanted them right away, not eventually. Only direct government support could grant them that wish, and Hoover opposed such support. In particular, both as secretary of commerce under Harding and Coolidge and after becoming president, Hoover successfully opposed the McNary-Haugen farm relief bill, a plan that would have had a government-funded export corporation restore the prices of various farm products to their pre–World War I parity levels by purchasing surplus output at those prices and disposing of it abroad. Farmers responsible for surpluses on which the corporation lost money were to be taxed to make up for those losses, while those responsible for crops sold abroad at a profit would receive a corresponding dividend.

Hoover opposed the McNary-Haugen plan because it called for "socialistic" government intervention in agriculture, because he thought that propping up farm product prices would only result in still larger farm surpluses, and because attempts to dispose of surplus crops abroad would violate antidumping laws. Hoover was hardly alone in harboring these objections. Many economists shared them, including Chase National Bank's Benjamin Anderson. When the McNary-Haugen bill was first taken up by Congress, Anderson

(1924, 8) observed, presciently, that it couldn't work unless the government could "exercise control over the production of agricultural commodities" by assigning every farmer some "permissible acreage of given commodities" and letting them all "farm only the acreage allowed them."

As president, Hoover continued to favor voluntary efforts to reduce farm output, which he attempted to assist through the establishment of a Federal Farm Bureau. However, as Joan Hoff Wilson (1977) points out, Hoover's voluntary scheme struck farmers as both too "complex" and too slow-going. So, they continued to press for "an immediate price-lifting solution guaranteed by the government" of the sort McNary-Haugenism promised (359). When the Depression started, the Hoover administration took the further step of using loans and grants to enhance both foreign and domestic demand for farm products, but that extra support hardly sufficed to make up for the Depression's further toll on crop and livestock prices, let alone achieve a pre–World War I parity of farm product prices. It fell to Roosevelt to grant farmers the sort of immediate and substantial aid they'd been seeking for more than a decade.

From Reform to Recovery

With the coming of the Depression, farmers' plight went from bad to worse in both absolute and relative terms. The average price of farm products fell below its prewar level and to a record low relative to prices of goods and services in general.

While farm legislation had previously been aimed solely at giving farmers their "fair share" of national income, once the Depression broke out its proponents began to emphasize its potential contribution to a general recovery. This tack was taken by Roosevelt during his presidential campaign, particularly in his September 1932 Topeka campaign speech (Roosevelt 1938, 1:693–711). Yet so far as specific policies were concerned, neither the Democratic platform nor Roosevelt himself went much beyond what had been the official Republican Party position on farm policy, "if indeed they went that far" (Nourse, Davis, and Black 1937, 12).

Roosevelt did, however, express his support for certain aspects of the domestic allotment plan, having been urged to do so by both Raymond Moley and Rexford Tugwell. By 1932 that plan, originally proposed by W. J. Spillman, an agricultural economist, and popularized by two others, Harvard's John D. Black and Montana State College's M. L. Wilson, was generally seen as best alternative to McNary-Haugenism, an option that itself seemed more futile than ever after the Depression struck. The basic thinking behind the domestic allotment plan was that while tariffs on farm products alone had proven ineffective in raising farmers' earnings, they could become effective if farmers could be induced to limit their output to levels consistent with domestic needs. The plan's "essential principle," Black told the House Agriculture Committee in 1929, "is paying a free-trade price plus the tariff duty for the part of [farmers'] crop which is consumed in the United States and this price without the tariff duty for the part of it that is exported" (US House 1929). Cheating was to be avoided by means of "a system of allotments to individual producers of rights to sell the domestic part of the crop in the domestic market."

A version of Black's plan, which had many progressive Republican supporters, including future agriculture secretary Henry Wallace, was taken up by Congress twice during 1932. But the Jones bill, named after Congressman Marvin Jones (D-TX), who became chair of the House Agriculture Committee when the Democrats gained control of Congress that year, was rejected by the Senate both times. Not that this mattered much: the bill would almost certainly have been vetoed by Hoover otherwise.

Once Roosevelt was in office, he asked Jones to assist Wallace, whom he'd just made his Secretary of Agriculture, in revising a bill Wallace had drafted that was also based on the domestic allotment plan.[2] The revised measure differed from Jones's earlier efforts mainly by replacing transferable allotment rights with direct payments made to farmers who agreed to limit output to allotted amounts, to be financed by taxes on food processors. The resulting Agricultural Adjustment Act,[3] promising in its long title to "relieve the existing national economic emergency by increasing agricultural purchasing power," flew through the House on March 22, 1933; gained the Senate's approval five weeks later; and was signed by Roosevelt on May 12. Mordecai Ezekiel, Wallace's economic adviser, called it "the greatest single experiment in economic planning under capitalist conditions attempted by a democracy in times of peace" (Schlesinger 1958, 46).

The Theory

By creating a government agency—the Agricultural Adjustment Administration—expressly charged with restoring farmers' purchasing power to levels last seen in the years just before World War I, the Agricultural Adjustment Act broke new and untested ground. Whether its combination of direct benefit payments and reduced farm output would suffice to achieve its immediate goal was doubtful enough. But even if it succeeded, just how were farmers' higher earnings supposed to translate into improved all-around prosperity?

Direct benefits to farmers were funded by taxes on food processors, which tended to be passed on to consumers. Crop-reduction programs likewise benefited farmers only by making food less abundant and more costly for everyone. Surely robbing Peter to pay Paul couldn't possibly make both Peter and Paul better off. Or could it?

It could, in theory. For direct benefits to do the trick, it sufficed for farmers, taken as a whole, to have a higher marginal propensity to consume than those, apart from farmers themselves, who bore the brunt of higher food prices. That, at least, is how economists might put it today. During the first years of the Depression, before John Maynard Keynes's *General Theory of Employment, Interest and Money* took the economics profession by storm, the same idea was stated more prosaically, if also more awkwardly, in a comprehensive Brookings study of the AAA. By initially shifting "purchasing power" to farmers from others, the study's three authors explained, the AAA intended to "exert a significant influence toward accelerating the release of [that] purchasing power into the general market" (Nourse, Davis, and Black 1937, 431).[4]

Roosevelt understood that as a means for improving overall prosperity, the AAA was a gamble. In his message transmitting the bill to Congress, he admitted that it took the government down "a new and untrod path" (Roosevelt 1938, 2:74). But Roosevelt considered the risk worth taking, and he promised the public that if the gamble failed to "produce the hoped-for results, I shall be the first to acknowledge it and advise you."

Cui Bono?

Did the AAA actually "produce the hoped-for results"? Roosevelt himself never suggested otherwise. All experts agree that the AAA's various efforts boosted overall farm earnings. According to the Brookings Institution's painstaking report, they boosted gross farm earnings by as much as $2 billion, about a quarter of which took the form of direct Treasury payments to farmers. Allowing for the burden of increased food prices still left farm families with combined net gains of between $1.5 billion and $1.9 billion, no small sum at a time when total US GNP was around $58 billion. A relatively recent econometric study reaches the complementary conclusion that between 1933 and 1935 the AAA raised the price of US agricultural products by between 31 and 33 percent (Madsen 2001, 352–53). Although AAA officials often boasted still bigger gains to farmers from their agency's programs, such estimates tended to credit the AAA for both its genuine contributions to farm earnings and improvements in those earnings for which other factors were responsible (Davis 1936).

A closer look at the AAA's contributions shows, however, that it is wrong to suppose that its policies benefited all (as opposed to certain farmers). For one thing, while southern and midwestern producers of tobacco, cotton, wheat, corn, and hogs benefited substantially, dairy, poultry, and livestock farmers in the Northeast lost out as a result of higher feed costs (Romasco 1983, 183). In the South, the AAA's largesse went mainly to farm owners rather than to those who did most of the actual farming, including tenants and sharecroppers.[5] Where AAA benefits went directly to cash-paying tenants, they tended to be fully offset by higher rents. And in the cotton-growing South, where benefits were instead paid only to landlords, who were supposed to split them fifty-fifty with their tenants and sharecroppers, the latter often ended up with no benefits at all. As Calvin Hoover, the AAA's consumers' counsel, explained at the time, tenants' and sharecroppers' gains depended "upon the charitable ness or unscrupulousness of the landlord" (quoted in Hoffsommer 1935, 498).

But an unjust division of AAA payments was the least of it. By paying landowners to take acreage out of cultivation, the AAA reduced their labor requirements, both directly and by allowing them to afford tractors and other labor substitutes. The reduced demand for farm labor, Camille Goldmon (2017, 60) says, was "the final nail in the coffin of many of the South's farm laborers, sharecroppers, and tenants," hundreds of thousands of whom found themselves homeless with no means of survival except those offered by New Deal relief programs (Henderson 2013). A Cornell agricultural economist estimated at the time that, all told, the AAA added roughly two million former farm tenants and workers to the ranks of the unemployed (Boyle 1936), while a more recent econometric study concludes that every 10 percent increase in AAA spending in the Cotton Belt reduced the number of sharecroppers and Black managing tenants there by between 1.4 and 1.9 percent (Depew, Fishback, and Rhode 2013). Because they made up most Cotton Belt tenants and sharecroppers, and were sometimes given even less consideration than their white counterparts, African American tenants and sharecroppers were the principal victims of the AAA's policies (Myrdal 1944, 256–61; Moreno 2002, 515–16).[6]

The question remains whether the AAA, in enriching some farmers while impoverishing others, helped lift the US economy as a whole from the depths of the Great Depression. Did it boost aggregate demand, as it was theoretically able to do, despite taxing consumers and further impoverishing some of the nation's poorer farmers?

According to two of the Brookings Institution's three experts, it did, because farmers were more inclined to spend extra funds that came their way than the groups from which those funds were diverted and because AAA programs often "advanced" purchasing power to farmers before grabbing it from food processors and ultimately food consumers:

> On the whole, we believe that the AAA was a quickening rather than a retarding factor in industrial activity. . . . With confidence renewed that he was to be enabled to keep his farm and continue supplying the market under more favorable commercial conditions, the farmer expanded his purchases of consumption goods and farm supplies up to the limit made possible by enhanced prices, better credit, and direct benefit payments. This expansion of orders . . . improved the financial position and the business confidence of certain classes of manufacturers and in turn enlarged their purchases of raw materials and equipment. This reacted favorably on employment, payrolls, and urban buying. Ultimately . . . there was a larger flow of national income from which to divert the larger share that went to the farmer. (Nourse, Davis, and Black 1937, 447–48)

The Brookings experts also saw no reason for doubting the AAA's claim that increased rural demand accounted for two-fifths of the rise in factory employment between the spring of 1933 and the fall of 1935. They noted, however, that AAA programs themselves only accounted for part of this increase, the rest having been due to "relief, public works, the Farm Credit Administration, and the drought" (Nourse, Davis, and Black 1937, 448).

Where Credit Is Due

For some, even the Brookings Institution's tempered conclusion gives the AAA too much credit. The dissenters included Joseph S. Davis, the third author of the Brookings study. In one of the study's footnotes, Davis claims that his colleagues' conclusion "conveys a materially exaggerated impression of the *extent* of the AAA's recovery contribution" (Nourse, Davis, and Black 1937, 448n27). Davis himself believed that if the AAA's contribution to recovery was positive at all, that contribution was minor. Elsewhere T. W. Schultz, the future Nobel Memorial Prize winner, concurred, saying that he doubted "if anyone would claim that the AAA has been a mighty or even a significant force in improving economic activity generally" (Ezekiel and Schultz 1935, 17).[7]

Although Davis didn't delve into his reasons for rejecting his coauthors' conclusions in that footnote, opinions he expressed two years earlier, when the AAA had been in business for nineteen months, offer hints. "On the basis of reasoning and experience to date," he wrote then, the AAA's contribution to recovery "has been minor, not major" (Davis 1935, 3). While allowing that

AAA programs boosted the earnings of certain groups of farmers, he attributed most of the post-AAA increase in both farmers' earnings and their demand for nonfarm goods and services to "other factors," including the Great Plains drought, the dollar's depreciation, and "huge outpourings of public funds other than through the AAA" (12).[8] Although Davis couldn't say just "what influence the AAA might have had" in the absence of these other factors, his best guess was "that as a force in general recovery . . . it quite failed to fulfill its advocates' promises and may even have retarded aggregate business recovery" (13).

Post–New Deal assessments of the AAA tend to support Davis's negative verdict. H. W. Arndt (1944, 48) considered it "extremely doubtful whether the AAA restriction policy did anything to increase total purchasing power." Whatever slight gains those restrictions may have achieved, he said, "must be set the waste of natural resources and manpower" they involved. In his review of the overall record of US farm relief policies published not quite a decade later, Murray R. Benedict (1953, 315) could find no evidence at all that the AAA served "as a stimulus to recovery in the economy as a whole." Because AAA payments were financed by food processing taxes that tended to be passed on to consumers, farmers' gains, so far as Benedict could determine, were mostly offset by consumers' losses. Regarding the AAA's primary objective of raising farm product prices to "parity" levels, Theodore Saloutos (1974, 397–98) observes that for the most part, it wasn't achieved. "Of the prices received for farm commodities," Saloutos says, "only one, that for beef cattle, had attained parity by August 1939. Corn was 59 percent of parity, cotton 66 percent, wheat 50, butterfat 59, hogs 60, chickens 93, and eggs 49. The income of the farm population[,] . . . after dropping to a low of $39,000,000,000 in 1933, had recovered to only $66,000,000,000 in 1939 but had not reached the $79,000,000,000 of 1929."

Still more recent research further reinforces these unfavorable opinions by showing that it wasn't just consumers outside of farm communities who bore the brunt of the AAA's largesse. Farmworkers also suffered. Drawing on county-level evidence, Price Fishback, William Horrace, and Shawn Kantor (2005, 22) conclude that instead of helping counties that received them, AAA grants slowed their growth. Because grants were rewarded to farmers who cut back production, even though farm owners themselves benefited from the payments and could spend more because of them, their increased spending tended to be more than offset by reduced spending by displaced former farm laborers, sharecroppers, and tenants (20). A later, complementary study using state-level data finds that AAA grants also failed to spur private employment in states that received them (Fishback and Kachanovskaya 2015). These findings suggests that while recipients of AAA grants may indeed have had higher marginal propensities to consume than those who footed the AAA's bills, the propensity to consumer of farm laborers, sharecroppers, and tenants whom those payments rendered redundant had been higher still.

The AAA Is Dead, Long Live the AAA

A complete assessment of the AAA's merits as a recovery measure must consider its longer-run consequences.

The AAA was sold to the public as an emergency measure that, if successful, would end once "the national economic emergency in relation to agriculture has been ended."[9] But as we've seen, its roots resided in proposals that predated the Depression. Moreover, the agency was expected to not just reestablish but also "maintain" agricultural commodity prices at their (high) pre–World War I levels, something it could hardly do once it ceased to exist.

It's not surprising, then, that many of those who took part in creating and overseeing them, including Roosevelt himself, looked forward all along to making the new government agency and its agricultural "adjustments" a permanent feature of US agricultural policy. "It was never the idea of men who framed the act," Roosevelt (1938, 4:432) said in an October 1935 statement that seemed contrary to the language of the law itself, "that the Agricultural Adjustment Administration should be either a mere emergency operation or a static agency. It was their intention—as it is mine—to pass from the purely emergency phases necessitated by a grave national crisis to a long-time more permanent plan for American agriculture."

And that is just what the AAA became. Despite the Supreme Court's January 6, 1936, ruling declaring the processing tax unconstitutional, the AAA survived. It did so even in name until 1953.[10] Since then, Bill Ganzel (2003) observes, "the basic policy of the federal government has remained to keep prices up by keeping production down. And this is a very real way in which the Great Depression continues to affect those of us growing up and living today."

As the Brookings Institution's AAA study notes, instead of being "swept from the boards by this [1936] Supreme Court decision," the AAA was merely "diverted into new channels under modified procedures" (Nourse, Davis, and Black 1937, 2). Less than two months after the court's decision, the AAA's crop-reduction component was resurrected as part of the Soil Conservation and Domestic Allotment Act (Davis 1936). Under that arrangement farmers, instead of being paid simply for not growing certain crops, were paid for "conserving" former cropland, either by growing grass or nitrogen-fixing legumes on it or by otherwise modifying it to limit soil erosion.

Two years later a new Agricultural Adjustment Act, guaranteeing minimum prices for cotton, corn, and wheat and otherwise supporting various other farm products, rose phoenix-like from its predecessor's ashes. To steer clear of the Supreme Court's 1936 ruling, instead of being funded by a tax on food processors, the new AAA relied on appropriations from the Treasury's general fund. In 1940 the new agency, which like its predecessor was originally to expire after two years, was made permanent, and in 1942 in *Wickard v. Filburn* the Supreme Court declared it constitutional.

In the Long Run . . .

Because Roosevelt and other proponents of the original AAA always had a permanent arrangement in mind, it seems reasonable to take both the original and the revived AAA's consequences into account in assessing the AAA's net benefits. Addressing those consequences a half century after the original law's passage, agricultural economist Don Paarlberg (1983) concluded that the program's tendency to benefit a minority of large farmers, present from the start, only grew worse over time. While producers of certain "basic" crops, which by 1983 accounted for only 20 percent of agricultural output, received 75 percent of the program's benefits, farmers of hundreds of other crops got no help from it at all, and 21 percent of the benefits paid went to just 1 percent of all participating farmers, who were generally far better off than the consumers and taxpayers who paid the bill for the government's largesse.

And that largesse has grown a lot since the 1930s, both absolutely and as a share of total farm earnings. When Paarlberg wrote, the government-provided share of total net farm income had already risen to almost 70 percent (Widmar 2019). Although direct farm payments made up a smaller share of total farm earnings afterward, they remained substantial for another three decades and they continued to be overwhelmingly aimed at relatively well-off large-scale farmers. "If the intent of commodity support programs is to assist low-income households," the President's Economic Report for 2005 observed, "then these programs are failing in this task today because the bulk of payments go to farm households with incomes above the U.S. nonfarm average" (The White House 2006).

At last, in 2014, Congress did away with direct farm subsidies by passing a new Farm Act. But while that measure reduced the flow of direct aid to farmers, it did so by substituting equally generous crop insurance subsidies along with other offsetting benefits (Dayen 2014). Consequently, although insurance companies now receive a bigger slice of the subsidy pie, large-scale farmers have suffered little if at all (C. Edwards 2018).

More recently still, thanks to the first Coronavirus Food Assistance Program, farmers have raked in more direct government aid than ever before (US Government Accountability Office 2022). In this program, as has been the case generally, the largest 1 percent of farms received one-fifth of all direct payments to farmers, amounting to almost $1.1 billion. While many people found themselves in desperate economic straights in 2020, thanks to the Coronavirus Food Assistance Program large-scale farmers earned *more* that year than they had in any year since 2013 (Associated Press 2022). A second COVID-19 relief package, including a similar amount of direct aid to farmers mostly aimed at the usual set of favored farm commodities, boosted farmers' earnings even more, raising their net income to an all-time record of $185.5 billion in 2022 (US Department of Agriculture 2024).

Nor has the harm done by post–New Deal farm policies been limited to regressive income redistribution. By encouraging intensive farming methods, including heavy applications of chemical fertilizers and pesticides, those policies have also had substantial adverse environmental consequences (Hoffpauir 2009). "To the extent then that agricultural assistance stimulates crop and livestock production," a trio of agricultural economists concluded some years ago (Lewandrowski, Tobey, and Cook 1997, 405), "and to the extent that such increases in output impose unintended and unaccounted for environmental costs on society, those environmental costs can be seen as a form of government 'policy failure.'"

How should one weigh the AAA's modest contribution to economic recovery in the 1930s, assuming it made one, against its ruination of tenant farmers and regressive and environmentally damaging long-run legacy? There may be no generally acceptable way of doing so scientifically. But it's hard to imagine a plausible social welfare function that would yield a positive balance, let alone a substantial one. And even if one did, it wouldn't follow that the AAA game was worth the candle. As Benn Steil (2024, 43) observes in his recent, captivating biography of Henry Wallace, whatever good the AAA did farmers in the 1930s might have been done "more cheaply, with less collateral damage, and with fewer lamentable legacy effects—just by mailing them checks."

9

The NRA

Everything's Relative

Writing in the *Washington Post* during the Great Recession, Barnard College professor David Weiman (2011) observed that "without Roosevelt's intervention, the economic recovery that lasted from 1933 to 1937 would have been weaker and shorter—not unlike our own recovery." Weiman was certainly right to claim that for its first few years the New Deal recovery was in many respects more impressive than the one he was witnessing. But it was more impressive not because it was exceptionally rapid compared to most business cycle recoveries but because the Great Recession recovery was exceptionally slow. As for Franklin Roosevelt's interventions, if some spurred recovery, others slowed it down.

Assessing the New Deal recovery three years after the start of Roosevelt's first term, Garfield Cox (1936, 2–3) reached a verdict that helps to put Weiman's in perspective. Comparing the pace of that recovery to recoveries from previous downturns, Cox found it far from satisfactory. He observed that all previous recoveries, once started, had brought business activity back to normal within fourteen months, whereas thirty-three months after the New Deal began, that activity was still "substantially below trend." Cox noted as well that "no previous recovery from depression has been punctuated by reversals so extensive as those which have interrupted the current expansion." Although the pace of the New Deal recovery quickened soon after Cox wrote, it did so only for fourteen months, when the recovery was interrupted yet again, this time by the most severe post–New Deal reversal of all.

Cox based his observations on a popular index of American business activity developed by Leonard Ayres, a well-regarded economist and statistician then serving as chair of the American Bankers Association's Policy

Commission. The ups and downs of Ayer's index during the 1930s closely resemble those of the Federal Reserve's more familiar monthly index of industrial production, on which Ayer's measure is partly based, but with a less pronounced upward trend. When Cox wrote, US industrial production was also well below the trend line to which a complete recovery would have restored it.

The most distressing fact about the New Deal recovery was the lack of new nonemergency jobs to match growth in real output. Instead of going hand in hand with increased employment, much of that growth was due to a remarkable increase in total factor productivity for which the New Deal was only partly responsible: for the most part, the productivity gains of the 1930s were a delayed response to pre-Depression innovations (Field 2003; Bakker, Crafts, and Woltjer 2016). So, despite increased output, the conventionally measured unemployment rate, counting persons on work relief as unemployed, stayed in double digits throughout the 1930s. In contrast, the highest unemployment rate recorded during the six months before October 1929 was just above 2 percent.

Concerning the situation in the spring of 1935, Ellis Hawley (1966, 131–32), a sympathetic critic of the New Deal, observes that the gains achieved until then "were hardly reasons for jubilation. Over ten and a half million workers were still unemployed, approximately twenty million people were still dependent upon relief, basic industries were still operating at little more than half their capacity, and the real income of the average family was still thirteen percent below that of 1929."

Even Hawley's statistics, unfavorable as they are to claims that New Deal policies rapidly revived the US economy, overstate those policies' success by concealing the extent to which jobs created between August 1933 and May 1935 were a result of mandatory "work sharing" rather than actual growth in the quantity of labor demanded by the private sector (Taylor 2011).

Yet thanks to gold flowing in from Europe, total spending itself grew substantially, if far from adequately, during the New Deal. By 1937, nominal GNP was 70 percent higher than it had been in 1933. The six million–dollar questions is why all that extra spending didn't translate into correspondingly large output and (especially) employment gains.

The Wages Puzzle

Part of the answer is that instead of taking advantage of their increased earnings to hire more worker hours, employers mostly used them to give *raises* to existing workers: manufacturing workers' hourly earnings rose by a remarkable 35 percent in the two-year stretch starting in mid-1933 and kept going up until the middle of the Roosevelt recession of 1937–1938.[1]

To anyone aware of the severe unemployment during those years, those substantial and persistent hourly wage gains pose a puzzle: How could wage rates rise so sharply with as much as one-fifth—and never less than one-tenth—of the labor force either unemployed or on work relief? With so many workers lacking nonemergency jobs and most plants operating at well below capacity, why would manufacturers confronting the choice of either giving their workers a raise or hiring more workers at going wage rates not prefer the second choice?

According to economic historian Christopher Hanes (2020, 1031–32), the "obvious answer" lies not in the ordinary workings of the laws of supply and demand but in New Deal legislation. "Starting in 1933," Hanes says, "the Roosevelt administration adopted 'New Deal' labor policies embodied in the National Industrial Recovery Act (NIRA), which established the National Recovery Administration (NRA) codes, and the 1935 National Labor Relations Act (NLRA), also known as the Wagner Act (named for New York senator Robert Wagner, who sponsored it). NRA codes boosted nominal wage rates, and imposed 'labor standards' such as overtime premium pay, by regulatory fiat. Both the NIRA and the NLRA promoted formation of labor unions and strengthened workers' bargaining power over employers. These policies could boost prices, as well as wages, as they gave an extraordinary boost to labor costs of production."

The NIRA

Although the March bank holiday and subsequent banking and monetary legislation ended the Great Contraction, pressure on the government to do something for the millions of workers left unemployed was "overwhelming" (Hawley 1966, 53). The Roosevelt administration's first response to this pressure was the Agricultural Adjustment Act. Its second response, passed five weeks later, was the NIRA. The NIRA was to be the locomotive responsible for hurtling the US economy toward a full recovery. Roosevelt (1938, 2:246) called it "the most important and far-reaching legislation ever enacted by the American Congress."

The NIRA consisted of three parts or titles.[2] Title II established the Public Works Administration and assigned it a budget of $3.3 billion. Title III contained various miscellaneous provisions, including one transferring the Reconstruction Finance Corporation's public works activities to the Public

Works Administration. Title I, which most concerns us, addressed industrial recovery and affirmed workers' right to engage in collective bargaining. Title I also provided for the establishment of industry "codes of fair competition." Those codes were supposed to assure adequate working conditions and set maximum working hours and minimum ordinary and overtime wage rates. Businesses operating under approved codes were to be exempt from federal antitrust laws. Four days after Congress passed the NIRA, the NRA was set up to see to the codes' development and enforcement.

Establishing minimum wage rates had in fact been the original aim of what became the NIRA. Like many at the time, Roosevelt believed that higher wage rates would translate into an overall increase in workers' "purchasing power" which, by enabling them to spend more, would in turn promote recovery. He therefore asked Labor Secretary Frances Perkins to suggest amendments to Hugo Black's "Thirty Hours" bill, a measure providing for minimum wage rates that, having first been introduced in 1932, was finally passed by the Senate that April.

At this time, Perkins (1946, 197) says, Roosevelt's "mind was as innocent as a child's of any such program as the NRA." But eventually Roosevelt decided to offer a substitute for Black's bill instead of amending it. The result was a scheme, based mainly on a pair of proposals made by the Chamber of Commerce and General Electric president Gerard Swope, in which industrial and trade associations would come up with codes establishing minimum wage rates and other working conditions that all firms in an industry would have to meet. Industries that abided by approved codes would be exempt from antitrust laws that would otherwise have kept them from colluding.[3]

Thanks to its businessmen's DNA, and despite the determined efforts of Hugh Johnson, the NRA's firebrand head, the NRA worked out far differently than Johnson, Roosevelt, Perkins, and other champions of higher wages intended. Although advisory boards featuring consumer and labor representatives took part in the code-writing process, that process was dominated by industry representatives, who took advantage of it to turn formerly (albeit imperfectly) competitive industries into so many cartels. While most codes also established minimum wage rates and sometimes wage rates were set above the minimum levels, the codes were often written so that whenever wage rates went up, product prices went up just as much.

"In practice," Ellis Hawley (1966, 33–34) observes, "the NRA became a mechanism that conflicting groups sought to use for their own ends, an agency that was unable to define and enforce a consistent line of policy." After initially raising hopes, the NRA ended up disappointing almost everyone, including those businessmen who hoped to profit by dominating the code-writing boards. Before the experiment ended, Roosevelt himself felt compelled to admit (privately, to Frances Perkins) that "the whole thing is a mess" (McElvaine 1993, 162).

The High-Wages Fallacy

Considering Roosevelt's own disappointment, it's hardly surprising that his critics mocked the NRA. But when William Randolph Hearst quipped that "NRA" really stood for "No Recovery Allowed," the nickname wasn't all that far from the truth. "It was unrealistic," Lester Chandler (1970, 239) writes, "to expect that the aggregate effects of efforts of individual industries to enhance their own profits by increasing their prices would be to raise total real output and employment." Even firms run by angels couldn't have turned the NRA codes into devices for boosting aggregate spending, the revival of which was crucial to recovery. To the extent that they raised prices or wage rates, those codes were bound to *reduce* the capacity of greater spending to boost employment. It doesn't follow, of course, that industries' *abuse* of NRA codes to establish and enforce monopoly pricing didn't make things worse: it did do so by further restricting output and, with it, firms' demand for labor. But it was mainly by boosting money wage rates, as government officials intended, that the codes undermined the employment-generating capacity of increased spending by reducing the number of worker hours that any given level of spending could pay for.

How could anyone have thought that forcing firms to pay higher wage rates would promote recovery? The belief that it would do so, which came to be known as the "high-wage doctrine," had its roots in the underconsumption theory of depression, which reached its peak of popularity during the 1920s. According to that theory, depressions happen when workers aren't paid enough, collectively, to buy the output their employers produce. The problem, Hartley Withers (1914, 83–84, emphasis added) wrote, was that while business owners might agree "that the workers of *other* industries should be better paid" so they could spend more, those same business owners weren't keen on increasing their *own* workers' wage rates. Instead "every company or firm would naturally wait for others to begin." Underconsumptionists favored government action to overcome this alleged free-rider problem.

The severe though short-lived depression of 1920–1921 gave a further boost to the high-wage doctrine's popularity, convincing many that instead of being a mere consequence of the collapse of spending that took place then, a concurrent 20 percent drop in wage rates was the *cause* of that collapse. Thanks to such thinking, especially as elaborated by William Foster and Waddill

Catchings' (1927) bestseller *Business without a Buyer*, by the time the Great Depression started, the high-wage doctrine had become conventional wisdom.

One of the doctrine's converts was Herbert Hoover. So convinced was Hoover of the high-wage doctrine's merit that in late 1929 he convened a series of conferences in Washington at which he secured major employers' pledges to resist cutting their employees' hourly wage rates so as to preserve "the consuming power of the country" (Rose 2010, 849). According to Jonathan Rose, while many employers did in fact comply with Hoover's request (850), others approved of his efforts only to the extent of "believe[ing] strongly in *other* employers paying high wages" (Lescohier 1935, 91, emphasis added).

Roosevelt was likewise won over to the high-wage doctrine. He differed from Hoover only in his chosen means for putting it into practice. Whereas Hoover merely tried to persuade businessmen to resist cutting their workers' wage rates, Roosevelt's NRA set aside that voluntarist approach in favor of a coercive alternative. Besides risking consumer and official boycotts, businessmen found guilty of violating NRA codes could be fined $500 or sentenced to six months in prison, where each day they remained in violation was reckoned a separate offense. Finally, if Roosevelt determined that an industry wasn't cooperating, he had the power to require firms in it to acquire a federal license, which he might suspend or revoke in the event of a violation. This final recourse was nothing less than the business equivalent of the death penalty (Josephson 1933).[4]

Had the high-wage doctrine been sound, Roosevelt's strategy would have been superior to Hoover's. But far from being sound, the doctrine was a crude fallacy, arising from an elementary confusion of "wage rates," meaning the amount businesses paid for a given quantity of labor (say, an hour's worth), with industries' "wage bill," meaning the total amount businesses spent on labor (Taylor and Selgin 1999). That "wages" could refer to either of these different things was the main reason for this confusion. While it's obviously true that, holding product prices constant, whatever increases industries' wage *bill* also increases workers' "purchasing power," compelling businesses to pay higher wage *rates* is likely to cause them to scale back employment so that the total earnings of their reduced workforce are no greater than, and may even be less than, what their larger workforce earned before. What's more, during a depression, when firms are making few if any profits, it's especially likely that many will be unable to pay higher wage rates unless they also hire fewer workers.

In short, although higher wage rates and increased employment are often concurrent results of increased spending, mandating higher wage rates doesn't itself generally serve to increase spending. And if it doesn't increase spending, it's likely to reduce employment.

Keynes on the NRA

Because underconsumptionist theories superficially resemble John Maynard Keynes's theory attributing depressions to a lack of spending, some have been tempted to treat Title I of the NRA as an application of Keynes's ideas. Frances Perkins (1946, 225), for one, claimed that by setting minimum wage rates, the NRA "constituted an effective demonstration of the theories which John Maynard Keynes had been preaching and urging."

But Keynes himself thought otherwise. In his famous December 1933 open letter to Roosevelt, Keynes censured as a "technical fallacy" the theory that by boosting wage rates (among other "prime costs") the NRA would raise workers' purchasing power:

> Rising prices are to be welcomed because they are usually a symptom of rising output and employment. When more purchasing power is spent, one expects rising output at rising prices. . . . [Therefore], it is essential to ensure that the recovery shall not be held back by the insufficiency of the supply of money to support the increased monetary turn-over. But there is much less to be said in favour of rising prices, if they are brought about at the expense of rising output. Some debtors may be helped, but the national recovery as a whole will be retarded. Thus rising prices caused by deliberately increasing prime costs or by restricting output have a vastly inferior value to rising prices which are the natural result of an increase in the nation's purchasing power. (Keynes 1933a)

Keynes (1933a) went on to say that while he approved of the NRA's attempts to achieve a more equal distribution of incomes "in principle," he also considered it a mistake to treat higher prices as an end in itself. "The stimulation of output by increasing aggregate purchasing power," he said, "is the right way to get prices up; and not the other way round." And the most reliable way to get purchasing power up, according to Keynes, was through "governmental expenditure which is financed by Loans and not by taxing present incomes"; in other words, by deficit spending. "The set-back which American recovery experienced this autumn was the predictable consequence of the failure of your administration to organise any material increase in new Loan expenditure during your first six months of office."

Keynes wrote this, it bears considering, a month before Roosevelt devalued the dollar and well before "hot money" started to pour into the United States from Europe. That inflow was to be the basis for an increase in US consumers' purchasing power far greater, according to most authorities, than anything Roosevelt's fiscal policies would ever achieve.

Code Blues

So much for the theory. Just how well does the evidence fit it?

Quite well, in fact. First, concerning the codes, these were of two sorts: NRA-approved codes, developed for and by representatives of specific industries, and a "blanket code," provided for by the President's Reemployment Agreement (PRA) of August 1, 1933, that firms could agree to abide by until the end of that year or until their industry-specific NRA codes were decided upon and approved, whichever came first. Almost all employers—Henry Ford was a notorious exception—quickly agreed to take part in the PRA, earning the right thereby to display the NRA's blue eagle showing that they were "doing their part" to end the Depression.

Both the blanket code and industry-specific codes prevented wage rate cuts and set minimum wage rates. The codes also tended to raise the wage rates of non–minimum wage workers and, indirectly, of *all* workers by mandating across-the-board cuts in individual employees' weekly hours and forbidding cuts in their total pay. "From June 1933 to June 1934," Frances Perkins writes (1946, 208), "average hourly earnings in manufacturing increased thirty-one per cent. The downward spiral of hourly earnings was checked and an upward spiral was set in motion."

And unemployment? Jason Taylor (2011) concludes that it was only owing to the codes' "work sharing" and shortened workweek provisions that unemployment, as conventionally measured, declined. These provisions made room for more workers at firms that abided by them, but they did nothing to boost firms' total demand for labor. On the contrary, Taylor finds that the PRA's work sharing provisions caused aggregate work *hours* to *decline* by over 9 percent. Industry-specific NRA codes tended to reduce the demand for labor still further, to the point of offsetting most of the job gains from work sharing. Data from manufacturing industries, as reported in a 1937 Cowles Commission study of the NRA (Roos 1937, 108, Table 1), support Taylor's findings, showing that total monthly man-hours of work in those industries fell from 1.1 billion in July 1933 to just 898 million in January 1934. Man-hours didn't return to their pre-NRA level until April 1935, when the codes were being flouted everywhere. Taylor calculates that had it not been for gold inflows and other developments that boosted total spending, the PRA and NRA codes combined would have reduced the quantity of worker hours demanded by as much as *one-third*, a calamitous decline in what was already a deeply depressed market for labor.

As if all this weren't bad enough, the NIRA's collective bargaining provisions—sections 7(a) and 7(b) especially[5]—inspired waves of strikes aimed at both organizing more workers and securing higher wage rates and lower hours. Workers went on strike 1,856 times in 1934 alone, more than at any time since World War I. Work stoppages included general strikes in San Francisco and several other cities that summer and the Textile Workers' Strike in September. The Textile Workers' Strike, the last of these stoppages, involved four hundred thousand workers across the whole Eastern Seaboard. Between April and October alone, strikes cost the nation over fourteen million worker days of labor, enough to account for a substantial downturn in industrial production (US Department of Labor 1936). According to Christopher Hanes (2020, 1034), one needn't look beyond PRA and NRA codes and increased union activity for the reason why wage rates rose faster than spending between 1933 and 1937: those two causes alone, Hanes says, supply "a plausible and *complete* explanation."

The Wagner Act

Hanes (2020) also shows that the timing of the New Deal's "anomalous" wage rate movements is *not* consistent with the alternative hypothesis that wage rates rose in response to an anticipated easing of monetary policy. That alternative explanation is especially hard to square with the upward wage rate movements that took place between November 1936 and October 1937, when both the Federal Reserve and the Treasury adopted anti-inflation policies that should have *reduced* the public's future price level expectations. It was just as these anti-inflationary steps were being taken that wage rates rose substantially *above* levels consistent with current spending.

But the NRA also can't explain those wage hikes, for after the Supreme Court declared it unconstitutional on May 27, 1935, it ceased to exist except as a minor bureau devoted to publishing economic reports. Instead, responsibility for the wage hikes belongs to the NLRA, better known as the Wagner Act, passed two months after the NRA was struck down.[6] Besides continuing many of the NRA's labor provisions, the Wagner Act, together with the National Labor Relations Board (NLRB), its enforcement agency, substantially strengthened workers' right to form unions and go on strike. Thanks mainly to the Wagner Act and the NLRB, Harold Cole and Lee Ohanian (2004) report, both the share of unionized workers and the number of strikes they held doubled between 1935 and 1939. Because the NLRB was able for a time to force firms to rehire workers fired for taking part in sit-down strikes, those strikes tended to be especially effective.[7]

Hanes (2020, 1056) shows that the nominal wage rate hikes of 1936–1937 coincided perfectly with the "wave of union membership drives and strikes" set in motion by passage of the Wagner Act. The hikes became especially pronounced after unions were further emboldened by the Supreme Court's April 12, 1937, decision declaring the Wagner Act constitutional. It took the recession of 1937–1938 to end both the strikes and wage rate increases, which the Wagner Act accomplished only by setting output and unemployment back to where they'd been just before the dollar was devalued.

Unconcealed Cartels

It would be a mistake, though, to attribute the harm done by the NRA solely to its wage rate–raising provisions, and it would be an even bigger mistake to imagine that the code-making process was dominated by organized labor. Instead, businessmen dominated the process from the very beginning, with the government's willing connivance. Labor leaders came second, with consumers bringing up the rear if not left entirely behind. The very haste to get codes in place practically guaranteed the last result. "It was not surprising," James MacGregor Burns (1956, 193) writes, "that in the haste and confusion Johnson dealt with the business and labor leaders closest at hand, those who were most vocal, best organized, most experienced in dealing with politicians and bureaucrats. Who could speak for that amorphous group, the consumers? A Consumers' Advisory board was set up but eased to one side; a member quit indignantly within a few weeks of its establishment."

Faulty economics in turn played into business leaders hands. As Hawley (1966, 12–13) explains, besides those who blamed the Depression on low wage rates, there were many, including some influential members of the Brain Trust, who blamed it on businessmens' irresponsible "chiseling" and "cutthroat" competition." According to them, the NRA could help end the Depression by forcing such chiselers into line. That meant setting antitrust legislation completely aside and encouraging the use of codes not simply to boost wage rates but also to at least maintain, if not boost, the prices firms charged for their products. It was this potential use of the NRA, rather than its use to increase wage rates, that businessmen, big ones especially, found most appealing. And it was business rather than labor representatives who dominated both the drafting of the NIRA's Title I and the subsequent writing of industry-specific codes. Of roughly 550 such codes, at least 400 prohibited firms they covered from setting the prices of their products below "cost," where in practice "cost" included some monopoly profit (57–61).

Nor were explicit price codes the only ones calculated to rule out not just "cutthroat" competition but real competition of any sort. "As code making proceeded," Hawley (1966, 57) writes, "industrialists succeeded in incorpo-

rating a whole series of provisions that were designed essentially to eliminate competition and establish business cartels." In fact, virtually all codes
included some sort of device or devices that could "be employed directly or
indirectly to fix or influence prices" ("Price Controls under N.R.A." 1934).

Thanks to the NIRA's suspension of antitrust laws for codified industries,
businessmen—big ones especially—were able to suppress price competition
with almost complete impunity, even resorting to intimidation for the purpose. For example, in a letter sent to one manufacturer, the secretary of a
code authority noted that the prices that manufacturer planned to charge for
its products were 10 percent lower than what other firms had in mind. "I feel
sure," the secretary wrote, "that you will want to revise your prices so that they
will bear a closer relation to those of your competitors [to avoid] an investigation to ascertain whether this price can be justified. . . . Such a procedure
is of course unpleasant and costly. I am sure this matter can be straightened
out without resorting to any such action" (Aiken 1936, 278).

Besides harming consumers, such anticompetitive practices drew the ire
of many small businessmen. As of March 1934, Idaho senator William Borah,
an NRA skeptic from the start, claimed to have received fourteen thousand
letters from such businessmen complaining that the codes made it impossible
for them to compete with their larger rivals (Horowitz 1993, 701). To investigate such complaints, Roosevelt established the National Recovery Review
Board that month, with Clarence Darrow as its chair. The new board eventually concluded that NRA codes "not only permit but foster monopolistic
practices" (Cole and Ohanian 2004, 792–93).

Notwithstanding the summer 1933 "boomlet"—a brief burst of industrial
activity the start of which roughly coincided with the NIRA's passage—the
use of NRA codes to enforce monopoly prices was bound to reduce output
and employment even with constant real labor costs, widening the gap between real and potential output and slowing down recovery accordingly. But
just *how much* did the codes slow it down? Hawley (1966, 132) lets the NRA
off lightly, saying only that it is doubtful that its encouragement of monopoly
pricing contributed anything to the 1933–1935 recovery. More recent research,
in contrast, suggests that the NRA's "contribution" was quite significant but
negative.

In a highly influential study, Harold Cole and Lee Ohanian (2004) compare wage and price changes in manufacturing and energy industries covered
by NRA codes to those in industries that weren't covered, excluding farming where, as we've seen, other government policies artificially limited output and boosted prices. They find that prices in the covered industries rose
substantially, while other prices didn't. Cole and Ohanian also construct a

TABLE 9.1. Predicted deviations from trend for various macroeconomic variables, 1934–1939, competitive (C) and cartel (M) models (Data from Cole and Ohanian 2004, tables 7 and 8)

	Output		Consumption		Investment		Employment		Wage Rates		
Year	C	M	C	M	C	M	C	M	C	M_C	M_M
1934	0.87	0.77	0.90	0.85	0.75	0.40	0.98	0.82	0.89	0.81	1.16
1935	0.92	0.81	0.91	0.85	0.97	0.62	1.01	0.84	0.91	0.83	1.19
1936	0.87	0.86	0.93	0.85	1.18	0.87	1.03	0.89	0.94	0.83	1.20
1937	0.98	0.87	0.94	0.86	1.14	0.90	1.03	0.00	0.95	0.83	1.20
1938	0.98	0.86	0.95	0.86	1.12	0.86	1.02	0.89	0.96	0.84	1.20
1939	0.99	0.87	0.96	0.86	1.02	0.88	1.02	0.89	0.97	0.84	1.20

M_C = cartel model, competitive sector; M_M = cartel model, cartelized sector

general equilibrium model in which employers and workers can form cartels and bargain over the division of the spoils. They then solve the model to come up with predicted paths of real output, consumption, investment, employment, and wage rates. Finally, they compare those variables' predicted paths to both their full-employment trend paths and paths predicted by an alternative purely competitive model. As table 9.1 shows, Cole and Ohanian's cartel-pricing model comes much closer to predicting the actual severity and persistence of the Great Depression than its perfectly competitive counterpart (although even the cartel model predicts a more rapid recovery than what actually took place).

More recently, Jason Taylor (2019, 99–101) has used industry-level data to compare the behavior of output in industries subject to lengthy (twenty pages or more) code provisions that generally provided for cartel pricing to those with shorter codes that generally did not. After controlling for various other factors, he finds that output fell by a very substantial *20 percent* in industries with the more elaborate codes but didn't fall at all in the rest.

"Hit Them All at Once"

The Supreme Court's May 27, 1935, Schechter Poultry ruling did away with official industrial codes. Yet it didn't put an end to the monopolistic practices those codes had encouraged. Instead, because the Department of Justice's Antitrust Division remained almost as disinclined to enforce antitrust laws as it had been before Schechter, firms in many industries kept on honoring their anticompetitive agreements (Hawley 1966, 166–68). For the entire 1933–1938 period, the number of antitrust cases averaged just 6.5 per year, as compared to 12.5 a year during the 1920s, itself a decade of notoriously lax antitrust enforcement (Posner 1970, 366).

But 1938, during which the Department of Justice filed ten antitrust cases, was a year of transition. In a message to Congress that April, Roosevelt signaled the change by observing that the US economy had "become a concealed cartel system" (Roosevelt 1941b, 2:308). He also said that "the *disappearance of price competition*"—something the NRA had deliberately sought—was among "the primary causes of the present difficulties" (310, emphasis added). Soon afterward Roosevelt put Thurman Arnold, a Yale law professor mainly known as the author of a pair of entertainingly mordant books on capitalism and the government, in charge of the Justice Department's Antitrust Division.

Most authorities agree that Roosevelt, far from planning to radically overhaul his administration's antitrust policies, merely intended his April speech to forestall more drastic antitrust legislation from Congress (Gressley 1964). Roosevelt asked Arnold, a loyal New Dealer who seemed unlikely to become a zealous trust buster, to take charge of an official investigation into the trust problem. But Roosevelt is supposed to have otherwise expected the new antitrust boss to maintain the status quo ante. If that's so, Roosevelt ended up with far more than he bargained for (Miscamble 1982). On being sworn in, Arnold promised that his enforcement of the antitrust laws would be "vigorous." And he meant it. During his five-year tenure the antitrust division brought ninety-three suits, a sum then equal to 44 percent of all the Justice Department's antitrust proceedings since the 1890 passage of the Sherman Antitrust Act (5). Writing in the *Saturday Evening Post,* journalists Joseph Alsop and Robert Kintner summed up Arnold's antitrust strategy as "hit hard, hit everyone and hit them all at once" (quoted in Brinkley 1993, 565).

Apart from more vigorous enforcement, Arnold's tenure at the Justice Department marked a fundamental change in the nature of antitrust policy. Instead of being a Brandeisian crusade against "bigness" as such, that policy became a technocratic endeavor to combat business agreements aimed, in Arnold's own words, at "maintaining prices which there is no purchasing power to support, and then cutting down production and creating unemployment" (Arnold 1938, 570). Arnold's policy was, in short, the very antithesis of the NRA's.

Arnold pursued the investigation into the concentration of economic power he'd been put in charge of just as doggedly as he went after antitrust violators themselves. According to Broadus Mitchell (1947, 361), that investigation, undertaken by the Temporary National Economic Committee (TNEC) established for the purpose, became "a full-dress inquisition" involving hundreds of witnesses, the proceedings and reports of which take up "31 volumes, 6 supplements, and 43 monographs." But what Mitchell found even more impressive than the shelf space those proceedings take up was the irony running through them. The New Deal had, after all, "done far more than any other [program] in the country's history to practice collective control and enterprise, through government alone and in cooperation with private interests. Here it was making an about-face, vehemently accusing its erstwhile business collaborators. Great frankness, or a better sense of humor, would have required the administration to blame itself for past actions. . . . [But] the President himself, and several leading participants . . . who had been intimately involved in government encouragement of business combination, confessed no embarrassment in now damning what they had helped produce" (361–62).

Embarrassed or not, the TNEC repudiated much of the thinking that had informed the NRA and many other New Deal programs, affirming instead, in its "Economic Prologue," "the traditional conviction of the people of the United States that the opportunity of the citizen to engage in business should not be restricted and that a system of free open competition is best calculated to preserve that opportunity" (US House 1939, 30). In its final report, published in March 1941, the TNEC endorsed Arnold's general agenda by recommending "the vigorous and vigilant enforcement of the antitrust laws" that he'd then been pursuing for two years (US Senate 1941b, 9).

Although war-planning bureaucrats eventually put Arnold's antitrust program on ice, encouraging him to accept Roosevelt's March 1943 offer of a court of appeals judgeship, Arnold "had the last laugh" when the antitrust division sprang back into life after the war, pursuing Arnold's agenda as aggressively as ever (Waller 2004, 607). Whatever it was that allowed the US economy to fully emerge at last from the Depression's dark shadow, it wasn't the eradication of competition.

Appendix: Great Expectations?

To say that the NRA hasn't made many friends among economists would be an understatement. Yet there have been notable exceptions, one of whom is Brown University's Gauti Eggertsson. In a pair of articles—"Great Expectations and the End of the Great Depression" and "Was the New Deal Contractionary?"—Eggertsson (2008, 2012) uses New Keynesian theory to argue that although the NRA didn't foster recovery by directly adding to workers' total earnings, it did so indirectly by giving people a new reason to expect prices to go up. With short-run nominal interest rates stuck at or very close to their zero lower bound, that expectation served, Eggertsson says, to lower real interest rates, thereby encouraging more borrowing and immediate spending in place of future spending, an outcome equivalent to a much-needed easing of monetary policy, albeit one accomplished by unorthodox means. Eggertsson thus reaches the paradoxical conclusion that NRA codes increased US producers' output despite—or rather *by*—raising their costs of production!

Not surprisingly, Eggertsson's paradoxical conclusion has provoked more than a few vigorous replies. First, although there's plenty of evidence that NRA codes led to a substantial onetime increase in the overall *levels* of nominal wage rates and prices, as they were designed to do, it's far from clear that the codes led people to revise their estimates of future inflation, as if they expected money wages and prices to continue rising beyond their code-mandated increases. After surveying various sorts of "narrative evidence," including mentions of "inflation" in period news articles and contemporary economists' inflation predictions, to see how these responded to various policy developments, Andrew Jalil and Gisela Rua (2016, 2017) conclude that while New Deal developments that opened the way to monetary expansion, including the May 12 passage of the Agricultural Adjustment Administration with its Thomas Amendment, the April 19 suspension of the gold standard, and Roosevelt's July 3 cable torpedoing the London Economic Conference, appear to have heightened inflation expectations, the coming of the NRA did not. Instead, according to Jalil and Rua's evidence, the NRA's establishment seems to have *reduced* the public's inflation expectations, most likely (they say) because people understood that the codes it was to enforce were the Roosevelt administration's *alternative* to monetary stimulus.

Other criticisms of Eggertsson's theory have to do with the limitations of his New Keynesian model. John Cochrane (2017) observes that such models have numerous equilibrium solutions for any assumed real (forward-looking) interest rate path, each of which implies a different path for the price level and output. The models' more controversial implications hold only for one way of solving them that's not obviously more compelling than others. And Michael Kiley (2016) shows that a minor departure from the standard New Keynesian treatment of price adjustment suffices to eliminate the paradoxical implications of these models even when they are solved the way Eggertsson and other New Keynesians solve them.[8]

Several more recent studies counter Eggertsson's argument with contrary empirical evidence. As Cochrane (2013) points out, Eggertsson's argument implies that when interest rates are stuck at their zero lower bound, *any* event that raises production costs—even a hurricane!—should prove stimulating. With this understanding in mind, Johannes Wieland (2019) looks at two adverse supply shocks that struck Japan at times when interest rates there were at their zero lower bound: eastern Japan's severe earthquake of March 11, 2011, and several world oil supply shocks. Wieland finds that despite increasing expected inflation and lowering forward-looking real interest rates, the shocks were sharply contractionary, just as unsophisticated intuition would lead one to expect.

Most recently, Yangyang Ji (2021) has used statistical evidence from the New Deal itself to counter Eggertsson's claims. Ji starts with a structural vector autoregression model, the variables of which are total factor productivity, the growth rate of real output, and the rate of inflation.[9] He then identifies New Deal aggregate supply and aggregate demand innovations using sign restrictions consistent with the uncontroversial assumption that supply shocks, including the enforcement of NRA and PRA codes, move total factor productivity and inflation in opposite directions. Ji's restrictions don't themselves restrict the response of output growth to adverse supply shocks, allowing that response to be either positive, as Eggertsson's New Keynesian theory predicts, or negative, as intuition and most other studies of the codes' consequences suggest. Ji can therefore test Eggertsson's theory by comparing his own estimate of the response of output to New Deal supply shocks to Eggertsson's prediction. He does, and Eggertsson's theory fails.

The fact that Eggertsson's model treats the economy's natural ("efficient") real interest rate as an exogenous variable rather than one that varies with the state of productivity also deserves comment. According to most theories, a more productive economy will have a higher natural rate, other things being equal (Williams 2003). This means that insofar as they made the US economy less productive, NRA codes should also have lowered the real natural rate. In that case, even if the codes also raised the expected rate of inflation, they may have left the New Deal economy's natural nominal interest rate as low as ever and the zero lower bound constraint as binding as ever.

Ellis Hawley's (1966) assessment of the NRA's initial and eventual effect on the public's mood is pertinent here, for it shows that that mood ultimately depended on not just the prospect of higher prices but also the economy's real performance:

> For a time the real drift of code policy was hidden behind a facade of propaganda, patriotism, and dramatic action. Yet popular hysteria could not be maintained indefinitely, particularly when the promised recovery failed to materialize, By the fall of 1933 the speculative summer boomlet was over, economic indices were falling again, and a mood of disenchantment was setting over the country. And with the change in mood, the realization began to dawn that essentially the codes reflected the interests of the larger and more highly-organized businessmen, that the NRA was busily promoting cartels in the interest of scarcity profits. . . . The millions that had once cheered the NRA parades were lapsing into indifference and hostility. (Hawley 1966, 66, 68)

Even many New Dealers themselves doubted that the NRA would sustain the burst of economic activity that marked Roosevelt's first few months in office. "Competent observers of trends," Raymond Moley (1966, 272) observes, "actually expected the late fall to usher in an economic relapse after the high hopes of the spring and summer. For the early recovery had been largely psychological. . . . Sustained confidence would have to have something more tangible than cheerful assurances from the White House." In short, however "great" the public's expectations may have been in the summer of 1933, there seems to be little basis for supposing that they stayed that way instead of giving way to pessimistic expectations that fall.

Taking account of all these criticisms of Eggertsson's theory, together with the mass of evidence pointing the other way, it seems reasonable to conclude that, for all its undeniable ingenuity, that theory shouldn't persuade us that the NRA promoted recovery or, for that matter, that a hurricane might have done so.

The NRA, Coda: The Brookings Report

In assessing the New Deal's contribution to economic recovery, it's only natural to lean heavily on recent research while discounting early appraisals uninformed by the discipline of econometrics, which was just getting under way in the 1930s. But some studies that predate the rise of that discipline contain such a wealth of information and analysis that they remain as valuable to scholars as when they first appeared. That is, they *can* be as valuable, provided they aren't forgotten.

A good example of this is the Brookings Institution's 1935 study *The National Recovery Administration: An Analysis and Appraisal* (Lyon et al. 1935). Although widely praised at the time of its release, it has long been out of print and is often overlooked by twenty-first-century writings on the New Deal.[1]

A Nonpartisan Assessment

Apart from having been prepared while the National Recovery Administration (NRA) was in full sway, the Brookings study is significant in several other ways. For starters, at almost one thousand pages, it's still the most exacting study of its subject. Its authors—a six-person team led by Leverett Lyon—were all highly regarded economists who enjoyed the NRA's full cooperation in drafting their report. "It would indeed be fortunate," a reviewer of the report wrote in October 1935, "if all of our government programs could be subjected to some such analysis as is offered in this survey" (Young 1935, 881).

The Brookings study was also free of any partisan taint. As the preface to it by Edwin Nourse, director of Brookings's Institute of Economics, notes, some of its authors had been "integral parts of the NRA organization." Lewis L. Lorwin was a lifelong advocate of economic planning and the founder, in 1934, of the National Planning Association. His views were among those that inspired the NRA, and he was "deeply invested" in its success (Misukiewicz 2015, 69). Another of the report's authors, Leon C. Marshall, was chosen by Franklin Roosevelt soon after the report appeared to head the NRA's Division of Review, a new administrative office charged with assessing "the effects of the administration of Title I of the National Industrial Recovery Act" (Roosevelt 1938, 4:257).

Although Harold Moulton, the Brookings Institution's president, was himself a very orthodox economist who later became an outspoken critic of the Roosevelt administration's deficit spending, Roosevelt thought highly enough of him, and of Brookings, to seek the think tank's advice in developing his administration's recovery strategy. "Quite frankly," President-elect Roosevelt wrote to Moulton, "we need help. Because I know of the splendid work that has been done by you and the Institute, and because of my old friendship for Mr. Brookings, I am hoping that you will be able to give us assistance in the preparation of a fairly definite plan between now and early March" (Saunders 1966, 53).

For his part, Moulton was determined to keep Brookings independent. For that reason, he only agreed to serve as its director after securing Robert Brookings's pledge that its trustees wouldn't interfere with its work. It was not, however, indirect pressure from the Roosevelt administration that Moulton feared. His chief concern, he told Brookings, was making sure that the nation's first think tank didn't fall under the sway of "the manufacturing interests of the country" (Critchlow 1984, 570).

In short, when the Brookings team set out to assess the NRA, its members had no axe to grind with either the Roosevelt administration or with planning as such, and there were no marching orders from aggrieved businessmen. Even so, their report is damning. Like most studies since, it finds that instead of promoting economic recovery, the NRA delayed it. The report's explanations for this failure are also essentially the same as those found in more recent works. What sets it apart from these works is the hundreds of pages of evidence upon which its conclusions rest, an amount rivaling anything to be found elsewhere.

Alas, the very thoroughness of the Brookings Institution's NRA report would limit its popularity even if it weren't hard to get hold of. Not many people want to read a thousand-page tome written by a committee almost nine decades ago! The following provides a quick review of the report's main findings and the arguments on which they're based.

Reform versus Recovery

The Brookings report concerns the NRA's bearing on recovery alone, not its longer-run consequences. "Our test of whether the NRA has furthered recovery," its authors state, "is whether the nation has enjoyed under it a larger production of goods and services than it would have enjoyed without it" (Lyon et al. 1935, 752). Recognizing that applying this test isn't simply a matter of noting that "recovery under the NRA has been quite disappointing" or of finding it "hard to believe that we would have made less progress without it" (754), the report's authors take great pains to control for other factors. Even so, they find not only that the NRA failed "to work out as planned" but also that the plan itself, meaning the thinking that was supposed to justify the NRA's codes, was "mistaken" (892). "Raising the prices of labor or goods," the report states, "is not the way to get a larger volume purchased. Instead the NRA should have sought the maximum enlargement of spending with the minimum increase in costs and prices, thus securing with the augmented expenditure the greatest gain in the number of units of labor and goods taken off the market" (873). Increased spending might have been promoted either by removing "the deterrents to the free and prompt utilization of the existing money of the country" or through monetary expansion. But "The NRA accomplished neither of these objectives."

The Brookings scholars trace the NRA's failure in part to its trying to be "all things to all men" and especially to its attempt to kill two birds with one stone. "Although the immediate concern of the National Recovery Administration was an attack on the business depression," the report states, the agency sought "both recovery and 'reform.' Indeed, it might even be said that it sought recovery *through* reform" (Lyon et al. 1935, 751). Organized labor wanted higher wage rates and shorter worker hours, while industrialists wanted relief from strict antitrust laws. To gain both groups' support, the NRA offered to meet all these demands while claiming, conveniently, that doing so was just what was needed to help end the Great Depression. According to the Brookings report, "The possibility that, despite their popularity with the two interest groups, such reforms might retard the emergence of the country from depression," wasn't a possibility the NRA's leaders were willing to entertain.

The Purchasing Power Theory

Nor, according to the report, were the NRA's procedures consistent with any coherent theory. Instead, like much of the New Deal, they were concocted on the fly. The hastily drafted legislation that created the agency included few particulars. The only guidance the new agency's administrators had to go by consisted of various and not always consistent "public statements emanating from different government officials" (Lyon et al. 1935, 756). It was therefore "a serious error to regard the NRA as a studied attempt to give institutional embodiment to an economic theory." Instead, the NRA's theory of recovery has to be inferred from the codes and other rules it enforced once it was established.[2]

Regarding those rules, because the NRA "could not compel a single producer to turn out one additional unit of product" (Lyon et al. 1935, 755), its administrators had to believe that codes governing the setting of prices and wage rates would stimulate production indirectly. According to the Brookings report, they ran with the high-wage doctrine's assumption that raising workers' wage rates "would expand the purchasing power of the nation for goods and services." Workers' increased demand for goods and services would in turn serve to "enlarge the volume of production and start the upward spiral of recovery" (757). But for this strategy to work, employers had to be willing and able to finance increased wage payments *before* the demand for their goods and services went up!

Was it reasonable, the report asks, to expect employers to pay higher wage rates without cutting worker hours? Its answer is an emphatic "no." Any hope that employers might do so by reducing dividends ignored the fact that dividend payments were "very small in relation to total payments to labor" (Lyon et al. 1935, 766), while any hope that they might manage by dipping into their profits ignored the fact that most were "operating in the red" and that any "attempt to squeeze blood from the turnip of business earnings would have aggravated the stagnation of business and investor expenditures" (771). Yet setting such unrealistic possibilities aside left only the still more absurd hope that employers would somehow secure "the wherewithal to pay . . . higher wages . . . from the increased spending of the benefited wage earners" (762).

Qui Bono?

Instead of enlarging payrolls, the higher wage rates called for by NRA codes tended to reduce total employment, a result precisely opposite the one desperately needed. "The basic difficulty in the spring of 1933," the Brookings report says, "was not that hourly wage rates were generally too low" (Lyon et al. 1935, 782). Owing in part to the downward "stickiness" of nominal wage

rates, real wage rates didn't actually fall all that much during the Great Contraction. To be more precise, they did not fall much for those lucky enough
to stay employed. For many who weren't so lucky, they fell to zero.

The thing most desperately needed wasn't higher wage *rates* but more
hours of employment, precisely the opposite of what the NRA codes achieved.
"It did not seem to occur to the NRA," the report caustically observes, "that
a high price for labor might restrict the amount used" (Lyon et al. 1935, 782).
Because NRA wage codes only applied to about half of all workers, mainly
those employed by relatively high-paying mining and manufacturing firms,
and because the codes often overcompensated for concurrent changes in the
cost of living, the NRA chiefly rewarded workers who "were already making
more income per hour than they made before the depression" (792). And it
awarded those workers at other workers' expense.

Farmers, farmworkers, and their families, who made up more than a quarter
of the population, were among those made worse off by the NRA codes. That
outcome was bitterly ironic, because one of the chief objectives of the New
Deal and of the Agricultural Adjustment Administration (AAA) in particular
was raising the prices of farm commodities relative to farmers' cost of living.

Whether the AAA helped to achieve that objective at all is, as we've seen,
a matter of some doubt. But whatever that agency's own shortcomings, the
NRA clearly tended to undermine its success. "The price-raising activities
of the NRA," the Brookings report observes, "have run flatly counter to the
efforts of the AAA to restore 'price parity' for agriculture" (Lyon et al. 1935,
794), boosting farmers' costs more than enough to offset whatever increase in
farm product prices the AAA managed to achieve by restricting farm output.

A Misleading Boomlet

Students of the NRA's influence on output have sometimes been misled by
the sharp but short-lived spike, or boomlet, in industrial production that
started around the time Roosevelt introduced the NIRA to Congress and
ended as the President's Reemployment Agreement's blanket code took effect. Some economists attribute that burst of activity to an upward revision of
the public's longer-term inflation expectations, a revision that, with nominal
interest rates stuck near zero, might have inspired a corresponding revival of
investment. The Brookings study pours cold water on this view (Lyon et al.
1935, 489). The boomlet, it insists, was instead the result of an arbitrage opportunity that was bound to be temporary. "The certainty and imminence
of impending cost and price increases," it says, "offered a well-nigh unprecedented incentive to speed up, to 'beat the gun,' and industry responded with

an acceleration of activity that perhaps has no parallel in the history of the country."[3]

But like a rainbow, the spree couldn't last. "Once the anticipated rise had materialized," the report continues, "the incentive to further activity was largely dissipated" (Lyon et al. 1935, 90). From then onward higher prices became "a continuing hindrance to the expansion of the physical volume of activity" (804).

More Jobs, Less Unemployment

Conventional unemployment statistics appear to show that despite limiting growth in the "physical volume of activity" in other respects, the NRA didn't stand in the way of a substantial reduction in unemployment. Even the Bureau of Labor Statistic's standard unemployment measure, classifying relief program workers as unemployed, shows that from the time of the NRA's establishment until it was declared unconstitutional in May 1935, the unemployment rate fell from its peak of over 25 percent to less than 18 percent.

Officials at the NRA were quick to credit it for this improvement. "As early as November 1933," the Brookings report observes, Hugh Johnson claimed that the NRA "had put 4 million men to work" (Lyon et al. 1935, 830). But that figure, the report says, was a mere "shot in the dark" that "probably exceeded the total increase in employment up to that time from all causes." According to the Bureau of Labor Statistics, 10.61 million workers were unemployed in 1935, compared to 12.83 million in 1933, a difference of just 2.22 million (Lebergott 1948, 50–53). The Brookings team determined, furthermore, that only about 1.5 million of those workers were employed in industries "materially affected by the NRA" (Lyon et al. 1935, 833).

But exaggeration was the least of it. Examining the evidence further, the Brookings team found that while the NRA may have put more people to work, its effect on the total quantity of labor employed was negative. As their report explains, the NRA influenced employment both by "work spreading" and by "changing the total amount of work done" (Lyon et al. 1935, 830). According to the Brookings Institution's estimates, had they not been accompanied by wage-rate increases, the NRA's work-spreading provisions alone, with no change in total hours, should have allowed firms to create 1.75 million more jobs, or 250,000 more than were actually created. It follows that the NRA had a *negative* effect on "the total amount of work done" and that it must therefore have had a similar effect on total real output, other things being equal. "In the last analysis," this part of the Brookings report concludes, "the NRA must be judged chiefly by what its program has done to increase the total amount of

work available. Merely dividing a smaller amount of work among more workers is neither recovery nor a good substitute for it" (844).

Reviving Nominal Income

The Brookings report's understanding of the real key to recovery is no less
in agreement with modern research than its account of the NRA's shortcomings. "A full utilization of the country's productive capacities," it says, "could
be achieved only by getting the national income high enough, in relation to
the [prevailing] price level for finished goods and services, to take off the
market a capacity output" (Lyon et al. 1935, 801). Somehow, "more money had
to flow into the markets for the current output." Instead of being something
that could be achieved by arbitrarily raising the prices of goods and services,
a revival of money earnings and spending was a prerequisite for sustaining
higher prices without curtailing output further.

"A program of income expansion," the report goes on to say, calls for one
or both of the following: "(1) the activation of idle and redundant cash balances through a revival of business confidence [and] (2) monetary expansion" (Lyon et al. 1935, 805). The NRA achieved neither. Although money
income grew, it did so mainly thanks to "the reopening of closed banks, gold
imports, and the financing by banks of the federal deficit" (806). Instead
of helping, by raising prices the NRA made the amount of money income
needed to clear markets higher than it would have been otherwise, hampering recovery.

Of course, output did recover somewhat between the passage of the National Industrial Recovery Act and the start of the Roosevelt Recession. But
that recovery took place despite rather than because of the NRA. As we've
seen, its cause was monetary expansion driven chiefly by gold imports. As
the Brookings report makes clear, had there been no NRA, that expansion
"would probably have done more than it did to expand the physical volume
of production" (Lyon et al. 1935, 807).

No Help to Debtors

The Roosevelt administration hoped that by getting prices closer to their
pre-Depression levels, the NRA would assist those who'd contracted long-
term debts before the Depression started. But the Brookings report sees this
as yet another promise the NRA failed to keep. "Debt charges are paid from
income, not from prices," the report notes (Lyon et al. 1935, 813). As we've
seen, the NRA itself did nothing to boost nominal incomes. Instead, by rais-

ing living costs, it harmed debtors, whose incomes grew less than their cost of living. These debtors included many farmers, whose long-term debts consisted mainly of mortgages and real estate and who, instead of gaining by the NRA's codes, suffered from their effect on the cost of consumer goods and farm supplies.

Nor were farmers the only debtors made worse off by the NRA. "It seems reasonably certain," the Brookings report says, "that the cost- and price-raising campaign of the NRA has, on the whole, increased rather than diminished the burden of private funded debt" (Lyon et al. 1935, 815).

A Great Fictitious Entity

Claude-Frédéric Bastiat famously defined the government as a "great fictitious entity by which everyone seeks to live at the expense of everyone else." According to this definition, and to the findings of the Brookings report, the NRA was a government institution par excellence.

In assenting "to the desires of labor on the one hand and industry on the other," the NRA overlooked "the fact that these interests usually get their ideas in reaction to limited individual situations, not from a consideration of the economy as a whole. One group of workers may improve its relative position by higher wage rates and one industry may benefit itself by higher prices, but this is merely because wages and prices are not similarly raised elsewhere. When the game is played universally it is self-defeating" (Lyon et al. 1935, 808). Actually, it was worse than that, for the NRA's price and wage codes ultimately served "to promote scarcity all around" when what the nation desperately needed was "abundance, not scarcity."

A Second Opinion

Because the verdict of the Brookings study is so harsh, it seems only fair to give the last word to someone who was even more intimately involved with the NRA's undertakings than any of its authors and no less qualified than any to judge its success. Charles F. Roos, who served as the NRA's principal economist and director of research on policy matters from July 1933 to September 1934, presumably fits the bill. It happens that two years after Brookings came out with its study, the Cowles Commission published one by Roos that, at just short of six hundred pages, is second only to the Brookings study in its comprehensiveness.

Yet when it comes to condemning the NRA, Roos's report may actually deserve first prize. "During 1934 and 1935," Roos (1937, 472) concludes, the

NRA "kept business in a churn, prevented re-employment, and consequently retarded American development." Throughout its existence, he continues, the NRA "was characterized by a lack of definite policy and of proper understanding of its objectives." In planning it,

> various economic panaceas equally or more contradictory, were borrowed from long agitated movements, both good and bad, and hastily thrown together into an ensemble of contradictions. To such, the NRA added a haphazard method of code writing involving the bargaining of two groups—industry and labor . . . for the purse of a third—the consumer. . . . As a result, despite laudable reform efforts to abolish child labor, to eliminate intolerable unfair trade practices, to make competition function more smoothly through open prices, and, most important, to promote discussion of economic issues, the NRA must, as a whole, be regarded as a sincere but ineffective effort to alleviate depression. (Roos 1937, 472)

The NRA was only one part of the New Deal, so it would be incorrect to suppose that its failure to shorten the Depression means that the New Deal as a whole didn't shorten it. But it is no less wrong to call the NRA's failure a mere "setback," as Noah Smith (2020) does. Although the NRA was not the New Deal, while it lasted it *was* a big part of what the New Dealers were counting on to get the US economy back on its feet. Far from being a mere hitch in their recovery program, the NRA's failure left them with no workable program at all.

A New Deal for Housing

To properly assess a New Deal program's contribution to recovery, one must distinguish that contribution from the same program's contributions to relief or reform. New Deal programs that offered badly needed relief to the Great Depression's victims or achieved reforms with indisputable long-run benefits didn't always shorten the Depression. Some almost certainly lengthened it.

But it's equally true that New Deal policies with relief or reform as their chief aim could also promote recovery. In theory, any policy that meant more federal spending, especially deficit spending, could help simply by boosting demand—as John Maynard Keynes would later suggest, semifacetiously—by instancing pyramid building. And this was far from the only way in which either relief or reform might go hand in hand with recovery.

None of the Roosevelt administration's first one hundred–day initiatives better exemplified the blurriness of the lines separating Roosevelt's three R's than the creation, on June 13, 1933, of the Home Owners' Loan Corporation (HOLC).[1] Although it was only active for a bit more than two years and was wound up in 1951, the HOLC's short life belied its lofty aims as well as its impressive achievements. In recommending it to Congress, Roosevelt explained that its immediate purpose was "to protect small home owners from foreclosure and to relieve them of a portion of the burden of excessive interest and principal payments incurred during the period of higher values and higher earning power" (Roosevelt 1938, 2:135). But Roosevelt first let Congress know that he considered the legislation an "urgently necessary step in the program to promote economic recovery."

The HOLC has been called "one of the great success stories of the New Deal" (Carrozzo 2008, 22), and this opinion is widely shared. To see why isn't difficult. During its brief career, the HOLC refinanced mortgage loans for a million homeowners, sparing many the extreme hardships of foreclosure. Lenders benefited as well by trading their delinquent mortgages for HOLC bonds. By many accounts, no New Deal program delivered more obvious benefits at so little cost. Some even claim that instead of costing taxpayers anything, the HOLC made a profit.

Yet it was not mortgage holders but mortgage *lenders* who benefited most from bargains the HOLC struck. The leg up that the HOLC gave them reflected its overarching purpose of promoting recovery: by boosting their capital, it hoped to do for mortgage lending and real estate investment what the Reconstruction Finance Corporation (RFC) tried to do for bank lending and business investment. But while the relief the HOLC offered to homeowners was palpable, its contribution to economic recovery is hard to pin down. Many claim, on the other hand, that its long-term influence on mortgage lending has been anything but benign.

Up, Up, and Away . . .

To understand the severity of the Great Depression mortgage crisis, one must step further back in time to consider the housing boom of the 1920s and the nature of the mortgage loans that financed a large part of it.

"In a decade of almost steady growth," Eugene Nelson White (2014, 117–18) says, "the behavior of residential construction stands out." Whereas the better-known boom of the first decade of the 2000s witnessed the construction of 1.3 million new homes, that of the 1920s, when the population of the United States was little more than a third as great, witnessed *twice* that number. For four years starting in 1924, residential construction accounted for more than 8 percent of the nation's GNP (Field 1992, 785), During 1925 and 1926 alone, the amount invested in new houses—almost $10 billion—was about equal to the value of new securities purchased in the peak stock market years of 1928 and 1929.

To some extent, the housing boom of the 1920s was just the economy's way of making up for the "crowding-out" of residential construction during World War I, when the government's heavy borrowing left little credit aside for the financing of new homes. But according to White (2014, 125), as happened during the 2000s, easy Federal Reserve policy also played a part by making it easier than ever for people to buy homes on credit.

. . . in Not-So-Beautiful Balloons

Mortgages, White (2014, 134, 138) explains, "supplied over $2 billion of the $3.3 billion in [home] financing for 1926," which was about twice the 1922 level. Hardly any of those mortgages resembled the long-term, amortized loans that have since become typical. Many weren't intermediated at all: that is, they were made directly by individuals to farmers and others and consisted of interest-only loans with terms of five years or less. When the loans matured, a final balloon payment, consisting of the loan principal, fell due. It was common for borrowers to refinance their loans at least once so as to have more time to accumulate the needed principal payment. Mortgages provided by commercial banks usually had similar terms.

But commercial banks didn't offer many mortgages in those days. Building and loan associations (B&Ls) were far more important. These were typically small local institutions, mutually owned and funded by members' dues, that is, by their weekly or monthly purchases of association shares (Fishback, Rose, and Snowden 2013, 12). B&Ls first rose to prominence during the last decades of the nineteenth century, when commercial banks either shied away or were prevented from lending on real estate. Until 1914, national banks weren't supposed to offer mortgages at all (Price and Walter 2019, 2).[2]

Yet the rise of B&Ls before 1900 was nothing compared to what came afterward. Between 1910 and 1929 their numbers more than doubled, from 5,869 to 12,342, while their assets quadrupled. When the stock market crashed in October 1929, roughly one American in ten was a B&L member. Even in 1930, as the economy was starting to spiral downward, B&Ls were writing one thousand mortgages a day and accounting for as much outstanding residential mortgage credit as commercial banks, life insurance companies, and mutual savings banks combined (Mason 2004, 61; Rose 2011, 1076).

Although it resembled other mortgages in being nonamortizing, the standard B&L mortgage had a longer term, usually between eleven and thirteen years. And while it also called for a balloon payment, the value of borrowers' shares, to which both their dues and dividends contributed, tended to rise over time until their equity sufficed to pay off the principal. Borrowers' share accounts thus served as sinking funds for their loans. Any share accumulations beyond the principal owed were the homeowner's, free and clear.

Thus, like those who took out interest-only mortgages with balloon payments, and unlike today's holders of amortized mortgage loans, B&L borrowers owed the entire principal of their loans for the loans' full life. It follows that if members defaulted, they "lost not only the house but also the accumulated value in the sinking fund" (Fishback, Rose, and Snowden 2013, 14–15). Even so, as long as B&L share values stayed the same or rose, these were attractive terms. They made it possible for borrowers to avoid having to come up with lump-sum balloon payments while enjoying a share of their association's profits. And so they did throughout the 1920s. Only if share prices fell could things possibly turn sour.

That Sinking Feeling

With the aid of hindsight, including knowledge of just how much mortgage-financed home buying went on during the 1920s, it's tempting to suppose that B&Ls and other mortgage lenders that came to grief afterward did so because they'd lent recklessly. But this supposition is hardly fair. Unlike banks, B&Ls seldom failed during the 1920s, and had it not been for the unprecedented severity of the subsequent downturn, most of their loans would have continued to perform well, while their capital would have sufficed to absorb losses from ones that didn't.

Two things had to go terribly wrong to cause the US mortgage industry to suffer as it did. One was a collapse in house values; the other was a collapse in household income and wealth. Had house prices remained stable, those who could not afford to keep paying their loans at least had the option of selling their properties at prices that would allow them to pay their debts. And if they didn't pay their debts, their lenders could at least make themselves whole by foreclosing. If, on the other hand, house prices fell dramatically but their owners' earnings didn't, although those owners would suffer a loss of equity, they could still go on paying off their debts (Wheelock 2008, 1378).

The Great Depression was great in part because in the United States at least it managed to pull the "double trigger" of collapsing house values and collapsing incomes, dealing a mortal blow to mortgage lenders by making it impossible for vast numbers of their clients to continue paying off their loans (Fishback, Rose, and Snowden 2013, 19). Between 1929 and 1933 house prices fell by a third, while the unemployment rate rose to 25 percent. In 1932, roughly 273,000 people lost their homes, as compared to only 6,000 in 1926. Yet the bottom still hadn't been reached. By the time of Roosevelt's inauguration, with roughly a third of all US mortgages in default and twice as many in arrears, lenders were foreclosing on one thousand loans *every day*.

This explosion of foreclosures was more than enough to ruin many mortgage lenders and the private firms that insured their loans (White 2014, 141). And the rot was tragically self-reinforcing: as mortgage credit dried up, borrowers facing balloon payments could find it difficult to refinance. So, more borrowers would default and more lenders would fail, in a vicious downward spiral. Finally, homeowners who managed somehow to keep up with their payments were paying with dollars that were worth a third more than their 1929 value (Fishback, Rose, and Snowden 2013, 29).

A similar negative feedback loop was tearing apart B&Ls, which were all the more vulnerable by virtue of having mortgage lending as their bread and butter. If any of a B&L's members failed to make payments because they lost their jobs or were earning less, the others all saw their share values dwindle and their hopes of paying off their loans go up in smoke. Members were also more likely to cash in their shares because they either feared further reductions or simply needed the money. When withdrawals rose to unprecedented levels despite both contractual and statutory withdrawal limits, B&Ls had to liquidate foreclosed properties at Depression prices, realizing large losses. By 1933, almost two thousand B&Ls had failed (Rose 2014, 30).[3]

Nor was the damage limited to homeowners and real estate lenders. The troubles of the mortgage industry contributed to the overall collapse in spending on residential construction, which (assessed in inflation-adjusted terms) would take almost a quarter century to return to its 1926 peak (Field 1992, 787). As construction fell to a mere trickle, hundreds of thousands of workers joined the ranks of the unemployed and, in many cases, those of mortgage deadbeats: all told, between a quarter and a third of workers unemployed during the depths of the Depression came from the building trades. So, still more foreclosures and as many more housing units added to an already severe glut.

Yet hundreds of thousands of nonperforming mortgages were still on lenders' books, thanks to state foreclosure moratoriums or to some combination of lenders' voluntary forbearance and their unwillingness to take possession of more unsaleable real estate. Such indulgences were, however, mere stays of execution: barring some other intervention, the mortgage pipers would have to be paid, and that many more delinquent homeowners would come home to find their locks changed and their belongings on the street.

A White Knight for Homeowners

Homeowners' and mortgage lenders' desperate straits cried out for some sort of remedy. The Federal Home Loan Bank Act, passed in July 1932, was supposed to help. Besides granting credit to illiquid B&Ls, much as Federal Reserve banks granted it to commercial banks, the new Home Loan banks could also lend directly to distressed homeowners. But their terms were so conservative that, of the forty-one thousand applications they received, only *three* were approved (Carrozzo 2008, 9). The Federal Home Loan Bank Board (FHLBB) itself recognized the need for an alternative. So, on April 13, 1933, when Roosevelt introduced legislation proposing a new agency, to be overseen by the FHLBB, which was charged with lightening homeowners' debt burden, the House hastened to make a law of the proposal, approving it in just two months with a whopping 383–4 majority. The bill then breezed through the Senate on a voice vote.

The HOLC's plan was ingenious in its simplicity. The HOLC would invite distressed mortgage holders and their lenders to apply to have it take their mortgages over. If the HOLC accepted an application, which it did provided it was convinced that the prospective borrower was both capable of making the lower payments and in need of help, it would contact the lender holding the original mortgage, offering to swap its own bonds, paying 4 percent interest, for the mortgage. By Depression standards, 4 percent was a good return, especially compared to what the mortgages in question were actually earning, which was typically nothing at all; it was also likely to be a better deal than what lenders could expect to earn by foreclosing on delinquent properties and then renting or selling them. The HOLC's loan purchases were thus financed by the loans' private market originators. If its offer was accepted, the HOLC acquired the loan, which it then replaced with a ten- or fifteen-year amortized loan for which it charged only 5 percent (and later just 4.5 percent).

But for all its simplicity, the HOLC's plan was no perpetual motion machine: what ultimately kept it humming—and the reason why no private market effort could have matched it—was the backing it got from the federal government. That backing consisted of not only the $200 million in starting capital the HOLC received from the Treasury but also the federal government's willingness to guarantee the interest on the HOLC's bonds and, starting in April 1934, the principal as well. That made those bonds as safe as Treasury securities (Fishback, Rose, and Snowden 2013, 112). The result was that holders of HOLC bonds didn't have to worry that by being too generous in its lending, the HOLC could itself go bankrupt.

Thanks to these guarantees, the HOLC's offers were eagerly swooped up. Between June 13, 1933, and June 27, 1935, when it stopped accepting them, it received applications from almost two million homeowners. By 1936 it had refinanced a million of their mortgages. Most of the homeowners it helped were many months in arrears on not just their loan payments but also their property taxes, which their HOLC loans also covered. It's therefore likely that had it not been for the HOLC, they would have lost their homes, doubling the number of foreclosures. That the HOLC wasn't being too strict in deciding who to help is evident enough from the fact that it ultimately had to foreclose on some two hundred thousand of its own clients, despite making every effort to avoid doing so. Figure 11.1 shows the progress of private and HOLC foreclosures.

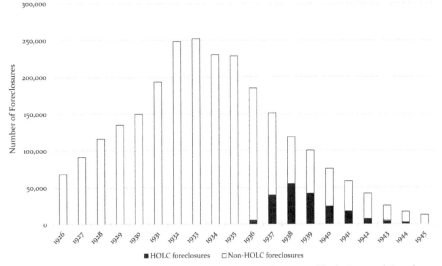

FIGURE 11.1. HOLC and non-HOLC foreclosures, 1926–1945. (Source: Fishback, Rose, and Snowden 2013, 22, Figure 3.1. Reproduced by permission of the University of Chicago Press.)

Four-fifths of those who received HOLC loans were, on the other hand, able to stay in their homes for good thanks to the improved terms. There can be no gainsaying the tremendous value of that deliverance. "The contributions of the HOLC," Peter Carrozzo (2008, 22) writes, "were very real." Thanks to it, "one million families were not afraid to receive their mail each day for fear off the eviction notice; one million families did not suffer the humiliation of carrying furniture and belongings out of their homes as neighbors watched; one million families were not forced to remove to a different neighborhood, into cramped houses with relatives and to transfer children to new schools; one million families did not have their credit destroyed and a sense of utter failure."

And a Bailout for Lenders

It would be a mistake, though, to regard homeowners as the HOLC's sole or even main beneficiaries. In fact, as Jonathan Rose (2011, 1074) points out, in important respects its strategy made it less a borrowers' than a lenders' program. Thus, the HOLC put less emphasis on achieving principal reductions for borrowers than on offering their lenders generous prices for their mortgages, which it did in part by appraising mortgaged properties very generously. That practice got lenders to take part in the program while boosting the number of qualified loan applicants. But it also lowered the number of distressed borrowers whose high loan-to-value ratios would otherwise have inspired HOLC efforts to get lenders to agree to "haircuts" on amounts they were owed.

Why did the HOLC take this approach? The explanation resides in its double-barreled purpose. Had relief been HOLC's sole aim, it might have preferred to devote more effort toward reducing distressed homeowners' debt burdens by striking harder bargains with their lenders. But because it was supposed to not only offer relief but also stimulate recovery, the HOLC chose instead to increase the relief it offered *lenders* by, in effect, boosting their capital, much as the RFC boosted the capital of commercial banks. The hope was that doing so would help revive investment in the real estate market.[4] "HOLC officials," Rose (2011, 1095) says, "appear to have been more concerned with the course of the housing market than with the availability of principle reductions. The most likely rationale was that even if borrowers' debts remained high, a strong housing recovery would allow borrowers to gain equity in their properties, and so the HOLC took as its mission to support such a recovery by increasing the size of the program."

How did the US housing market respond to the HOLC's support? Most assessments of that support refer only to the relief it offered homeowners, neglecting its overarching macroeconomic purpose. It isn't hard to see why. As David Wheelock (2008, 144) notes, "It is difficult to determine the extent to which the HOLC contributed to a rebound in the housing market, let alone to the macroeconomic recovery." Wheeler himself claims that by taking one million bad loans off of private lenders' books, the HOLC must have helped revive private mortgage lending. But the extent to which it did is anything but clear.

A publication for students (Hanes and Hanes 2002, 101) says that "by February 1939, the HOLC had refinanced 992,531 loans totaling over $3 billion. The refinanced loans not only halted countless foreclosures but reduced delinquent property taxes. This permitted communities to meet their payrolls for school, police, and other services. Millions were also spent on repair and remodeling of homes. Thousands of men gained employment in the building trade. Thousands more jobs were stimulated in the manufacture, transportation, and sale of construction materials."

But while they all credit the HOLC with reducing foreclosures, economic historians are not so sure its undertakings led to any substantial change in residential repairs or new construction. In a 2011 study, Charles Courtemanche and Kenneth Snowden (2011, 307) recognize that the HOLC's "primary goal was to break the cycle of foreclosure, forced property sales and decreases in home values." They also uncover evidence that HOLC refinancing did in fact "cut short" the vicious cycle of debt and deflation of the early 1930s by boosting both home values and homeownership rates (309). But they find no evidence that it stimulated new home construction (335). In another study published that same year, using data from 2,800 US counties, Price Fishback and his coauthors (2011) find some evidence that the program stimulated both home sales and home and apartment construction but only after setting data for counties with fifty thousand inhabitants or more aside. When bigger counties are included, as seems more appropriate for assessing the program's overall effects, the HOLC doesn't seem to have made any difference. Finally, although it's certainly true that the HOLC spent money repairing homes it foreclosed on, private lenders did so as well, for the same reason: to profit as much as possible from the properties they took possession of.

TANSTAAFL

Whatever the HOLC's macroeconomic achievements, they were a bargain if, instead of costing taxpayers anything, its undertakings helped fill the Treasury's coffers. That's what most assessments of those achievements suppose. Peter Carrozzo (2008, 23), for example, says that "upon congressionally-ordered liquidation in 1951 and a final accounting, the HOLC ultimately turned a slight profit." In his history of the corporation, C. Lowell Harriss (1951, 159–62) puts that profit at $14 million, a figure he seems to have arrived at by simply subtracting the HOLC's cumulative capital loss of $338 million from its total operating income of $352 million (Wheelock 2008, 144).

But Harriss's accounting is wrong. According to Fishback, Rose, and Snowden (2013, 112–14), if the HOLC's loan financing activities are considered apart from its other undertakings and if account is taken of all its interest expenses, including the foregone interest on the Treasury's $200 million investment in it, the HOLC actually *lost* $53 million, or about 1.8 percent of the $3 billion it lent. Considering the relief those loans provided, this was still a good deal. But if one instead treats economic recovery as the goal of the HOLC's refinancing efforts, while relying on econometric assessments of its loans' macroeconomic consequences, those $53 million look more like money poured down a drain.

There is also an important sense in which the HOLC placed a much greater burden on taxpayers than the $53 million loss itself suggests. Thanks to government guarantees, the HOLC was able to borrow for between one and two percentage points less than it would otherwise have had to pay to acquire all the mortgages the HOLC acquired. But because those guarantees put taxpayers on the hook for any substantial losses the HOLC incurred, they amounted to a taxpayer-financed subsidy. Had it not been for this subsidy, and assuming it operated on the same scale, the HOLC's total losses would have been several hundred million dollars greater (Fishback, Rose, and Snowden 2013, 119).

In the event, the gamble the HOLC took with taxpayers' money paid off: the federal government never had to make good on its bonds (Fishback, Rose, and Snowden 2013). But things might have turned out much differently. Had the HOLC been liquidated in 1938 instead of staying open until 1951, it would almost certainly have ended up insolvent, and taxpayers would have been on the hook for substantial losses. On the other hand, as Lowell Harriss (1951, 124) points out, had it waited a few more years to dispose of its properties instead of selling most before the war started and the rest by 1944, it really would have turned a tidy profit.[5]

Seeing Red

Many also claim that the HOLC's activities had costly unintended consequences—consequences that now cast a dark shadow over its more immediate and admirable accomplishments. The corporation stands accused of having invented, employed, and institutionalized the discriminatory lending practice subsequently known as "redlining."

The conventional story starts as follows: having been asked by the FHLBB to survey real estate risk levels in larger US cities, the HOLC complied by producing detailed reports on each, together with "security maps" for many. Those maps assigned letter grades—A, B, C, and D—to different neighborhoods while coloring them green, blue, yellow, and red, respectively. Neighborhoods considered likely to appreciate were graded A and colored green, those that had "reached their peak" were graded B and colored blue, those understood to be declining were graded C and colored yellow, and those seen as already fallen and therefore particularly "hazardous" were graded D and colored red. Predominantly African American neighborhoods were unfailingly red.

So far, the story is correct. But some versions of it go on to claim that the HOLC based its own lending on these maps, thereby systematically discriminating against African American homeowners,[6] while many more have it sharing its maps with both private mortgage lenders and the Federal Housing Authority (FHA), which began insuring private mortgages in August 1934. Because the FHA tended not to insure low-valued homes located in the red zones, these last versions (e.g., Aaronson, Hartley, and Mazumder 2023) hold the HOLC indirectly responsible for the systematic segregation caused by redlining.[7]

Of course, discrimination and segregation had been rampant and rising sharply for at least three decades before the 1930s. But redlining reinforced it by making a property's proximity to minority households a reason for refusing to mortgage it. Because of such discrimination, according to Jacob Faber (2020, 744), by 1960 some two million more African Americans were living in highly segregated city neighborhoods than would have been the case otherwise.

Whodunnit?

It's true that the HOLC created those multicolored maps and shared copies of them with the FHA. It's also true that the FHA discriminated against the red-colored areas where almost all African Americans lived, intensifying racial segregation. But it doesn't follow that the HOLC was to blame for that outcome.

Thanks to research by Amy Hillier, Price Fishback, and others, it's now possible to conclude that the HOLC was mostly if not entirely innocent of the charges often laid against it. First of all, the HOLC didn't invent discriminatory lending practices. According to Hillier (2003, 398), mortgage companies had long been systematically discriminating against African American neighborhoods when the HOLC was established. More importantly, despite the prevalence of discriminatory lending, the HOLC itself didn't practice it. On the contrary, the HOLC vowed not to put residents of poorer minority neighborhoods at a disadvantage, and the numerous mortgages it purchased from them leave no doubt that it kept that promise. A 1940 census showed that 4.5 percent of all HOLC mortgages went to nonwhite borrowers, as compared to 2.5 percent of mortgages from other lenders (Fishback et al. 2024).

As for those notorious multicolor maps, HOLC staff couldn't possibly have made much use of them in deciding which mortgages the HOLC should purchase, for the simple reason that the maps weren't drawn until *after* the HOLC did most of its lending. Like other materials the HOLC produced as part of the FHLBB's City Survey Program, which was launched in September 1935, the maps weren't intended to guide its own mortgage purchases. Instead, their purpose was to assist it in "gauging the risks of the enormous portfolio of loans it had already accumulated, and in managing the resale of its foreclosed real estate holdings" (Fishback et al. 2024, 3).

The possibility remains that other lenders and government agencies, the FHA in particular, based their own mortgage approval practices on the HOLC's security maps. But the evidence for this is extremely slim. The FHLBB treated all City Survey Program materials, including the maps, as highly confidential, precisely because it feared that others might interpret and use them in ways that "were not intended" (Hillier 2003, 399). Private lenders never got any copies, and HOLC staff were instructed to keep their own copies to themselves.

The FHLBB did, however, supply security maps to "a handful of government agencies," including the FHA. But there's no evidence that the FHA based its own assessment of mortgages' riskiness or its willingness to insure them on those maps. Instead, the FHA began developing its own risk rating system, using block-level information and maps based on the same, eight months *before* the start of the FHLBB's City Survey Program. Alas for the HOLC, and to the enduring confusion of many subsequent scholars, the FHLBB came up with letter and color grading systems very similar to those found on the HOLC's maps.

If circumstantial evidence can also be thrown on the scales in assessing the HOLC's culpability, that evidence also tends to exonerate the HOLC, while making the FHA look as guilty as a cat in a goldfish bowl. The HOLC could hardly keep distressed mortgage holders in their homes without making risky loans. Although it certainly screened out applicants it considered unqualified because they didn't need its help or appeared unlikely to pay off even its more generous loans, the HOLC had no reason to discriminate against particular neighborhoods or minorities. The FHA, in contrast, was supposed to play it safe. Its goal was reviving the construction of new homes, almost all of which were destined to be sold to relatively affluent white home buyers, by insuring "economically sound" mortgages only. In practice, that meant not insuring mortgages in predominantly African American neighborhoods. It also meant not insuring mortgages—including ones for African Americans seeking to move into mostly white neighborhoods—that reduced the value of others the FHA had insured.

Far from making a secret of its discriminatory practices, the FHA recommended them in early editions of the manuals it supplied to its underwriting staff. Section 233 of the 1935 version (US Federal Housing Authority 1935), for instance, tells them to "investigate areas surrounding the location [of a property] to determine whether or not incompatible racial and social groups are present, to the end that an intelligent prediction may be made regarding the possibility of the location being invaded by such groups. If a neighborhood is to retain stability it is necessary that properties shall continue to be occupied by the same social and racial classes." If that doesn't seem explicit enough, we have Homer Hoyt, the FHA's principal housing economist, declaring in another FHA publication that "the presence of even one nonwhite person

in a block otherwise populated by whites may initiate a period of transition"
(Hoyt 1939, 54, quoted in Fishback et al., 2024, 3).

Finally, the security maps of the FHA's Chicago office were deliberately
destroyed by one of its staff members soon after that office was served notice,
in 1969, of a class action suit brought against it for discrimination (Sagalyn
1980, 16; Fishback et al. 2024). In a court of law, this would qualify as evidence of consciousness of guilt. Because such evidence is also circumstantial,
a judge might advise jurors to infer nothing from it. Nothing, that is, that isn't
reasonable, given other evidence.

Appendix: The HOLC's Country Cousin

The HOLC's mortgage refinancing program wasn't the New Deal's first. That
honor belongs to the corporation's agricultural counterpart: a sweeping farm
mortgage refinancing program initially provided for by the May 1933 Emergency Farm Mortgage Act. That companion to the Agricultural Adjustment
Act charged a newly overhauled Farm Credit System, composed of twelve
government-sponsored federal land banks, a land bank commissioner, and
their overseer, the Farm Credit Administration, with refinancing outstanding
farm mortgages and supplying new farm credit on generous terms. Those
terms were in turn made possible by a combination of direct Treasury subsidies and low-cost funds raised using government-guaranteed bonds. The
RFC contributed the program's first $200 million. The rest came from the in-
dependent Farm Mortgage Credit Corporation (FMCC), established in January 1934 at Henry Morgenthau's urging (Glock 2021, 152).[8] The FMCC was
authorized to issue up to $2 billion in guaranteed federal land bank bonds.

As we saw in discussing the banking crisis, American farmers struggled
throughout the 1920s, often unsuccessfully, to keep up with their debts. When
the Depression struck, many who had managed to do so until then fell behind.
Between 1931 and 1932 alone the delinquency rate on farm mortgages more
than doubled, from 23 percent to 50 percent (Saulnier, Halcrow, and Jacoby
1958, 161). Although creditors, including the federal land banks themselves,
commercial banks, insurance companies, and other private-sector lenders,
were reluctant to foreclose on farms while agricultural land prices tumbled,
many had to do so to satisfy their own creditors. Unless indebted farmers got
some sort of relief, the foreclosure rate was certain to climb even higher.

So, it wasn't surprising that as soon as the farm mortgage relief program
was up and running, applications flooded in. At first the federal land banks
and the land bank commissioner received some seventy-five thousand applications *every month*, although by the fall of 1933 the rate had tapered off to

about ten thousand a month, where it stayed for several years (Preston 1936, 677). At the program's peak halfway through the decade, it had processed a million applications, just over two-thirds of which were ultimately approved (Rose 2013, 10). By 1937 the federal land banks and the land bank commissioner had made 1.1 million loans worth almost $3 million, matching the scale of the HOLC's residential program. Like the HOLC's loans, most emergency farm mortgages—about 90 percent—replaced mortgages with less favorable terms, including many granted by commercial banks and life insurance companies. By 1939 the federal land banks and the land bank commissioner owned more than 40 percent of all farm mortgages, as compared to the 13 percent share that federal land banks held before the Depression (Rose 2013, 7).

The farm mortgage program also resembled the HOLC in having, besides its immediate purpose of helping indebted farmers stay afloat, the ultimate goal of promoting recovery. Farm mortgage refinancing was among the few specific elements of Roosevelt's recovery strategy that he was clear about from the very start of his 1932 presidential campaign. "Farm mortgages," Roosevelt (1938, 1:656) explained in accepting the Democratic Party's nomination, "reach nearly ten billions of dollars today and interest charges on that alone are $560,000,000 a year. . . . Our most immediate concern should be to reduce the interest burden on these mortgages. Rediscounting of farm mortgages under salutary restrictions must be expanded and should, in the future, be conditioned on the reduction of interest rates. Amortization payments, maturities should likewise in this crisis be extended before rediscount is permitted where the mortgagor is sorely pressed. That, my friends, is another example of practical, immediate relief: Action."

Roosevelt hoped that besides allowing farmers to meet their payments, refinancing their mortgages would leave them money to spare for capital improvements. By relieving commercial banks of nonperforming farm mortgage, he also hoped to provide a fillip to bank lending. Of sums spent refinancing mortgages in 1933 and 1934 alone, commercial banks received $368,405,000. Insurance companies, which were also important mortgage lenders and almost as badly in need of help, received $203,447,000 (Preston 1936, 677).

Because many of the farm mortgages outstanding in May 1933, including $1.1 billion worth held by the twelve federal land banks, were already amortized over long (thirty- to forty-year) periods, farm mortgage relief was less a matter of lengthened amortization periods than was the case for HOLC residential mortgage relief. Instead, relief mainly took the form of substantially reduced interest rates, principal payment deferrals, payment period extensions, and relaxed collateral requirements. Thanks to government guarantees, the RFC and the FMCC were able to borrow at rates considerably below what private-sector lenders had to pay. That advantage translated into correspondingly cheap federal land bank and loan bank commissioner mortgages. The federal land banks' initial emergency rate, set at 4.5 percent, was applied to both their new mortgages and, retroactively, those already on its books. The June 1935 Farm Credit Act lowered the rate still further to just 3.5 percent, where it ultimately stayed until June 30, 1944. The rate on loan bank commissioner loans was 5 percent.

When authorized rates were set below contractual rates on outstanding federal land bank mortgages, farmers paid the lower rates. The Treasury then indemnified the federal land banks for lost interest revenue. The Treasury also compensated the federal land banks and the land bank commissioner for deferring principal payments, as the federal land banks did by putting those payments off until July 1938 and as the loan bank commissioner did by deferring them for its loans' first three years. Although deferments were at first allowed on loans in good standing only, the 1935 Farm Credit Act extended the privilege to those in arrears (Rose 2013, 14). The mortgage program's reduced loan collateral requirement finally consisted of the land bank commissioner's willingness to lend up to 75 percent of farms' "normal" value, as opposed to the standard 50 percent, together with local farm credit authorities' rosy appraisal, based on crop prices that prevailed before World War I, of farms' "normal" value (Noyes 1940; Rose 2013, 15). In more than a few cases, 75 percent of farms' appraised value was more, if not considerably more, than the farms were worth (Case 1960, 175).

Was the New Deal's farm mortgage program successful? As was true of the HOLC's program, deciding that it helped mortgage holders and lenders is easy. Establishing that the benefits those groups received were worth the costs born by others is another matter. According to Jonathan Rose (2013, 24), scholars have as yet made no attempts to determine "whether the Treasury's costs were justified by the benefits delivered to borrowers, lenders, and farm land markets." One thing, though, is clear: because it relied less on lengthened amortization periods and more on outright subsidies than the HOLC, the farm mortgage program was no bargain. The Treasury's direct support of it alone cost more than half a billion dollars (Rose 2013, 13–14).[9] According to Jonathan Rose (19–20), the program's overall rate of return was probably somewhere between *minus* 6.6 percent (the return for a 2 percent discount rate) and *minus* 9.6 percent (the figure for a 7 percent discount rate).

Even those negative returns depended on a heavy dose of good luck. Despite their generous terms, by the end of 1939 the delinquency rate on federal land bank mortgages was 20.5 percent, while that on the land bank commissioner's loans was a whopping 25.9 percent (Noyes 1940). Having already had to foreclose on 83,313 mortgages, those agencies were facing much higher foreclosure rates that would have saddled them with vast amounts of unsalable farm property. Had it not been for World War II, which revived farm earnings and property values, the federal land banks and the land bank commissioner would almost certainly have ended up having to be bailed out, at a probable cost of several hundred million more dollars.

A dearth of relevant research makes it even more difficult to say much about the farm mortgage program's contribution to overall economic recovery. By improving banks' bottom lines, the program presumably reduced bank failures, thereby enhancing credit availability or at least limiting its further erosion. Nor can there be much doubt that the program boosted farmers' capital expenditures both directly, by reducing the share of their earnings devoted to paying off creditors, and indirectly, by making it easier for them to qualify for production loans (Saulnier, Halcrow, and Jacoby 1958, 219). But until some econometricians put their minds to it, no one can say even in very rough terms how much either of these consequences contributed to recovery.

There are, on the other hand, good reasons for concluding that however valuable it may have been as a component of countercyclical macroeconomic policy, the New Deal policy of subsidizing farm mortgages had regrettable long-run consequences. Although Murray Benedict (1934, 46–7), one of the nation's better-known agricultural economists, was fully convinced of the need for emergency mortgage relief while the Depression lasted, he warned in 1934 that failure to end subsidized lending once the emergency was over could bring the Farm Credit System to a "disastrous" end for which "the great middle class rather than the wealthy will pay the bill" (47). Several years later, when the emergency was in fact over, while federal land banks were still lending at 3.5 percent, Benedict (1942, 25) renewed his warning. "A policy of subsidizing interest rates in normal times," he wrote then, "is not to be recommended since it tends to stimulate borrowing and may lead to the placing of excessive valuations on land. . . . [I]f the present favorable terms and interest rates lead [American agriculture] into extensive speculation and borrowing, the burden in any succeeding serious depression may be even more onerous than that of the thirties."

Despite Benedict's warnings, the Farm Credit System went on supplying not just low-cost farm mortgages but also cheap agricultural credit of all kinds. In the late 1970s, for example, when the prime rate was 19 percent, the system was lending for 14 percent (Sunbury 1990, xiii). According to Ben Sunbury, a Federal Credit Administration senior staff associate at the time, such terms "made a hero of the System" during good times and a very popular hero at that: by 1983 the Federal Credit System was lending $80 billion *every year* (xiv). But the system was also counting on both rates coming back down and agricultural land prices, which rose sharply during the 1970s, at least staying up.

Although it took four decades, the "succeeding serious depression" Benedict warned about finally arrived in the shape of the severe agricultural slump of the 1980s. Between 1981 and 1987 the value of US farm assets fells by $300 billion, or about 30 percent (Barnett 2000, 376). In parts of the Midwest, farm values fell even more. As farmers' collateral withered away, so did the Farm Credit System's capital. In just the first three months of 1985, it lost $522 million (Hill 2010, 37). Finally, on September 4, 1985, which farmers dubbed "Black Wednesday," the system's governor announced that it could no longer endure the losses. By the end of 1987, those losses added up to almost $5 billion. The collapse of the Farm Credit System ultimately cost US taxpayers a cool $1 billion, no small sum even if it was soon overshadowed by the vastly greater cost of the savings and loan association bailout.

The Farm Credit System, Sunbury (1990, 242) says, "got in trouble" because it "was underselling the competition on loans" instead of "charging the going rate and building up reserves." Cheap credit, like opioids, is good for killing pain. Alas, it is also dangerously habit-forming.

The RFC, Part 2

While the Home Owners' Loan Corporation was giving homeowners new mortgages, Jesse Jones's Reconstruction Finance Corporation (RFC) was expanding the scope of its own lending far beyond the limits Herbert Hoover had envisioned. But it was during Hoover's tenure that the RFC first started to exhibit symptoms of chronic mission creep.

Minding the Gap

The RFC's support for railroads was the first inkling of what was to be a steady expansion of its involvement in lending to nonfinancial enterprises. The Emergency Relief and Construction Act of July 21, 1932, extended its remit to include lending to state and local governments for relief and public works and to various agricultural credit agencies. Although he ultimately signed off on it, the extension worried Hoover, who complained prior to the law's passage that the direction the RFC was taking risked turning it into "the most gigantic banking and pawn-broking business in all history" (Hoover 1932b).

Hoover's worries proved prophetic. "Slowly, almost imperceptibly," James Stuart Olson (1982, 43) writes, "as it poured billions of dollars into the economy" under Jones's leadership, the RFC "evolved into a major New Deal agency[,] . . . making loans to banks, savings banks, building and loan associations, credit unions, railroads, industrial banks, farmers, commercial businesses, federal land banks, production credit associations, farm cooperatives, mortgage loan companies, insurance companies, school districts, joint-stock land banks, federal intermediate credit banks, and livestock credit corporations."

In this evolutionary process, no step was more controversial than the RFC's decision to start lending to all sorts of ordinary businesses. Despite its other efforts and officials' attempts to cajole bankers into lending more, by late 1933 the volume of bank lending, commercial lending in particular, had hardly budged from its level when the RFC was established. New Dealers feared that by denying businesses the working capital they needed, bankers' excessive caution threatened to undermine the efforts of their flagship recovery agency, the National Recovery Administration (Olson 1982, 137).

In response to such concerns, in September 1933 the RFC first offered to supply short-term funds to banks, mortgage loan companies, and other private lenders for up to six months at just 3 percent interest, on the condition that they relend them to business firms for 5 percent or less. But the program was almost stillborn (Olson 1982, 139–40): by December, the RFC had only lent $2 million under it. The bankers explained that with prevailing money rates well below 5 percent—a fact they attributed to the limited demand for credit— the allowed spread just wasn't big enough to cover their risks and still leave them with a profit. Some months before the RFC's new initiative began, one banker tried to warn the Senate Finance Committee that the government was erring by putting the credit expansion cart before the purchasing power revival horse. "The administration," he said, is "misinterpreting the real problem with the economy. . . . Banks were accumulating excess reserves . . . because there was so little consumer purchasing power in the economy. . . . Even hundreds of millions in RFC and Federal Reserve credit would not address the problem" (159).

But government officials weren't buying it. Franklin Roosevelt even accused bankers of "hoping by remaining sullen to compel foreign exchange stabilization" (Olson 1982, 138). A July 1934 Bureau of the Census survey of over six thousand firms nationwide supplied grist for their mill by reporting that 45 percent of them had trouble getting loans, with small firms having the most trouble. Ultimately the claim that a serious "credit gap" existed became conventional wisdom (369). If the bankers wouldn't fill the gap even using cheap RFC credit, the thinking went, why not have the RFC itself do so? So, on June 19, 1934, the 73rd Congress passed the Industrial Advances Act (US Public Law 417), giving both the Federal Reserve and the RFC permission to go into the commercial lending business.

Alas, the performance of the RFC's new Business Loan Division mainly served to prove that the bankers had been telling the truth all along. Because Jessie Jones was determined to keep the RFC from lending to firms that bankers themselves had reason to avoid, the RFC stuck to its own strict credit standards. Besides having to sport the Blue Eagle, firms to which it lent had to be financially solvent and capable of posting adequate security. They were also supposed to show that they'd tried and failed to secure private-sector credit (Olson 1982, 163). Individual RFC loans were also limited to $500,000 and (more importantly) to five years' maturity. Finally, the loans were made at prevailing market rates. When, some years later, the American Bankers Association sent out a survey asking businessmen whether the RFC's credit standards were "appreciably less rigid than those of commercial banks," 93 percent of those who responded said that they were either just as rigid or even more rigid (Kimmel 1939, 120). In short, whatever their other merits, the RFC's commercial lending practices seemed tailor-made for testing whether bankers could be trusted to not overlook good borrowers.

And the bankers passed that test with ease. By September, the RFC had received fewer than 1,200 business loan applications and had approved only 100 of them, for a grand total of $8 million in loans. Two months later, an influential study commissioned by Henry Morgenthau and undertaken by Charles O. Hardy and Jacob Viner (1935) determined that very few worthy businesses were actually being refused credit by ordinary banks. The low initial volume of RFC lending was therefore no surprise, given that its lending policies were no less strict than those of most commercial banks (Kimmel 1939, 120, 144). Although Hardy and Viner didn't say so, the simple truth was that as long as it continued to conduct its lending as any responsible commercial bank might, the RFC had little to offer.

Not to be daunted, the RFC tried relaxing its lending terms, particularly by gaining permission, at the end of June 1935, to lend for up to ten years and beyond its original $500,000 limit. But the changes made little difference. After climbing to 412 during the last quarter of 1934, the number of loans authorized by the Business Loan Division fell off rapidly. By the end of 1936 it had lent only $80 million to ordinary businesses, compared to the $2 billion it lent to banks and the $600 million it lent to railroads. During the 1938 downturn the RFC lowered its lending standards still further, but by the close of that year it had still authorized only $384 million in loans to some six thousand businesses, of which it disbursed only $157 million (Kimmel 1939, 370). "Even with liberalized regulations and more statutory authority," Olson (1982, 172) says, "the RFC's business loan program never got off the ground. . . . For more than three years Jesse Jones had criticized and cajoled bankers, telling them to increase the volume of commercial and working capital loans or the country would stay mired in the depression indefinitely. But when the RFC started making those loans, Jones found himself agreeing with them: the number of applications was low and the credit worthiness of prospective borrowers left much to be desired" (177).

That the RFC's Business Loan Division eventually managed to make a considerable number of business loans was a result of its having ultimately been willing to take risks that ordinary banks wisely avoided taking: most of its borrowers "were at, or under, the margin of creditworthiness when judged by the ordinary standards of commercial banks" (Saulnier, Halcrow, and Jacoby 1958, 253–57). Little wonder, then, that by February 1939 the division had racked up some $28 million in bad loans, meaning loans that had foreclosed, were in the process of doing so, or were in default (Klemme 1939, 373–74). This was a loss rate well beyond what any commercial banker would have tolerated. It was also, Jones admitted in his seven-year report to the president, "a substantially larger percentage of losses" than any of the RFC's other divisions had incurred (Jones 1939, 10).

And it was not helping the US economy to recover.

A Capital Bank

As its title suggests, the best-known history of the RFC, James Olson's (1982) *Saving Capitalism: The Reconstruction Finance Corporation and the New Deal, 1933–1940,* is nothing if not a sympathetic review of that agency's undertakings. Yet according to Olson, most of those undertakings—or most of them until World War II began—were no more successful than the RFC's commercial lending venture. The Business Loans Division itself eventually sputtered out (163–64). The experience of the Export-Import Bank, of which the RFC "was firmly in charge" starting in 1936, "was no different," its commercial loans having been "hardly enough to affect recovery" (153, 164, 174). RFC support of state relief agencies and public works "did little to stimulate . . . employment" (20). The RFC's early agricultural lending projects were also failures (21, 144), as were its efforts to keep the financial system from crashing (29) and to raise commodity prices by financing gold purchases (110). The RFC's loans to railroads "had not improved the railroad bond market" (23), and its Mortgage Company, formed in 1935 with $10 billion in capital, was a "cumbersome failure" that "never lived up to its expectations." The RFC's other attempts to "buttress the real estate mortgage markets" (156, 174, 176) fared no better. The one exception to this otherwise dismal record was the RFC's preferred share purchase program. But as we've seen, although that program set the stage for recovery by helping to stabilize and repair the nation's banks and trusts, it was also supposed to get banks lending again, and so far as that goal was concerned it too was a failure.

Olson recognizes two other success stories among the RFC's many flops: the Electric Home and Farm Authority, which financed consumer appliance purchases, and the Commodity Credit Corporation (CCC), which made no-recourse loans to farmers secured with crops that the CCC would end up owning and storing if their value fell below the amounts lent. But the Electric Home and Farm Authority, Gregory Field (1990, 55) notes, "was never more than a minor league operation": when Roosevelt shut it down in 1940, it had arranged a grand total of just a quarter of a million sales, worth $36.1 million, or less than 2 percent of all electrical appliance installment sales over the same period (57). Olson's favorable appraisal of it, Field says (58–59), seems to be due in part to Olson's belief that the agency financed 70,000 refrigerator sales in 1934 alone. In fact it negotiated only 4,886 sales for the entire period from its foundation through June 1935.

As for the CCC, while the $1,885 million in loans it made through the end of June 1941 certainly helped prop up the prices of various farm commodities, they did so only by saddling the CCC with losses equal to almost 10 percent of that sum and with far more crops than it knew what to do with. The CCC would have lost a lot more had droughts not severely reduced the 1934 and 1936 corn harvests (Shepherd 1942, 591–98). Even with the help of those droughts, had it not been for World War II, which dramatically increased the demand for all sorts of farm products, the CCC would have ended up costing taxpayers a great deal of money; and even if it hadn't lost money the CCC could not be said to have helped US farmers taken as a whole, let alone shortened the Great Depression (Johnson 1954, 11).[1]

But the RFC had one client that benefited immensely from its exceptional lending capacity: the federal government itself, and particularly its executive branch. The RFC's status rendered it "free from the most part from the annual pilgrimages other agencies made to beg for appropriations" (Olson 1982, 43). Government officials were quick to recognize the potential advantages of this unusual arrangement, which allowed them to secure funding for their various projects without having to have an appropriations bill provide for it. Once they did, appropriations could be dispensed with altogether. As a former Federal Reserve official observed some years later, the RFC's own undertakings "could be enlarged indefinitely, as they were to almost fantastic proportions" (43). "In the end," Joseph Mason (2009, 98) writes, the RFC can be said to have helped achieve "tremendous New Deal expansions off the government's balance sheet, though little more."

While the Hoover administration took little advantage of the RFC's ability to finance "backdoor spending," Roosevelt was quick to turn the agency into "the capital bank for the New Deal"—a device for financing all sorts of executive undertakings, such as the Treasury's gold purchases, and for providing seed money to other alphabet agencies. Under Jesse Jones, who later wrote of

Roosevelt's inclination "to use the RFC as a sort of grab bag or catchall in his spending programs" (Jones 1951, 4), the RFC steered vast amounts of money, directly or indirectly, into every congressional district. "On any given day," Olson (1982, 49) says, "there was a line of senators and congressmen waiting outside" Jones's office, all wanting to make sure their states and districts got their fair share. By the end of the decade, the RFC had handed out more than $7.2 billion (Sprinkel 1952, 215). "Next to the President," pollster and then-aspiring reporter Samuel Lubell wrote of Jones in a January 13, 1940, *Saturday Evening Post* article, "no man in the Government and probably in the United States wields greater powers" (quoted in Fenberg 2011, 368).

And Jones was just getting started.

"Unlimited Power To Do Anything"

When, following Germany's invasion of the Low Countries on May 10, 1940, Roosevelt promised to equip the nation with "production facilities for everything needed for the Army and Navy for national defense," it was only natural for him to look not just to Congress but also Jesse Jones for some of the billions that effort would cost (Roosevelt 1941b, 4:202). But if the RFC was to contribute any substantial amount, its lending capacity had to be considerably enhanced, and it would have to be allowed to take greater risks than ever.

Despite the grumblings of many legislators, Congress eventually gave the RFC all the support it needed, and then some, approving an administration proposal that allowed the RFC "to take any action deemed necessary" by the president and the federal loan administrator "to expedite the defense program" (Cho 1953, 87). Asked at a Senate Banking Committee hearing held toward the end of the war just what he understood this language to mean, Jones explained: "We can lend anything that we think we should[,] . . . any amount, any length of time, any rate of interest, and to any-body" (US Senate 1945, 27).

For the duration of the war, the RFC's defense-related activities overshadowed its other undertakings to the point, Olson (1982, 217) says, where it "ceased to be a recovery agency and came to resemble its ancestor, the War Finance Corporation" (216). But Olson here understates things, for during World War II the RFC was nothing less than the government's principal financial agent (Cho 1953, 319). By June 30, 1947, when its authority to do so expired, it had authorized $1.85 billion worth of "national defense" loans to private firms, or about $300 million more than its ordinary industrial loans. It also lent hundreds of millions to other government agencies for war-related purposes. But its biggest contribution by far consisted of its financing, to the tune of *more than $21 billion,* eight wartime subsidiaries, including an $8 billion Defense Plant Corporation that, at the war's end, owned around 11 percent of the total US industrial capacity (109).

All told, the RFC's defense-related wartime commitments amounted to about $25 billion, with actual disbursements of some $23.5 billion (Cho 1953, 162). During the same period, the RFC handed just $90 million to financial institutions, less than 3 percent of its pre-1935 disbursements to them. In short, if the RFC was promoting recovery during the war, it was doing so fortuitously by serving as a conduit for military spending.

It is owing to that RFC role, and despite his awareness of the failure of so many of its projects, that Olson credits the RFC with saving capitalism. Olson has in mind not the RFC's activities prior to 1940, when it was ostensibly serving as a New Deal recovery agency, but its contribution to "massive federal spending" afterward, which he, like most people, credits with ending the Depression (Olson 1982, 220). The war, Olson says, saw to "the fulfillment of [the RFC's] 1930's expectations" (224). Perhaps so. But whatever it did for the US economy, World War II was not a New Deal project.

A Parade of Scandals

That Congress allowed the RFC to become so powerful was mainly a result of what Hyo Won Cho (1953, 320) calls its "unbounded confidence" in Jesse Jones. However, as Cho, a student of the agency's "evolution," remarks, "a sound government principle cannot be built upon faith in one man, for officials are mortal and fleeting."

After having held the RFC's purse strings for a dozen years, during the last five of which he served concurrently as federal loan administrator and secretary of commerce, Jesse Jones had to let go when Roosevelt offered both of his jobs to Henry Wallace.[2] Jones, who detested Wallace, ultimately persuaded Congress to deny him the position of federal loan administrator. But Jones himself never worked for the federal government again.

Until Roosevelt's death, the post of federal loan administrator was filled by Fred Vinson, the future US Supreme Court chief justice, after which it went to Jones's former special assistant, John Snyder. Then, on June 30, 1947, Harry Truman signed an amendment that drastically overhauled the RFC. Besides depriving the agency of many of its former powers, then considered redundant, the amendment did away with the position of federal loan administrator, returning control of the RFC to its board of directors. That board thus secured the ability to unilaterally make and manage any loan approved by three of its five directors.

The outcome of this lack of overarching supervision was a panoply of postwar RFC loans, the sole aim of which seemed to be that of gratifying the directors themselves, their close acquaintances, and others who bribed their way into one or more directors' good graces (Cho 1953, 215–69). Although suspicions of RFC favoritism and insider dealing were as old as the agency itself, and earlier suspicions were far from groundless, its directors' postwar misconduct was far too brazen to stay undercover for long. The big reveals took place between April 1950 and May 1951 during hearings held then by a special RFC subcommittee of the Senate Banking Committee, known as the Fulbright Committee after its chair, Arkansas senator J. William Fulbright (US Senate 1950).

The Fulbright Committee hearings, concerning RFC loans to Texmass Oil, to Lustron Corp. (a manufacturer of prefabricated all-metal homes), to the Kaiser-Frazer automobile company, and to Boston's Waltham Watch Company, among other doubtful enterprises, make for painful if spellbinding reading (see also Knerr 2015; Hemmings Contributor 2018; Vox 2022; Carosso 1949). One of the main lessons from the hearings is drawn in the committee's February 5, 1951, interim report. "In a five-man Board," that report says, "it is possible for the individual members to avoid, obscure, or dilute their responsibilities by passing the buck from one to the other, or to subordinate employees" (US Senate 1951, 4). And how! The report goes on to summarize the frequent "improper use" of the RFC's "vast authority" that resulted from outsiders' influence over its directors, including a "large number of instances in which the Board of Directors has approved the making of loans, over the adverse advice of the Corporation's most experienced examiners and reviewing officials, notwithstanding the absence of compelling reasons for doing so and the presence of convincing reasons for not doing so."

Three months later, Herbert Hoover summed the situation up dryly before the full Senate Banking Committee. "It would appear," he said, "that the test of public interest has been very little applied in recent years" (Cho 1953, 275).

The Fulbright Committee's revelations only served to turn the volume up on what had already been "a clamor for abolition of the RFC from the Congress as well as from the public" (Cho 1953, 322). The clamorers included none other than Jesse Jones himself, who expressed his opinion to the committee in a letter dated April 10, 1950. "As for the future of the RFC," he wrote, "I think it should be given a decent burial, lock, stock, and barrel." The first and most compelling reason Jones offered for taking this position was simply that "none of the conditions which prompted the creation of the RFC exist today" (278). What Jones didn't say was that most of those conditions had ceased to exist by sometime in mid-1935.

Still, neither the Truman administration nor the Democratically controlled 82nd Congress chose to bury the RFC, decently or otherwise. Instead, they arranged, against all reason, to extend its life until 1956. But the Fates had another plan in store. On November 4, 1952, Dwight Eisenhower won by a landslide, and the Democrats lost control of both houses of Congress. The following June the new government passed the Reconstruction Finance Corporation Liquidation Act, calling for the corporation to be dissolved two years ahead of schedule (15 USC 14 §1–7, June 30, 1957).[3] Just as it had taken a Republican president to give birth to the RFC, so too did it take one to kill it.

Fiscal Stimulus?

When we think of government policies to promote economic recovery to-day, the main if not only policies that come to mind are versions of fiscal or monetary "stimulus," that is, Treasury or Federal Reserve actions aimed at deliberately boosting overall spending. It may therefore surprise many to learn that, according to most economists, the Roosevelt administration didn't make much use of either of these now conventional depression-fighting tools.

Here I consider the contribution of New Deal fiscal policy to recovery. Later chapters will look at the part played by postdevaluation monetary policy and the influence of Keynesian economic theory.

Fallen Spending, Deflation, and Reflation

The proximate cause of the Great Depression was a dramatic collapse of overall spending on goods and services, or what economists call "aggregate demand," between 1929 and early 1933.[1] A collapse in spending can mean either that fewer goods and services, and ultimately fewer production inputs, are sold, or that prices fall, so that a given amount of spending purchases more goods and services than before. In practice, reduced spending tends to have both consequences, where the greater its effect on prices, the less severe its effect on quantities sold. During the Great Contraction, total spending as measured by nominal GDP fell by about 45 percent, while real GDP fell by about 26 percent. The difference was the extent to which prices of final goods and services fell.

Falling output prices prevent inventories from accumulating but don't themselves revive production. For that to happen, firms' input prices must also decline, as will tend to happen as they cut back production. If prices of all sorts decline enough in response to reduced demand, it's possible, in theory, for that decline alone to bring about a full recovery.

It's possible, but in an economy with many outstanding fixed debts, it's also unlikely, because renegotiating those debts is often difficult if not impossible. Because deflation increases the real value of such debts, without adding to their holders' ability to pay them, it tends to further impoverish not just debtors but also their creditors, including bankers, who must suffer from higher default rates. If creditors in turn retrench, and especially if banks and other financial intermediaries either reduce their lending or fail, the resulting credit squeeze will cause spending to shrink still further while also undermining industrial productivity. In short, the greater the extent of indebtedness when demand collapses, the greater the risk that deflation, instead of offering a way out, only makes the downturn that much deeper (Bernanke 1983b). "Thus," Frederick Lewis Allen (1940, 54) observes, "a theoretically flexible economic structure became rigid at a vital point. The debt burden remained almost undiminished."

In fact, Irving Fisher (1933, 345–46) notes in summarizing what he called the "debt deflation" theory of the Depression, "The debts of 1929 were the greatest known, both nominally and really, up to that time." A more recent study affirms Fisher's claim while also showing that during the 1920s the ratio of American's indebtedness to their earnings increased by a remarkable 39 percent, a surge like none ever seen since (Fackler and Parker 2005). Under such circumstances, Fisher (1933, 344) says, "the very effort of individuals to lessen their burden of debts increases it, because of the mass effect of the stampede to liquidate in swelling each dollar owed. Then we have the great paradox which, I submit, is the chief secret of most, if not all, great depressions: The more the debtors pay, the more they owe. The more the economic boat tips, the more it tends to tip. It is not tending to right itself, but is capsizing."

Three years later John Maynard Keynes argued much as Fisher had, albeit using jargon peculiar to his *General Theory of Employment, Interest and Money*. There the "wage-unit" is the price of a unit (e.g., one hour's worth) of labor and "the quantity of money in terms of wage-units" is the total amount of labor units the nominal money stock can purchase. "The method," Keynes (1936b, 268–69) explains, "of increasing the quantity of money in terms of wage-units by decreasing the wage unit increases proportionately the burden of debt; whereas the method of increasing the [nominal] quantity of money whilst leaving the wage-unit unchanged has the opposite effect. Having regard to the excessive burden of many types of debt, it can only be an inexperienced person who would prefer the former." The problem, Keynes goes on to explain, is that "if the fall of wages and prices goes far, the embarrassment of those entrepreneurs who are heavily indebted may soon reach the point of insolvency—with severe adverse effects on investment" (264).

In short, given the circumstances in the United States when the Depression broke out, deflation was the least reliable and therefore the least desirable of theoretically conceivable remedies: the more it was relied upon, the more debtors' impoverishment, loan defaults, and firms' inability to secure needed funding would bar the way to recovery. It was true, nonetheless, that so long as spending remained depressed, controls that *prevented* prices from falling in response to that reality could make matters even worse. As we've seen, neither the Hoover administration nor the Roosevelt administration appreciated this unpleasant truth.

More surefire ways to fight recessions and depressions consist of means for reviving spending. The idea here is to bring equilibrium prices back to their pre-downturn levels, a procedure that Fisher and his contemporaries called "reflation." Broadly speaking there are two ways to do this: expansionary monetary policy and expansionary fiscal policy. The first consists of steps that increase the money stock, meaning the sum of currency and bank deposits available for the public to spend. The second consists of either reduced taxation or increased government spending. "Fiscal stimulus" is just another name for a deliberately increased government deficit aimed at combating a recession or a depression.

A Deficit Deficit

Although many consider record New Deal spending proof that fiscal stimulus played an important part in the New Deal recovery effort, most economists say otherwise. Their view owes much to a 1956 study by Massachusetts Institute of Technology economist E. Cary Brown (1956). After calculating the magnitudes of annual Great Depression fiscal deficits, Brown concluded that fiscal policy was "an unsuccessful recovery device in the 'thirties—not because it did not work, but because it was not tried." While federal fiscal policy was, according to Brown, "more expansionary throughout the 'thirties than it was in 1929," in most years after 1933 it wasn't sufficiently so to offset reductions in state and local government spending. "The direct effects," Brown says, "on aggregate full-employment demand of the fiscal policy undertaken by all three levels of government was clearly relatively stronger in the 'thirties than in 1929 in only two years—1931 and 1936—with 1931 markedly higher.... The trend of the direct effects of fiscal policy on aggregate full-employment demand is definitely downward throughout the 'thirties."[2]

As for the exceptional spending and deficits of 1931 and 1936, far from reflecting any deliberate resort to fiscal stimulus by either the Hoover administration or the Roosevelt administration, both were consequences of Congress's acquiescence, partial in the first instance and complete in the second, to World War I veterans' demand for early payment of bonuses originally scheduled for 1945, and both got through only after Congress overrode presidential vetoes.

Although Brown's study has been especially influential, he wasn't the first economist to claim that fiscal stimulus contributed little to recovery during the 1930s. Brown himself quotes Alvin Hansen, "the American Keynes," to the same effect. "Despite the fairly good showing made in the recovery up to 1937," Hansen (1941, 84) wrote, "the fact is that neither before nor since has the administration pursued a really positive expansionist program" (see also Hansen 1963). A few years later Sherwood Fine (1944, 124–25), one of Hansen's students, concluded a detailed study of federal spending during the 1930s by observing that "the experience of the Roosevelt administration with fiscal policy cannot be judged to have been very successful. . . . [T]he meager results achieved . . . reflect more the restricted scale of spending than any absolute failure of compensatory spending per se."

Later research mostly reinforces these earlier conclusions. According to Larry Peppers (1973), because Brown relied on a naive estimate of full-employment tax revenues—one he arrived at by multiplying actual revenues by the ratio of full-employment to actual GNP—he *overstated* the New Deal's full-employment deficits. By Peppers's reckoning, federal fiscal policy was even less expansionary in 1933, 1937, 1938, and 1939 than it was in 1929.[3] Christina Romer (1992, 767) likewise concludes that "fiscal policy contributed almost nothing to the recovery" of the 1930s. Comparing actual real GNP values for the 1930s to projections based on the assumption that the federal government altogether abstained from countercyclical fiscal policy (i.e., that it maintained a fixed fiscal surplus to GNP ratio), she finds only trivial differences.

Still more recent studies also tend to reach a similar verdict. Price Fishback (2010, 386) summarizes them thus: "During the Hoover Presidency Congress doubled federal spending and ramped up federal lending through the Reconstruction Finance Corporation. The Roosevelt Congresses then spent nearly double the Hoover levels. But both administrations collected enough taxes in a variety of new forms to maintain relatively small deficits throughout the period. Relative to a Keynesian deficit target designed to return to full employment, the deficits were minuscule." Figure 13.1 shows the modest size of real (deflation-adjusted) Depression-era federal spending, receipts, and deficits relative to the post-1929 decline in real GNP.

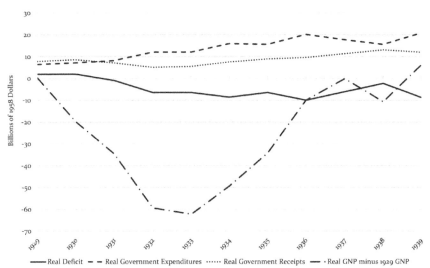

FIGURE 13.1. Actual minus 1929 real GNP, real federal expenditures, revenues, and budget surpluses, billions of 1958 dollars, 1929–1939. (Source: Fishback 2010, Figure 4. Reprinted by permission of Oxford University Press.)

In principle, with a large enough fiscal "multiplier"—the ratio of the change in total domestic product resulting from a given stimulus to the size of that stimulus—even apparently modest levels of government spending and deficits can make a big difference. But most fiscal multiplier estimates, including almost every estimate covering the New Deal period, assign it a value of less than 1.5 (Ramey 2011; Fishback 2017, 1447). A recent study by Valerie Ramey and Sarah Zubairy (2018; see also Ramey and Zubairy 2015), using data for 1889–2015, is especially compelling because the authors specifically consider multiplier values for situations of high unemployment and low interest rates, when fiscal policy is supposed to be especially potent. After trying all sorts of alternative specifications, Ramey and Zubairy come up with multiplier values below 1.0 in all except one or two special cases. Their findings imply that, even under depressed conditions, government spending tends to crowd out some private spending.[4]

The Consensus Challenged

The modern consensus on New Deal fiscal policy has not, however, been without its critics. Nathan Perry and Matias Vernengo (2014, 363–64) question the modest values so many studies assign to the Depression-era fiscal multiplier, claiming that those values simply can't explain "the impact of the federal government's fiscal policy on employment.... [O]nce the reduction in unemployment is properly understood," they write, "it is clear that fiscal policy did not fail and also it can hardly be argued that it was not tried."

But the employment numbers Perry and Vernengo have in mind are Michael Darby's, and, as we've seen, although those numbers may accurately account for the number of persons that had either emergency or nonemergency jobs, they're a poor guide to the extent of recovery, which also depends on the ratio of emergency to ordinary jobs. In fact, as we learned from the Brookings Institution's National Recovery Administration (NRA) report, even Lebergott's more conservative employment statistics convey a misleading picture of the extent of the 1933–1937 recovery: once again, much of the job growth during that time, including almost all of the growth up to 1935, was a result of "work sharing," that is, mandated workweek reductions that caused existing jobs to be divvied up by larger numbers of workers (Lyon et al. 1935; Taylor 2011). Such gains did not require or imply any increase in either firm revenues or aggregate demand.

A second challenge to the prevailing view of New Deal fiscal policy also questions standard estimates of the government spending multiplier. According to Margaret M. Jacobson, Eric M. Leeper, and Bruce Preston (2023), by leaving the gold standard, Franklin Roosevelt made way for "unbacked fiscal expansion," meaning deficits not tied to future, offsetting taxes. Jacobson, Leeper, and Preston claim that, because it involves an increase in the public's perceived wealth, such expansion is more capable than future tax-backed deficits are of boosting overall spending. A *lot* more capable: according to them, the Depression-era unbacked fiscal expansion multiplier was in the very hefty range of 3.5 to 4.5, or as much as three times the *highest* values found in most other studies. Together with other features of their model, these high values lead Jacobson, Leeper, and Preston to conclude, in stark contrast to the prevailing consensus, that fiscal stimulus was the true cause of the post-1933 recovery and that gold inflows only played a secondary role.[5]

Jacobson, Leeper, and Preston's case rests on a theory that's both well argued and plausible. Even so, there are good reasons for not accepting their conclusions, starting with their account of Roosevelt's fiscal policies. Parts of that account are true: By setting aside the gold standard, Roosevelt made a policy of unbacked fiscal expansion *possible*. Roosevelt was also committed to raising the general price level. And he made "emergency" spending an exception to his administration's efforts to balance the federal budget. Finally, it's true that between the end of the bank holiday and 1937 the federal debt doubled and prices rose substantially.

On the other hand, as we'll see in detail shortly, until well into his second term, Roosevelt did *not* consider deficits helpful for raising prices or otherwise promoting recovery.[6] It's therefore wrong to claim, as Jacobson, Leeper, and Preston do, that Roosevelt turned to fiscal policy, much less that he "leaned entirely on" it (Jacobson, Leeper, and Preston 2023, 10) *for that purpose.* Instead, he mainly relied on the *direct* consequences of his gold policies—gold purchases followed by formal devaluation—and on President's Reemployment Agreement (PRA) and NRA codes and the reductions in farm out sponsored by the Agricultural Adjustment Administration (AAA) to get prices up. If prices did in fact rise because of unbacked fiscal expansion, as Jacobson, Leeper, and Preston claim, that outcome could only have been unintentional.

Furthermore, Jacobson, Leeper, and Preston's results depend heavily on developments during Roosevelt's first year in office. In that year, "emergency" spending jumped from zero (allowing for consistent treatment of Reconstruction Finance Corporation loans) to just over $4 trillion, most of which was deficit financed. This was by far the biggest case of unbacked fiscal expansion before the war. (The still larger 1936 deficit was a result of supposedly "backed" nonemergency spending in the form of the Veterans' Bonus.) The same brief period witnessed a substantial upward price-level movement. This is the movement Jacobson, Leeper, and Preston attribute to early New Deal spending initiatives.

But the year in question was also one during which dollar depreciation, the PRA and NRA codes, and AAA policies (as well as drought) boosted prices independently of any fiscal expansion. Although Jacobson, Leeper, and Preston deny that these other developments can account for the observed rise in prices, their reasons aren't compelling. They note, for example, that Romer (1992) "makes a forceful case that the dollar depreciation after April 1933 cannot account for the sustained increases in subsequent price levels" (Jacobson, Leeper, and Preston 2023, 33). But Romer never denies that formal devaluation contributed to an arbitrage-based increase in prices of traded commodities. She merely insists that other factors were responsible for gold inflows once that arbitrage had worked itself out, while other studies—notably Hausman, Rhode, and Wieland (2019)—argue convincingly that dollar depreciation boosted prices (and output) independently of any fiscal stimulus that spring.

As for the PRA and NRA codes and the AAA farm output restrictions, Jacobson, Leeper, and Preston make no attempt at all to either deny or control for their influence. They don't so much as mention the AAA; and although they remark that the NRA "likely slowed recovery" (Jacobson, Leeper, and Preston 2023, 33), they don't say that it did so by restricting output and thereby *raising prices independently of any concurrent fiscal stimulus*. Robert J. Gordon (1980) finds that while they were in effect, NRA codes accounted for an annual percentage increase in the GNP deflator of about 8.5 percent, an amount equal to the *entire* increase during that time. Although Christopher Hanes (2013) doesn't estimate the magnitude of the NRA's influence on prices, he notes that "the exact timing of the inflation anomalies is entirely consistent with the operation of the NRA and unionization" (5). The sharp decline in industrial output after July 1933, when the blanket code went into effect, is also consistent with the predicted consequence of that code but not with Jacobson, Leeper, and Preston's fiscal stimulus story.

The large multiplier estimates that Jacobson, Leeper, and Preston's conclusions rest upon are also suspect. The imprecision of those estimates is evident from the fact that values ranging roughly from 0.5 to 9.5 fall within the standard error bands surrounding them. And the error bands they choose to display are themselves unusually narrow: chances are almost one in three that the "true" multiplier actually falls beyond their already wide range. The bottom line is that there is no reason to suppose that Jacobson, Leeper, and Preston's exceptionally high multiplier estimates are as reliable as the much lower estimates arrived at in other studies using all sorts of techniques.

Finally, Jacobson, Leeper and Preston's chosen sample period of April 1933 through June 1940 rules out any test of their hypothesis that abandoning the gold standard changed the effectiveness of government spending, emergency or otherwise.

For all these reasons, and despite their argument's considerable ingenuity and intuitive appeal, it seems only prudent to conclude that Jacobson, Leeper, and Preston's main finding—that fiscal rather than monetary expansion was responsible for most of the recovery of the 1930s—is best taken *cum grano salis*.

New Deal Spending

If economists haven't found much evidence that New Deal deficit spending contributed much to the post-1933 recovery, it's partly because, instead of reflecting a "Keynesian" strategy decided upon in advance, the Roosevelt administration's deficit spending was the unplanned result of two conflicting forces: Roosevelt's fundamentally orthodox fiscal policy views on one hand and the economic and political realities he confronted once in office on the other.

Notwithstanding both popular beliefs and the claims of some experts, Roosevelt's arrival in Washington did not itself launch a fiscal revolution. Instead, as Julian Zelizer (2000, 332) remarks in his brilliant essay on the topic, "fiscal conservatism . . . remained normative for most of the New Deal." David

Kennedy (2011) is more pointed: Roosevelt, he says, "was a bold and visionary innovator," but despite portrayals of him by conservative critics then and since, "the Beelzebub of the Budget he was not." Instead, Roosevelt was no less devoted to "budget-balancing orthodoxy" than Herbert Hoover. Indeed, to judge from his unsparing criticism of Hoover's deficit spending during the 1932 campaign, Roosevelt considered himself the more fiscally orthodox candidate.

In its most doctrinaire version, fiscal policy orthodoxy made an annually balanced budget the rule, the only exceptions being those for financing major wars, borrowing for "self-liquidating" public works (meaning ones that would eventually pay for themselves), and "honest miscalculation of revenues and expenditures" (Chandler 1970, 123). By the 1920s, however, that extreme view had already given way to the understanding, shared by many economists and public officials, that "increased expenditure on public works could be a powerful instrument against depression unemployment" (Stein 1966, 193–94). By then, Herbert Stein says, "no one demanded, or as a practical matter expected," that such expenditure "would be financed out of current taxation." The federal budget ought to be balanced, an expert consensus then held, but only in the long run. This was the version of fiscal orthodoxy to which Hoover himself subscribed.

Roosevelt was likewise willing to tolerate deficits for the sake of countering unemployment. He made this clear during his Pittsburgh campaign speech when he said that he had no intention of balancing the federal budget at the cost of "starvation and dire need on the part of any of our citizen" (Roosevelt 1938, 1:810). But Roosevelt also made it clear that he'd rather fund relief spending by either cutting other government spending or raising taxes than by running deficits. To that end, he promised that if elected he'd immediately cut nonrelief spending by "at least 25 percent."

Upon taking office, Roosevelt set out to deliver on that promise. Although the Economy Act of March 20, 1933, didn't cut federal spending by 25 percent, it did trim the government's $3.6 billion budget by $500 million, mostly by eliminating some government agencies and by cutting government salaries, pensions, and veterans benefits. The Economy Act also strengthened Roosevelt's ability to make further cuts through executive authority. "Too often in recent history," Roosevelt (1938, 2:50) told Congress in recommending it, "liberal governments have been wrecked on the rocks of loose fiscal policy." Nor was Roosevelt merely pandering to other more sincere fiscal conservatives. According to Frank Freidel (1956, 96), far from being "a hypocritical concession to delighted conservatives," the Economy Act "was an integral part of Roosevelt's overall New Deal, and a key aspect of his thinking both then and later."

In proposing his first "hard boiled" budget for fiscal 1934, instead of trying to take full advantage of his recent abandonment of the gold standard, Roosevelt sought to limit that fiscal year's deficit to just $120 million. He hoped that with the help of partial and then complete repeal of prohibition and correspondingly revived liquor tax revenues, the deficit would soon give way to a surplus ("Budget for 1934 Nearly Balanced" 1933). But Roosevelt's hopes, roseate to begin with, were frustrated by numerous developments he failed to anticipate, including disappointing liquor tax yields and a congressional override of his veto of an appropriations bill that added $228 million to the federal budget without providing for "a similar sum by additional taxation" (Roosevelt 1938, 3:173–81).

On April 8, 1935, in what would be his administration's greatest intentional burst of spending by far, Roosevelt signed the Emergency Relief Appropriations Act, providing for a record $4.88 billion in relief spending including $1.4 billion for the Works Progress Administration. That May, on the other hand, he demonstrated his determination to limit deficit spending to relief by successfully vetoing a spending package that would have paid out the Veterans' Bonus that year.

With the economy improving in 1936, Roosevelt took another stab at cutting the deficit, this time by trimming outlays on relief and public works while resisting tax cuts (Lee 1982, 64). Instead of supposing that the public favored unbacked fiscal expansion, Roosevelt understood that he could best improve his reelection prospects by sticking to his promise to balance the budget. According to the very first Gallup poll, taken the previous September, 60 percent of the American public "thought expenditures for relief and recovery were 'too great,' while only nine percent deemed them 'too little'" (74). Moreover, like many at the time, far from worrying that a dose of austerity could jeopardize an incipient recovery, Roosevelt believed it would help the recovery along by boosting businessmen's confidence, particularly by quelling their fear of inflation and another boom-bust cycle (Leff 1984, 205). Observing in his State of the Union address that January that "national income has grown with rising prosperity," Roosevelt asked Congress whether this was any reason to "put off the day of approaching a balanced budget and of starting to reduce the national debt" (Roosevelt 1938, 5:15). The question was of course rhetorical. It matters here mainly because it shows how Roosevelt still took for granted the need to eventually reduce the national debt.

Alas for Roosevelt, just three days later the Supreme Court dealt another blow to his hope of balancing the budget when, in *United States v. Butler*, it declared unconstitutional the AAA's tax on food processors, which was yielding $500 million a year. As if that wasn't bad enough, a day later another

Veterans' Bonus bill started making its way through Congress, to be passed, like the last one, by both the House and the Senate. As we've seen, although Roosevelt exercised his veto again, Congress was able this time to override it, hence the biggest of all "New Deal" deficits and the only one big enough (according to most economists) to have given a substantial boost to overall spending. Joshua Hausman (2016) puts the Veterans' Bonus in perspective by observing that it might have allowed every veteran to buy a new Ford V8 and represented roughly the same share of GDP (2.1 percent) as President Barack Obama's 2009–2010 Recovery and Reinvestment Act.

But because Roosevelt opposed the Veterans' Bonus, it can hardly serve as an example of his administration's willingness to take advantage of post–gold standard opportunities for unbacked fiscal expansion. On the contrary, Roosevelt was still clinging then to the ideal of a fully balanced budget. According to David Kennedy (2011), in what was to be Roosevelt's last attempt to balance the budget, in May 1937, he "warmly embraced the conventional budgetary counsel of Treasury Secretary Henry Morgenthau . . . , sharply contracting government spending." No sooner did Roosevelt propose this new round of austerity than a new downturn began, which would end in a collapse second only at the time to the initial Great Depression downturn itself.

For many, including Kennedy, Roosevelt's fiscal tightening was among the causes of the 1937 collapse. Yet even that debacle didn't immediately weaken his commitment to fiscal conservatism. Still hoping to regain businessmen's confidence by affirming his administration's resolve to limit deficit spending, Roosevelt gave his blessing in advance to a November 10, 1937, speech by Henry Morgenthau promising yet another "determined movement toward a balanced budget" (Leff 1984, 211; see also Burns 1956, 323). "There is no evidence," Harvard's John H. Williams (1942, 239) observed several years later, "that the [Roosevelt] administration, as distinct from some persons within it and some economists offering advice from the outside, ever had a conscious interest in fiscal policy as an instrument of recovery prior to the new depression in 1938."

It wasn't until April 1938, many months after the Roosevelt Recession began, that Roosevelt, after much prodding by the administration's Keynesians and a very sharp decline in stocks and other economic indexes, finally agreed to resort to fiscal "pump priming" (Burns 1956, 327). And even this supposed embrace of Keynesianism—to the tune of some $3 billion in additional relief spending and public works—was more fling than genuine love affair. "Many historians," David Kennedy (1999, 358–59) writes, "have hailed that decision as establishing the first deficit deliberately embraced for purposes of economic stimulus. But in a $100 billion economy, with more than ten million persons unemployed, $3 billion was a decidedly modest sum, not appreciably larger than most earlier New Deal deficits, considerably less than the unintended deficit of 1936, and far short of the kind of economic boost that Keynes envisioned as necessary to overcome the Depression once and for all."

In fact, according to James MacGregory Burns (1956, 335), Roosevelt was never won over by Keynesian thinking. To him "the idea of gaining prosperity by the deliberate creation of huge debts . . . seemed but another fanciful academic theory," and by 1938 he'd "had a bellyful of such theories." While he was prepared to try some emergency pump priming of the sort plenty of non-Keynesian economists had long favored, Roosevelt never saw deficit spending as a key to "full-scale economic recovery," and while he may have sounded like a Keynesian during his January 5, 1939, budget message when he offered the economic gains made since the previous spring as proof that "wise fiscal policies . . . can do much to stimulate" national income (Roosevelt 1941b, 3:13), he still looked forward then to the day when revenues would "provide a surplus which can be applied against the public debt that the Government must incur in lean years." If this was no longer the Roosevelt who hoped to balance the budget within a year or two, neither was it someone whose thinking had progressed far from what Stein (1966, 193–94) describes as the "conventional wisdom of the 1920s."

New Deal Taxes

Despite Roosevelt's attempts at "economy," New Deal spending was far from modest by the standards of the day. On the contrary, as a share of GNP, the Roosevelt administration's spending during the 1930s was roughly twice Hoover's, just as Hoover's had been roughly twice Coolidge's. Aside from the 1936 Veterans' Bonus, the increase was mostly due to "emergency" spending. The 1935 Emergency Relief Appropriations Act alone cost almost $1 billion more than *total* federal expenditures during Hoover's last year in office.

But the Roosevelt administration's doubling of federal expenditures didn't lead to a persistent increase in deficit spending compared to its levels during Hoover's last years in office. Even using Jacobson, Leeper, and Preston's preferred measure, the deficit–to–gross debt ratio, New Deal deficits were markedly larger only in 1934 and 1936, and only those of 1934 were larger because of increased emergency (hence supposedly "unbacked") deficit spending. Setting aside those two spikes, New Deal deficits tended to decline between 1933 and 1938.

New Deal deficits were less impressive than New Deal spending because the Roosevelt administration went to considerable lengths to boost tax revenues and did so even when it meant relying heavily on taxes that mostly burdened low-income Americans. For that reason, the administration chose not only to retain and then repeatedly extend most of the excise taxes imposed as part of Hoover's 1932 budget—taxes Herbert Stein (1966, 210) considers "the purest act of pre-revolutionary fiscal policy"—but also to increase taxes on gasoline and tobacco, revive the liquor tax upon the repeal of Prohibition, and introduce its AAA tax on food processors.

Because they fell on consumers, either directly or indirectly, excise taxes, which eventually funded 60 percent of the government's "ordinary" revenues (Leff 1984, 147), tended to be deflationary even when fully offset by government spending. Such taxes therefore had little to recommend them from a countercyclical fiscal policy perspective (Brown 1956, 868; Leff 1984, 39). But because excise taxes were revenue workhorses, to an administration not much less determined to limit deficits than Hoover's had been, they made perfect sense. At the height of the New Deal, Mark Leff (1984, 38) points out, the tax on food processors alone "accounted for one-eighth of total tax revenues," which was more than the yield from either the personal income tax or the corporate income tax. For this reason, after the tax on food processors was struck down, Roosevelt "continued to suggest processing taxes to balance the budget and to fund farm subsidies" (Leff 1984, 44).

What was true of excise taxes was truer still of the Social Security payroll tax that the government began collecting in January 1937. According to Leff (1984, 45), when Roosevelt first came up with his plan for funding Social Security, his advisers warned that because it would draw purchasing power from consumers for the purpose of establishing a $47 billion reserve fund without making any like disbursements from that fund for many years, the plan would be dangerously deflationary. Still, Roosevelt insisted on it, saying that it would assist in balancing the budget while projecting "an image of fiscal responsibility" (47). According to Sherwood Fine (1944, 114), the regressive Social Security tax diverted "more than a billion dollars of purchasing power . . . away from an industrial establishment sensitively attuned to consumer demand" in the midst of a severe economic downturn. "Running along, as we are, on a low level," Alvin Hansen (1939b, 283) wrote afterward, when various amendments to the Social Security Act were under consideration, "we cannot afford . . . the luxury of a Social Security Program which turns out in effect to be essentially a compulsory savings program, and which thereby seriously curtails the volume of consumption expenditures."

Although the Roosevelt administration eventually added progressive taxes to its otherwise highly regressive tax strategy, Leff (1984, 147) argues persuasively that New Deal progressive taxation was more "symbolic" than substantive, its purpose having been "to propitiate and quiet the clamor on the left" for "soaking the rich," including corporations, without asking too much from the economy's middle-class cash cows. While progressive taxes may have achieved Roosevelt's aim of stealing the thunder of Huey Long and other proponents of radical income redistribution (Moley 1935, 310; see also Amenta, Dunleavy, and Bernstein 1994), they also tended "to counteract the reflationary program of the administration," especially by "weigh[ing] onerously upon business investment" (Fine 1944, 126–27).

The most controversial Roosevelt administration tax of all—the undistributed profits tax introduced in 1936—was supposed to make it harder, in Roosevelt's words, for big businesses to "gobble up" smaller ones (quoted in Fine 1944, 173). In fact, that tax harmed small and medium-sized businesses more than big ones: bigger firms could turn to capital markets to finance new investment, whereas smaller ones depended far more heavily on retained earnings for that purpose.[7] But the real reason for this extremely unpopular tax was Roosevelt's desire to fill the $620 million revenue shortfall created by that year's Veterans' Bonus and the Supreme Court's elimination of the food processing tax. The undistributed profits tax therefore satisfied both the "symbolic" part of New Deal tax strategy and its orthodox "revenue imperative" (183).

Given that imperative, it's not at all surprising that the Roosevelt administration never considered using tax *cuts* to stimulate business spending. Although some of the administration's Keynesians suggested the option, their advice fell on deaf ears. "In the late 1930s," Joseph Thorndike (2010, 122) observes, "the notion of countercyclical tax cuts . . . remained in the land of economic theory, not political reality." Robert Musgrave (1987–1988, 174) is still more emphatic: expansionary tax cuts, he says, were "unthinkable" during the 1930s and would remain so until "after the fiscal watershed of World War II." When the Revenue Act of 1938 did at last roll back some business taxes, abolishing the hated undistributed profits tax altogether, it did so at the behest of the growing conservative consensus, and without the benefit of Roosevelt's signature. Countercyclical fiscal policy, Keynesian or otherwise, had nothing to do with it.

In truth, Keynesian economics had little influence on the New Deal, which was drawing to a close just as the administration's Keynesians started feeling their oats. But that's a subject for another chapter.

FDR's Fed

Despite the harm done by National Recovery Administration and President's Reemployment Agreement codes and the Roosevelt administration's failure to pursue a more expansionary fiscal policy, the US economy did recover considerably between March 1933 and the spring of 1937. The Lebergott–Bureau of Labor Statistics unemployment rate shed fourteen percentage points from its 25 percent peak, while industrial production more than doubled. Behind these gains, or a substantial part of them, was a 60 percent increase in total spending as represented by nominal GDP. If New Deal fiscal policy didn't revive spending, what did?

A Money-Fueled Recovery

It's tempting to answer "New Deal monetary policy." During the period in question, the money stock (M2) rose by more than 50 percent, boosting the overall demand for goods and services and, with it, both equilibrium prices and real output. After examining the contributions of both fiscal and monetary policy to the New Deal recovery, Christina Romer (1992) concludes that monetary expansion was responsible for "nearly all" of it. According to her calculations, if instead of growing as rapidly as it did the US money stock had only grown at its average historical rate, "real GNP would have been approximately 25 percent lower in 1937 and nearly 50 percent lower in 1942 than it actually was" (759). In short, the four years following Franklin Roosevelt's election witnessed a "Great Expansion" of money and real output that reversed much of the Great Contraction of the preceding four years.

For those accustomed to thinking that monetary expansion can only spur real activity if it lowers short-run interest rates, Romer's argument raises the question of how such expansion, however rapid it was, could have made any difference at a time when short-term rates were persistently close to their "zero lower bound." Romer's own explanation, which several other economists (Bernanke, Reinhart, and Sack 2004; Eggertsson 2008) also accept, is that by raising the expected rate of inflation, gold inflows lowered longer-term *real* interest rates, thereby encouraging business investment and spending on consumer durables. Christopher Hanes (2019) offers and makes a compelling case for a second explanation, namely that although gold inflows couldn't reduce short-term nominal interest rates, they succeeded in reducing medium- and long-term nominal interest rates, much as quantitative easing is supposed to have done during the Great Recession. Hanes's argument implies that gold inflows may have boosted real activity even if they failed to convince the public that inflation was in the offing. I'll have more to say about this in chapter 15, which assesses the various causes of the 1933–1937 recovery.

As we've seen, Roosevelt's gold policies and troubles in Europe both contributed to post–bank holiday growth in the US money stock. It follows that if monetary policy is taken to include gold policy, as it surely should be when any sort of gold standard prevails, New Deal monetary policy contributed to economic recovery. If, on the other hand, monetary policy is understood, as it is today, to mean Federal Reserve actions, then New Deal monetary policy contributed nothing to recovery and may even have cut it short.

Since we've already discussed Roosevelt's gold policy, I here turn to consider New Deal monetary policy understood in its modern, more narrow sense.

Sources of Money Growth

To appreciate just what the Fed did and didn't do to promote recovery, we must first consider the possible causes of monetary expansion. Fundamentally, there are just two. One is growth in the stock of high-powered or base money; the other is an increase in the base money multiplier, meaning the ratio of the money stock (bank deposits plus currency) to the stock of base money. Because the base money multiplier declined persistently throughout the 1930s, any monetary growth that took place then had to be due to growth in the monetary base.

Once gold coins and Treasury certificates ceased to be an important part of the publicly held money stock, base money consisted mostly of Federal Reserve notes and member bank reserve balances. The chief exceptions were circulating national banknotes and, after the passage of the Silver Purchase Act of June 19, 1934, circulating Treasury-issued silver certificates. But neither of these was an important factor in the monetary expansion that took place. After hovering around $900 million between March and August 1933, the volume of national banknotes fell rapidly as the bonds national banks were required to back them with became unavailable. As for Treasury's silver purchases, although they directly added about $1 billion in silver certificates to the money stock between 1934 and 1938, that was less than one-fifth of the growth in high-powered Federal Reserve liabilities during that time. Furthermore, by buying substantial quantities of silver abroad, the Treasury indirectly *reduced* the US base money stock by lowering the US trade surplus. In short, as Cornell economist Paul Homan (1936, 166) pointed out at the time, rather than serving any genuine monetary policy end, the silver purchase program was "essentially political bribery, purchasing the support of silver-producing states."[1]

The outstanding quantity of Fed-supplied base money itself depended on (1) the value of commercial paper ("bills") and Treasury securities the Fed acquired through its discounting and open market operations and (2) the amount of gold (or, starting in March 1933, Treasury gold certificates) deposited with it. Whereas the Federal Reserve System controlled the first determinant, it had little if any influence over the second.

Figure 14.1 shows index numbers for these last-mentioned contributors to the US monetary base, and for the US money stock, between March 1933 and May 1937, with March 1933 = 100. The dashed line represents the Fed's gold holdings, the dashes-and-dots line shows its holdings of commercial bills and Treasury securities, and the solid line shows the narrow money stock (currency in circulation plus bank demand deposits). Because Fed discounting of commercial paper "went out of fashion" after the bank holiday (Friedman and Schwartz 1963, 501), Treasury securities made up almost all of the Fed's nongold holdings afterward. The discount rate, in turn, became almost irrelevant: having been set at 1.52 percent in February 1934, it was left there until the summer of 1937.

The remarkable conclusion that emerges from this figure is that monetary expansion between the bank holiday and the spring of 1937 was *entirely* due to growth in the Fed's gold or gold certificate holdings. The Fed's bill and security holdings didn't increase at all. Instead, they first declined from $3.5 billion in March 1933 to just $2.2 billion that summer. Modest Fed security purchases between April and December had them back up to $2.65 billion later that year. But during the first months of 1934 they declined again to around $2.45 billion, where they remained for the rest of the period.

So, although the Fed let its balance sheet and bank reserves grow passively in response to gold inflows and may be said to have contributed to money growth to that extent, its positive actions contributed nothing. Commercial

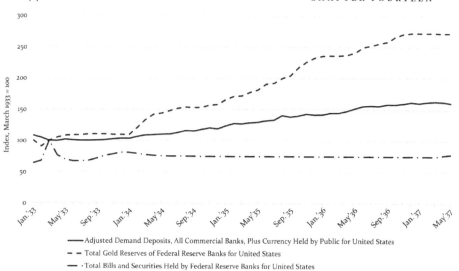

——— Adjusted Demand Deposits, All Commercial Banks, Plus Currency Held by Public for United States

– – Total Gold Reserves of Federal Reserve Banks for United States

—– · Total Bills and Securities Held by Federal Reserve Banks for United States

FIGURE 14.1. US money stock and monetary base components, March 1933–May 1937, index numbers, March 1933 = 100. (Data from FRED®, Federal Reserve Bank of St. Louis, https://fred.stlouisfed.org/graph/?g=135ID.)

banks, for their part, limited gold's influence by allowing their reserve ratios to increase, causing the base money multiplier to decline correspondingly. Consequently, the money stock didn't even grow as rapidly as the Fed's gold holdings.

A Once-Emboldened Fed

Why did the Fed contribute so little? It certainly wasn't because there was no case for additional monetary stimulus: for all the progress the US economy made between 1933 and 1937, at the end of that stretch, with industrial production only modestly above its 1929 level (and per capita output actually below it, thanks to population growth), and with unemployment still in the double digits, the economy was still running well below full capacity.

Nor was it because Fed officials' hands were tied. Even during the Great Contraction, when Herbert Hoover was still in office and many Fed officials not only felt duty-bound to uphold the gold standard but also believed that the Fed should stick to rediscounting "real bills" (short-term commercial paper), the Fed seemed to show more initiative. Between the stock market crash and Britain's suspension of the gold standard the twelve reserve banks reduced their discount rates, increasing member bank borrowing, with New York lowering its own rate from 6 percent to just 1.5 percent. The run on the

US gold stock triggered by Britain's suspension compelled the reserve banks, and the New York Fed especially, to jack those rates back up again. But the same run would eventually help inspire two rounds of Fed open market security purchases, including purchases of longer-term Treasury notes and bonds, that were to *quadruple* its security holdings, inviting subsequent comparisons of their program with the Federal Reserve's quantitative easing program of November 2008 through March 2009 (Bordo and Sinha 2016, 4).

The story of those early large-scale asset purchases and Hoover's role in them is among the most interesting chapters in Fed history. Besides spotlighting Hoover's efforts to promote expansionary monetary policy, it serves as a useful foil by which to set off the Fed's later passivity.

The basic facts of the story are as follows: having been persuaded to do so by its chairman, New York Fed governor George Harrison, the Federal Reserve's Open Market Policy Committee (OMPC) agreed on February 24, 1932, to have Fed banks purchase up to $250 million worth of government securities at a rate of $25 million a week. No actual purchases took place then. But when, at its April 12 meeting, the OMPC resolved to have the system purchase *$100 million* worth of securities every week for five weeks, it meant what it said. The *New York Times* called the decision "the boldest of all central bank efforts to combat depression" ("Cite Past in Reserve Move" 1932). Yet the OMPC wasn't finished: on May 17 it approved a second $500 million round (Meltzer 2003, 358–63).

But that was all. As the Fed's security purchases mounted, so did concerted opposition to them (Epstein and Ferguson 1984, 968). There were several reasons for this, but the chief one was that the Depression had caused many banks to shy away from risky loans and instead hold safe but lower-yielding Treasury bills and notes (969). By pushing rates on those securities even lower, the Fed banks' open market purchases lowered such banks' already slim earnings even more (970). The hardest-hit ones included many Chicago banks, dozens of which fell victim to the banking crisis that June. At last, in early July, Chicago Fed governor James McDougal, who had only reluctantly taken part in the Fed's open market purchases, called it quits. Other Fed governors, some of whose banks were also running short of gold, then began to express their own reluctance to continue in what was supposed to be a system-wide undertaking. Thus, as the end of July approached, the program ground to a halt (977).

Although they didn't last long and ultimately proved painful to many of the nation's banks, the Fed's large-scale open market purchases proved effective in promoting recovery. They were responsible, first of all, for reversing the contraction of bank reserves and the monetary base that had been going on for several months. Between February 24 and May 18, member bank reserves rose from under $1.9 billion to almost $2.2 billion (Anderson 1949, 272), even as banks dramatically reduced their borrowing from the Fed. Between July 1932 and January 1933 commercial bank deposits grew by more than $1 billion (King 1935, 242). Money market pressures were reduced correspondingly. Yields on Treasury securities not only declined but declined "dramatically" (Bordo and Sinha 2016, 30), while premiums on private market securities, which had risen by two percentage points between June and December 1931, fell by half that amount between February and April (Meltzer 2003, 352, 361). After a lag lasting about a month, wholesale prices, which had long been sinking, started to climb decisively for the first time since 1929 (King 1935, 242). Finally and most importantly, real activity—pig iron production, department store and mail order sales, imports and exports, and factory employment—rose (243). According to an econometric study by Michael Bordo and Arunima Sinha (2016, 30), the Fed's security purchases boosted the US economy's growth rate by 0.07 percent, a remarkable result for a program that only lasted several months.

What if the program had continued? Bordo and Sinha have an answer to that as well. According to a counterfactual simulation they performed, had the Fed kept its $100 million a week purchases going for another two-quarters while announcing its intention to do so at the very start of its purchases, yields would have fallen twice as much, and the economy's growth rate would have increased by a full one-half of 1 percent, considerably more than the 0.13 percent growth rate improvement the Fed's 2008–2009 first quantitative easing program is said to have achieved. Consequently, Bordo and Sinha (2016, 32) conclude, "the Great Contraction would have been attenuated significantly earlier." Never one to mince words, Allan Meltzer (2003, 372–73), goes further: "It seems likely," he writes, "that had the purchases continued, the collapse of the monetary system during the winter of 1933 might have been avoided."[2]

Hoover's Stimulus

To an extent that's likely to surprise many, Hoover was personally responsible for the Fed's bold 1932 undertaking. From the very start of the Depression, he saw the revival of long-term investment, particularly real estate construction, as essential to combating the Depression. He also believed that the best way to revive investment was to get long-term interest rates down. Finally, Hoover happened to be very close to George Harrison, who held similar beliefs and whose advice Hoover sought so often that at least one Hoover aide considered Harrison "mightily close to the 'top man' in the administration." Hoover therefore endeavored "to reshape the Federal Reserve System in line with his and Harrison's views" (Glock 2019, 309–10).

Hoover's first move, in September 1930, consisted of engineering the resignation of two Fed Board members who didn't share his or Harrison's views and replacing one of them with Eugene Meyer, who did. The resulting shift in the balance of opinion at the Fed Board was significant enough to cause longtime board member Charles Hamlin to bemoan its "Hooverizing" (Glock 2019, 311). But a shift in opinions alone wouldn't alter the Fed's capacity to buy Treasury securities, which was constrained by the strict collateral requirements for Federal Reserve notes.[3] To recall, those requirements called for full backing of the notes with either gold or commercial paper, with gold making up no less than 40 percent of the mix.

The problem, Benjamin Anderson (1949, 262) explains, was that as the Fed bought government securities, banks gained reserves. As they gained reserves, they found it less necessary to borrow them from the Fed, which they normally did by having it rediscount their commercial paper. Banks could also use reserves exceeding their needs to buy back commercial paper the Fed had already discounted for them. So, the more bonds the Fed banks bought, the more they had to rely on gold rather than commercial paper to collateralize their notes, and the less "free gold" they had left. Having already had their free gold depleted by runs following Britain's departure from the gold standard, the Fed banks were unwilling to embark on a program of large-scale security purchases until they once again had gold to spare, hence Hoover's subsequent moves.

On October 7, 1931, after consulting with Harrison and other bankers, Hoover issued a statement including several reform proposals. One called for the establishment of what became the National Credit Corporation; another anticipated the Reconstruction Finance Corporation alternative. Either institution would stand ready to discount bank assets other than commercial paper that the Fed itself could not discount. A third proposal called for relaxing the Fed's own eligibility provisions.

Next, in early 1932, Hoover took aim at the "free gold" problem. Having outlined a plan at that January's Open Market Policy Conference, Ogden Mills, then Hoover's undersecretary of the treasury, worked with Harrison and Eugene Meyer to draft legislation providing for the temporary use of Treasury securities as collateral for Federal Reserve notes. Then, on February 10, Hoover invited both Republican and Democratic leaders to a nonpartisan conference at the White House, where the legislation was discussed, and Glass and Steagall each agreed to introduce bills based on it. The bills, having already been sold by the administration to Congress, sailed through, leaving only one last task for Hoover to perform, which was signing off on the new law on February 27.

Or so it seemed. In fact, Hoover wasn't yet finished, for despite this first Glass-Steagall Act and the fact that the Open Market Policy Conference had authorized $200 million in Treasury bond purchases in February, when the OMPC met in April, the Fed banks still hadn't bought any. It was then that Mills, now Hoover's treasury secretary, famously put his foot down. "For a great central banking system to stand by," he told the conference attendees, "with a 70 percent gold reserve without taking active steps in such a situation was almost inconceivable and almost unforgivable. The resources of the System should be put to work on a scale commensurate with the existing emergency" (quoted in Epstein and Ferguson 1984, 968). Under pressure from the White House and also from Congress, which threatened to take inflationary measures of its own, the last hesitating members of the Open Market Committee gave in, authorizing the Fed's Executive Committee to buy not just $200 million but as much as half a billion dollars' worth of Treasury securities.

In view of the lengths Hoover went to in encouraging them, Peter Temin's (1996, 312) characterization of the Fed's 1932 security purchases as "a temporary aberration in Hoover's deflationary story" hardly seems fair. It's difficult to imagine any president doing more than Hoover did to get the Fed to pursue an aggressively expansionary monetary policy. To suppose, as Temin seems to do, that Hoover might have gone further by devaluating the dollar is to overlook the very real "political constraints and fears" that "continued to tie policymakers' hands" (Eichengreen 1992a, 293) then, constraints and fears that left Roosevelt himself "undecided" on the devaluation option until mid-March 1933 (331), when circumstances had changed decisively.

The Fed's New Deal

Despite the steps Hoover took, the Fed remained far more constrained while he was in office than it would be during the New Deal. Over the course of the Roosevelt administration's famous first hundred days, many of the constraints on Federal Reserve actions that Hoover had left in place went by the wayside. The new administration repeatedly renewed the 1932 Glass-Steagall Act, allowing Treasury securities to continue to serve as collateral for Federal Reserve notes. But far more important than that were the steps Roosevelt took that rendered previous gold constraints irrelevant, starting with the holiday suspension of gold payments and concluding with the dollar's formal devaluation. After those changes, the Fed enjoyed greater freedom than ever to expand the monetary base independently of additions to its gold holdings.

Having swept aside many long-standing constraints on the Fed's capacity to fuel monetary growth, the Roosevelt administration then took steps that greatly enhanced its control over Fed policy. Although the Thomas Amendment and the Gold Reserve Act had already awarded Roosevelt substantial money creation powers he could employ without the Fed's cooperation, his influence on Fed policy itself at first remained limited. It was mainly by appointing Marriner Eccles as the Fed's new governor in November 1934 that Roosevelt saw to it that the Fed played his administration's tune.

Unlike Eugene Black, the Fed's previous governor whom Roosevelt also appointed but who stepped down after Roosevelt forced the Fed banks surrender their gold, Eccles was said (by the *New York Evening Post)* to have "views on monetary policy . . . even more liberal than those already embraced by the New Deal" (quoted in Conti-Brown 2016, 28). In fact, it was Henry Morgenthau who recommended Eccles to Roosevelt after concluding that, with Eccles at the Fed's helm, the administration and in particular the Treasury could count on the Fed's cooperation.

But Eccles was willing to take Black's place on one condition only: Roosevelt had to let him author a radical Fed overhaul. Eccles was determined to prove Morgenthau correct by substantially increasing both the administration's direct influence on Fed policy and Eccles's own control over it while reducing the say of the system's twelve reserve bank governors.

Eccles's proposal became the Banking Act of 1935, which Roosevelt signed that August. The act replaced the former Federal Reserve Board with the present seven-member presidentially-appointed Board of Governors. It also changed the composition of the Federal Open Market Committee, which had been established by the Banking Act of 1933 to coordinate the Fed's open market operations. That committee's voting members originally consisted solely of the twelve Fed bank governors (as they were then styled). The 1935 act established the arrangement still in place today by having the committee consist of only five Fed bank presidents—New York's and four others chosen on a rotating basis—plus the seven politically appointed members of a reconstituted Federal Reserve Board henceforth to be known as the Board of Governors. Besides allowing the Board of Governors to make up a majority of the Federal Open Market Committee, the new law also allowed it alone to set Fed bank discount rates and reserve requirements.

These reforms, Peter Conti-Brown (2016, 32) says, amounted to nothing less than the subordination of monetary policy to administration, and particularly Treasury, policy. "It is no surprise," Conti-Brown observes, "that the

Eccles Fed of the 1930s saw less of a need to declare formal independence from government, as the Banking Act of 1935 had done in a declaration of independence from private bankers. Even during a brief and painful interlude of further recession in 1937–1938, the Fed's policy during the 1930s was fully congenial to the administration's."

Fed economists Mark Carlson and David Wheelock (2014, 31) agree that "New Deal legislation limited the Fed's ability to conduct an independent monetary policy." The Fed, they say, "was forced to cooperate with the Treasury in the 1930s, and fully ceded monetary policy to Treasury financing requirements during World War II." "Forced" isn't quite the right word, however. Although the Fed's powers were certainly limited, the fact remains that during his tenure at the Fed Eccles was happy to have it take a back seat to the Treasury. Although he was, as we've seen, an unrelenting champion of fiscal stimulus, Eccles viewed monetary stimulus as a substitute so poor as to be practically worthless. He made his position perfectly clear in a now-famous exchange with representatives Paul Brown (D-GA) and Alan Goldsborough (D-MD) during the hearings on his Banking Act:

MR. BROWN. Do you not think it is fair for us to ask what you would do if given this power under present conditions! It seems to me that we ought to know, that Congress ought to know your attitude as chairman of the Board.

GOVERNOR ECCLES. I can speak only for myself with reference to the matter....

MR. BROWN: When I say "your" I am referring directly to you.

GOVERNOR ECCLES. Yes; I understand. Under present circumstances there is very little, if anything, that can be done.

MR. GOLDSBOROUGH. You mean you cannot push a string.

GOVERNOR ECCLES. That is a good way to put it, one cannot push a string. We are in the depths of a depression and, as I have said several times before this committee, beyond creating an easy money situation through reduction of discount rates and through the creation of excess reserves, there is very little, if anything that the reserve organization can do toward bringing about recovery. I believe that in a condition of great business activity that is developing to a point of credit inflation monetary action can very effectively curb undue expansion. (US House 1935, 377)

It was owing to such thinking that Eccles's Fed made no attempt to supply banks with reserves beyond what gold inflows provided. On the contrary, instead of endeavoring to reinforce those inflows or at least welcome them, Eccles bemoaned the Fed's inability to *counter* them. "There appears to be nothing that the United States can do," he wrote in dismay on October 22,

1935, "to prevent the inflow of gold" (Eccles 1935, 2). By the following April Eccles was telling Morgenthau that "a *loss* of gold, even in considerable volume, would be a distinct gain to the United States" (Eccles 1936b, 3, emphasis added). Eccles wrote this when consumer price and farm commodity price indexes, although rising, were still 20 percent and 30 percent below their pre-Depression levels, respectively. And he wrote it even though he was to advise Roosevelt two months later that Roosevelt's best hope for securing another term lay in overcoming voters' fears "that the monetary and fiscal policies which shattered the last three Republican administrations will be reverted to" (Eccles 1936a).

Eccles's hawkish stand reflected his own fear that unless something were done to reduce them, the excess reserves banks were accumulating might allow them to "more than double the volume of credit in this country," a possibility that in Eccles's view "posed a grave danger of harmful inflation" (Eccles 1936b, 1). As far as Eccles was concerned, Fed security purchases, let alone aggressive ones of the sort the Fed made in 1932, would only raise the risk of undesirable inflation still further. Consequently, under Eccles's leadership, with the Roosevelt administration's evident support, the Fed's only deliberate monetary control actions were those taken in 1936 and 1937 for the sake of not encouraging but rather *limiting* money growth. According to many experts, those steps, far from helping to spur recovery, were at least partly to blame for the severe Roosevelt Recession that began in the last quarter of 1937. But that's a subject for our next chapter.

To sum up, if ever an administration had control over Fed policy and monetary policy more generally, Roosevelt's was it. It follows that if monetary policy did less than it might have to end the Great Depression, the Roosevelt administration must bear most of the blame.

The Recovery So Far

By 1937 the New Deal was drawing to a close. The final curtain dropped on what many consider the genuine or "first" New Deal when the Supreme Court ruled the Agricultural Adjustment Act unconstitutional in January 1936. By then a "second" New Deal," including the Works Progress Administration (May 6, 1935), the Wagner Act (July 6, 1935), and the Social Security Act (August 14, 1935), was itself nearing completion. Unlike parts of the first New Deal, none of the Second New Deal's efforts had economic recovery as its chief aim.

It therefore makes sense to step back from our assessments of particular New Deal policies to view the overall progress of economic recovery up to the spring of 1937, when that recovery reached its peak. How much had economic conditions improved? What role did New Deal policies play in the improvement and in the ups and downs along the way? If New Deal policies can't account for some of those ups and downs, what can?

A Three-Stage Recovery

"Between 1933 and 1937," Christina Romer (1992, 757, 760) writes, "real GNP in the United States grew at an average rate of over 8 percent per year," while unemployment fell from 25 percent to 11 percent. Noting that such gains were "spectacular even for an economy pulling out of a severe recession," Romer wonders how they can be reconciled with "the conventional wisdom that the U.S. economy remained depressed for all of the 1930s."

There are two obvious answers to Romer's question. One is that an economy with 11 percent unemployment is still quite depressed. The other is that instead of lasting, the "spectacular" New Deal recovery gave way to another

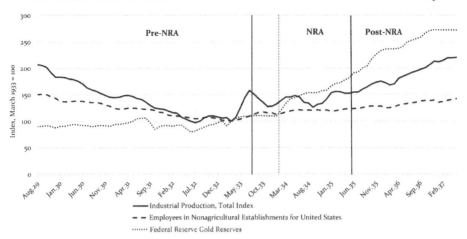

FIGURE 15.1. Industrial production, nonagricultural employment, and Fed gold reserves, August 1929 through May 1937. (Data from FRED*, Federal Reserve Bank of St. Louis, https://fred.stlouisfed.org /graph/?g=1pDBF.)

recession that, by undoing much of it, left the US economy considerably more depressed for the rest of the decade. The real challenge isn't that of squaring the New Deal recovery with the Great Depression's persistence: it's reconciling that recovery, however limited it may have been, with the claim that some New Deal policies stood in recovery's way.

This challenge can also be met. But meeting it requires that instead of thinking in terms of a single recovery period lasting from March 1933 until May 1937, we divide that stretch into three parts: a pre–National Recovery Administration (NRA) period lasting until August 1, 1933; an NRA period lasting from then until the Schechter Decision of May 27, 1935; and a post-NRA recovery.[1] Figure 15.1 shows index numbers for industrial production, nonagricultural employment, and the Fed's gold reserves, with March 1933 = 100, from the start of the Depression until May 1937. The figure's solid vertical lines separate the three periods; its dashed vertical line marks the date of the dollar's devaluation.

Many factors, of course, contributed to the progress of recovery during each of these periods, and no chart can do more than suggest the importance of a few. What this one suggests, strikingly, is that between them the negative contribution of the NRA and the positive contribution of gold inflows explain a great deal. Those ups and downs in output and employment that can't be traced to the influence of either are for the most part easily accounted for by other developments we've addressed.[2]

The basic story is this: During the pre-NRA period, the various steps taken to resolve the banking crisis, including indefinite suspension of the gold standard, the Reconstruction Finance Corporation's bank bailout, the passage of the Agricultural Adjustment Act, with its Thomas Amendment, and the establishment of the Federal Deposit Insurance Corporation, all contributed to a pronounced recovery by generally reviving the public's confidence, especially by replacing the fear that prices would keep falling with positive inflation expectations (Temin and Wigmore 1990; Eggertsson 2008; Jalil and Rua 2016).

Until the NRA's passage, those expectations remained largely unfulfilled. Despite the flotation of the dollar and the Treasury's gold purchase program, the consumer price index hardly budged. Prices of tradable farm commodities, on the other hand, rose sharply as the dollar depreciated. According to Joshua Hausman, Paul Rhode, and Johannes Wieland (2019), that increase alone may have raised industrial output by redistributing income toward farmers with relatively high marginal propensities to consume, as the Agricultural Adjustment Act intended. But really substantial increases in both the price level and output had to await the June 16 passage of the National Industrial Recovery Act (NIRA), which boosted output in part by causing industrial firms to build up their inventories before NRA codes raised the costs of doing so.[3]

The fact that six weeks after the NIRA's passage only four industries had established "codes of fair competition" led to the passage of the President's Reemployment Agreement (PRA) of August 1, 1933, with its "blanket code" alternative. Because most industries quickly complied with the blanket code, the PRA's passage can be said to mark the true start of the NRA era. It also marked the end of the pre-NRA boom: a slump between then and November erased half of all pre-NRA output gains. Most studies (e.g., Hawley 1966; Weinstein 1980; Cole and Ohanian 2004) liken the adoption of NRA codes to an adverse supply shock, where the blanket code mainly raised labor costs, whereas industry-specific NRA codes often served to enforce monopoly prices and correspondingly reduced output. Although the number of persons employed increased somewhat while the PRA was in effect, that gain was entirely due to work sharing: there was no increase in total *hours* of labor employed (Taylor 2011). Total labor hours only started rising after 1934, when support for and compliance with industry codes began to erode (Higgs 2009).

Despite the NRA, conditions improved after November 1933 and especially after the dollar's devaluation at the end of January 1934. The initial improvement may reflect the fact that by November most industries had switched from the PRA's blanket code to their own heterogeneous (and presumably less onerous) industry codes. But from January 1934 onward gold inflows and corresponding growth in the Fed's gold reserves were the main forces driving recovery. Devaluation directly inspired the first wave of gold shipments by making dollars cheap. Then, when initial arbitrage opportunities had been spoken for, unrest in Europe kept the gold coming (Eichengreen 1992a, 345–46).

Codes of fair competition continued nonetheless to limit output by suppressing competition, as did the NIRA's collective bargaining provisions (Eichengreen 1992a, 344). As we saw in assessing the NRA, the latter provisions inspired waves of strikes that can account not just for slower progress but also for at least some of the substantial dip in industrial production between April and October 1934.

Although the NRA wasn't declared unconstitutional until May 27, 1935, its adverse effect on output diminished before then owing to the "compliance crisis" it faced starting in March 1934 (Taylor 2019, 129–56). When the Supreme Court rendered its decision, most of the NRA's codes of fair competition had been dead letters for months. Monopoly power declined correspondingly, allowing the gold that had been pouring into the country and (as gold certificates) onto the Fed's balance sheet to finally have something like its full, if still limited, effect on economic activity for the first time, and to go on doing so until May 1937 (Romer 1992, 1993). Even so, output rose less than it might have thanks in part to a second surge in labor actions inspired by the Supreme Court's April 12, 1937, Wagner Act decision. Those strikes—especially the series of sit-down strikes beginning with the General Motors strike of December 30, 1936, through February 11, 1937—amounted to yet another severe negative supply shock that, according to Joshua Hausman (2016), was among the causes of the 1937–1938 recession.

Our brief overview of the New Deal recovery is revealing not only because it shows how a small number of causes can explain quite a lot but also because it hardly mentions many other factors of potential importance, including deficit spending and monetary policy in the usually understood sense of the term. As we've seen, during the time we're considering, the Fed did next to nothing to influence money growth, while New Deal deficits other than the one caused by the 1936 Veterans' Bonus were too small to have mattered. It's therefore just as well that one can explain the progress of recovery without having to assume any substantial role for either Fed intervention or deficit spending.

A Consumption-Led Recovery

There is, however, one part of the story of the New Deal recovery that our one-chart account doesn't tell. It concerns what was happening to investment. If the slow recovery from the Great Recession was a jobless recovery, the New Deal recovery was an investment-less one. That is, the recovery consisted

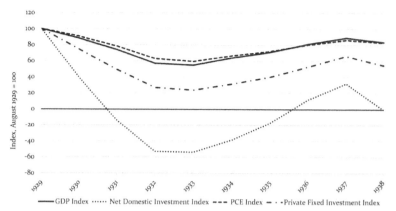

FIGURE 15.2. Consumption and investment spending, 1929–1937, index numbers, 1929 = 100. (Data from FRED®, Federal Reserve Bank of St. Louis, https://fred.stlouisfed.org/graph/?g=1pDBK).

almost entirely of increased spending on and production of consumption goods. As figure 15.2 shows, GDP and personal consumption expenditures displayed nearly identical patterns of decline and recovery between 1929 and 1937, with GDP ending up just 11 percent below its initial level and personal consumption expenditures only slightly lower. In contrast, in 1937 gross private fixed investment—that is, investment in land, buildings, machinery, and technology—was still less than two-thirds its 1929 level.

But it's the progress of *net* fixed investment, meaning fixed investment beyond that needed to merely compensate for capital depreciation, that best illustrates the investment-less nature of the New Deal recovery. "Throughout the entire period of recovery," Harvard's Sumner Slichter (1938, 105), observed, "managers were unwilling to embark upon plans for major improvements or for expansion in substantial volume, and the purchases of capital goods were mainly confined to replacements. . . . Compared with 1928, when industrial production was almost at the same rate as 1937, purchases of capital goods by producers were, in 1937, down about 20 per cent. The limited demand for capital goods is particularly impressive because the long depression had created the need for large replacements." In fact, net investment went *negative* relatively early in the Depression, in 1931, staying that way until 1936. Although net fixed investment rose in response to that year's massive bonus payment, which "was peculiarly calculated to aid sales of luxury, semiluxury and all types of durable consumers' goods" (Fine 1944, 105), it dried up again with the general collapse of 1937 so that, by 1938, the stock of private fixed capital was still more than $8 billion below its value in 1930.

"Obviously," Robert Higgs (1997, 567), points out, "regardless of what else might have been happening, no one could expect a resumption [of full employment] when the economy—its labor force continuing to grow—went a decade without any increase of the capital stock." The lack of investment meant disproportionately high and persistent unemployment in heavy industries. In October 1935, the unemployment rates for the construction industry, coal mines, and other mines and quarries were 67 percent, 44.5 percent, and 50.7 percent, respectively, as compared to 14.7 percent for wholesale and retail trades (Patch 1936). This was so despite a sharp upturn in production of capital goods that began with the NRA's compliance crisis and continued with its dismantlement (Bendiner 1935).

Looking at the situation toward the end of 1935 and observing how the recovery until then had been "mostly a consumption goods recovery," Leonard Ayres drew much the same conclusion Higgs was to draw:

> In this country a full recovery cannot be attained merely by increasing the output of consumption goods, nor can it be in any progressive industrial country. . . . If we are ever again to have a real recovery and a real prosperity it must come through a large-scale business revival in the durable goods industries. It will require the production of almost twice as much iron and steel as we are making now, and the manufacturing of about twice as much cement, and the use of nearly twice as much lumber, and the transportation by railroads and trucks of almost twice as much freight. It must produce large volumes of capital goods, as well as consumption goods. (*Commercial and Financial Chronicle* 1935b, 3758)

Nor was Roosevelt himself unaware of the lopsided nature of the New Deal recovery. During his May 22, 1935, address to Congress explaining his veto of that year's Veterans' Bonus bill, in response to the argument that paying the bonus would "increase the purchasing power of the consuming public," he observed "that retail trade has already expanded to a condition that compares favorably with conditions before the depression" and that paying the bonus "would not improve the conditions necessary to expand those industries which have the greatest unemployment" (Roosevelt 1938, 4:187).

The poor record of net investment had a close counterpart in that of bank lending, which followed a similar pattern, collapsing between 1929 and 1934, recovering only slightly between 1934 and 1937, and falling back again with the Roosevelt Recession until wartime activity revived it. To some extent the failure of bank lending and, more generally, of investment to recover before then was a lingering result of the banking crisis: deposits at failed banks remained unavailable for investment until those banks were liquidated, and it generally took years—for failed national banks, an average of just over six years—for that to happen (Anari, Kolari, and Mason 2005). Thus, despite having ended, the banking crisis continued to take its toll until the end of the decade (Anari, Kolari, and Mason 2005; Calomiris and Mason 2003b).

If some part of the supply of credit went missing in action during the 1930s, it was also true that businessmen's *demand* for credit and their general willingness to invest had dried up. If some recent estimates by Max Breitenlechner, Gabriel Mathy, and Johann Scharler (2021) are reliable, although bank credit remained tight until 1936, it ceased to be so afterward, notwithstanding the incomplete liquidation of failed banks. It follows that low activity after that date reflected businessmen's low demand for rather than a shortage of funds. According to Ayres and many others, businessmen had simply lost their nerve, and no matter how completely the banking system itself recovered, investment could only revive once they got it back. Recovery would come, Ayres said, "when our people have sufficient confidence in the future to make new investments in that future. It will be based on the firm confidence in the future that will lead business men to improve and enlarge their plants, and to extend their enterprises, with borrowed money" (*Commercial and Financial Chronicle* 1935b, 3758).

The French Connection

Our story of a New Deal recovery ultimately fueled by monetary growth, but limited in its completeness and occasionally checked altogether by adverse supply-side developments for which New Deal policies were often to blame, has a close French counterpart that lends it further credence and is worth reviewing for that reason.

To recall, France was one of the few countries and the only major one to take longer to recover from the Great Depression than the United States. France was also the only country that resorted to policies closely resembling—indeed inspired by—the New Deal, including NRA-style codes. And it was the only country that did not experience a substantial improvement in output after devaluing its currency. As Barry Eichengreen (1992a, 349) observes, France's example shows, even more clearly than that of the United States, that "devaluation was necessary but not sufficient for economic recovery."

France's first stab at New Deal–style industrial planning consisted of the so-called Flandrin experiment, an attempt by the conservative ministry of Pierre-Etienne Flandrin (November 1934–May 1935), directly inspired by the NRA, to cartelize French industries and reduce workers' working hours. Flandrin's experiment went no further, and his government fell after six months. But several weeks after decisively winning France's May 3, 1936, parliamentary election, the Popular Front—an alliance of French radicals, socialists, and communists—implemented an NRA-inspired plan of its own. That plan was so aggressive that recent scholars have dubbed it "a sort of NIRA on steroids" (Cohen-Setton, Hausman, and Wieland 2017). As Barry Eichengreen (1992a, 375–76) explains, "Employers were compelled to sign the *Accord de Matignon* granting trade union recognition, collective bargaining privileges, and wage increases. . . . [T]he work week was shortened again, but this time without any corresponding reduction in pay. The government legislated an annual paid vacation and a 40-hour week. Wages were raised by 7 percent for high-paid workers and by up to 15 percent for the lower paid. . . . Other elements of the French 'New Deal' raised the school-leaving age and nationalized the armaments industry." The Matignon Agreements' mandatory wage rate increases went into effect at once, raising nominal labor costs by between 7 and 15 percent (Cohen-Setton, Hausman, and Wieland 2017, 279). The rest of the Popular Front's plan, including its forty-hour week provision, was phased in industry by industry between then and the end of the year.

The Bank of France in the meantime had been struggling to maintain France's gold standard. During the latter months of 1934 it managed, with the help of import quotas and fiscal retrenchment, to regain some of the reserves it lost immediately following the US devaluation. But the Bank of France suffered further large reserve drains in 1935 and the first months of 1936. By resorting to capital controls, the government was able to check those losses as well for a time. But the bank endured further losses that September as rumors of an impending devaluation spread. As so often happens, those rumors proved self-fulfilling. Seeing the handwriting on the wall, on September 26 the French Parliament allowed the Bank of France to suspend gold payments. A week later the franc's gold value was formally lowered by 25 percent (Eichengreen 1992a, 353–77).

France's devaluation did not, however, hasten economic recovery there as devaluation did elsewhere. Instead, France's industrial production rose only slightly and temporarily. Its industrial production then fell again, after which it took until early 1938 to reach its level *just prior to* the franc's devaluation (Eichengreen 1992a, 383). Although the Popular Front offered various excuses for this outcome, according to Eichengreen (384) the straightforward explanation was that the French government's New Deal–inspired policies had "imparted to the economy a negative supply shock on a massive scale":

> Pressure for wage increases was unrelenting. Though there was a decline in strike activity immediately following the *Accord de Matignon,* there were new

outbreaks over the course of the subsequent year. Between 1936 and 1937, average weekly hours fell from 46 to little more than 40. Workers demanded further increases in hourly rates to prevent weekly earnings from falling with the reduction of hours. . . . The increase in wages consistently outstripped the concurrent rise in prices. Instead of falling, as was typical in countries depreciating their currencies, real wages rose dramatically in Paris, and modestly elsewhere in France, between 1936 and 1937. (Eichengreen 1992a, 384)

Compared to France's overall increase in real wage rates, Eichengreen points out, the NRA-inspired US increase was modest (Eichengreen 1992a, 385). It's not surprising, then, that France's New Deal proved so detrimental to its economic recovery.

Two studies published since Eichengreen wrote lend support to his conclusions. Noting how after 1936 France's industrial output was persistently 30 percent below its long-run trend, Paul Beaudry and Franck Portier (2002) consider various possible explanations, including technological stagnation, only to conclude that the best is the simplest: French output fell 30 percent because between them the Blum government's labor market legislation and strikes caused total hours worked to fall 25 percent. A decline in the ratio of investment to output, itself traceable to France's New Deal legislation, accounts for the remaining five percentage points by which output fell.

According to the second study, by Jérémie Cohen-Setton, Joshua Hausman, and Johannes Wieland (2017, 495), although taken alone France's decision to devalue the franc would have had a "substantial positive effect . . . on production," that effect was entirely offset by the French New Deal's hours restrictions. Because that same combination of policies led to a substantial increase in expected inflation and an accompanying decline in ex ante real interest rates (285), Cohen-Setton, Hausman, and Wieland's findings are strikingly at odds with the predictions of New Keynesian models. Evidence from France's New Deal therefore casts further doubt on claims that the NRA helped the US economy to recover.

The Role of Expected Inflation

Our three-part breakdown of the New Deal recovery is also helpful for understanding the part that heightened inflation expectations played in it. As Temin and Wigmore (1990), Eggertsson (2008), and others have argued, when short-term interest rates are near to or at their zero lower bounds, heightened inflation expectations can promote recovery by lowering anticipated real interest payments.

Briefly, the expected inflation channel appears to have played an important role during the pre-NIRA period. With the passage of the NIRA, its significance dwindled; but once gold started pouring into the country, it became important once more. Concerning the first of these stages, there's little doubt that several steps the Roosevelt administration took during that period succeeded in replacing fears of deflation with either hopes for or (for fiscal conservatives) fears of inflation. But the steps that did this were all ones that heralded increased growth of the money stock.

In contrast, as we noted in discussing the NRA, although that measure was generally expected to lead to a onetime upward shift in money wages and prices, it also appears to have reduced forecasted inflation, presumably because the NRA's codes, unlike expansionary monetary policies, actually limited the potential for *persistent* upward price and wage rate movements (Jalil and Rua 2016, 2017).

This brings us to the postdevaluation period. Jalil and Rua's research deals only with events before 1934. However, in a paper published some years earlier Christina Romer (1999) considers the possible bearing of devaluation on inflation expectations. She first notes how in theory any direct effect of devaluation on either the price level or the rate of inflation should be short-lived. She then goes on, for good measure, to test the hypothesis that devaluation led to a substantial increase in inflation expectations and finds, sure enough, that it did not.

While devaluation may not have directly reopened the expected inflation channel, it was an initial cause of gold inflows that subsequent developments helped to sustain for the rest of the decade and beyond. Although they at first came as a surprise, those inflows eventually gave rise to heightened inflation expectations. Romer maintains that it was only owing to their effect on expected inflation that gold inflows contributed to the recovery. "Nominal interest rates were already so low," she says, that "the main way that the monetary expansion could stimulate the economy was by generating expectations of inflation and thus causing a reduction in real interest rates" (Romer 1992, 775).

Alas, heightened inflation expectations turned out to be a double-edged sword. Instead of just helping to keep the recovery going, as theory says they should have, those expectations ultimately doomed it. How they did so will become clear in due course.

Quantitative Easing Avant Les Lettres

Several studies made during the last two decades—Bernanke, Reinhart, and Sack (2004), Anderson (2010), Jaremski and Mathy (2018), and Hanes (2019)— compare the gold-based expansion of the Federal Reserve's balance sheet during the 1930s to central banks' more recent resort to quantitative easing, meaning substantial long-term asset purchases undertaken when short-term interest rates have reached their effective (often zero) lower bound. Theories of quantitative easing suggest that it can influence real output in several ways, all involving a reduction in long-term interest rates. One is by raising inflation expectations. Another is through a "portfolio balance" effect. By purchasing longer-term securities, central banks reduce the supply of longer-duration assets, reducing the term premium and therefore the yield on other long-term as well as medium-term securities.

According to Christopher Hanes (2019), the portfolio effect channel may also have been relevant in the 1930s, when a substantial share of Europe's "hot money"—Roosevelt's own term for gold flowing from there into the United States—was invested in long-term Treasury securities both directly and indirectly through deposits to US banks. Consequently, Hanes (2019, 1171) says, gold inflows were "accompanied by substantial declines in medium- and long-term *nominal* yields."

The Golden Avalanche

From the evidence he reports, Hanes draws the conclusion that like their present counterparts, "American monetary authorities" in the 1930s resorted to "policies that increased high-powered money" (Hanes 2019, 1170). Hanes's statement is somewhat misleading, because gold inflows were the only reason why the Fed's balance sheet grew after 1933, and Fed policies weren't responsible for those inflows. If any American authorities were responsible for them, it was Treasury officials who supplied the Fed with gold certificates equal in value to the gold they purchased. And Treasury officials only did that much with increasing reluctance.

When economists spoke of "the gold problem" during the 1920s and early 1930s, they had in mind the *shortage* of gold stemming from the combination of inflated money stocks, diminished gold output, and the uneven distribution of existing monetary gold, a disproportionate share of which had piled up in the vaults of the Bank of France and the Federal Reserve System (Gay 1931; Williams 1931; League of Nations 1932). That "gold problem" is generally understood to have been a factor of fundamental importance in propagating the Great Depression, the deepening of which eventually led Federal Reserve officials themselves to plead for the gold standard's suspension.

It may therefore come as a surprise to many to learn that by 1936, US economists and policymakers, instead of complaining that there wasn't enough gold, were worrying that there was too much. "The world may have been devastated by deflation," Max Harris (2019, 3) writes, "but inflation remained a bug bear as the economy grew apace." But when one considers how, after having hardly budged for more than a decade, the US monetary gold stock *tripled* between March 1933 and May 1937, with no end to the inflows in sight, policymakers' concerns become easier to understand, if not easy to justify.

Several developments accounted for the "new" gold problem. The best known, as we've noted more than once, was the growing fear of another European war. That fear caused Europeans to shift their savings to the United States by either depositing them in US banks or buying American securities, $1.2 billion of which were sold to them between 1934 and 1939. It also increased European governments' demand for armaments, which American arms makers were only too happy to help satisfy.

The dollar's devaluation also contributed to the gold inflow, though not by doing much to slant the balance of trade in favor of the United States. As Bernanke, Reinhart, and Sack (2004, 319n33) observe, although the dollar's devaluation "improved the competitiveness of U.S. exports and raised the prices of imports . . . in an economy that was by this time largely closed, the direct effects of devaluation seem unlikely to have been large enough to account for the sharp turnaround." Because of this and also because the dollar's devaluation was one of many devaluations that tended to have offsetting effects, its main consequence, together with that of the rest, was simply to substantially increase the relative price of gold and with it world gold output. For this reason, it wasn't just gold that had been aboveground before the Depression that found its way to the United States. It was also new gold, and plenty of it.

From Russia, without Love

All told, world gold output grew from $889 million in 1933 to $1.39 billion in 1939 (Lehmann 1940, Table 1). Just how unanticipated this change was when the "original" gold problem was on experts' minds can be judged from the fact that those experts were then predicting that world gold output would *shrink* 20 percent by the end of the decade (League of Nations 1932). Most of the increased gold output came from mines in the British Empire, and especially in South Africa, which until the mid-1920s accounted for roughly half of world gold output. In 1922, for example, South Africa's gold mines yielded about 200 metric tons of gold. The Soviet Union's Siberian mines, in contrast, produced just 6.2 tons.

But this was about to change. Starting around that time, the Soviet government made its own distinct and substantial contribution to what would eventually be reckoned a gold "glut" by centralizing and investing heavily in Siberia's gold mining industry. As a result, Siberian gold output grew exceptionally rapidly, to 25 tons in 1929, 68 tons in 1932, and 185 tons in 1936. The last figure was almost half of South Africa's impressive output that same year (Lehmann 1940).

Remarking in September 1936 on the vastly increased output of subsidized Russian gold, John Maynard Keynes (1936c, 417) anticipated recent arguments for quantitative easing by claiming that Russia's gold output was "bound to exert a great influence in keeping rates of interest down," thereby increasing the odds that prices would start moving "steadily upwards." Russian gold thus removed "the most important obstacle in the way of cheap money," offering hope for economic recovery without any need for radical policies. "The importance of large supplies of gold now in sight," Keynes wrote, "lies in the fact that they may make possible by more or less orthodox methods adjustments, highly desirable in themselves, which we should be less likely to secure by other means. The muse of History is ironically disposed. Communist efficiency in the extraction of gold may serve to sustain yet awhile the capitalist system" (418).

Were Keynes referring only to the United States, he might have added Nazi bellicosity to communist "efficiency." Between them, it seems, Stalin and Hitler were then doing more to hasten the US recovery than the American president himself!

Too Much of a Good Thing

Yet in one of the Great Depression's more bemusing plot twists, instead of welcoming all that foreign gold, US authorities came to dread it. What's more, they came to dread it for precisely the reason that Keynes saw it as a godsend, namely, because it seemed likely to lead to more bank lending and higher prices.

What concerned those authorities was the extent of lending and inflation that could result if, as the economic recovery then under way continued, banks found it worthwhile to dispose of all the excess reserves they'd accumulated. As the consumer price index was still 20 percent below its 1929 level at the end of 1936, this fear may seem extravagant. But US officials weren't just worried that prices might rise more than enough to compensate for past deflation. They feared a sudden orgy of bank lending that, instead of merely assisting a business revival, would fuel an unsustainable boom. So it happened that, in the summer of 1936, those officials decided to take steps aimed at putting a lid on inflation before it got out of hand.

The muse of history is, indeed, ironically disposed.

The Roosevelt Recession

At the start of 1937, things were looking up for the US economy. The Supreme Court had struck down the National Industrial Recovery Act (NIRA) and the Agricultural Adjustment Act, the prime movers of the original New Deal's recovery plan. But like a glider released by its tow plane, the recovery itself kept going.

In truth, the glider analogy doesn't quite work, because instead of gradually declining, economic activity started rising faster than ever. Whereas in 1934 and 1935 real GNP grew by 7.7 percent and 8.1 percent, respectively, in 1936 it grew by a whopping 14.1 percent. Between May 1935, when the NIRA was struck down, and April 1937, unemployment fell by a third. Bank lending, which had long been stagnant, also started to revive. But the most obvious sign of improvement came from the stock market, which after having bounced around a slightly downward trend while the NIRA was in effect, rose by a hefty 70 percent.

The improvement was no mystery. As we've seen, instead of promoting recovery as they were supposed to do, National Recovery Administration (NRA) codes held it back, offsetting much of the increased spending that gold imports allowed with higher wage rates and prices instead of allowing that increase to pay for more jobs and greater output. By setting those codes aside, the Supreme Court made it legal for firms to use their increased earnings to hire more labor and produce more goods instead of paying higher wage rates and charging higher prices, and that change did more to promote recovery than the NRA itself ever did.

Seeing the Light

Things were so good in fact that many believed the long-awaited recovery to be just around the corner. Franklin Roosevelt himself must have thought so, or else he wouldn't have reminded Congress that January that "your task and mine is not ending with the end of the depression" (Roosevelt 1937).

But the optimism didn't last long. In May, according to the National Bureau of Economic Research business cycle chronology, the economy started shrinking again: expenditures fell, inventories accumulated, and already meager profits evaporated. Soon it was obvious to all that the United States was in the throes of yet another severe downturn. In little more than a year from that time, real US GNP shrank 18.2 percent, undoing a substantial part of the gains that had been achieved after Roosevelt took office.

Because the 1937–1938 downturn was both very steep and short-lived, even quarterly GNP numbers don't do it justice. To really appreciate its severity, one must look at the Federal Reserve's monthly index of industrial production, which tracks the output of manufacturing firms, mines, and utilities. Between May 1937 and June 1938, that index fell by almost *one-third*, a truly stupendous drop that, seen on a chart, brings to mind an economy jumping off a cliff.

What came to be known as the Roosevelt Recession, especially among the president's detractors, has posed a challenge to economic historians. But unlike the challenge of explaining the 1929 downturn, the problem here consists not of a lack of obvious suspects but of a surfeit, a very different sort of whodunit.

Fear of 'Flation

Most accounts of the 1937 crash blame it on demand-side shocks, including a sudden switch to contractionary monetary and fiscal policies. That switch was itself partly informed by the belief that a full recovery was in sight, a belief encouraged by the fact that markets for stocks and some commodities were again booming. But the switch was also a reaction to banks' large holdings of excess reserves. Together these developments suggested to many that unless steps were taken to prevent it, the United States was headed for what Federal Reserve chairman Marriner Eccles called a "dangerous inflation." Eccles's worries were shared by many administration officials, including Roosevelt. "I am concerned—we are all concerned," he told the press that April, "over the price rise in certain materials" (Roosevelt 1941b, 1:141).

Dangerous inflation? In retrospect at least, those officials' fears seem tragicomic. Inflation sufficient to get prices back to their 1926 level had long been one of the Roosevelt administration's main objectives. One could even say that Roosevelt regarded its achievement as the sum and substance of a complete recovery. In the late spring of 1937, the consumer price index was still about 20 percent below its level in mid-1926. So, what harm could a little more inflation have done? And if the still-depressed price level wasn't proof enough that the recovery was far from complete, there was the fact that even with the help of job sharing, conventionally measured unemployment was still in the low double digits. Upon hearing that American officials had begun to worry then about inflation, John Maynard Keynes is said to have quipped that they "professed to fear that for which they dared not hope" (Hughes 1986, 539).

Alas, despite Keynes, those officials were in earnest, and their fears soon led to action. What particularly concerned them was the large quantity of reserves banks had accumulated since the bank holiday, most of which were "excess" reserves, or reserves beyond those needed to meet banks' minimum legal requirements. Fed officials feared that, as the recovery continued, a revived demand for credit would lead first to a rapid expansion of bank lending and the money stock and thence to the "dangerous inflation" Eccles warned about. That Europe's gold was then pouring into the US banking system faster than ever, and that the Fed's limited security holdings meant that it couldn't rely on open market sales to offset that inflow, only made the need for other action seem that much more acute.[1]

Although the Fed's capacity for open market sales was limited, the Banking Act of 1935 had given Fed officials another way to neutralize member banks' excess reserves: the authority to as much as double their minimum reserve requirements. Those officials now chose to put that power to use. On Bastille Day 1936, a divided Board of Governors voted to raise member bank reserve requirements by 50 percent effective August 15. Because rates didn't budge and gold kept pouring into the country, sentiment grew in favor of further increases. Finally, at the end of January 1937, the board elected to raise the requirements by another third—to the maximum level allowed—this time in half steps taken on March 6 and May 1, respectively.

A Doubling Debacle

While the Fed's first two reserve requirement increases seemed to do little harm, the third coincided with the start of the 1937 downturn. According to many experts, this was no coincidence. So far as they're concerned, instead of merely serving to head off inflation, the Fed's doubling of its reserve requirements was one of the chief causes, if not *the* cause, of the 1937 collapse.

Their argument, the best-known version of which is in Milton Friedman and Anna Schwartz's (1963) *Monetary History of the United States*, is that while Fed officials viewed excess reserves as redundant reserves, the banks themselves didn't see them so (520–31). Instead, having been traumatized by runs in the early years of the Depression, they accumulated excess reserves deliberately, for safety's sake: unlike required reserves, excess reserves could be used to meet runs without risk of legal penalties. Thanks to low interest rates, this precaution, besides being prudent, was also cheap.[2]

So when the Fed increased banks' required reserves, and especially when it did so for the third time, instead of doing nothing, the banks proceeded to rebuild their excess reserve cushions. With only so many reserves in the system, that meant reducing their required reserves by paring down their loans, investments, and deposits. The resulting decline in bank credit and the money stock helped bring about the 1937–1938 recession, just as the Great Contraction of 1929–1933 led (once again, according to Friedman and Schwartz) to the first Great Depression downturn.

Reserve-ations

Popular as it is, the theory that the Fed triggered the 1937 collapse by raising banks' reserve requirements has never lacked critics. It's no surprise that these include Lauchlin Currie, Marriner Eccles's personal economic adviser, and other Fed officials who were behind the policy (Phillips 1997). But many outside the Fed have also declared it innocent. According to Benjamin Anderson (1949, 440), Chase National Bank's chief economist at the time, "Reducing the [banks'] excess reserves could not reduce the volume of business unless real differences were made thereby in interest rates, and unless restrictions were imposed thereby upon the use of money and credit. Now the evidence is overwhelming that nothing of this sort occurred."

Several more recent writings draw renewed attention to and supplement the evidence Anderson had in mind. L. G. Telser (2001) shows that instead of lending less, Fed member banks met their increased reserve requirements by selling government securities. Haelim Park and Patrick Van Horn (2015) also find that Fed's reserve requirement changes didn't lead member banks to reduce their lending. For that reason they also conclude that the Fed "cannot be blamed for instigating the economic downturn of 1937–38." Finally, by examining data for individual Fed member banks, Charles Calomiris, Joseph Mason, and David Wheelock (2023) are able to show that even after they'd been doubled, the Fed's reserve requirements weren't binding on most Fed member banks. Although those banks did increase their reserves, they did so for reasons unrelated to their legal requirements, and they did it not by lending less but by either selling off government securities, as Telser claims, or reducing their balances with correspondents.

And a Rejoinder

But the Fed's defenders may not have the last word. Their criticisms of the Friedman-Schwartz story have been criticized in turn by Gauti Eggertsson and Benjamin Pugsley (2006), who claim that the Fed's doubling of reserve requirements didn't have to cause a credit crunch to trigger the 1937 downturn. They argue that the Fed's decision mattered not because it led to an immediate tightening of credit but because it signaled a reversal in the government's stance on inflation: having long promised to get prices back to their pre-Depression levels, in 1937 the Roosevelt administration made it clear that it had abandoned that objective in favor of steps aimed at putting a lid on inflation.

Eggertsson and Pugsley (2006, 152) consider this official about-face "one of the most peculiar policy mistakes in U.S. economic history." But they regard it so not because it led to any immediate clamping down on credit but instead because it "created pessimistic expectations of future growth and price inflation that fed into both an expected and an actual deflation." Owing to the presence of "sticky" nominal wages, prices, and interest rates, the collapse of expected inflation was accompanied by an equally severe contraction of output.

Rebirth Control

The Fed's doubling of reserve requirements was only one of two monetary policy changes that may have contributed to the Roosevelt Recession, whether through an expectations channel or otherwise. The other, which some consider more important, was also part of the government's effort to forestall inflation. This was the Treasury's decision to "sterilize" gold inflows.

As we've seen, after Hitler was named Germany's chancellor, gold fleeing Europe became the chief cause of US monetary base growth and, starting in 1935, accompanying fears of unwanted inflation. The Fed couldn't keep all that gold from adding to banks' reserves. But it could and it did force banks to hold on to reserves they'd accumulated. The Treasury, on the other hand, could keep gold inflows from increasing banks' reserves. Normally, after drawing on its Fed balance to buy gold at the official price of $35 an ounce, the Treasury would replenish its Fed account by depositing an equivalent sum in gold certificates in it. The monetary gold stock and monetary base (bank reserves plus circulating currency) would then grow in step with the Treasury's gold purchases. To sever the link between these, the Treasury just had to quit depositing those certificates. Doing that "sterilized" the gold inflows.

From December 1936 until February 1938, except for a onetime "desteril-ization" of $300 million in September 1937, the Treasury sterilized all the gold that came its way with the express aim of arresting that gold's "inflationary potentialities." Because the Fed's nongold portfolio remained essentially fixed during this time, the Treasury's policy slammed the brakes on the monetary base growth that had been promoting recovery, insofar as other New Deal policies allowed it to, since 1934.

Friedman and Schwartz assign roughly equal blame for the 1937–1938 con-traction to the Treasury's decision to sterilize its gold purchases and the Fed's doubling of reserve requirements, Doug Irwin (2012), on the other hand, be-lieves that the Treasury was the main culprit. According to Irwin, sterilization was far more contractionary than the Fed's reserve requirement increases. That was so in part because reserve requirements were less binding than Friedman and Schwartz and many others have supposed. But the reduced annual growth rate of the monetary base, from an average of 17 percent be-tween 1934 and 1936 to zero, also had a far greater effect on overall money stock growth than the concurrent change in the base money multiplier. For these and other reasons, including the almost identical timing of gold ster-ilization and the 1937–1938 contraction, Irwin concludes that the Treasury's policy was the main cause of the contraction. As for Eggertsson and Pugsley's alternative theory, Irwin (2012, 250n7) considers it unlikely that "animal spir-its" (by which he means the public's loss of confidence in the government's willingness to boost prices) "could sink the economy as much as occurred during 1937–38 in the absence of some tangible change in government policy or some real shock."

Regardless of which theory one prefers, it seems safe to conclude that the *combination* of increased reserve requirements and gold sterilization proved lethal to the New Deal recovery. Here it's worth noting that each responsible party acted as if it didn't know, or didn't care, what the other was up to. While both Marriner Eccles and Treasury Secretary Henry Morgenthau saw a need to clamp down on money growth to head off inflation, Eccles favored doing so by raising the Fed's reserve requirements, while Morgenthau tried to per-suade Eccles that sterilizing gold inflows was the better option. Instead of the two men coming to an agreement or otherwise coordinating their actions, Eccles went ahead with the Fed's first reserve requirement increase without even bothering to tell Morgenthau, let alone gain his approval. When that in-crease seemed to make little difference, Morgenthau proceeded with his ster-ilization program after securing Eccles's last-minute and grudging support for it. Then, despite Morgenthau's objections, Eccles had the Fed go through with its further reserve requirement increases. It's as though two doctors, sharing the same overanxious patient, each insisted on administering a powerful sedative whether the other did the same or not and so ended up putting their patient in a coma.

Here again the analogy falls short, because it's far from obvious that the US economy needed a sedative at all. The analogy also fails in another respect: The US economy didn't just get a double dose of sedatives: it got a triple dose.

Austerity, New Deal Style

Worries about overspeculation and looming inflation that caused the Fed and the Treasury to tighten monetary policy had as their fiscal counterpart the fear that the federal debt was reaching unsustainable levels. That fear led to a renewed attempt during the spring of 1936 to clamp down on deficits by reining in federal expenditures and collecting new taxes.

Although Henry Morgenthau was the new austerity effort's prime mover, Roosevelt was solidly behind it. "People complain to me," he told a gathering at New York's National Democratic Club that April, "about the current costs of rebuilding America, about the burden on future generations. I tell them that whereas the deficit[] of the federal government this year is about $3,000,000,000, the national income of the people of the United States has risen from $35,000,000,000 in the year 1932 to $65,000,000,000 in the year 1936, and I tell them further that the only burden we need to fear is the burden our children would have to bear if we failed to take these measures today" (quoted in Boeckel 1936, 2). The difference between fiscal 1936 receipts and revenues turned out to be almost twice Roosevelt's $3 billion estimate, making for the largest peacetime deficit in the nation's history. Added to the deficits of the preceding five years, it raised the total federal debt to $34.5 billion.

The Roosevelt administration reacted to the government's record indebtedness by pulling hard on the reins. Federal expenditures, which thanks to the Veterans' Bonus had risen to $8.7 billion in 1936, were reduced to $7.4 billion in 1937, while tax revenues were boosted by the undistributed profits tax introduced in mid-1936 and the Social Security tax first collected in January 1937 (Velde 2009, 19–20). The result, Larry Peppers (1973, 206) says, was "a restrictive shift of unprecedented size" in fiscal policy. In just one fiscal year, the full-employment surplus—an estimate of what the federal surplus would be were the economy operating at its full-employment potential—leaped from a modest but nonetheless stimulating 0.57 percent to a very austere 2.82 percent.

Not surprisingly, Fed officials, led by Eccles, were quick to pin the blame for the 1937 downturn on the government's decision to turn off the fiscal tap. Drawing on a 1938 report prepared by economist Lauchlin Currie, his personal assistant, Eccles (1939, 8) himself attributed the collapse to a "too rapid withdrawal of the government's stimulus." "From 1934 to 1936," Currie (1938, 3) had written, "the largest single factor in the steady recovery movement was the excess of Federal activity-creating expenditures over activity-decreasing receipts." During 1936, those net outlays averaged $335 million per month. In contrast, from September through March 1937, the average was just $60 million. After briefly considering other possible causes, Currie blamed the recession entirely on this "withdrawal of the Government's contribution" to overall spending.

Fiscal Policy: Mountain or Molehill?

That the federal government slowed economic activity by withdrawing most of its fiscal stimulus seems beyond dispute. But Currie's claim that its doing so alone accounts for the severity of the 1937 downturn won't stand close scrutiny. For one thing, by comparing net government outlays between March and September 1937 to those for 1936, he exaggerates the extent of the retrenchment. Because of the Veterans' Bonus, the government's net contribution to fiscal 1936 spending was an exceptionally high $4.1 billion, as compared to $3.2 billion and $3.1 billion for 1934 and 1935, respectively. On the other hand, the period from March to September 1937 was a *low*-water mark for net government expenditures. The government's monthly contribution was still $264 million that January, and by mid-1938 it had bounced back to about $300 million per month, a value exceeding the averages for 1934 and 1935, and only slightly below the exceptionally high monthly average of $335 million for 1936.

Even so, there *was* a cutback, and it was substantial. But timing is another problem for Currie's thesis. As Kenneth Roose (1951) observes, there's a lag of more than six months between December 1936, when net government spending started to drop, and the initial decline in income, which didn't fall below its 1936 average until January 1938. Yet a large share of government spending in the 1930s, including relief payments, became income with no lag at all, and contemporary estimates put the income lag for government payments of all sorts at just one month.

But there's a still bigger problem with Currie's thesis, which has to do with his assumption that until 1937 "the largest single factor in the steady recovery movement was the excess of Federal activity-creating expenditures over activity-decreasing receipts" (Currie 1938, 3). That assumption is crucial, for if expansionary fiscal policy *wasn't* an important driver of the pre-1937 recovery, then reducing it, even substantially, couldn't have caused or even contributed all that much to the 1937 crisis.

In fact, as we've seen, most experts deny that fiscal stimulus contributed much to the 1933–1937 recovery: recall E. Cary Brown's conclusion, so opposite Currie's, that fiscal stimulus simply "wasn't tried." If the federal government's net contribution to spending was lower in 1937 than it had been in 1934 and 1935, it was also no greater in those two years than it had been in 1929. The year 1936 alone witnessed an exceptional fiscal contribution, thanks to the Veterans' Bonus. But those bonus payments, which began only midway through that year, can only account for a small part of the overall increase in income between April 1933 and May 1937.

If Currie's attempt to blame the Roosevelt Recession on fiscal retrenchment is unconvincing, so is his attempt to exonerate monetary policy. Currie notes, correctly, that from their nadir at the start of the bank holiday, demand ("checkable") deposits grew by some $10 billion by the middle of 1936 and that this growth went hand in hand with growth in spending on consumer durables. But he goes on to claim that the buildup in deposits can only have been due to the government's deficit spending, whereas statistics reveal the overwhelming importance of gold imports (Friedman and Schwartz 1963, 499–500).

Parceling Out Blame

Allowing that fiscal retrenchment played some part in the 1937 crash, how important was it compared to monetary tightening? Weighing the two factors' contributions econometrically, Jonian Rafti (2015) affirms Friedman and Schwartz's rough guess that each was responsible for about half of the overall decline in income. But because he assumes a generous fiscal policy multiplier of 1.4, meaning that every $1 reduction in net government spending reduced total income by that amount plus 40 cents, Rafti's estimate of the fiscal contribution may be on the high side. At the other extreme, Christina Romer (1992) puts the period's fiscal policy multiplier at just 0.233, implying a much smaller fiscal contribution. Most other estimates of the contribution of fiscal policy (e.g., Velde 2009) fall somewhere between Rafti's and Romer's. It's therefore likely that the cutback in net government spending was to blame for less, perhaps much less, than half of the 1937 downturn.

To be clear, this conclusion does *not* mean that a sufficiently expansionary fiscal policy couldn't have *prevented* the Roosevelt Recession. However small the fiscal multiplier, a big enough *boost* in net government spending might in principle have made up for any decline in spending of other sorts. Still, it doesn't follow that the recession was mainly brought about by the Roosevelt administration's cutbacks and new taxes.

Striking It Poor

Because serious recessions generally involve correspondingly severe reductions in overall spending, it's not surprising that economists seeking the cause of the 1937 collapse should suspect either monetary or fiscal tightening. But adverse supply shocks can also cause or at least aggravate economic downturns. That happened when the Organization of the Petroleum Exporting Countries restricted its oil exports starting in 1973. It happened again when the COVID-19 outbreak spread worldwide during 2020. And some experts claim it happened in 1937 and that at least part of the problem then was neither foreigners' machinations nor mother nature (or both) but rather New Deal policies.

Several supply-side developments sent shock waves through the US economy that year, striking the automobile industry especially hard. One was an increase in the cost of labor and raw materials. Thanks mainly to European rearmament and the Spanish Civil War, the materials needed to make a small car, which would have cost General Motors, Ford, or Chrysler less than $90 in the summer of 1936, cost almost $106 a year later. But that was the least of it. Owing mainly to more aggressive union tactics, and despite persistent unemployment, labor costs rose even more (Hausman 2016). The union tactics included numerous strikes, among which were many production-paralyzing sit-down strikes. According to the Bureau of Labor Statistics, there were 4,740 strikes in 1936. It was an all-time record. Yet there were more than twice as many strikes in 1937 (Crowther 1938). The 1937 strikes involved the loss of almost 28.5 million man-hours of work, another record.

Sit-down strikes, the main cause of lost work hours, were rare before the Depression. They became common only after members of the United Auto Workers took over two Flint, Michigan, auto body plants on December 30, 1936 (White 2010). Between then and late February 1939 there were some six hundred such strikes, thanks to which the automobile industry alone ended up losing about 4.5 million man-hours.

Strikes and the Wagner Act

The surge of strikes and of sit-down strikes especially is often blamed on the July 1935 passage of the National Labor Relations Act, better known as the Wagner Act. Harold Cole and Lee Ohanian (2004, 785), for example, claim that by giving "even more bargaining power to workers than the NIRA," the

Wagner Act led to a significant increase in strike activity, especially so once its constitutionality was held up by the Supreme Court. Sit-down strikes became much less frequent, on the other hand, after the Supreme Court decided, with its February 1939 decision in *National Labor Relations Board v. Fansteel Metallurgical Corporation* (306 U.S. 240), that the National Labor Relations Board (NLRB) lacked authority to order employers to reinstate workers fired for taking part in them.

But the Wagner Act's bearing on strike activity isn't as straightforward as it may seem to be at first glance. For one thing, the timing is off. Although Roosevelt signed the act on July 5, 1935, the total number of strikes, and the number of major sit-down strikes, didn't rise considerably until the last weeks of 1936. Nor does Cole and Ohanian's claim that the number of strikes rose "after the Supreme Court upheld [the NLRB's] constitutionality in 1937" quite fit: striking reached its zenith in March 1937, a month before the Supreme Court's decision.

And while it's certainly true that the National Labor Relations Act strengthened workers' collective bargaining rights, it and other "little Wagner Acts" passed by state governments also established boards to adjudicate disputes over those rights. The whole point of those boards was to make it unnecessary for unions to resort to militant tactics. Consequently, as John Spielmans (1941, 725) observes, as tempting as it may be to connect the strike wave to the New Deal's "promise . . . to lend support to labor in its struggle," treating that wave as "proof of the unhappy effects of the Wagner Act" would be "rash."

The more subtle truth is that the Wagner Act encouraged strikes not by granting workers more rights but by failing to adequately clarify those rights. By allowing workers to organize under "majority rule," it tried to rule out employer-dominated "company" unions. But it left unsettled federal law regarding the legality of "closed shops," meaning unions that compelled all workers in any unionized firm to take part in them and their tactics (Hogler 2005). The NLRB was therefore in no position to settle disagreements between unions seeking to establish closed shops and employers bent on stopping them. Frustrated by what they considered the Wagner Act's failure to deliver on its promises, and encouraged by Roosevelt's reelection in November 1936, union organizers decided to force the issue. The Flint strike was their big gamble, and that strike's surprising success inspired hundreds of others like it.[3]

A Cost-Push Recession?

Strikes, however encouraged, and the Wagner Act's general strengthening of workers' bargaining power, substantially boosted labor costs at a time when many firms were already hard-pressed by high raw materials prices. Cole and Ohanian (2004, 785) claim that union activity "significantly reduced firm profitability" by temporarily shutting down plants and otherwise boosting the cost of labor. Benjamin Anderson (1949, 446) considered the increased cost of labor rather than shrinking demand to have been the "main factor on the industrial side in bringing the revival of 1935–1937 to a close." Anderson's opinion is borne out by the fact that industrial production started to decline in December 1936, whereas new orders didn't reach their peak for another five or six months (Slichter 1938, 99). Low profits also took their toll on investment. "In a free enterprise economy," Kenneth Roose (1948, 246) says, "given sufficiently low profits, an increase in costs . . . can lead to an almost complete cessation in investment." And that, he said, was what happened when input costs, "of which labor costs were the most important," began rising during the first quarter of 1937.

Could increased union activity alone really have boosted labor costs enough to throttle business investment? Chris Hanes (2020) thinks so. Using earnings and other data for before and after the Great Depression, he comes up with a series of projected average hourly earnings (AHE) inflation rates for 1929–1939. Comparing that series to actual Depression-era AHE inflation, Hanes finds that the actual series rose well above projected levels in 1933–1935 and again in 1937–1938. A figure from Hanes's paper comparing actual hourly earnings to his AHE projections, with standard error bands around the last, suggests a kneeling Bactrian camel complete with gastrointestinal tract (figure 16.1).

Hanes goes on to consider several explanations for the camel's humps, only to rule out all of them except New Deal labor policies. He finds that the first hump coincides with the dates of the NRA codes, while the second matches "a wave of strikes associated with unionization supported by New Deal labor policies" (Hanes 2020, 1051). Employers, Hanes says, "raised wages and overtime premiums as they entered into agreements with unions or attempted to forestall union threats." The wage hikes were also quite large, especially compared to firms' still-depressed profits. Finally, Hanes performs a simple regression of his estimated AHE anomaly against the number of manufacturing workers involved in strikes and a small set of control variables. The results, he finds, fit the data quite well, reproducing "not only the rise of anomalous [wage] inflation in 1933 but also the diminution of anomalous inflation in 1936 and the second round of anomalous inflation in late 1936–1937" (1058).

A somewhat earlier study by Joshua Hausman (2016) also finds that New Deal labor supply shocks in the automobile industry and elsewhere reduced

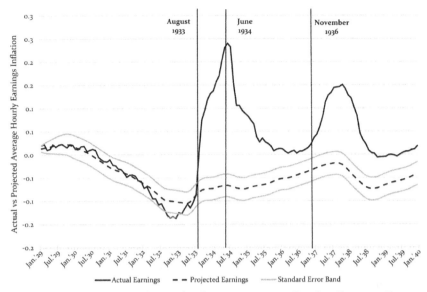

FIGURE 16.1. Actual and projected average hourly earnings, 1929–1939. (Data from Hanes 2020, Figure 5. Data courtesy of Christopher Hanes.)

overall real output substantially. Automobile production, Hausman notes, made up a much bigger share (3.5 percent) of US GDP in 1937 than it does today. Most car production inputs were also supplied domestically back then. Using a statistical model that fits pre-1937 auto sales to fiscal, monetary, and other economic determinants, Hausman concludes that had it not been for adverse auto industry supply shocks, the Roosevelt Recession would only have been two-thirds as deep.

✷ ✷ ✷

In *Murder on the Orient Express,* Hercule Poirot eventually figures out that, except for the victim, all of the Express's passengers belong to the same household, and all had a hand in the killing. One might say much the same thing of the many suspects in the killing of the 1933–1937 recovery. All bear some guilt. And all were offspring of the New Deal.

The Keynesian Myth

In *The Money Makers,* his book about New Deal monetary and fiscal policy, Eric Rauchway (2015) says that Franklin Roosevelt "conducted an active monetary and fiscal program of recovery . . . working along lines suggested by Keynes." Rauchway's book's subtitle in turn declares that between them "Roosevelt and Keynes ended the Depression." Other accounts likewise claim that "the beliefs of Keynes and FDR proved successful at alleviating the Great Depression" (Rust 2021) and even that "without John Maynard Keynes, FDR's New Deal may never have happened" (Future Hindsight n.d.).

Our survey of post–bank holiday New Deal policies suggests that many of those policies contributed little to the recovery and that some actually hindered it. Readers who take Keynes's influence on the New Deal for granted may be tempted to view that conclusion as one that implicitly condemns Keynes or Keynesian economics. But no such condemnation is implied for the simple reason that despite what one reads everywhere, the New Deal was not particularly Keynesian and was in some ways quite un-Keynesian.[1]

According to Rexford Tugwell (1957, 290), "the Keynesian myth" (as he styles it) first became fashionable in the later 1930s, when Keynes's *General Theory of Employment, Interest and Money* began to sweep the board of macroeconomic thought. The myth was later reinforced by Roy Harrod's *Life of Keynes* (1951). As Eric Rauchway (2015, xxix) tells us, in a 1950 letter to Dennis Robertson, Keynes's colleague at Cambridge in the 1930s, Harrod admitted that he'd deliberately exaggerated Keynes's influence on Roosevelt's policies because "in the mind of the general public you have to have One Man. There isn't room for more."

Tugwell himself dismisses the claim that Keynes influenced Roosevelt's thinking or otherwise played an important part in shaping New Deal poli-

cies. Another New Dealer, Leon Keyserling, who served as an attorney for the
Agricultural Adjustment Administration and helped draft some other major
New Deal legislation, does so as well, though in starker terms. "With all due
respect to Keynes," Keyserling wrote in 1972, "I have been unable to discover
much reasonable evidence that the New Deal would have been greatly different if he had never lived, and if a so-called school of economics had not taken
on his name" (Keyserling, Nathan, and Currie 1972, 135).

That Keynes had little influence on New Deal policies is only part of the
truth too many popular accounts of the New Deal fail to tell. It's also true that
had Roosevelt actually taken Keynes's advice, the Great Depression might not
have been so severe.

Brains and Keynes

Any account of Keynes's role in shaping New Deal policies should begin with
an appreciation of two facts. The first is that despite his stature in Great Britain, Keynes was not well known in the United States until after he published
The General Theory in 1936. The second is that far from feeling any need
to seek advice from a British economist, Roosevelt came to office accompanied by a corps of advisers unmatched by any other in the history of the US
presidency.

Historians of the New Deal have found it convenient, if perhaps never
entirely accurate, to divide Roosevelt's many advisers into various factions.
All agree that the most important of these were the "planners," led by Tugwell, and the "trustbusters," led by Harvard law professor Felix Frankfurter.
The trustbusters' ideal was one of rivalrous competition, which they wanted
to encourage by breaking up large corporations and banks. The planners, in
contrast, had nothing against large-scale enterprises or collusion as such: to
their way of thinking, uncoordinated competition could be more dangerous
than desirable, and at least some of the trustbusters' efforts were counterpro-
ductive. Rather than try to prevent firms from colluding, the planners merely
wanted to transfer control of that collusion from businessmen to bureaucrats
like themselves, who would manage it rationally, in the public interest, instead of just trying to make a buck.[2]

As diametrically opposed as their ideals were in many respects, these factions had at least one important belief in common: both treated the Great Depression "less as a problem to be solved than as an opportunity to be exploited
for radical surgery on U.S. business and finance" (Best 1991, 11). Nor was it
obvious how either of their programs, which predated the Depression, would
help end it. The generally held verdict that their favorite reforms "never

contributed much to economic recovery" (Hawley 1966, 15) should therefore not come as a surprise. It shouldn't be necessary to add that the reforms favored by trustbusters and planners had nothing to do with policies aimed at enhancing aggregate spending that later came to be identified with Keynesian economics. The simple truth is that, when it came to fiscal and monetary policy, most of Roosevelt's closest advisers, including members of the original Brain Trust, weren't Keynesians even in a loose sense.

This isn't to say that Roosevelt received no Keynesian advice beyond the bits Keynes himself offered. Besides the trustbusters and planners, a third group of advice givers—the inflationists—also influenced his thinking. This group's most important members, neither of whom was a genuine New Dealer, were Irving Fisher and George Warren, the last of whom had an important ally in Henry Morgenthau (Stanton 2007). Although they were fiscal conservatives, Fisher, Warren, and Morgenthau favored suspending the gold standard and otherwise trying to raise prices by means of what may loosely be called monetary policy. Expansionary *fiscal* policy, particularly large-scale spending on public works, had their own New Deal proponents in Frances Perkins, Harold Ickes, Harry Hopkins, and Marriner Eccles. But calling the policies these New Dealers favored "Keynesian" is one thing; claiming that Keynes was their "patron saint" (Mitchell 1947, 125) is quite another. In fact, there's no evidence that any of them came to think as they did because of Keynes.[3]

Until *The General Theory* made its big splash in 1936, Keynes's own arguments appear to have impressed only one of Roosevelt's close advisers: trustbuster Felix Frankfurter. In the fall of 1933 Frankfurter was on sabbatical to England where in early December, after visiting Keynes at Cambridge, he encouraged Keynes to write the open letter published in the *New York Times* later that month. Keynes gave Frankfurter an advance copy, which Frankfurter sent to Roosevelt on December 12 (S. Edwards 2018, 1–2).

If Tugwell (1957, 404) is right in saying that Roosevelt "never . . . read anything Keynes wrote, except perhaps some newspaper pieces commenting on his [Roosevelt's] own actions," that letter would have been one of Roosevelt's main helpings of Keynes's advice. But the letter didn't impress Roosevelt. "You can tell the Professor," he told Frankfurter, "that in regard to public works we shall spend in the next fiscal year nearly twice the amount we are spending in this fiscal year, but there is a practical limit to what the Government can borrow." From that terse reply and other evidence, William Barber (1996, 83) concludes that Keynes's pleas "had little impact on Roosevelt's thinking."

Nor were the two men's minds ever to really meet. The discord in their thinking became evident in May 1934 when the men themselves met for the first and only time. To judge by the impressions each shared with Frances

Perkins after their one-hour meeting, that event, which Frankfurter hoped would establish a rapport between them, was unsuccessful. "I saw your friend Keynes," Roosevelt said. "He left a whole rigmarole of figures. He must be a mathematician rather than a political economist" (Perkins 1946, 226). Keynes, for his part, told Perkins that although he admired the president very much, he expected him to be "more literate, economically speaking." According to Arthur Schlesinger (1960, 406), Keynes later told Alvin Johnson, the New School's director who was himself an economist, "I don't think your President Roosevelt knows anything about economics." However much the men may have respected one another, so far as economic policy was concerned, each might have spoken a foreign language that the other couldn't understand.

The Wrong Rs

As Tugwell (1970, 103) points out, Roosevelt's "less than enthusiastic" response to Keynes's advice was due not to his having disagreed with Keynes but instead to his belief that Keynes was merely telling him "to do what he had already been doing for some time.'" But was he?

Keynes himself certainly didn't think so. One purpose of his open letter was to encourage Roosevelt to spend more—*much* more—on public works and to finance that spending by borrowing more instead of raising taxes (Keynes 1933a). As we've seen, Keynes was quite right to think that Roosevelt needed such encouragement. But that wasn't all. Keynes also disapproved of much that Roosevelt had "already been doing." Among other things, he questioned Roosevelt's priorities, wondered whether the president was quite sure what he was doing, and called some of the advice he was taking "crackbrained and queer." It was here also that Keynes compared the gyrations in gold's price that some of those policies were abetting to "a gold standard on the booze." In short, while Keynes applauded Roosevelt's willingness to reject orthodox policies in favor of "bold experimentation," he also blamed the president for conducting the wrong experiments while clinging to some of the most obstructive orthodoxies.

Keynes also faulted Roosevelt for ranking his three R's—reform, relief, and recovery—incorrectly. Instead of making recovery his administration's first priority, Keynes (1933a) said, Roosevelt was "engaged on a double task, Recovery and Reform." Keynes argued that he ought to have deferred reform until recovery was achieved.[4] He was especially critical of the National Recovery Administration, the planners brainchild, describing it, accurately, as pretending to promote recovery while actually impeding it.[5]

Nor was Keynes less critical when, not long after meeting Roosevelt in

1934, he once again shared his thoughts with the *New York Times,* this time in the shape of some brief "notes" on the New Deal (Keynes 1934). Here Keynes took aim at the National Recovery Administration again, objecting to its "excessive complexity and regimentation" and especially to its "impractical and unnecessary" attempts to regulate prices. He noted as well the lack of business confidence, "for some of which the administration may be to blame." And he complained that, despite a temporary boost, the government was still not spending, or not deficit-spending, enough. Keynes repeated many of these complaints, more trenchantly, in a February 1, 1938, letter to the president (Keynes 1982 [1938]).

Even this cursory review of Keynes's public and private remarks on the New Deal should suffice to show why it's misleading to claim that Keynes "staunchly defended the New Deal through 1933, and continued to do so into 1934" (Rauchway 2013). Keynes certainly pinned his hopes for the future of American capitalism on the Roosevelt administration. He admired Roosevelt's boldness and particularly applauded his decision to abandon the gold standard. And he approved of some New Deal undertakings considered as *long-term reforms.* But in 1933 and 1934, Keynes's verdict on the New Deal *as a program for recovery* was, on the whole, negative. And he made no bones about it.

Anchors Aweigh

Of all the steps Roosevelt took during his first year in office, none pleased Keynes more than his decision to abandon the gold standard. But much as Keynes, who famously condemned the gold standard as a "barbarous relic" in his *Tract on Monetary Reform* (Keynes 1923), welcomed that decision, he had nothing to do with it.

That the gold standard might eventually have to go was a possibility Roosevelt recognized as early as October 1932, when he wisely chose not to mention the topic in his campaign speeches. "I do not want to be committed to the gold standard," he privately explained to his aides at the time. "I haven't the faintest idea whether we will be on the gold standard on March 4th or not; nobody can foresee where we shall be" (Fuller 2014, 86).

On the eve of the inauguration, Roosevelt and his advisers still hadn't given up on the gold standard. According to Sebastian Edwards (2017, 3), although they considered "tinkering with the currency," they viewed doing so as "an option with a rather low priority." Events, more than economic doctrine, were to ultimately seal the gold standard's fate: the banking crisis, which had been triggered by a run on the dollar, compelled Roosevelt to restrict both gold exports and domestic ownership of gold, while gold's subsequent appreciation, which Roosevelt would eventually encourage through his gold purchase program, put paid to any prospect of a restoration of the dollar's former gold value.

Had Roosevelt wished to permanently devalue the dollar all along, he didn't need to turn to any British economist to gain an expert's approval of that decision. Days before the inauguration Irving Fisher, who according to Joseph Schumpeter (1951, 223) was "the greatest economist the United States has ever produced," urged Roosevelt to begin his presidency by announcing that the United States was abandoning the gold standard in favor of a "managed currency." That step, Fisher maintained, "would reverse the present deflation overnight and would set us on a path toward new peaks of prosperity" (Barber 1996, 25). But Roosevelt wasn't yet prepared to go that far. Instead, he settled for his March 6 bank holiday proclamation suspending both gold exports and internal gold payments, steps that could hardly be avoided since gold withdrawals were about to exhaust the New York Fed's reserves. As we've seen, subsequent executive orders extended and reinforced these prohibitions until, on April 20, Roosevelt issued his proclamation formally suspending the gold standard.

Roosevelt's next major step away from the gold standard consisted of his bombshell cable of July 3, 1933, effectively withdrawing his support for the currency stabilization goals of the World Economic Conference then being held in London. The other participating nations hoped that the United States would cooperate with them to restore the international gold standard and the system of fixed exchange rates that went hand in hand with it by agreeing to stabilize the then free-floating gold value of the dollar. Although it was understood by then that the dollar would be devalued, the thought was that by working together the assembled delegates could avoid "competitive" devaluations that might delay the gold standard's revival, if not prevent it altogether. The US withdrawal left Roosevelt free to devalue the dollar as much as he liked or to let it keep floating forever.

Keynes's role in Roosevelt's decision to not support the conference's currency stabilization agenda has been exaggerated. Keynes approved of the steps Roosevelt took during the bank holiday and of his decision to officially let the dollar float that April. Keynes also understood that Roosevelt was prepared to permanently devalue the dollar if that would help to raise the US price level. Keynes believed that Roosevelt's willingness to devalue the dollar made his cooperation crucial to any successful international stabilization plan. "There is one man in the world," Keynes wrote in the *Daily Mail* that June, "who seems to take seriously the business in hand to which others do not more than pay lip service, namely, President Roosevelt, [but] we are all talking as though that man is defeating the alleged objects of the conference" (Rauchway 2015, 70).

But it doesn't follow from any of this that it was Keynes who convinced Roosevelt to torpedo the London Economic Conference. The only evidence for that claim consists of Raymond Moley's (1939, 236) statement that Roosevelt's thinking had been "greatly influenced" by Keynes's (1930) *Treatise on Money*. But that statement, which Rauchway (2015, 51) takes at face value, simply isn't credible. For one thing, Moley contradicts himself. Elsewhere in his memoir he says that Roosevelt's views "seemed to approximate those" found in Keynes's *Treatise*, which suggests something other than his actually having gotten them from Keynes (Moley 1939, 225n20). And in a later work Moley (1966, 4) affirms Tugwell's (1957, 404) claim, mentioned earlier, that Roosevelt "never . . . read anything Keynes wrote." "During all the time I was associated with [Roosevelt]," Moley says, "I never knew him to read a serious book." Assuming that there was any truth at all to Moley's and Tugwell's testimonies, it's far-fetched to suppose that Roosevelt made an exception of Keynes's longest and most abstruse work!

But the most important reason for doubting Moley's claim is simply that there's nothing in the *Treatise on Money* that could possibly have inspired Roosevelt's July 1933 decision. While it's true that in his 1923 *Tract on Monetary Reform* Keynes disparaged attempts to restore the then dismantled gold standard, by 1930, when he published the *Treatise*, "the facts had changed" and so had Keynes's thinking.[6] "Today," Keynes wrote then (1930, 2:338), "the reasons seem stronger . . . to accept, substantially, the fait accompli of an international standard. . . . For to seek the ultimate good *via* an autonomous national system would mean not only a frontal attack on the forces of conservatism, . . . but it would divide the forces of intelligence and goodwill and separate the interests of nations." Such words could hardly have inspired Roosevelt to torpedo the London Economic Conference! Nor are there any other passages in the *Treatise on Money* that are likely to have done so.

Instead of Keynes, the experts whose views almost certainly informed Roosevelt's decisions were Fisher and, above all, Warren. Although Fisher, like Keynes, was never one of Roosevelt's official advisers, unlike Keynes he corresponded with Roosevelt often and met with him on numerous occasions throughout the New Deal. Between late February and early June 1933 alone Fisher sent Roosevelt no fewer than seven letters, all addressing the currency question. In a March 2 letter, Fisher wrote that "the present situation in currency cries to heaven for reflation (up to a reasonable price level about half way back) and, *after such reflation*, for stabilization" (Allen 1977, 568n35, emphasis added). According to William Barber (1996, 33), just before the London Economic Conference began Fisher wrote to Roosevelt again advising him that the United States "should not wait for action by other countries, nor make our action dependent on theirs, nor tie up our standard to theirs irrevocably." The cable's endorsement of "efforts to plan national currencies with the objective of giving those currencies a continuing purchasing power which does not vary in terms of commodities" might have been written by Fisher himself, who long favored the idea.[7]

Warren also urged Roosevelt not to commit to any definite plan to stabilize the dollar. Ever since Roosevelt took office, Warren had been trying to win him over to his theory that as the price of gold rose, so would other commodity prices. After Roosevelt let the dollar float, commodity prices started to rise rapidly while gold depreciated, in apparent confirmation of the theory. Then when it seemed that the United States was about to please Britain by stabilizing the dollar, gold depreciated and prices fell. Between them, these events and Warren's advice played an important role in convincing Roosevelt to resist getting "trapped" (Warren's term) by any proposal to stabilize the dollar's gold value while commodity prices were still well below their pre-Depression levels. The Committee for the Nation, a lobbying group made up, according to Henry Wallace (1934, 60), "largely of businessmen interested in the export trade," with which both Fisher and Warren worked closely, joined them in advising Roosevelt against tying the hands of the United States (Bratter 1941, 532; Pearson, Myers, and Gans 1957, 5603).

In short, US experts appear to have done all the persuading necessary to get Roosevelt to fire off his July 3 cable. Keynes's contribution to Roosevelt's sabotaging of the London Economic Conference consisted of little beyond the support he gave to Roosevelt after the fact by publishing an article in the *Daily Mail*, the title of which called his decision "Magnificently Right."

Sober Advice

While Roosevelt's withdrawal from the London Economic Conference left little doubt that the old gold dollar was history, it offered no clue as to where the dollar's gold value would settle or even whether it would settle at all instead of continuing to float. Nor does Roosevelt himself seem to have known yet. He wanted more advice, and once again he turned for it to US experts, not to Keynes. Some advice came from Fisher and from Yale economist James Harvey Rogers, one of Fisher's many students. But it was George Warren's thinking that ultimately prevailed, and Warren was the least Keynesian of the bunch.

To recall, it was Warren's theory, according to which a sufficient increase in gold's price, however achieved, was sure to deliver on Roosevelt's promise to restore the prices of farm products to their 1926 level, that inspired Roosevelt's ill-fated gold-buying spree. But apart from convincing Roosevelt and Henry Morgenthau, Warren's theory won few converts either in or outside of the Roosevelt administration. "Almost ridiculous" and "hardly worth serious refutation" were the brusque opinions of James Warburg (1934, 136) and Rex Tugwell (1968, 403), respectively, concerning the theory, and they matched those of most economists. Even Fisher, whose views superficially resembled Warren's, insisted that raising gold's price alone wouldn't raise other prices: monetary expansion was needed to get people to spend more. By February 1934, when Roosevelt and Morgenthau quit buying gold and fixed the dollar's official gold content at 59 percent of its former level, Warren's critics had every reason to feel vindicated if not to gloat: the wholesale price index was only 3 percent higher than it had been at the start of the gold buying program in October 1933.[8]

Whether he gloated or not, Keynes was among the most unsparing of those critics. In his December 1933 open letter, it was Warren's theory that Keynes called "crack-brained," observing that it rested on a "set of fallacies." Instead of supposing that gold's appreciation would *cause* higher prices, Keynes (1933a) told Roosevelt, he ought to have gotten both gold's price and those of other commodities up by other means and *then* devalued the dollar accordingly. Because the gold purchase plan put the gold depreciation cart before the price-raising horses of expansionary monetary and fiscal policy, its main result consisted not of higher equilibrium prices but rather of those disturbing "gyrations of the dollar" that seemed to Keynes "more like a gold standard on the booze than the ideal managed currency of my dreams."

In view of Keynes's harsh remarks, it's more than a stretch to claim that "in the general outline of his beliefs, Warren had support from John Maynard Keynes" (Rauchway 2014, 4), much less that those beliefs had secured Keynes's "moral endorsement" (Mitchell 1947, 140–41). In truth, it was Warren's opinions *rather than* Keynes's that Roosevelt heeded. But as Roy Harrod understood, once one discerns that in the mind of the general public "you have to have One Man," a little truth stretching is hard to resist.

The Keynesian Myth, Continued

Big Spenders

What then of New Deal fiscal policy? Here too, John Maynard Keynes's influence has been greatly exaggerated because there were plenty of American proponents of deficit spending during the New Deal who weren't influenced by Keynes and also because Franklin Roosevelt long remained unpersuaded by either their or Keynes's own fiscal policy advice.

Eccles and Currie were only two of many advocates of deficit spending whose thinking wasn't inspired by Keynes. There were plenty of others, many of whom had been calling for bigger deficits long before Roosevelt was elected. For example, as Julian Zelizer (2000, 352–53) notes, years before Keynes began arguing for compensatory fiscal policy to make up for inadequate private investment, William Truffant Foster and Waddill Catchings (1927) had proposed it as a cure for "underconsumption" (see also Gleason 1959).

The Great Depression naturally caused such proposals to multiply. In January 1932, for example, thirty-one economists submitted a report to Congress outlining a plan for $5 billion in spending on public works, to be entirely financed by new borrowing. The report noted that economists had long favored "the construction of public works in periods of depression in order to relieve unemployment and restore purchasing power" (75 Cong. Rec. 1656, 1932). As J. Ronnie Davis (1968, 476–77) reminds us, far from resembling the "classical" straw man, with his unshakable belief in Say's Law, that Keynes erected as a foil against which to display his own more enlightened views, University of Chicago economists, including Frank H. Knight, Henry C. Simons, and Jacob Viner, were among the more outspoken advocates of deficit spending to counter unemployment and deflation. "As far as I know," wrote Knight in May 1932, "economists are completely agreed that the Government should spend as much, and tax as little as possible, at a time such as this"

(75 Cong. Rec. 10323, 1932). As we've seen, Viner went on to form the New Deal's original Brain Trust and to include Lauchlin Currie in it.[1]

Nor were economists alone in calling for deficit spending to combat unemployment. As Joseph Thorndike (2010, 97–98) notes, "many political and business leaders of the 1920s believed that government had a useful role to play in fighting recessions and curbing unemployment. They placed particular faith in the efficacy of increased spending on public works [and] generally agreed that debt finance was the only plausible answer" to the question of how to pay for them. The sharp 1920–1921 depression was a potent catalyst for such thinking—so potent that it caused the ultraconservative Warren Harding to convene the Conference on Unemployment on September 26, 1921. Sherwood Fine (1944, 10) calls that event, which led to "a record expansion of all types of public works by a majority of cities," one of the "most serious attempts" by the United States "to alleviate depressed conditions by a large public works program." Yet Harding himself wasn't keen on involving the federal government in such efforts. It was instead Harding's secretary of commerce who strongly believed that properly timed public works, undertaken by all levels of government, could be a powerful weapon against business downturns. His name was Herbert Hoover.

For the remainder of the 1920s, Hoover (who also served as Calvin Coolidge's commerce secretary) was the federal government's most persistent advocate of countercyclical spending on public works. Even so, Hoover's efforts produced few results, in large part because the rapid recovery from 1920–1921 took the wind out of countercyclical public work advocates' sails. The prevailing thinking, especially among the Republican Party's leaders, was of the same sort that could see little reason for patching a roof so long as the sun was shining.

Once in office, President Hoover at first redoubled his efforts to organize countercyclical public works spending, particularly by proposing what came to be known as "the Hoover Plan" for preventing another economic depression. Among other things, that plan would have had the federal government defer construction during good times in order to create a public works "reserve fund," to be spent when private spending flagged. At $3 billion, the sum Hoover proposed for the fund was almost equal to the entire 1929 federal budget. But thanks once again to the Republican Party leadership, which now held that a "new era" made it unnecessary to prepare for another depression (Howenstine 1946, 495), the Hoover Plan fared no better than Hoover's earlier efforts.

It took the Depression itself to call Republicans' complacency into question. When it did, the movement for compensatory public works seemed to gather steam at last. After the 1929 crash, Hoover promised to make "a special effort" to expand construction work at all levels of government. By early 1930 he'd succeeded in getting twenty-nine state governors to agree on a plan to undertake $1.3 billion worth of combined state and federal public works projects. Thanks to Hoover's efforts, during the first two years of the crisis overall spending on public works tripled.

But the Depression proved to be a double-edged sword, because so far as fiscal conservatives were concerned, the deeper it got, the more important it was to balance the federal budget. In December 1931 James Garfield, who headed the public works subcommittee of the President's Organization on Unemployment Relief, dismissed calls for multimillion-dollar public works bond issues as unsound. "The problem of unemployment," he said, "cannot be solved by any magic of appropriations from the public treasury" (quoted in Hopkins 1936, 59). In a radio address the following March, Ogden Mills, Hoover's recently appointed treasury secretary, expressed the same sentiment. "The foundation upon which the structure of restoring prosperity must rest," he said, "is the unimpaired credit of the national Government" (US Department of the Treasury 1932, 262). By then, with the election looming, Hoover was himself singing the fiscal-conservative tune. A balanced budget, he said, was "the very keystone of recovery" without which "the depression will be prolonged indefinitely" (Slichter 1932).[2]

Thus it fell to what William Dale Reeves (1968, 5) calls "a determined public works faction in the Senate," led by New York Democrat Robert Wagner and Wisconsin Republican Robert La Follette Jr., to take up the cause of increased federal spending on public works in the teeth of the administration's opposition. Wagner and La Follette and other members of the coalition introduced a series of bills proposing billions of dollars in public works to be financed by bond sales, to little avail. Both Wagner and La Follette introduced amendments that would have made a $5.5 billion public works program part of the July 21, 1932, Emergency Relief and Construction Act. But both senators knew perfectly well by then that such large-scale proposals didn't stand a chance with a Republican administration. The act ended up providing for only a bit more than $320 million in public works expenditures. It was to be the only federal spending on public works authorized by the 72nd Congress.

Under Construction

The 73rd Congress ended up spending a lot more on public works than Hoover ever spent, starting with the Public Work Administration's (PWA) $3.3 billion program, provided for by Title II of the National Industrial Recovery Act. But Keynes had nothing to do with this breakthrough. And although Roosevelt didn't veto the measure, as Hoover surely would have, he only signed off on it grudgingly: his chief aim in signing that legislation was the establishment of what he then considered the New Deal's centerpiece—the National Recovery Administration (NRA)—to which the rest of the National Industrial Recovery Act was devoted.

Far from being an integral part of the New Deal, the PWA, name and all, was La Follette's June 1932 amendment, dusted off for the new Congress. Disappointed by Hoover, La Follette and other members of Congress's public works faction supported Roosevelt in the 1932 election. They knew that some New Dealers—Frances Perkins especially—were keen on public works, and they expected Roosevelt to be so as well. But as Reeves (1968) reports, the faction soon learned that the sailing might not be all that smooth. When several shared their hopes over dinner that March with Raymond Moley and Rexford Tugwell, the two Brain Trusters warned them not to press the President too hard, as he "was leery of the arguments for public works" (12).

Still the public works faction pressed on, preparing a draft bill calling for $5 billion in public works, or half a billion less than Wagner and La Follette had each proposed the previous summer. For his part, Roosevelt wondered how the government could possibly spend that much if it tried, a concern that was far from groundless in those as yet unprogressive times. Although Frances Perkins answered with a list that the Construction League, a contractors' association, had prepared with that very question in mind, Roosevelt wasn't convinced, and neither were Lewis Douglas, his budget director, Tugwell, or the other Brain Trust planners (Martin 1976, 263–68).

In the end, Roosevelt compromised by accepting a reduced PWA budget of $3.3 billion. But he never ceased being "leery" of public works. What's more, he deprived those $3.3 billion of much of their potential stimulus effect by drawing on them to finance almost all of the federal government's ordinary construction activities as well as its spending for relief and national defense. Roosevelt also allowed Harold Ickes, the PWA's head, to use its resources slowly and deliberately so as to avoid waste. It was largely owing to Ickes's husbanding, Herbert Stein (1990, 207) says, that it took the Roosevelt administration until 1937 to get annual public works spending up to $710 million. Taking account of not just federal spending on public works but also spending by all levels of government relative to GDP, until World War II the Roosevelt administration never even managed to best the public works spending record set under Hoover in 1930.

Roosevelt's lack of enthusiasm for voluminous public works was, as we've seen, one of the things Keynes tried to counter in his December 1933 open letter. There he urged Roosevelt to make spending, especially on projects "which can be made to mature quickly on a large scale," his first domestic priority. "Could not the energy and enthusiasm, which launched the NIRA in its early days," Keynes (1933a) wrote, "be put behind a campaign for accelerating capital expenditures, as wisely chosen as the pressure of circumstances permits? You can at least feel sure that the country will be better enriched by such projects than by the involuntary idleness of millions."

Keynes returned to this theme in the "Agenda for the President" he published in the London *Times* soon after returning from his 1934 trip to the States. "For six months at least," he wrote, "and probably for a year, [recovery] will mainly depend on the degree of direct stimulus to production deliberately applied by the Administration. Since I have no belief in the efficacy for this purpose of the price and wage raising activities of the NRA, this must chiefly mean the pace and volume of the Government's emergency expenditures" (Keynes 1934). Keynes went on to recommend monthly expenditures of $400 million, "financed out of loans, and not out of taxation," or, according to Lauchlin Currie's later estimates, roughly half again as much as the government's total net "activity-creating" expenditures at the time.

Balancing Act

As Richard Adelstein (1991, 177) observes, far from taking Keynes's advice that he ratchet up the federal government's deficit spending, "Roosevelt held fast to the ideal of a balanced budget and remained the chief opponent within the administration of an aggressive program of public works." Rather than make spending on public works a central component of the New Deal's recovery program, Roosevelt viewed such spending as a mere "auxiliary" to the New Deal's essential recovery "schemes" (Kazakévich 1938, 476).

As we've seen, despite Roosevelt's desire to avoid large deficits, for three fiscal years during the 1930s—1934, 1936, and 1939—his administration's deficits were higher than Hoover's largest. But the 1936 deficit was only as large as it was because Congress overrode Roosevelt's Veterans' Bonus veto. Although federal expenditures more than doubled between 1933 and 1937, federal receipts also rose considerably. Therefore, Roosevelt's deficit spending never quite reached 7 percent of GDP in any fiscal year before the United States entered the war, and no two consecutive New Deal budgets packed a greater fiscal stimulus punch than Hoover's one-year budgets for 1930 and 1931 (Lee 1982, 65). "In brief," E. Cary Brown (1956, 869) says, wrapping up his classic reappraisal of "Fiscal Policy in the 'Thirties," "it took the massive expenditures forced on the nation by the second world war to realize the full potentialities of fiscal policy."

If these facts seem surprising, it's partly because, as Keynes's reputation grew to gigantic proportions during the 1950s and 1960s, historians became increasingly inclined to reinterpret the New Deal generally, and Roosevelt's recovery strategy in particular, as practical applications of Keynes's thinking. According to this revisionist view, if deficit-financed spending on public works didn't go far enough, it must have been the fault not of Roosevelt himself but of either his opponents or his more conservative associates. The generally excellent Zach Carter (2020, 292), for example, says that Henry Morgenthau "urged Roosevelt to pursue a balanced budget to improve the confidence of businessmen in his leadership." In truth, Roosevelt needed no urging.

Popular accounts give Roosevelt both too much and too little credit. In truth, Julian Zelizer (2000, 332) says, fiscal conservatism was not a constraint on but "a key component" of the New Deal, and this was so not just because some of Roosevelt's more important appointees and advisers were fiscal conservatives but also because Roosevelt was one himself. Hence, Roosevelt condemned Hoover's deficits during the 1932 campaign also promised during that October's campaign speech in Pittsburgh to balance the federal budget, provided he could do it without letting anyone starve (Roosevelt 1938, 1:795–812).[3] Far from seeing "a complete and honest balancing of the Federal budget" as a goal at odds with ending the Depression, Roosevelt considered it the only "sound foundation" for a "permanent economic recovery" (807).

Nor did Roosevelt change his tune once in office. Determined to keep his promise, he offered the rabidly orthodox Lewis Douglas the post of budget director, assuring him in doing so that he "was absolutely committed to economy and a balanced budget" (Browder and Smith 1986, 82). Roosevelt then had Douglas draft the legislation that became the Economy Act of March 1933, slashing the federal budget by $243 million. Roosevelt had originally hoped to cut government spending by more than twice that amount. "Too often in recent history," he told Congress in a message defending his plan, "liberal governments have been wrecked on rocks of loose fiscal policy" (Roosevelt 1938, 2:50). According to Arthur Schlesinger (1958, 10), whose account of Roosevelt's efforts is nothing if not sympathetic, "Roosevelt spoke with deep sincerity. His fiscal notions were wholly orthodox. He saw little difference so far as budgets were concerned between a household or a state government on the one hand and the federal government on the other." Although the Economy Act failed to balance the budget and Roosevelt, unlike Douglas, was willing to run "emergency" deficits for the sake of financing public works, he went on trying to balance the budget, especially by finding new ways to increase tax revenues, until after the outbreak of the Roosevelt Recession, when it became all too clear that the cause was lost.

Zelizer is justifiably scornful of what he calls "Whiggish" attempts to portray Roosevelt and the New Dealers generally as Keynesians. In fact, a strong case can be made that Roosevelt's fiscal conservatism was even less "Keynesian" than Herbert Hoover's had been because, as Herbert Stein (1966, 223) explains, resorting to aggressive deficit spending required more than "a new, Keynesian model of the economic system," and even a determined Keynesian would have hesitated to advise heavy deficit spending under the conditions that prevailed during Hoover's presidency. "What was necessary," Stein says, "was a change in the basic facts. There had to be a coordinated or permissive monetary policy, so that government deficits would not force up interest rates to an undesired degree. There had to be either international economic independence or international economic cooperation so that domestic expansionary policy would not be hamstrung by adverse international trade reactions or flight from the currency. . . . The Government's fiscal policy did not begin to change until after these facts had changed."

By February 1934, the basic facts that Stein lists *had* changed. Yet Roosevelt wouldn't be persuaded to engage in deliberate deficit spending for several more years. Only the limited extent of the recovery, together with his unwillingness to withdraw needed relief spending, kept him from actually balancing the budget. Still, in 1937 with another overwhelming election victory behind him and the economy appearing to be making real progress, Roosevelt decided to have another crack at it.

The Keynesian Conversion

Roosevelt's apostasy is supposed to have finally come about as a result of the 1937–1938 recession.[4] In mid-April 1938 in a belated response to that crisis, Roosevelt asked Congress to fund several large-scale government spending programs, to be financed by borrowing rather than increased taxation. Some suppose that Keynes himself finally won the president over to his thinking, for Keynes (1982 [1938]) had written to Roosevelt again that February chiding him for having done little since Keynes's 1934 visit to arrange for spending at the required scale, particularly on housing, public utilities, and transport, and going so far as to blame the downturn on Roosevelt's having "greatly curtailed" public works spending earlier that year. Only "a large scale recourse" to such spending, Keynes wrote, could "maintain prosperity at a reasonable level."

But there are good reasons for supposing that if anyone got Roosevelt to change his mind about deficits, it was not Keynes but Eccles and Harry

Hopkins, with help from Lauchlin Currie, Eccles's economic adviser; Leon Henderson, an economist then working for the Works Progress Administration; and Beardsley Ruml, a director of the New York Federal Reserve Bank and one of five members of Roosevelt's National Resources Committee. Eccles had tried to discourage Roosevelt's attempts at budget balancing with a 1936 memo on the subject, only to have Morgenthau resolve to "dynamite" his arguments (as Eccles later told his staff) lest Eccles should end up displacing him as Roosevelt's fiscal policy adviser. The dynamite worked for a while. But when the economy nose-dived in the fall of 1937, no amount of high explosives could prevent many from thinking that Eccles had been right all along.

The big spenders, with Harry Hopkins taking the lead, then mounted a full-court press. That November, at Hopkin's urging, Currie, Leon Henderson, and Bureau of Labor Statistics head Isador Lubin met with Roosevelt to discuss the recession, which they blamed on the government's austere fiscal policy. The spenders' next move came just after Roosevelt's 1938 annual message several weeks later. With the recession approaching its nadir, Eccles testified before the Senate's Special Committee to Investigate Unemployment and Relief. Asked what would happen if the government raised public spending by $1 billion, he did not hesitate to say that provided the spending "worked quickly enough, and went into consumer-buying powers," it "would act as a great stimulus . . . and would tend, I think, to stop the depression." Eccles tactfully insisted that he was merely answering a question, not recommending a policy (US Senate 1938, 73 and 80), but his message was nonetheless clear.

Finally, that March while Roosevelt was vacationing in Warm Springs, Georgia, Hopkins resolved to win him over to a definite plan for large-scale compensatory spending. For help drafting a memorandum for the purpose he turned to Leon Henderson and Aubrey Williams, the Works Progress Administration's second-in-command, arranging for them to do the job a stone's throw away from the Little White House. Henderson and Williams were to be helped in turn by Currie, who equipped them with a paper of his own (Currie 1938) elaborating upon his previous arguments blaming the 1937 downturn on fiscal austerity.

In most respects, Hopkins's plan went off like clockwork. On April Fools' Day, he took delivery of the requested memo, which he immediately passed on to Roosevelt. A day later, the president was on his way back to Washington with definite plans for a new, large-scale spending program.

Yet to some extent Hopkins's victory was sheer luck, for instead of being mostly written by Henderson, with Williams's help, the memo that changed Roosevelt's mind was to a considerable extent Beardlsey Ruml's handiwork. Ruml happened to be on the *Southerner* passenger train, en route from New

York to a business meeting in Atlanta, when Williams boarded it at Union Station. Like Currie and Eccles, Ruml was a champion of compensatory spending, with a well-established reputation as Washington's "ideas man." So, Williams talked him into coming to Warm Springs to help draft the memo Hopkins had requested. It was Ruml who put forward the memo's thesis "that the competitive capitalist system has been sustained from the beginning by federal intervention to create purchasing power." The thesis was tendentious, but it seems nonetheless to have helped overcome Roosevelt's remaining qualms about "inessential" deficit spending (Collins 1978, 382–83).

Just how much credit Eccles, Hopkins, and their economist colleagues each deserve for getting Roosevelt to finally ask Congress, on April 14, to spend another $3.75 billion on public works and relief (Roosevelt 1941b, 2:21–33) isn't clear. Dean May (1976, 98) says that Currie's views "provided the most convincing justification for a resumption of spending policies forced by circumstances upon a reluctant president," while Patrick Renshaw (1999, 35) gives Eccles top honors. But what matters is that together the administration's own big spenders supplied all the wheels needed to bring the president around. Keynes was wheel number six.

What's more, it's not clear that Roosevelt's newfound willingness to tolerate deficit spending meant that he'd fully embraced Keynesian thinking. Renshaw doesn't think so. Roosevelt's April 14 spending request, he says, "did not mark his conversion to Keynesian notions about how to manage the trade cycle of a capitalist economy" (Renshaw 1999, 350). Frank Freidel (1969, 14) claims that Roosevelt never ceased to be "a staunch believer in a balanced budget." John Kenneth Galbraith, who knew all the actors involved, agrees. In his opinion, despite their temporary victory, Eccles and Currie "did not, at any time, persuade F.D.R." to overcome his dislike of deficits (Galbraith 1984, 5). "It is my view," Galbraith says, "supported by the weight of modern historical judgment, that Roosevelt remained committed to the deeper canons of conservative finance—the broad principle of the balanced budget—until the advent of war swept this issue aside." It was presumably the Roosevelt Galbraith remembers, rather than one convinced that with unemployment topping 16 percent even pyramid building might be worthwhile, who in July 1939 told Henry Morgenthau he was "sick and tired of having a lot of long-haired people around here who want a billion dollars for schools, a billion dollars for public health. Just because a boy wants to go to college is no reason why we should finance it" (Polenberg 1975, 261).

Julian Zelizer (2000, 352–53) likewise considers the view that the 1938 deficit signaled Roosevelt's conversion to Keynesian thinking "misleading." Relative to what Keynes considered necessary, Zelizer points out, the 1938 deficit was very modest: as a proportion of US GDP, it was in fact smaller than the 1936 bonus payment deficit passed over Roosevelt's veto. "Moreover," Zelizer says, "within a year . . . a conservative congressional coalition of southern Democrats and Republicans" was able to push deficit spending back down until World War II took the lid off government spending altogether. Thus, far from being a watershed, the 1938 deficit turned out to be little more than an "augury of the timid, halfhearted way in which Americans would embrace Keynesianism for most of the next forty years" (Brinkley 1995, 104).

But did Americans ever really "embrace" Keynesianism? Although Renshaw (1999, 337) claims that "what could be called a 'Keynesian approach' to economic management had emerged by 1945," the vast amounts the US government spent in "defense of democratic existence" (Roosevelt 1941a) can hardly be attributed to the influence of Keynesian economics. If a "Keynesian approach" did take hold, the proof would have to come afterward, such as during postwar reconstruction. Yet Robert Skidelsky (2001, 498–505), who is nothing if not devoted to Keynes, doubts that it did so even then. "To be sure," he says, "governments consumed a larger share of the national income than before the war and this contributed to stability. But this was because of the extensive post-war nationalizations and expansion of the social services. Neither had an explicit warrant in Keynesian theory; neither was undertaken for Keynesian reasons. Nor for that matter was America's recession-proof military spending." It could well be the case, in other words, that long after the New Deal, Keynesian economists were still telling presidents "to do what they'd already been doing."

✳ ✳ ✳

To return to where our discussion of Keynes's influence began, the New Deal, considered as a program for ending the Great Depression, had relatively little in common with Keynesian economics, considered as a body of advice for doing the same. It follows that to point out the New Deal's shortcomings isn't to criticize either Keynes's own beliefs or those of later Keynesians. If this seems paradoxical, it's only because so many people, including both the New Deal's critics and its champions, wrongly view it as an exercise in Keynesian economic policy, when it was nothing of the kind.

The popular tendency to identify the New Deal with Keynesian economics has had an unfortunate effect on discourses concerning the merits of each. That tendency causes fans of Keynesian economics to rush to the defense of New Deal policies that Keynes himself disparaged. It even causes some to claim that the New Deal brought the Depression to an end, an opinion

Keynes (and everyone who lived through the Depression) would have considered risible. On the other hand, the identification of the New Deal with Keynesian economics causes the New Deal's conservative critics to treat its failure to end the Depression as proof of the wrongheadedness of Keynesian thinking. To think clearly about what the New Deal did or failed to do, one has to recognize that the New Deal and Keynesianism were very different things, just as Roosevelt and Keynes were very different men.

Fear Itself

> There is no place for industry, because the fruit thereof is uncertain.
> THOMAS HOBBES ON THE STATE OF NATURE

In assessing the New Deal's contribution to ending the Great Depression, it's tempting to look only at its policies and programs aimed at that result. But the New Deal was much more than a recovery plan: as its name suggests, it was a novel policy *regime,* and regime changes can have economic consequences beyond those of particular policies they herald.

Regime change can be beneficial. We've already encountered the claim that the Roosevelt administration's willingness to sacrifice sacred cows of economic orthodoxy spurred recovery by boosting inflation expectations. But regime change is a double-edged sword that can slash away at confidence no less than at despair, and many claim that the New Deal ultimately left business confidence in tatters.

"A Gigantic Question Mark"

Economic historian Robert Higgs (1997) is among the better-known proponents of that negative verdict. Higgs claims that whatever hopes the New Deal may initially have raised, it eventually became a source of "pervasive uncertainty among investors about the security of their property rights in their capital and its prospective returns" (564). It was because of this uncertainty, Higgs says, that investment failed to revive after its Hoover-era collapse, causing the Depression to linger on. "The outpouring of business-threatening laws, regulations, and court decisions, the oft-stated hostility of President Roosevelt and his lieutenants toward investors as a class, and the character of the antibusiness zealots who composed the strategists and administrators of the New Deal . . . could hardly have failed to discourage some investors from making fresh long-term commitments" (586).

Higgs wasn't the first to blame the Depression's persistence on what he calls "regime uncertainty." As he himself notes, the accusation dates from the Depression years themselves, when the New Deal stood accused, mainly by conservative businessmen and columnists, of undermining "business confidence." "Before a new factory is built or an old one is enlarged," Dupont's president Lammot du Pont II told members of the National Association of Manufacturers on December 7, 1937, "industry must know with some reasonable degree of certainty the conditions that will prevail once the wheels begin turning" ("Text of du Pont's Address before Industrialists" 1937). Instead, thanks to the New Deal, industry found itself "blanketed by a fog of uncertainty":

> Uncertainty rules the tax situation, the labor situation, the monetary situation and practically every legal condition under which industry must operate. Are taxes to go higher, lower, or stay where they are? We don't know. Is labor to be union or non-union; is the A.F.L. or the C.I.O. to dominate it, and in any event what will be expected of the employer? It is impossible even to guess at answers. Are we to have inflation or deflation, more government spending or less? Industry is without a scrap of knowledge on either subject. Are new restrictions to be placed on capital, new limits on profits? Industry doesn't know. The whole future is a gigantic question mark. ("Text of du Pont's Address before Industrialists" 1937)

Some days later, on New Year's Eve, Alfred Sloan of General Motors bemoaned the failure of the economy's normal "forces of recovery," blaming it on "fear as to the future of American enterprise and the rules upon which it is to be conducted. In other words," Sloan continued, "our difficulties are political economic rather than purely economic. It seems to me that there is one remedy, and only one. Confidence must be reestablished on a firm foundation by demonstrated fact and understanding as to objectives and methods before American business can go forward with confidence. Panaceas will accentuate the lack of confidence that is already existing" (quoted in Akerlof and Shiller 2009, 71–72). "What Mr. Roosevelt has done," wrote conservative columnist David Lawrence, "is to break down the spirit and faith of the business and financial world in the actual safety of a citizen's property and his savings. To strike down this bulwark of the whole economic system is to breed panic and fear of indescribably dangerous proportions" (quoted in Allen 1940, 310).

Nor were Roosevelt's critics all either businessmen or conservatives or both. Already in June 1934, when Roosevelt was still trying to gain businessmen's cooperation and despite the many steps he'd taken that were supposed to make investment more attractive to them, John Maynard Keynes (1934) saw "no likelihood that business of its own initiative will invest in durable goods of sufficient scale [to end the Depression] for many months to come." The problem, Keynes said, was that "the important but intangible state of mind, which we call business confidence, is signally lacking," and confidence was lacking because the business world had been "driven so far from its accustomed moorings into unknown and unchartered waters. The business man, who may be adaptable and quick on his feet in his own particular field, is usually conservative and conventional in the larger aspects of social and economic policy. At the start he was carried away, like other people, by the prevailing enthusiasm. [But now] he is sulky and bothered [and] even begins to look back with longing to the good old days of 1932."

Several years later when the sulking had given way to an outright revolt, Raymond Moley (1939, 373) drew a conclusion very similar to Keynes's. "Confidence," Moley wrote, "is the existence of that mutual faith and good will which encourages enterprises to expand and take risks. . . . And in an age of increased governmental interposition in industrial operations . . . the maintenance of confidence presupposes both a general understanding of the direction in which legislative and administrative changes tend and a general belief in government's sympathetic desire to encourage the development of those investment opportunities whose successful exploitation is a sine qua non for a rising standard of living. This, Roosevelt refused to recognize."

Jacob Viner also believed that the main reason the Depression lingered on "was that businessmen were just living in an atmosphere of lack [of] long-run confidence, and therefore were not investing and were not optimistic" (Fiorito and Nerozzi 2009, 90). So did Joseph Schumpeter (1942, 64–65), who in *Capitalism, Socialism, and Democracy* blamed both "the subnormal recovery" up to 1937 and the slump that followed on the "general change in the attitude of government to private enterprise" since 1933. "So extensive and rapid a change in the social scene," he wrote, "naturally affects productive performance for a time, and so much the most ardent New Dealer must *and also can* admit."

Even a radical socialist could appreciate how, in an economy still dependent on the exertions of private businessmen, government hostility toward them could thwart recovery. Six-time Socialist Party presidential candidate Norman Thomas (1938, 260) considered businessmen's "lack of confidence . . . a great factor" in the 1937–1938 downturn while claiming that Roosevelt had contributed to that lack of confidence through both his actual policies and "the jitters which he gave to an already jittery investing class because of the uncertainties with regard to his future program. . . . There is a point," Thomas said, "where taxes and regulations which reduce the hope of profit, and policies which rightly or wrongly inspire among big and little investors 'lack of confidence,' do keep money out of business and industrial expansion and drive investors to those bond issues which governmental expenditures supply in lavish abundance. The difficulty is that there is no mathematical formula for finding in advance the precise point beyond which this governmental regulation of the profit system cannot safely go" (261).

Scared Stiff

As opinions such as Thomas's suggest, the New Deal gave businessmen the willies in two different ways. One was by heightening regime uncertainty in the strict sense: as the Roosevelt administration's policy experiments multiplied, with no clear end in sight and no telling what might come next, businessmen no longer felt able to plan for the future. The other was by employing rhetoric that vilified those same businessmen or coming up with laws that seemed deliberately aimed at punishing them.

That the New Deal would involve "bold, persistent experimentation" was, as we've seen, something Roosevelt made clear during his 1932 campaign. "It is common sense," he said at Oglethorpe University, "to take a method and try it. If it fails, admit it frankly and try another. But above all, try something" (Roosevelt 1938, 1:646). Such experimentation was bound to complicate business planning. But it complicated it all the more because Roosevelt didn't fully heed his own advice.

The trouble, Jacob Viner remembered, was that Roosevelt "was never able to admit a failure" (Fiorito and Nerozzi 2009, 98). This was so, for example, with respect to the National Recovery Administration (NRA), which Roosevelt refused to kill even after most of his close advisers urged him to have done with it. As late as March 1935, when those advisers all recognized that it was moribund, he was calling it "a very live young lady" and looking forward to renewing it for another two years ("President Pushes Extension of NRA" 1935).

Because of Roosevelt's reluctance to "admit it frankly" when experiments failed, increasing numbers of them ended up running at once, confronting businessmen with "an unprecedented multiplication of administrative rules and regulations" (Rozwenc 1949, v). In the fall of 1934, W. M. Kiplinger asked regular readers of his business newsletter to share their thoughts on New Deal policies. "'The indefiniteness of Washington,'" he wrote in summing up over two thousand letters he received,

> is a subject of complaint by three out of four businessmen. They say business itself contains enough natural hazards, and on these are now superimposed a

whole new set of political hazards. The objection is not so much to any single policy by itself. The objection is rather to a hodgepodge of policies which are sometimes conflicting, which are explained in different ways by different sets of officials, and which create in business minds the impression that the government is in a great state of indefiniteness and confusion.

This confusion makes fear. . . . It's a vague fear, but it is more potent than any tangible situation. (Freidel 1964, 95)

Businessmen's confusion was further compounded by the New Dealers' shifting priorities. "Roosevelt's style," Albert Romasco (1983, 14–15) says, "left businessmen, whose affairs required stability and predictability, in a state of suspended animation about the New Deal. They were reduced to guesswork about Roosevelt's recovery program." The legislation passed during 1935, for example, marked such a decisive shift in the Roosevelt administration's priorities—mainly toward reform and away from recovery—that many historians consider it a regime change in itself, a "Second New Deal" (Wilson 1966). "The impact of these multitudinous measures upon a bewildered industrial and financial community," Benjamin Anderson (1949, 362) recalled some years later, "was extraordinarily heavy."

The Second New Deal also brought a change for the worse in the Roosevelt administration's demeanor toward businessmen. In his 1934 letter, Keynes had urged Roosevelt to dispel the "atmosphere of disappointment, disillusion, and perplexity" to which the New Deal was contributing by assuring businessmen that "they know the worst." But starting in the spring of 1935 Roosevelt, instead of following Keynes's advice, did just the opposite. Upset by the Supreme Court's NRA decision, convinced that business organizations were sabotaging the New Deal,[1] egged on by progressives in his own administration, and determined to steal a march on Huey Long and other radicals, Roosevelt adopted an increasingly scornful public attitude toward businessmen that seemed calculated to heighten rather than quell their fears.

Nor was the change one in rhetoric alone. Roosevelt took direct aim at "economic royalists"—a set indistinguishable in practice from the merely wealthy and all sufficiently "big" businessmen—by recommending in his June 19 message to Congress several new taxes specifically aimed at wealthy individuals and large corporations, including a graduated tax on corporate income (Roosevelt 1938, 4:270–77). And Roosevelt intended this to be a mere start. "Ultimately," he said, he planned to do more to "discourage unwieldy and unnecessary corporate surpluses." The press dubbed Roosevelt's plan a "Wealth Tax" with good reason, for unlike previous revenue plans, this one was less concerned with raising revenue than with soaking the rich.

To say that the Wealth Tax plan upset businessmen would be a heroic understatement. According to Raymond Moley (1939, 316), coming as it did little more than six months after Roosevelt's annual budget message advising against *any* new taxes, and with no other warning whatsoever, it threw them into "paroxysms of fright." Never before had there been a tax proposal so clearly aimed at penalizing wealth and, in the case of corporations, mere bigness. As Fred Clausen, chairman of the Chamber of Commerce's Committee on Federal Finance, pointed out during the Ways and Means Committee hearings on the plan, the tax meant that a company with $800 million in capital that earned $8 million—a return on investment of just 1 percent—would be taxed at a higher rate than one that made $120,000 on an investment of just $600,000, a 20 percent return (Thorndike 2009, 43). Other businessmen and business representatives lined up at the same hearings to condemn the plan, all echoing the words of George H. McCaffrey, director of research at New York's Merchants Association, who said that the tax would "impair business confidence when every attempt should be made to increase it" (43).

One ought, of course, to be wary of such complaints. Businessmen are never happy to pay new taxes, and they don't mind exaggerating the adverse consequences of having to pay them. They may even consider doing so part of their duty to their shareholders. But businessmen weren't the only ones to worry that the Wealth Tax would stifle recovery. Besides economists, many journalists shared their dim view, including the *Philadelphia Inquirer*'s editorial staff. "Without warning," they groused, Roosevelt "bears down upon the slowly reviving forces of returning prosperity with a tax program to lure hosannas from the something-for-nothing followers of Huey Long, 'Doc' Townsend, Upton Sinclair, and the whole tribe of false prophets" (Thorndike 2009, 42).

Power Play

The 1935 Revenue Act wasn't the only measure that had businessmen shuddering that summer. Less than a week after it became law, with only relatively minor revisions, Roosevelt signed the still more controversial Public Utility Holding Company Act, granting the Securities and Exchange Commission the power to break up the nation's utility holding companies.

On the eve of the Depression, Paul Mahoney (2012) explains, most US electric and gas companies were directly controlled by trusts or holding companies. Groups of smaller utility holding companies were in turn controlled by a smaller number of larger holding companies and so on, for several layers.

Three gigantic holding companies at the apex of this holding company pyramid ultimately controlled more than 80 percent of the nation's power companies.

Up to that time, the consolidation of the utilities industry had awarded consumers and investors with falling electricity prices and robust returns. Even after the crash, utilities held up well. Then, in June 1932, Insull Utility Investments, one of three holding companies at the top of the pyramid, failed, forcing many other holding companies to fail in turn. Some 600,000 utility shareholders faced huge losses.[2]

The Insull empire's collapse turned Samuel Insull, its septuagenarian founder, into a symbol of the greed and corruption many blamed for the whole boom and bust. The Insull collapse also encouraged Roosevelt, who had already crossed swords with utilities as New York's governor (Bellush 1955, 208–42), to make reforming them part of his New Deal. Roosevelt threw down the gauntlet during his September 21, 1932 campaign speech in Portland, Oregon, assailing the "Insull monstrosity" and calling its business methods "wholly contrary to every sound public policy" (Roosevelt 1938, 1:727–42).[3]

Roosevelt's election left no doubt that a reform of the electric utility industry was coming. But no one knew just when or what form it would take: some New Dealers favored regulation, others wanted to ban utility holding company pyramiding, and still others wanted to ban utility holding companies altogether. This uncertainty caused surviving utility share prices, which had still been outperforming the market despite Insull's downfall, to plummet.

Utility reform stayed on Roosevelt's back burner until July 1934, when he appointed the National Power Policy Committee to study the utility companies and propose legislation. The committee didn't complete its report until late January 1935. In the meantime, investors remained on edge, with many fearing the worst. In a column titled "Utility Baiting," the *Commercial and Financial Chronicle* (1935a, 351) reported on what it called the "wholesale slaughter" of utility holding companies. "The attack of the Administration upon the utility industry," it noted, "does not seem to abate with the passage of time." Instead, "the plans of the President to conduct a vigorous, and apparently an indiscriminate, attack upon utility holding companies [are] proceeding with dispatch."

Electric Shock

The administration finally introduced its bill on February 6, 1935, ending the suspense, but confirming investors' worst fears. The bill included what quickly became known as a "death sentence" provision, granting the Securities and Exchange Commission the power to not just put a stop to pyramiding but also force utility holding companies to disband altogether. That drastic step would expose those companies' many shareholders to large fire-sale losses.[4] In less than a month the bill had called forth a larger flood of criticism than had any prior New Deal measure (Mahoney 2012, 44).

But although the administration had made up its mind, the final outcome remained very much in doubt. The bill now went on a six-month-long legislative roller-coaster ride during which the death sentence itself was condemned, miraculously pardoned and rehabilitated, and threatened with judicial murder once more. In mid-August, a compromise was reached: the revised bill would ban pyramiding. But it would allow individual holding companies to survive provided each controlled a geographically contiguous set of operating companies. At last, on August 26, 1935, Roosevelt signed the Public Utility Holding Company Act, better known as the Wheeler-Rayburn Act. Yet even that didn't quite settle things. The industry fought back by filing a suit challenging the new law's constitutionality. It wasn't until March 28, 1938, that the final curtain came down on the dispute with a Supreme Court ruling in the government's favor.[5]

Our concern isn't with the Wheeler-Rayburn Act's constitutionality or its overall merits. It's with the economic consequences of the fears that haunted investors and businessmen while the threat of drastic reform dangled over the utility industry like the sword of Damocles. In his first open letter to Roosevelt, Keynes (1933a) reminded him that he was "engaged in a double task, recovery and reform," and that "for the first, speed and quick results are essential." He went on to say that "on the other hand, even wise and necessary reform may, in some respects, impede and complicate recovery. For it will upset the confidence of the business world and weaken its existing motives to action before you have time to put other motives in their place."

Whatever might be said in favor of Roosevelt's assault on utility conglomerates, it flew in the face of Keynes's advice.

No Love Lost

Having dealt with the utilities, Congress adjourned. Soon after, Roosevelt received a letter, dated August 26, from Roy Howard, an influential newspaper editor and publisher who had backed Roosevelt's 1932 campaign. "Businessmen who once gave you sincere support," the letter warned, "are now not merely hostile, they are frightened." Howard went on to urge the president to "undo the damage that has been done by misinterpretation of the New Deal" by posting a public reply to his letter promising "a breathing spell to industry" ("Text of the Roosevelt-Howard Letters" 1935). To Howard's surprise and the business community's immense relief, Roosevelt's reply, published in early September, didn't just grant the requested breathing spell. It said that Roosevelt's legislative program had "reached substantial completion." New Deal experimentation had finally run its course. Or so it seemed.

And how the public breathed! Moley (1939, 318) later recalled its response, which "astonished" Roosevelt. "Thousands of letters and telegrams came in congratulating the president. Stock issues hit the highest level since September 1931 and the Gallup poll showed later a spectacular rise in Roosevelt's popularity." According to Gary Dean Best (1991, 110–11), "Businessmen, business writers, and business periodicals hailed the beginnings of the long-awaited recovery. Only a few skeptics warned that despite any boom that might occur, the foundations for a genuine recovery had not yet been laid."

Alas, as some of those skeptics feared, the breathing spell turned out to be just that: an opportunity for businessmen to gulp some air before the next wave broke over them. That wave was not long in coming. No sooner did Congress reconvene than Roosevelt went on the offensive again. Instead of offering the usual bland account of economic conditions, with suggestions for improving them, he made his 1936 State of the Union address the occasion for what many considered an antibusiness diatribe:

> We have returned the control of the Federal Government to the City of Washington. To be sure, in so doing, we have invited battle. We have earned the hatred of entrenched greed. The very nature of the problem that we faced made it necessary to drive some people from power and strictly to regulate others. I made that plain when I took the oath of office in March, 1933. I spoke of the practices of the unscrupulous money-changers who stood indicted in the court of public opinion. I spoke of the rulers of the exchanges of mankind's goods, who failed through their own stubbornness and their own incompetence. I said that they had admitted their failure and had abdicated. . . . [B]ut now with the passing of danger they forget their damaging admissions and withdraw their abdication. . . . They seek the restoration of their selfish power. (Roosevelt 1938, 5:13–14)

Roosevelt then deftly turned the tables on those businessmen who complained that his policies undermined their confidence:

> Their weapon is the weapon of fear. I have said, "The only thing we have to fear is fear itself." That is as true today as it was in 1933. But such fear as they instill today is not a natural fear, a normal fear; it is a synthetic, manufactured, poisonous fear that is being spread subtly, expensively and cleverly by the same people who cried in those other days, "Save us, save us, lest we perish." I am confident that the Congress of the United States well understands the facts

and is ready to wage unceasing warfare against those who seek a continuation of that spirit of fear. (Roosevelt 1938, 5:17)

Roosevelt's verbal assaults on big business went on for the rest of that year, reaching a sort of apotheosis during his famous Madison Square Garden campaign speech that October. Comparing "business and financial monopoly" and other manifestations of "organized money" to an "organized mob," he promised that they'd met their match. And he made no bones about having a personal score to settle. "They are unanimous in their hate of me," he said. "And I welcome their hatred" (Roosevelt 1938, 5:568).

Sticks, Stones, and Votes

Roosevelt knew he was putting the recovery at risk by declaring war on "organized money." He understood that even if he were unstinting in his support for it, federal spending couldn't be expected to make up for the lack of private investment. He also knew that Roy Howard was far from alone in suggesting that Roosevelt's hostile stance was discouraging investment.

But there was good economics, and there was good politics. Jacob Viner once told Roosevelt that he didn't think "renewing his [Roosevelt's] warfare against business" was a good idea (Fiorito and Nerozzi 2009, 17). "Viner," Roosevelt said in reply, "you don't understand my problem. If I'm going to succeed and if my administration is going to succeed, I have to maintain a strong hold on my public. In order to maintain a firm hold on the public I have to do something startling every once in a while. I mustn't let them take me for granted." Above all, having "to maintain a strong hold on the public" meant having to stay in office, and in 1935 that meant heading off the threat posed by Huey Long, whose aggressively redistributionist "Share the Wealth" movement had become immensely popular. Until Long was assassinated that September, the Roosevelt administration feared that, by running as a third candidate in the 1936 election, he might divert enough votes from Roosevelt to hand the Republicans a victory. This fear played no small part in shaping both Roosevelt's rhetoric and some Second New Deal legislation, including the Wealth Tax (Snyder 1975).

Words, every child learns, aren't sticks or stones. But that doesn't make them inconsequential. If startling words can gain votes, they can also discourage investment, all the more so if businessmen believe the sentiments to be ones shared by large segments of the public. Businessmen realize, Schumpeter (1939, 1046) wrote, "that they are on trial before judges who have the verdict in their pocket beforehand, that an increasing part of public opinion is impervious to their point of view, and that any particular indictment will, if successfully met, at once be replaced with another." In the same vein, Kenneth Roose (1954, 224) observed some years later that "in a political and social environment which was infected with such hatreds and distrusts, the risks and uncertainties of investment decision were seriously increased." But as usual it was Raymond Moley (1939, 132–33) who put it most piercingly: Roosevelt's "vague, veiled threats of punitive actions," Moley said, "tore the fragile texture of credit and confidence upon which the very existence of business depends."

The Unkindest Cut

In the midst of Roosevelt's war of words, Congress passed the 1936 Revenue Act, including the notorious "undistributed profits tax." That provision taxed firms' retained net earnings (i.e., those not paid out as dividends) at rates that rose with the share of retained to total earnings. The maximum rate was 27 percent for a share of 60 percent or more. The administration hoped that, besides raising another $600 million in revenue, the new tax would stimulate spending by discouraging corporations from hoarding cash.

But to many the new tax, the first word of which came in Roosevelt's supplemental March 3, 1936, budget message to Congress, was just another New Deal assault on business. "No other single measure, except possibly utility legislation, was so disapproved of by business" (Roose 1954, 212–13). Writing in 1938, Willard Thorp, director of economic research for Dun & Bradstreet, remarked that "with respect to no other legislative action of the last several years has business presented such a strong and unified front" (213–14n16). Thanks to this concerted opposition, and despite Roosevelt's refusal to sign any tax bill that excluded it, the undistributed profits tax was omitted from the 1938 Revenue Act and allowed to expire at the end of that year.

Rightly or wrongly, businessmen saw the undistributed profits tax as confirming the then widespread belief that the government was out to get them. As George Lent (1948, 111–12) observes in his comprehensive assessment of the tax, "With the major exception of public utilities and railroads, American industry has expanded largely through the reinvestment of corporation earnings." The undistributed profits tax therefore "raised a fundamental issue over the proper direction and control of business investment and expansion."

A Bark Worse Than Its Bite

How much did the undistributed profits tax really matter? According to Lent (1948, 175), its direct consequences "do not appear to have been so serious as its most violent critics have charged, or so desirable as its most ardent proponents have claimed." The tax ended up raising only $145 million and $176 million in 1936 and 1937, respectively, with only 2.5 percent of firms paying the maximum 27 percent rate. Most others instead managed, through increased dividend payments or otherwise, to keep the surcharge at 7 percent, its lowest level.

Nor do the tax's direct effects on investment seem to have been as severe as many feared they might be. Although it reduced retained earnings, to the extent that it did so by boosting dividends and other firm expenditures, the tax supplied others with means for purchasing more securities. And larger firms were able, Lent says, to make up for most of their loss of internal funds by selling securities or borrowing from banks. It was mainly small and medium-sized firms that found themselves placed "at a disadvantage in securing funds for growth" (Lent 1948, 158, 161, 188).[6]

But while the undistributed profits tax may not have severely reduced businesses' access to funds, it doesn't follow that fears raised by the tax didn't reduce their desire to invest. According to Roose (1954, 224), by tending "to increase the uncertainty concerning the nature of the economic system of the future," those fears did just that. "It would be a hardy investor indeed," Moley (1939, 311) wrote, "who would venture his money in an enterprise that had no opportunity to acquire the very essentials of permanent corporate health." It's perhaps because they harbored such doubts that in a survey of three thousand Illinois manufacturers, 83 percent of them reported having "deferred or abandoned plans for plant expansion or rehabilitation" because of the tax (Lent 1948, 132).

More recent research by Ellen McGrattan, using a model in which uncertainty about future dividend tax rates plays a central part, lends support to Roose's claim. "If, in addition to raising individual income tax rates," McGrattan (2012, 1516) finds, "the government introduces a tax on the undistributed profits of corporations, as the U.S. government did in 1936, then investment is . . . negatively impacted. The introduction of such a tax would naturally affect the recovery in the second half of the 1930s." In fact, McGrattan says, "tax rates on undistributed profits . . . led to [a] dramatic decline in investment" (1539).

Sent Packing

No survey, however brief, of confidence-shaking New Deal schemes would be complete that overlooked the court-packing plan originally hatched the day after Christmas 1936. Still seething from the Supreme Court's overturning of the National Industrial Recovery Act and Agricultural Adjustment Act,

Roosevelt had been looking for a way to bring the Supreme Court to heel, and he thought his attorney general had found it. The plan couldn't have been simpler: the administration would author a bill to add up to six new justices to the bench, ostensibly for the sake of reducing the heavy burden being borne by the then-present justices.

Alas, the plan's real purpose also couldn't have been more transparent. No sooner was it unveiled on February 5, 1937, than its critics—including many Democrats—condemned it as an assault on the Supreme Court's independence. Although the administration pulled no punches in trying to push the measure through, it ultimately failed, thanks in part to a scathing Senate Judiciary Committee report on the bill saying that it "should be so emphatically rejected that its parallel will never again be presented to the free representatives of the free people of America" (US Senate 1937, 23). A month later Senate majority leader Joseph T. Robinson, who'd been leading the administration's charge in the Senate, died of a heart attack, and a week after that the bill was sent back to committee, where the court-packing provision itself died.

The judicial implications of Roosevelt's court-packing effort don't concern us. But its effects on business confidence do. Although Roosevelt himself never revealed the "kind of economic reform that his 'reinvigorated court' was supposed to approve" (Moley 1939, 364), according to Gary Dean Best (1991, 151), Roosevelt's "determination to dominate the court convinced business and other critics that Roosevelt had in mind another sweeping program of business control akin to the NRA." Considering the almost universal unpopularity of the original NRA, and the extent to which it impeded recovery, that would seem to have been a frightening prospect indeed.

✶ ✶ ✶

Such were the more noteworthy instances of New Deal proposals, rhetoric, and actual policies said to have shaken businessmen's confidence and undermined their willingness to invest. The vehement response these provoked may itself seem sufficient proof that they hindered economic recovery. But it isn't: by the time the New Deal entered its second phase, hissing Roosevelt at the Trans-Lux and other displays of Roosevelt-hating had become a sort of national pastime among businessmen and the relatively well-to-do. At least some of this hating, Frederick Lewis Allen (1940, 234) observes, "was a form of conscious self-indulgence in the emotional satisfaction of blaming a personal scapegoat for everything that went wrong." It follows that "a good deal of the bitter anti-Roosevelt talk [cannot] be taken at its face value" and that we must look at other evidence before deciding the merit of the regime uncertainty hypothesis.

Fear Itself, Continued

Proving It

Nothing seems more plausible on its face than the claim that policy shocks such as those we've surveyed, coming as they did from a president who was often openly hostile to businessmen, discouraged investment. It's no doubt largely owing to this, and to businessmen's own insistence that New Deal policies frightened them, that the regime uncertainty hypothesis has gained adherents among economists.

But *proving* that regime uncertainty really mattered is an altogether different kettle of fish. It means establishing, first, that regime uncertainty is *theoretically* capable of causing a substantial and persistent decline in investment spending and, second, that it did in fact account for low investment levels during the New Deal.

Of these challenges, the theoretical one has been met reasonably well. Numerous studies show how, in theory, bad news, uncertainty shocks, risk shocks, and such might lead to substantial reductions in investment, employment, and output. Some years ago, for example, Ben Bernanke (1983a) showed how even risk-neutral firms' propensity to proceed with irreversible investment projects can be very sensitive to "downside uncertainty." Bernanke thus added a little formal flesh to the bare-bones reasoning of John Maynard Keynes, Schumpeter, and other Depression-era writers who worried about businessmen's shaken confidence. Since Bernanke's paper appeared, numerous other works, including Pindyck (1991), Dixit and Pindyck (1994), Bachmann and Bayer (2013), and Stokey (2016), have built on its "wait-and-see" hypothesis.

Related strands of research explore the role of "animal spirits," "sunspots," and business sentiments in propagating business cycles. Roger Farmer (2021), for example, constructs a model in which investment spending depends on exogenous shocks to would-be investors' beliefs, meaning their confidence or optimism. The model implies that even a temporary bout of pessimism can permanently lower an economy's capital stock, output, employment, and consumption. Not surprisingly, a permanent adverse investment shock has similar but larger long-run effects. Farmer's analysis implies furthermore that offsetting increases in government consumption (relief spending, for example) can't compensate for adverse investment shocks because they don't make up for the lost capital investment.

These and other theoretical studies lend credence to the late Depression-era complaint that the New Deal's "stimulated revival" was no substitute for "a more normally balanced expansion, predicated upon long-run undertakings by business leadership in an environment sufficiently secure from interference to justify assumption of risk" (Crum, Gordon, and Wescott 1938, 43).

Regime-Change Dummies

Unlike some Depression-era writers, Farmer doesn't identify confidence shocks with any sort of government interference. Instead, he treats them as random autonomous events, the dimming and brightening of what Keynes called "animal spirits." Whether certain New Deal events also qualify as confidence shocks is something statistical evidence alone can establish. Alas, designing suitable statistical tests is anything but easy.

One approach to the challenge has been to identify certain events during the Depression as policy shocks and to then assign dummy variables to the dates on which they occur. The economic significance of the events—their bearing on investment and other macroeconomic variables—can then be assessed empirically using statistical models that control for other fundamental determinants of the same variables.

In a study that took this approach some years ago, Thomas Mayer and Monojit Chatterji (1985) conclude that of six political shocks they identify, only one—the outcome of the 1938 presidential election—influenced investment as the business confidence hypothesis predicts. That shock to confidence is also the only supposedly positive shock those authors consider. The other supposedly negative shocks appear, in contrast, to have had no effect at all on investment or to have influenced it the "wrong" way, that is, by encouraging instead of discouraging it. On the whole, Mayer and Chatterji conclude, "the data reject the hypothesis that the New Deal frightened off business investment" (913).

But Mayer and Chatterji's test leaves a lot to be desired. They themselves suggest one reason why, namely, that most investment in the 1930s "consisted of replacing worn-out equipment to keep factories running," making it "less likely to be sensitive to political shocks" (Mayer and Chatterji 1985, 918). As we've seen, for much of the period under study, capital was actually being consumed faster than it was being replaced. For that reason alone, one might not expect to find large investment effects of negative political shocks. Instead of causing investment to fall much further, such shocks were more likely to have mattered by precluding an investment *revival*.

A more serious shortcoming of Mayer and Chatterji's study concerns the political shocks they look at and their understanding of how would-be investors should have responded to them. Of the six specific shocks they consider, three consist of the outcomes of the elections of 1934, 1936, and 1938. Because they reinforced the Democratic majority, the 1934 and 1936 election outcomes are classified by Mayer and Chatterji as negative shocks, meaning ones that should have discouraged investment, while the 1938 election, which resulted in large Republican gains, is considered a positive shock. The remaining three shocks, all supposedly negative, consist of the January 1937 General Motors (GM) sit-down strike and two compound shocks: one comprising policy developments between March and June 1933 and the other comprising those for May through August 1935.

To call Mayer and Chatterji's reckoning of New Deal policy shocks idiosyncratic is being generous. For starters, it leaves out several of the era's most notorious negative shocks, including Roosevelt's July 27, 1933, announcement of the President's Reemployment Agreement (marking the actual start of widespread industrial codes); his February 6, 1935, introduction of utility holding company legislation; his January 3, 1936, address to Congress renewing his war against "economic autocracy"; his March 3, 1936, budget proposing the undistributed profits tax; and his February 5, 1937, unveiling of his court-packing plan. Mayer and Chatterji's account also leaves out the positive shocks consisting of the May 27, 1935, Schechter decision and Roosevelt's September 7, 1936, "breathing spell" pledge. All except the first of these developments came as a surprise; and although utility legislation of some sort was long anticipated, the administration's extreme plan, with its notorious "death sentence," was not.

As for Mayer and Chatterji's compound shocks, although these do encompass some notorious negative shocks, they lump them together with others generally considered positive. The March through June 1933 period, for example, witnessed the resolution of the banking crisis and the removal of the US economy's "golden fetters," both of which are generally assumed to have assisted recovery by replacing fears of further deflation with positive inflation expectations. The passage of the National Industrial Recovery Act is also generally supposed to have boosted output, if only because it gave business-men a reason to anticipate higher input costs. It's hardly surprising, then, that Mayer and Chatterji find no evidence that the events of March through June 1933, considered as a whole, lowered investment. Mayer and Chatterji's second compound shock, for May–August 1935, suffers from the same drawback as the first, bundling negative shocks with positive ones, the latter consisting of the May 27, 1935, Schechter decision, which put paid to the National Recovery Administration (NRA), and Joseph Robinson's July 14 death, which did the same to Roosevelt's court-packing gambit.

Turning to Mayer and Chatterji's third and final nonelection shock—the GM sit-down strike of January 1937 (which actually began on December 30)—that event ended on February 11 with GM's formal recognition of the United Auto Workers union as its workers' sole bargaining agent. Because the re-gression results for this strike dummy assign "wrong" (positive) coefficients, some of them significant, to almost all the investment variables they consider, Mayer and Chatterji conclude that the strike didn't discourage investment.

But this finding too deserves scrutiny. It is, first of all, highly counter-intuitive. The GM strike is generally considered the most important strike in American labor history. It was also among the most disruptive: lasting forty-four days, it involved 136,000 GM workers and prevented almost 300,000 cars from being built. Forcibly removing the strikers was unthinkable, if only be-cause of the damage it was likely to do to GM's equipment and plant. Yet the alternatives of either letting the strike continue indefinitely or yielding to the United Auto Workers' demands can hardly have lifted businessmen's spirits! Nor need we rely on intuition alone to suspect that something is amiss with Mayer and Chatterji's results. A painstaking study of (mostly) Depression-era strikes' effect on industry stock returns by John Dinardo and Kevin F. Hallock (2002, 219) finds that the strikes had "large, negative effects," particularly so when they were long-lasting, led to violence and resulted in union recogni-tion.[1] The GM strike checked all three boxes, and how!

It seems likely, on closer consideration, that Mayer and Chatterji's econo-metric results refer to the GM strike's short-run consequences only rather than its more adverse longer-term effects. As Joshua Hausman (2016, 429) explains, although from auto industry executives' perspective GM's union-ization was a negative supply shock, since it was bound to eventually compel them to raise their products' prices and reduce output, its more immediate effects where quite different. At first, *anticipated* auto price increases "brought auto sales forward." The resulting rush of orders, combined with a produc-tion backlog due to the strike itself, was an exceptional poststrike surge in the quantity of automobiles produced, with GM running its plants overtime

(452). When GM finally got around to raising auto prices, sales plummeted. That's when auto industry production and investment really flagged, enough, Hausman claims, to have contributed substantially to the 1937–1938 downturn.

Shocking Elections

We still haven't gotten to the most serious shortcoming of Mayer and Chatterji's study: its understanding of how election outcomes influence investment. Mayer and Chatterji argue that because the 1934 and 1936 election results reinforced the Democratic majority, they ought to have discouraged investment. Instead, those results seem to have made little difference or to have made a positive difference. The 1936 election appears, for example, to have led to a significant *increase* in orders for foundry equipment. Mayer and Chatterji therefore conclude that the New Deal hadn't "frightened off" business investment after all.

But it isn't simply bad outcomes that frighten investors; it's also not knowing what's in store, hence "regime *uncertainty*." When election *campaigns* with uncertain outcomes unnerve investors or otherwise convince them to avoid committing themselves to further investments, election *results* can come as a relief and can do so even when the results themselves are disappointing. In that case, instead of declining further following an unwanted election outcome, business activity may merely increase less than it would have had the election gone the other way.

In fact, conventional wisdom long had it that "the months leading up to a presidential election are apt to be months of uncertainly" during which "business is likely to run below normal" (Putney 1936). Although the pattern that wisdom predicted didn't actually hold for most elections before 1936 (Ogburn and Jaffe 1936), it did for some, and there are good reasons for supposing that the 1936 election was one of them. Precisely because the stakes in it were so high, the campaign leading to that election was expected to have an exceptionally chilling effect on business, as *CQ Researcher*'s Bryant Putney reported at the time:

> The impact of the New Deal policies on business has been greater than under any previous peacetime administration, and the resistance of the business community to these policies is likely to reach its high point doing the months leading up to the election. . . . The growing schism between business and the administration, widened by the unexpected stand taken by the President in his [January 3] message, foreshadows a determined fight to defeat him, while the importance attached to that result by the business world may tend to check recovery pending the outcome of the election. . . . Under such conditions it is

at least questionable whether any large-scale expansion of private enterprise will take place during 1936. (Putney 1936)

The circumstances Putney describes are precisely the sort that inform Ben Bernanke's "wait and see" hypothesis. "It seems reasonable to suppose," Putney (1936) says, "that if industry sees a chance of escaping regulation it may withhold decisions on proposed expansions until after the election." Leonard Ayres likewise considered it likely that industrialists and investors would adopt a wait-and-see policy during the months leading to the election. "In the second half of the year," Ayres observed in December 1935, "we shall be engaged in the election campaign, which will largely center on problems concerning the relationships between government and business. It seems probable that during such a year the volume of business discussion will reach unprecedented heights, while physical production and new enterprise will be restricted to modest progress" (*Commercial and Financial Chronicle* 1935b, 3759).

A Run of Regimes

Jason Taylor and Todd Neumann (2013) also investigate the macroeconomic effects of New Deal policy shocks using a dummy variable approach. Like Mayer and Chatterji, they treat entire stretches of time as distinct regime-change shocks; in fact, they consider no other sort. But Taylor and Neumann's identification of relevant shocks is more plausible, as is their understanding of the shocks' significance. And unlike Mayer and Chatterji, Taylor and Neumann find that New Deal regime changes often impeded economic recovery.

I say "regime changes" because Taylor and Neumann recognize six distinct New Deal regimes. In chronological order, these are the hundred days regime (March–July 1933); the President's Reemployment Agreement regime (starting August 1, 1933, and ending for each industry when it adopted its own NRA codes); an NRA regime (starting for each industry when it adopted its own codes and ending with the May 27, 1935, Schechter decision); a National Labor Relations Board regime (April 1937 through October 1938); and a Fair Labor Standards Act regime, starting in November 1938 and lasting through the end of Taylor and Neumann's sample period. Unlike Mayer and Chatterjie, Taylor and Neumann (2013, 590) find that most of the regime-change shocks they consider had significant effects on output, wage rates, and other macroeconomic variables "that cannot be fully explained . . . by fiscal or monetary policy" or other factors their study controls for.

Turning to particulars, Taylor and Neumann (2013, 590–91) find that their hundred days regime led to significant *increases* in wage rates, prices, and output, "suggesting a positive demand shock." That's just what one would expect given the ending of both the banking crisis and the gold standard during that period and the fact that the NRA hadn't yet led to the establishment of industry codes. The PRA regime also boosted wage rates, but unlike the hundred days it had hours and output falling "sharply." These were predictable consequences of the blanket codes the agreement introduced. As NRA "codes of fair competition" were adopted, employment fell again, as did output (although the coefficient on the last is not significant). These too are expected consequences, in this case of industrial cartelization. Finally, the Supreme Court's April 1937 upholding of the National Labor Relations Act boosted wage rates and lowered output and hours, much as the PRA appears to have done.

Unfortunately, although Taylor and Neumann's study reports the effects of New Deal regime changes on employment, hours, wages, prices, and output, it doesn't investigate their effects on investment. Consequently, the study offers only limited support for the "regime uncertainty" or "business confidence" hypotheses: regime changes that reduced output presumably discouraged investment in the means of production. But *by how much?* For answers to that question, one must turn to other research.

Counting on Confidence

In principle, instead of identifying particular confidence shocks by which to test the regime uncertainty hypothesis, one can test it using continuous measures of the extent of policy uncertainty. Until relatively recently, no such measures existed. But economists were inspired to develop several because of the Great Recession, the persistence of which was blamed by many on US policy experiments, including the Fed's resort to unconventional monetary policy, and the uncertainty those experiments bred. The best-known result of these efforts, the Economic Policy Uncertainty Index developed by Scott Baker, Nicholas Bloom, and Steven Davis (2016), measures uncertainty by the number of articles in various newspapers containing the terms "uncertainty," "uncertain," "economic," or "economy" together with any of the following: "congress," "legislation," "white house," "regulation," "Federal Reserve," and "deficit."

Not surprisingly, the Economic Policy Uncertainty Index reaches its highest levels during the Great Depression and its second highest during the Great Recession. A study using the index to investigate the 2007–2009 financial crisis also finds "a strong negative relationship between policy uncertainty and capital investments," with that uncertainly accounting for almost a third of the decline in such investment that took place then (Gulen and Ion 2016, 561).

Such evidence is highly suggestive. Still it falls short of establishing that scary policies or the threat thereof hindered investment and recovery during the New Deal.

Work by Sharon Harrison and Mark Weder (2006) comes considerably closer to doing just that. They develop a Great Depression–era time series for what they call "sunspots": changes in confidence that can't be attributed to past or current changes in such economic "fundamentals" as the growth rate of output, the real money stock, the price level, and real interest rates. Because their research predates the work of Baker and his colleagues, Harrison and Weder use a proxy for the level of policy uncertainty or what they call a lack of business "confidence": the interest rate spread between Baa- and Aaa-rated securities. Like Baker et al.'s measure of policy uncertainty, Harrison and Weder's lack of confidence measure reaches its highest level—roughly seven percentage points higher than usual—during the Great Depression and its second highest, of about half the Great Depression level, during the Great Recession.

To get their "sunspot" series, Harrison and Weder perform a vector autoregression using their confidence measure and the previously mentioned fundamental variables. The sunspots consist of the errors—the unexplained residuals—from this regression. Figure 20.1 shows how those authors' "extrinsic confidence" index—an index of Depression-era confidence levels based on "sunspots" alone—changed between 1929 and 1940. Because the extrinsic confidence series is independent of output, it neatly avoids the problem of reverse causation.

What remains to be considered is whether and to what extent changes in "extrinsic confidence" can account for the actual behavior of investment, output, and other macroeconomic variables during the Depression. To answer that question, Harrison and Weder start with a standard dynamic general equilibrium model in which equilibrium values depend in part on agents' expectations, which in turn depend on their confidence. They then feed their sunspot (or extrinsic confidence) values into the model after scaling them to make the maximum decline in output predicted by their model match the actual maximum decline. Finally, they compare the changes in various macroeconomic variables predicted by their model to actual changes.

The results are striking. Although its predictions are driven by "sunspots" alone, "the model," the paper's abstract reports, "can explain well the entire Depression era," including "the decline from 1929 to 1932, the subsequent slow recovery, and the recession that occurred in 1937–1939" (Harrison and Weder 2006). Harrison and Weder's model replicates Depression-era changes in output and investment especially well. Although it predicts both lower real wage

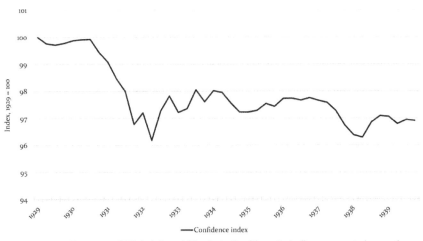

FIGURE 20.1. Harrison and Weder's (2006) "Extrinsic Confidence Index," 1929–1940, index numbers, 1929 = 100. (Data courtesy of Sharon Harrison and Mark Weder.)

rates and a more substantial recovery of employment after 1933 than actually occurred, those discrepancies are readily explained by appeal to the nominal wage-boosting effects of NRA codes and, after those were struck down, the Wagner Act's strengthening of labor unions' bargaining power. In only one respect does Harrison and Weder's model fall short, namely by predicting a less severe decline in consumption than actually took place.

Timing Is (Almost) Everything

Impressive as Harrison and Weder's findings are, they still don't clearly confirm the regime uncertainty hypothesis. Although the findings suggest that "sunspots," or changes in "extrinsic confidence," can go a long way toward explaining the persistence of the Great Depression, they make no attempt to link the sunspots to New Deal policy developments. Instead, by referring to sunspots as a "continuing sequence of pessimistic animal spirits," Harrison and Weder (2006) suggest that they're inscrutable.

Of course, the term "animal spirits" alludes to Keynes. But as we've seen, Keynes himself, far from thinking that animal spirits were the only possible "nonfundamental" cause of changes in businessmen's confidence, was keenly aware of the adverse effects of various New Deal policy developments on that confidence. It's therefore reasonable to look into whether any clear relation exists between those developments and Harrison and Weder's sunspot series or something akin to it.

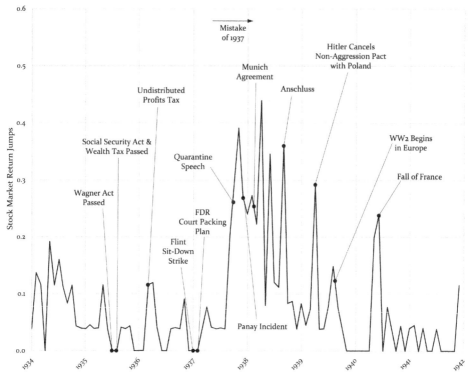

FIGURE 20.2. Stock return "jumps" and Depression-era shocks, 1934–1942. (Based on Mathy 2016, Figure 7. Data courtesy of Gabriel Mathy.)

Gabriel Mathy (2016) has tried doing just that. Mathy starts by constructing yet another measure of Depression-era uncertainty—"jumps" in stock returns. He then comes up with a timeline of events that are supposed to have contributed to that uncertainty, including many of the New Deal policy shocks discussed here and in chapter 19. Comparing the events to the timing of stock return jumps, Mathy finds little evidence for the regime uncertainty hypothesis. Figure 20.2 shows the results.[2]

"Other than the NIRA's [National Industrial Recovery Act] passage," Mathy (2016, 186) says, "none of these [New Deal policy] events line up with high volatility and jumps. . . . While policy uncertainty could absolutely create uncertainty shocks, the evidence doesn't show that policy uncertainty played a large role in the weak recovery."

But Mathy's shouldn't be the last word on this topic. Unlike Harrison and Weder's "sunspot" series, his stock jump measure of uncertainty doesn't correct for "fundamental" determinants of stock returns. So, it can't distinguish

changes in uncertainty driven by the ups and downs of the business cycle itself from "extrinsic" or "autonomous" changes having other causes, including
New Deal policy shocks. (The same goes for other "raw" uncertainty measures, including Baker et al.'s, all of which tend to rise during severe downturns.) If one performs an exercise similar to Mathy's using key dates from
our own narrative of "shocking" New Deal developments along with those
for other major events while replacing Mathy's stock jump measure of uncertainty with Harrison and Weder's extrinsic confidence series, the results, seen
in figure 20.3, seem both intuitively reasonable and broadly consistent with
the regime uncertainty hypothesis.

It would of course be interesting to see the outcomes of other such studies
using different "extrinsic confidence" measures. In the meantime, the regime
uncertainty hypothesis supplies an explanation for persistence of the Great Depression that, while hard to prove, is also hard to dismiss. And as we shall see,
a look into developments *after* the New Deal makes dismissing it harder still.

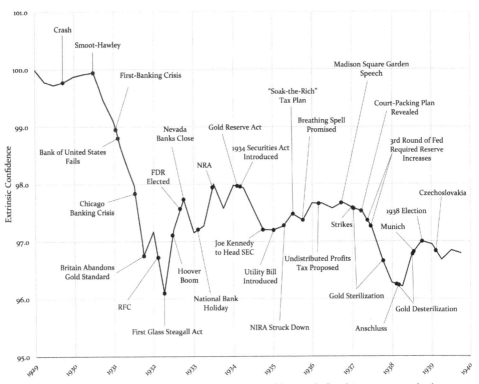

FIGURE 20.3. Harrison and Weder's (2006) "Extrinsic Confidence Index" and Depression-era shocks,
1929–1940. (Data courtesy of Sharon Harrison and Mark Weder.)

PART III

After the New Deal

War, and Peace

Thanks to the Roosevelt Recession, in the spring of 1938 the New Deal's Keynesians finally found themselves in the saddle, displacing the planners, reformers, and trustbusters whose legislative programs had all petered out. The Keynesians' rise was symbolized by Franklin Roosevelt's proposal, in his message to Congress on "stimulating recovery" that April, for several billion dollars in extra spending on relief and public works (Roosevelt 1941b, 2:221–35).

Although it marked a significant change because it was informed by Keynesian reasoning and undertaken despite Treasury opposition, Roosevelt's 1938 spending program didn't pack much of a punch. As David Kennedy (1999, 358–59) points out, "with more than ten million persons unemployed, $3 billion was a decidedly modest sum, not appreciably larger than most earlier New Deal deficits, considerably less than the deficit of 1936, and far short of the kind of economic boost that Keynes envisioned as necessary to overcome the depression once and for all." Moreover, the crisis that finally gave the Roosevelt administration's Keynesians the upper hand also proved fatal to its more ambitious plans, Keynesian or otherwise. Thanks to it, voters sent many Democrats, and New Deal democrats especially, packing that November. Although Democrats retained a strong majority in Congress, the election's real winners consisted of a group of Republicans and Southern Democrats that came to be known as the "conservative coalition," which was to dominate Congress for the next three decades.

While some historians have since labeled the Keynesian ascendancy a "Third New Deal," the Keynesians themselves saw their preferred policies as far less radical, if more expensive, alternatives to the more aggressive interference with private enterprise that most New Dealers favored. Even so, the large-scale spending plans they favored were hardly likely to sail through the new Congress. On the contrary, the conservative coalition, having been reinforced by the 1938 election results, showed its mettle in June 1939 by scuttling that year's $3 billion–plus Works Financing Act—the "Great White Rabbit" ("The Presidency: Revolving Rabbit," *Time*, July 3, 1939) that was supposed to continue Roosevelt's 1938 spending program. Not for nothing did the *New York Times'* Arthur Krock report, just after the 1938 elections, that "the New Deal has been halted" ("Taxpayers Revolt" 1938).

Far Off

Although the New Deal may have ended, the Depression certainly hadn't. At the start of 1939, 6.25 million workers, or about 12 percent of the labor force, were completely unemployed; another 3.25 million, or roughly 5 percent of the labor force, were on work relief. Adults were working only four-fifths as many hours as they had in 1929, industrial production was still 10 percent below its 1929 peak, and real private nonresidential investment languished at two-thirds its pre-Depression level. A year later the situation was roughly the same.

Of course, the situation in March 1933 had been far worse. But if "recovery" meant returning to anything like the state of employment throughout most of the 1920s or that decade's trajectory for industrial output, the US economy still had a very long way to go. "Despite the New Deal's exertions and innovations," David Kennedy (1999, 166) writes, "and contrary to later mythology," the New Deal and the Depression had been "Siamese twins, enduring together in a painful but symbiotic relationship that stretched to the end of the decade." That most other formerly depressed economies, with the noteworthy exception of France, were by then faring much better than the United States only gave Americans further grounds for aggrievement.

Nor were the New Dealers themselves, Roosevelt included, unaware of their recovery program's failure. Observing, in his 1939 State of the Union address, that the United States continued to "suffer from a great unemployment of capital," while Europe's dictatorships had "solved, for a time at least, the problem of idle men and idle capital," Roosevelt wondered whether the United States could "compete with them by boldly seeking methods of putting idle men and idle capital together and, at the same time, remain within our American way of life" (Roosevelt 1941b, 3:1–12). That May, Henry Morgenthau privately bemoaned the fact that the unemployment problem was almost as bad as when Roosevelt first took office. "I am just wearing myself out and getting sick," he complained to two congressmen serving on the Ways and Means Committee. "Because why? I can't see any daylight" (Folsom 2008, 143). "Even the staunchest defenders of the New Deal," Hugh Norton (1977, 91) observes, "were forced to admit that it had largely failed in its efforts" to end the Depression.

Over the Hill

An equally weighty acknowledgment of the New Deal's failure to achieve recovery came from the Keynesians' most influential spokesman, Harvard's Alvin Hansen. The acknowledgment was implicit in Hansen's "secular stagnation hypothesis," a hybrid of British-style Keynesianism and the version of Frederick Jackson Turner's "frontier" thesis Stuart Chase popularized in the book that gave the New Deal its name (Nettels 1934; Chase 1932).

According to Turner, American enterprise had depended for its unique vitality on continued westward expansion. The closing of the western frontier therefore threatened to stifle American prosperity. Between them, World War I and the Roaring Twenties put Turner's thesis on ice. But the Depression and Chase's book gave it a new lease on life. The prosperity of the 1920s, Chase wrote, was a mere "flash in the pan" (Chase 1932, 126): not only had the frontier passed, but population growth was grinding to a halt, leaving markets for everything from shoes to automobiles at their "saturation points." As for technological progress, instead of helping, it would only bring that much more unemployment. Chase (1932, 82) even suggested, facetiously, that it might "be a jolly good thing to declare a moratorium on inventions for at least a decade." But, moratorium or no moratorium, American progress had run out of steam. "For the first time in our national history since the opening of the West, we have to deal with a roughly static rather than an expanding structure. There is no prairie, no mountain, no forest to which we can escape; there are no elastic real estate values to muffle the impact of our industrial blunders. Our luck has run out; we have at last to face real things in a real world" (74).

To his credit, Hansen rejected Chase's jaundiced view of technological progress. "There can be no greater error," he said in his December 1938 American Economic Association presidential address, "than that which finds in the advance of technology, broadly conceived, a major cause of unemployment" (Hansen 1939a, 10). But in other respects Hansen shared Chase's pessimism. "We are passing," Hansen said, "over a divide which separates the great era of growth and expansion of the nineteenth century . . . into no one knows what" (1). In the past, the exploitation of new territory and population growth had between them supplied outlets for roughly half of the nation's capital formation. Now those outlets were "rapidly being closed," leaving only the outlet "created by the progress of technology" (9–10). But technological progress only helped if it gave rise to whole new industries, and there was little prospect that the future would see anything "as rich in investment opportunities as the railroad, or more recently the automobile" (10).

Hansen's secular stagnation or "economic maturity" thesis implied that none of the Roosevelt administration's efforts to achieve economic recovery, including such fiscal "pump priming" as its April 1938 spending program provided for, could achieve a lasting recovery. Instead, eliminating unemployment would take a massive and *permanent* increase in government spending. In other words, the heart of American private enterprise could no longer be expected to keep on beating on its own. It needed a Big Government pacemaker.

War!

Despite the conservative coalition, a pacemaker is just what the US economy got. But Keynesian thinking had nothing to do with it. On September 1, 1939, Germany invaded Poland. The war Europe had long dreaded was about to engulf it. Although the United States wouldn't join the conflict until December 1941, it at once started shipping substantial quantities of arms and other matériel to Europe. When France fell in June 1940, the United States itself began mobilizing in earnest. According to Robert G. Gordon and Robert Krenn (2010), by the time the Japanese attacked Pearl Harbor, the US economy had been running at full capacity for several weeks. The number of unemployed workers had fallen from 7.7 million to just 3.4 million, and US industrial production rose 25 percent above its 1920s pinnacle. Before long, material and labor shortages had the government placing limits on "nonessential" construction and production.

The claim that World War II and the government spending that went along with it ended the Great Depression has long been conventional wisdom. But the claim hasn't gone unchallenged. When Christina Romer (1992, 767) says that fiscal policy "contributed almost nothing to the recovery," she doesn't just mean that it contributed nothing before the war: she means that it contributed nothing until as late as 1942. Brad DeLong and Lawrence Summers (1988, 467) make the complementary claim that by the time the US government started cranking up its war effort in earnest, "more than five-sixths of the Depression decline in output relative to trend had been made up."

But such revisionism has been revised in turn by Gordon and Krenn (2010) and also by J. R. Vernon (1994). Vernon shows that the recovery was no more (and probably less) than half complete at the start of the last quarter of 1940 and that it took a big dose of fiscal medicine to complete it. Gordon and Krenn take Vernon's argument a step further by showing that federal government spending began to play a decisive role as soon as France fell, with the federal government's overall share of GDP doubling between then and December 1941. US defense spending alone grew almost tenfold, from $1.5 billion to $14.3 billion, while the number of active military personnel rose from just 335,000 to more than 1.8 million.[1] These magnitudes pale in comparison with later wartime figures. Nevertheless, Gordon and Krenn show, by the close of 1941 the government's contribution was already large enough to account for almost 90 percent of the recovery that took place between January 1939 and then.

As for those more impressive post–Pearl Harbor statistics, Robert Higgs (1992, 55) warns against taking them at face value. As soon as the United States declared war on Japan, he says, the government "began imposing such pervasive and sufficiently effective controls that, by the beginning of 1943, the economy became a thoroughgoing command system." Consequently, the superficially remarkable "wartime boom" of 1942–1945 is in truth little more than a statistical artifact.[2] Before Pearl Harbor, on the other hand, relatively few controls were imposed. For that reason, despite being the furthest thing from a Keynesian, Higgs agrees with Gordon and Krenn: "in 1940 and 1941," Higgs says, "the economy was recovering smartly from the Depression."

But there is a deeper sense in which the wartime recovery, however and whenever it started, was no recovery at all. "In the crucial respect of waste of economic resources," Broadus Mitchell (1947, 396) observes, "the war was, particularly for the United States, a deepening of the depression." Tens of millions who had been either unemployed or employed in peacetime activities now took part in activities that, however crucial, continued to reduce instead of enhancing their own and the world's living standards. To label such a state of affairs "full employment" was, Mitchell says, but "a flattering unction": the employment thus generated was "for purposes which, by very definition, could have no place in a normal economy." In short, the war was but a temporary solution to the problem of economic depression, and the more temporary the better. The point may seem trite. But it's a necessary response to those—and there are many—who declare that World War II ended the Depression and just leave it at that.

To their credit, the Roosevelt administration's Keynesians did not leave it at that. Instead of treating the ongoing wartime recovery as a real solution to the problem of unemployment, they saw in it a successful test of their own preferred solution, namely a substantial increase in peacetime government spending. Alas for them and their recommendations for postwar policy, the test proved to be a mixed blessing. Although it showed that sufficiently aggressive government spending could always counter unemployment, it also took the wind out of the Keynesians' sails. It did so, most obviously, by turning the once-urgent problem of unemployment into yesterday's news and instead confronting the government with entirely different but no less urgent challenges. But it also did so, ironically, by causing many—conservatives especially—to doubt that capitalism needed to be on life support after all.

Medical Referral

The change in the government's priorities was evident in Roosevelt's rhetoric and especially in his January 1941 State of the Union address, better known as his "Four Freedoms" speech (Roosevelt 1941a). "The immediate need," he said then, was "to change a whole nation from a basis of peacetime production of implements of peace to a basis of wartime production of implements of war" and to "prepare . . . to make the sacrifices that the emergency—almost as serious as war itself—demands." Although Roosevelt also insisted that "this is no time for any of us to stop thinking about the social and economic problems which are the root cause of the social revolution," including unemployment, the fact remained that mobilization supplied an immediate solution to many of those problems, if only by drawing millions of young men into the armed services.

The result was that despite Roosevelt's admonition, many *did* stop thinking about unemployment and other prewar problems. What's more, Roosevelt himself eventually seemed to quit thinking about them. During a December 1943 press conference a reporter, having noticed that Roosevelt was no longer using the term "New Deal," asked why. Comparing the prewar US economy to a sick patient, Roosevelt explained that while "Dr. New Deal" had been a perfectly competent internist, the patient had since been "in a pretty bad smashup" (Roosevelt 1950, 3:571). Since Dr. New Deal knew nothing about mending broken arms and legs, "Dr. Win-the-War" had taken over. If there was to be a "new" New Deal, it would have to wait until the war ended.

But would there be? The war didn't just change the government's priorities. It also changed the public's outlook for the future. According to Alan Brinkley (1995, 171), the spectacle of a fully employed economy—despite the government intervention that gave rise to it—caused many to reconsider the once widespread belief that capitalism was chronically if not mortally ill. Just as World War I had sent Frederick Jackson Turner's original frontier thesis into cold storage, World War II deprived Alvin Hansen's version of its once considerable appeal, undermining support for Keynesians' ambitious plans for keeping the postwar economy on its feet.

That the Keynesians found themselves fighting an uphill battle was first made clear by the fate of the National Resources Planning Board (NRPB). Established in 1939 as the last of a series of similar boards, all charged with helping to coordinate New Deal policies, when the war broke out its focus changed to domestic postwar planning. With that objective in mind, the NRPB produced a stack of reports and pamphlets several feet high, including several by Hansen, its most prominent adviser. Not surprisingly, those documents all stressed the need for public works and relief planning on a large scale to avoid a postwar collapse. Hansen himself looked forward to seeing Congress agree to cede to the administration its power of the purse so as to give it a free hand with which to regulate compensatory spending (Rosen 2005, 228).

Such a vision would have gotten a cold reception from the conservative coalition under the best of circumstances. But Roosevelt's decision to publish the NRPB's recommendations in early 1943 was particularly ill-timed so far as its ambitious recommendations were concerned: the 1942 midterm election had given Democrats another thrashing, leaving them with a paper-thin majority only in the House and a much-reduced one in the Senate. Not surprisingly, given the circumstances, the 78th Congress turned a deaf ear to the NRPB's proposals. But that was just for starters. The Senate's "antistatists," led by Robert Taft (R-OH), also planned to reduce the NRPB's budget to just $200,000, only to be one-bettered by the Appropriations Committee, which quit funding it altogether.

Jobs for All

When the NRPB was officially abolished that August, Roosevelt transferred many of its duties to the Bureau of the Budget, turning that bureau into the Keynesians' new unofficial headquarters. There, at the Fed and at the Office of War Mobilization and Reconversion (while Fred Vinson was in charge of it) they soldiered on, producing more papers, reports, and forecasts. According to Michael Sapir, one of the economists then working at the Bureau of the Budget, the "whole tone and emphasis" of these productions "was on the drastic primary impact of curtailed government outlays" on postwar "income and employment in the private economy" (Sapir 1949, 278). Demobilization, they argued, would have "a strong deflationary tendency" and would leave some 8 million to 12 million workers without jobs unless the government ran huge peacetime deficits.

One of the bureau's more important documents was a joint Federal Reserve–Bureau of the Budget memorandum on postwar employment written by Hansen and Gerhard Colm, the Bureau of the Budget's principal fiscal policy expert. That memorandum, which was circulated confidentially in October 1944 (Nourse 1956, 194), made achieving "full employment," meaning "productive work for all who are willing and able to work," the administration's first post-war economic policy priority. Fearing more congressional backlash, Roosevelt tabled the memo. But that didn't stop him from drawing on it when, on October 28, 1944, he gave his famous campaign speech at Chicago's Soldier Field (Roosevelt 1950, 4:369–78). Reminding the crowd of 150,000 that the "Second Bill of Rights" he'd proposed in his State of the Union address that January included Americans' "right to a useful and remunerative employment," he now explained that guaranteeing that right would take "close to sixty million productive jobs" and a corresponding "expansion of our peacetime productive capacity." Roosevelt promised that the government would "do its part" to finance the needed expansion. But having taken Congress's temperature, he was careful to add that the effort was to be a joint government-private market undertaking:

> I believe in free enterprise—and always have.
> I believe in the profit system—and always have.
> I believe that private enterprise can give full employment to our people.
> If anyone feels that my faith in our ability to provide sixty million peace-time jobs is fantastic, let him remember that some people said the same thing about my demand in 1940 for fifty thousand airplanes. (Roosevelt 1950, 4:376)

What Roosevelt didn't say that day was that fifty thousand B-17s in 1940 cost about $10 billion and that if the Keynesians' estimates were right, avoiding mass unemployment after the war would cost at least that much every year for several years at least and (if the secular stagnation thesis was correct) perhaps forever. Hansen himself thought that maintaining full employment would cost the government "some $18 billion annually," or close to four times what John Maynard Keynes had thought necessary in 1934. Other estimates of the required annual spending ran the gamut from Walter Salant's relatively sanguine range of $10 billion to $15 billion (Jones 1972, 126) to Paul Samuelson's especially gloomy $25 billion (Samuelson 1944; see also Samuelson 1943).

Needless to say, such large-scale deficit spending couldn't be flipped on like a switch. Yet the liberation of Paris that August made it obvious to everyone, apart perhaps from Hitler, that Nazi Germany's days were numbered. If the government was to keep its promise to avoid a severe postwar depression, it had no time to spare to start planning for peace. Alas, the Battle of the Bulge that December put to rest all talk of starting the process of economic reconversion before Germany threw in the towel.

The Employment Act

In his January 6, 1945, address to Congress, President Roosevelt once again called for a national program to ensure full employment. "The Federal Government must see to it," he said, "that these rights become realities. . . . This means that we must achieve a level of demand and purchasing power by private consumers . . . sufficiently high to replace wartime Government demands" (Roosevelt 1950, 4:503).

Roosevelt and the Keynesians whose recommendations he was now taking found their main champion in Congress in Montana senator James Murray, a staunch New Dealer who chaired the War Contracts Subcommittee of the Senate Military Affairs Committee. On January 22, 1945, Murray introduced his subcommittee's Full Employment Bill, based on a draft prepared by several Keynesian economists, as S. 380. A month later, Congressman Wright Patman (D-TX) introduced the House equivalent as H.R. 2202. The bills' centerpiece consisted of a national production and employment budget that was to include an estimate of the level of GNP consistent with full employment, the private sector's expected contribution, and the gap between these that the government would have to fill.

Although the text of both bills was the same, the fates they suffered in their respective chambers couldn't have been less alike. S. 380 wended its way through the Senate with relatively little opposition. Even so, by the time it passed the Senate on September 28, 1945, with minor amendments only, by a vote of 71 to 10 (with fifteen senators abstaining), both Germany and Japan had surrendered, and Roosevelt, who never got around to endorsing it, had been dead for more than five months.

Yet the conservative-leaning House Executive Expenditures Committee, to which H.R. 2202 had been assigned, was taking even longer, having only begun hearings on it days before S. 380 passed the Senate. It was during those hearings that the anti-Keynesians at last took to the offensive, assailing the very idea of a "right" to employment, exposing the vagueness of the concept of "full" employment, and casting doubt on the Keynesians' ability to forecast the course of private spending and employment with any reasonable degree of accuracy (US Senate 1945).[3] The anti-Keynesians' acerbic testimony informed a clamorous series of "close votes and compromises" (Wasem 2013, 99). President Harry Truman, for his part, was not at all inclined to weigh in on the Keynesians' behalf. On the contrary, in a May 17, 1945, letter to Securities and Exchange Commission chair Ganson Purcell, instead of worrying that a lack of postwar spending would bring mass unemployment, Truman conveyed his fear of a "speculative financial boom" like that of 1928 and 1929 and associated inflation (Truman 1945a).

When the dust settled, an Executive Expenditures Committee subcommittee found itself drafting a substitute for H.R. 2202. The resulting bill scrapped everything beyond the original measure's preamble. Instead of establishing workers' "right to employment," the Employment-Production Act of 1945 merely had the government "aiding and assisting" the unemployed; and instead of mandating Keynesian compensatory spending as specified by a national production and employment budget, it merely provided for a strictly advisory "economic report of the president." Finally, instead of assigning responsibility for drafting that report to the Bureau of the Budget, the watered-down bill assigned it to a new Council of Economic Advisers, to be appointed by the president, while creating a separate Joint Economic Committee to be charged with advising Congress on economic affairs. Both the Council of Economic Advisers and the Joint Economic Committee were to be advisory bodies only: neither could "authorize programs, pass laws, or appropriate funds" (Truman 1945a, 145). It was this tepid substitute for H.R. 2022 that the House eventually passed by a vote of 255 to 126.

It remained for the Conference Committee to decide between the House and Senate bills or something in between. The committee did so by choosing the House alternative while weakening it still further by downplaying or omitting altogether its references to government spending, public works, and loans. The conference report was accepted by the House on February 6, 1946, by a vote of 320 to 84, and was unanimously agreed to by the Senate two days later. At last, on February 20, more than six months after Emperor Hirohito announced Japan's unconditional surrender, President Truman signed the Employment Act of 1946 into law.[4]

Shock Therapy

Much as later Keynesians like to portray the Employment Act of 1946 as a triumph for their way of thinking, the fact remains that even if that act hadn't been so toothless, it would have come too late to compel Congress to take steps to avoid the mass postwar unemployment that Keynesians had long been predicting. In fact, Truman's Council of Economic Advisers didn't even bother to come up with a general plan for compensatory fiscal policy. Nor did Truman himself propose such a plan. "Compensatory spending," Leon Keyserling, the second chairman of the Council of Economic Advisers, recalled years later, "was never tried during the Truman administration; it was never needed" (Sundquist et al. 1981, 105). Instead, the items on Truman's fiscal policy wish list were a reduced deficit (and eventually a surplus), as little inflation as the elimination of controls would allow, and economic growth.

In any event, the gutted Employment Act ultimately let the 79th Congress determine precisely what the government's fiscal policy would be (Olson 1966, 97). That Congress, having emasculated its original Full Employment Bill, didn't put the Keynesians' recommendations into practice on its own initiative goes without saying. The upshot was that postwar economic reconversion went ahead without the benefit of peacetime compensatory spending. Instead, between fiscal year 1945 and fiscal year 1946, government outlays fell by 40 percent, from $92.7 billion to $55.2 billion, while the deficit fell from almost $50 billion, or 21 percent of GDP, in 1945 to just $16 billion, or about 7 percent of GDP, in 1946. In fiscal year 1947, federal revenues *exceeded* outlays for the first time since 1930, and by 1948 the surplus had risen to nearly $12 billion! In the meantime, the military returned some ten million Americans to civilian life (Eskin 1946).

According to most American Keynesians, fiscal surpluses were the last thing those Americans needed.[5] Instead, as we've seen, they thought it would take annual deficits of at least $10 billion and, according to Samuelson (1943), perhaps $25 billion to provide for their employment. Samuelson spoke for most Keynesians when he warned that "were the war to end suddenly . . . , were we again planning to wind up our war effort in the greatest haste, to demobilize our armed forces, to liquidate price controls, to shift from astronomical deficits to even the large deficits of the thirties—then there would be ushered in the greatest period of unemployment and industrial dislocation which any economy has ever faced" (51). Leon Henderson (1944, 8) likewise predicted that "if the war on both fronts were over by Christmas, we would probably have the most precipitous slump in our history. Beside it, 1929 and what followed would look like a picnic."

If the Keynesians were right, the US economy was headed for disaster: not only were deficits about to give way to surpluses, but most wartime controls, instead of being removed only gradually as they'd recommended, would be lifted soon after V-J Day, while the rest would be gone within a year. In short, the US economy was about to experience, at close to the fullest conceivable amperage, what historian Jack Stokes Ballard (1983) called the "shock of peace."

Keynesian economists weren't alone in dreading that shock. Writing in November 1944, the Swedish economist and future Nobel Prize winner Gunnar Myrdal feared that 14.5 million people would find themselves unemployed after the war and that, unless the government provided for them somehow, it could look forward to "a high degree of unrest" if not "an epidemic of violence" (Henderson 2010, 4). *Newsweek, Time, United States News,* and most of the liberal-leaning press also "feared a gradual slide into a major depression" rivaling that of the early 1930s, with between five million and seven million former workers and soldiers on the dole by end of 1945 (Hinchey 1965, 125). Not to be outdone, *Business Week* put peak unemployment at nine million, or about 14 percent of the labor force. But even that was nothing compared to Senator Harley Kilgore's (D-WV) prediction that the new depression would be far *greater* than the Great Depression, with *eighteen* million men and women failing to find jobs (126). Finally, Leo Cherne of the Research Institute of America and Boris Shishkin, an economist for the American Federation of Labor, topped all the others by forecasting nineteen million and twenty million unemployed, respectively, or unemployment rates in excess of 35 percent! (Taylor and Vedder 2010, 6).

But not everyone took part in such foreboding. The chief exceptions were businessmen, the very people who had been the previous decades' outstanding pessimists. More than a few now looked forward to a postwar boom (Wasem 2013, 47), and many nodded their heads when Russell Leffingwell, a J. P. Morgan and Company partner then serving as president of the Council on Foreign Relations, predicted in 1945 that instead of unemployment, the main economic challenge confronting the government would be inflation (Krooss 1970, 217). That same year Robert Wood, the chairman of Sears, Roebuck, staked $300 million on the prospect of a postwar boom. There were exceptions, of course: Seward Avery, the chair of Sears's chief rival, Montgomery Ward, believed the economists' forecasts and had his company stand pat (Fitzgerald 1995). But for most businessmen the mood then and during the immediate postwar period "was one of cautious confidence and optimism" (Krooss 1970, 219).

So far as most government economists were concerned, optimistic businessmen such as Wood were living in a fool's paradise. But because the government failed to heed their warnings, they couldn't do a thing about it. Instead, they were reduced to waiting, in helpless trepidation, for the Great Depression to return with a vengeance.

Yet those optimistic businessmen were to have the last laugh, for it never did.

The Phantom Depression

It was supposed to be a debacle.

As World War II drew to a close, the nation's leading economists feared that once the armed services demobilized, at least eight million men and women, perhaps many more, would be unemployed. That meant an unemployment rate of at least 12 percent, or almost as high as the rate before Hitler raided the Low Countries, setting off the "wartime boom." If their forecasts were reliable, the postwar economy could end up being no closer to recovery than the prewar economy had been.

A Worst-Case Scenario

Of course, such dire predictions weren't unconditional. Most of them assumed a worst-case scenario, one in which, in Alvin Hansen's words (1943, 5), the government chose to "just disband the Army, close down the munitions factories, stop building ships, and remove all economic controls" without compensating for these steps by substantially increasing its spending on public works and other employment-generating programs.

But that worst-case scenario is just what played out in fact. The government *did* "just disband the Army." Thanks to Operation Magic Carpet, which used everything from tank landing ships to the *Queen Mary* to deliver military personnel from overseas, within ten months of V-J Day more than 8 million of the 12.2 million military personnel on active duty that June had been discharged. By mid-1947, only 1.5 million—a million fewer than the military had planned on—were still enlisted.

And the government *did* close munitions factories and other facilities that had been engaged in war production, many of which were established solely for that purpose (Higgs 2004).[1] Some ended up being demolished; others were deactivated and put on standby for the next war. The rest were cleared of wartime inventory in anticipation of their conversion to civilian uses.

The government also stopped building ships. As soon as the war was over, the US Navy terminated or canceled most of its ship construction contracts. Most of the shipyards established under the government's Emergency Ship-building Program, including the seven large Kaiser shipyards in Richmond, California, and the Pacific Northwest, quickly shut down (Shipbuilding History n.d.).

Finally, the government quickly dispensed with most wartime controls. Soon after Roosevelt appointed him acting chairman of the War Production Board in late August 1944, Julius Krug released a report announcing that most of the production controls then in place would be lifted as soon as the war was over. The report also affirmed Krug's "deep commitment to the quick restoration of the free-market economy" (Brody 1975, 296). "The free enter-prise system," it explained, "would remain the basis of our economic activity; should Government intervene to maintain high levels of unemployment, it would do so by means of fiscal policy; controls would not be used to restore prewar economic relationships or to accomplish social or economic reforms, and wartime controls would be abandoned as rapidly as possible" (US Bureau of Demobilization 1947, 818).

Krug was true to his word. On November 3, 1945, when the War Produc-tion Board was replaced by the Civilian Production Administration, of al-most 650 of its control directives that had been in play at the war's height, only 55 were still in effect (Bernstein 1965, 258). Krug's plans were bound to under-mine attempts by the Office of Price Administration (OPA) to keep a lid on prices and were fervently opposed by Chester Bowles, the OPA's head, for that reason. But Harry Truman let Krug have his way, and the OPA soon faced a flood of petitions for price increases, forcing Bowles to choose between ap-proving each request or giving up on price controls altogether. By V-J Day controls on fuel and processed food prices had already been removed, and by year's end many more were to go by the wayside.[2]

As for government spending and deficits, to the Roosevelt administration's Keynesian economists they amounted to a mere drop in the ocean. About half of 1945's GDP had been war production, paid for by the government. Between then and 1947 defense-related federal spending fell by more than 75 percent, while the share of GDP consisting of current federal expenditures fell by one-half, from about 32 percent to about 16 percent. Finally, that year's wartime deficit of $32 billion, instead of being replaced by a peacetime deficit of at least a third of that amount as Keynesian economists had recommended, became a peacetime *surplus* of $2.5 billion. These cutbacks were even larger—*considerably* larger—than the government's economists had allowed for in their most pessimistic forecasts.

The Shoe That Didn't Drop

Yet peace did not bring mass unemployment, at least not according to official statistics. Far from returning to prewar levels, the unemployment rate never rose above 4.26 percent until 1949 and was generally between 3.5 and 4 percent, levels comparable to if not below those for the Roaring Twenties. The total number of unemployed persons reached its peak of 2.7 million, not quite half of whom were recently returned veterans, in March 1946, and was generally closer to 2 million. Such levels were well within wartime forecasts of postwar "frictional" unemployment, meaning short-term unemployment of workers seeking (and eventually finding) jobs, as opposed to unemployment resulting from a lack of job openings. As such, they were consistent with the accepted meaning of "full" employment. Hansen, for example, had said in 1943 that were full employment achieved after the war, between two million and three million persons might still be searching for jobs at any time.

In fact, the postwar unemployed seldom stayed so for long. Almost all veterans who wanted jobs got them quickly (Modell 1989, 206). That relatively few were on the market at any time during the process of demobilization was all the more remarkable considering the huge numbers pouring in, not to mention the fact that the 1944 Serviceman's Readjustment Bill (the GI Bill) made it easier for ex-servicemen to stay unemployed by offering them fifty-two weeks of unemployment compensation at the enhanced rate of $20 per week.

For contemporary testimony regarding the immediate postwar employment story, we can do no better than turn to the document that was among the few relatively immediate and substantive fruits of the 1946 Employment Act, namely the first *Economic Report of the President,* published on January 8, 1947. During 1946, that report states,

> civilian employment approached 58 million. This was the highest civilian employment this Nation has ever known—10 million more than in 1940 and several million higher than the wartime peak. If we include the military services, total employment exceeded 60 million. Unemployment, on the other hand, remained low throughout the year. At the present time it is estimated at about 2 million actively seeking work. This is probably close to the minimum unavoidable in a free economy of great mobility such as ours.

Thus, at the end of 1946, less than a year and a half after VJ-day, more than 10 million demobilized veterans and other millions of wartime workers have found employment in the swiftest and most gigantic change-over that any nation has ever made from war to peace. At its peak during 1946 aggregate employment was substantially in accord with the objectives stated by the Congress in the Employment Act. (The White House 1947)

That is, the level of employment was in accord with the objectives of the 1946 Employment Act even though the act's original sponsors had said that it couldn't possibly be so without the help of huge peacetime deficits.

More Guns, Less Butter

Employment is ultimately not an end in itself but a means for procuring life's necessities, if not its luxuries, and averting depression, as that concept is generally defined, means avoiding not just unemployment but also a substantial decline in the real output of goods and services. In light of this understanding, official postwar statistics pose a puzzle, for if the official postwar unemployment numbers are ones Truman might have boasted about, those for real output tell a very different story: between 1945 and 1946, according to the most recent Commerce Department data, real GDP fell by almost a fifth, implying, in Bob Higgs's (1999, 602) words, "by far the largest annual fall ever in U.S. economic history, exceeding even that of the worst year (1932) of the Great Contraction." The monthly Industrial Production index paints an even starker picture: it was *34 percent* lower in February 1946 than it had been a year earlier, a drop exceeding that of the *entire* Great Contraction! Even allowing for a postwar decline in working hours, a temporary decline in the size of the labor force, and the strike wave of 1945–1946, such huge declines in standard output measures can't possibly be reconciled with other statistics showing that the economy was at or near full employment (Brecher 1997, chap. 6).

So, which official numbers are lying, the ones for unemployment or those for output? According to Bob Higgs and several other economic historians, it's the output numbers that deceive. And their arguments are compelling. The shortcomings of those numbers start with the Commerce Department's occasional revisions of its real GDP data. Every now and then, Richard Vedder and Lowell Gallaway (1991, 11–12) explain, that department's Bureau of Economic Analysis revises the way it calculates the deflator it uses to convert nominal GNP data into constant-dollar equivalents. Since 1958, when the Bureau of Economic Analysis came up with its first estimates of postwar real GNP, each revision has increased the weight assigned to consumer purchases relative to government purchases, and each has thereby made the 1946 down-turn look worse than its predecessor did.

Thus, if instead of consulting the latest (1990) real GNP numbers one consults those from 1958, one finds that instead of losing a fifth of its value between 1945 and 1946, real GNP declined by just 7.8 percent. According to Vedder and Gallaway (1991) and also according to Hugh Rockoff (1998, 86–87), the older estimate is probably closer to the truth. It's also likely to be closer to what Edwin Nourse, Truman's Council of Economic Advisers chair, had in mind when he wrote the 1947 *Economic Report of the President.*

Scholars have also come up with new estimates of inflation during the 1940s, all of which tend to revise wartime inflation figures upward while revising the postwar ones downward. The revisions imply opposite adjustments to real GNP. As Milton Friedman and Anna Schwartz (1982, 101) explain, the government's resort to price controls during the war and its rapid removal of the same controls afterward make such revisions essential. Wartime controls, they say, "meant that price increases took indirect and concealed forms not recorded in the indexes. The large rise in price indexes when price control was repealed in 1946 consisted largely of an unveiling of the earlier concealed increases. Hence, the recorded price indexes understate the price rise during the war and overstate the price rise after the war. This defect is reflected in the national income estimates in an overestimate of the wartime rise in income in constant prices, and hence an underestimate of the wartime rise in the implicit price index." While the price indexes that Simon Kuznets prepared for the Commerce Department after the war had prices rising by 15.6 percent between 1942 and 1945, and by about 20 percent between 1945 and 1947, Friedman and Schwartz's own revised indexes have prices rising by 27 percent during war and by just 9 percent afterward. The estimated severity of the postwar slump drops correspondingly. Using somewhat different methods, Vedder and Galloway (1991, 10) arrive at an estimate of inflation during the immediate postwar years somewhat below Friedman and Schwartz's. They conclude that real GNP fell only "by a bit over seven percent" between 1945 and 1946.

Yet even such revisions, substantial as they are, fail to address the most serious shortcoming of wartime output measures, namely, their tendency to overstate, perhaps dramatically, both the nominal value of war matériel and the extent to which it should be considered part of national output at all. As Higgs (1992, 45–47) reports, Kuznets, whose wartime and postwar deflators are among those that have been called into question by Friedman and Schwartz and others, had his own grave misgivings about the Commerce Department's valuation of wartime output. "A major war," he observed, "magnifies" the usual challenges involved in estimating national income, because war

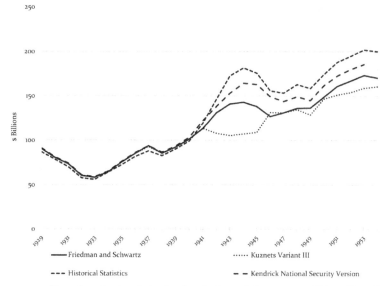

FIGURE 22.1. Alternative estimates of net national product, 1929 dollars, 1929–1955. (Adapted from Rockoff 2020, Figure 3. Data courtesy of Hugh Rockoff.)

matériel isn't sold at anything resembling "market" prices and also because wars blur "the distinction between intermediate and final products" (45).

Such considerations persuaded Kuznets to come up with several alternative measures of wartime and postwar GNP, all of which imply a less impressive wartime boom, or no boom at all, and no postwar slump. For example, according to Higgs (1992, 46), "whereas the Commerce Department's latest estimate of real GNP drops precipitously in 1946 and remains at that low level for the rest of the decade," Kuznets's "wartime" estimate "*increases* in 1946 by about 8 percent, then rises slightly higher during the next three years." Another Kuznets GNP estimate—what he called "peacetime" GNP—revises the record still further by valuing goods produced for military use at their nonmilitary surplus values only. According to that estimate, between 1945 and 1947 real output rose by almost 18 percent!

More recently, Hugh Rockoff (2020, 38) has created a chart comparing real *net* national product (GNP minus depreciation) estimates by Kuznets, the Commerce Department's Bureau of Economic Analysis national income and product accounts, and others, including Kuznets's "peacetime" series, for both the 1930s and 1940s. The chart, reproduced here as figure 22.1, shows especially clearly just how unsafe it is to conclude, from the usual national income and product accounts estimates, that despite low unemployment, the US economy suffered a severe slump just after World War II.

The Market's Verdict

While some statistics suggest that there was no serious postwar contraction, they don't settle the matter. But there is other evidence one can look at to decide whether the US economy was depressed in 1946 or not, and it all tells the same story: if there *was* a postwar slump, nobody seemed to notice.

Consider the stock market. As a rule, recessions are bad for stock prices, and severe recessions and depressions have *always* been bad for them. During the 1920–1921, 1929–1933, 1937–1938, and 2007–2009 contractions, for example, the S&P common stock index fell by 24, 79, 32, and 40 percent, respectively. Yet during the 1945 contraction it *rose* 18 percent. Former Bureau of Labor Statistics commissioner Geoffrey Moore (1983, 147) observed that since the Panic of 1873 there had been only two occasions when a business recession wasn't associated with a decline in stock prices. One was during the very mild—and all but forgotten—recession of 1926–1927, which that era's bull market completely ignored. The other was in 1945. Nor have things changed since Moore wrote. For the whole postwar period up to now (May 2024), the average S&P 500 drop during contractions has been about 29 percent, while the median drop has been about 24 percent. In short, if there was a severe 1945–1946 downturn, the stock market's response to it was sui generis.

Much the same may be said about the bond market's reaction, allowing, of course, for the fact that recessions tend to raise rather than lower bond prices while lowering bond yields. Because yields on short-term marketable securities, such as Treasury bills, tend to be most sensitive to changes in overall business conditions, these might be expected to decline most. Treasury bill yields did in fact fall during all contractions except for two between 1919 and 1970. The exceptions were 1920–1921 and, once again, 1945 (Moore 1983, 153, Table 9.4).

A final source of clues concerning the performance of the US economy immediately after the war consists of contemporary magazines and newspapers, which one can search through for references to a major slump. But one will search postwar periodicals for such references in vain, because there aren't any.

* * *

To conclude, there was no postwar slump, let along a postwar "Great Depression." Instead of being a mere intermission in a two-act Great Depression tragedy, the war left the Depression behind, ushering in a period of remarkable prosperity in the United States and abroad that was to continue, with only relatively minor interruptions, until the 1970s. And it appeared to do this with little help from the federal government (Levinson 2016).

The question is how.

The Fate of Rosie the Riveter

Before we seek an explanation for the US postwar recovery, there's a loose end to my account of it that needs tying up.

In questioning wartime and postwar output measures, while taking the same period's unemployment statistics at face value, I set aside a hypothesis that disputes the unemployment numbers themselves. According to this hypothesis, when the war ended, many would-be women workers left the labor force not because they didn't want to keep working but because they faced impossible odds of staying employed. If that was the case, official figures substantially understate the real extent of postwar unemployment, and no matter how high it was, US postwar output was well below its potential.

Frances Coppola (2022) has recently defended the hypothesis in question with great vehemence. "There was never full employment," she says. "The low unemployment of the post-war years is a massive statistical fudge. In fact, over five million people lost their jobs immediately after the end of the war, most of whom never worked again. But they were never listed as unemployed—because they were women."

In defending this claim, Coppola (2022) takes the accuracy of conventional wartime and postwar output measures for granted. "The fall in real GDP in 1945–46," she says, "dwarfs both the Great Recession and the Covid-19 recession. Only the Great Depression was worse." Observing further that it "is extremely odd for unemployment to be so low in a recession of such severity," Coppola concludes that it's not postwar output statistics but postwar unemployment statistics that mislead. Those unemployment statistics are low, she says, only because they exclude millions of discouraged women workers. "Faced with discrimination, harsh pay cuts, and unfair job downgrades," she says, "many women did indeed opt to leave the workforce. But it is hard to see how dropping out of a labour market that did not want them and was determined to push them out is in any way 'voluntary.'" Had these supposedly discouraged women been included among the unemployed, unemployment rates for the immediate postwar years would be twice as high.

Veterans and Interlopers

For reasons given in chapter 22, it simply isn't safe to infer the true extent of postwar unemployment from postwar output measures and especially from the dramatic decline in those measures from their notoriously inflated wartime levels. It remains true nonetheless that the total (civilian and military) labor force shrank considerably between mid-1945 and mid-1946 and that much of that decline was due to women workers' withdrawal. It's also true that discrimination against women workers and in favor of returning (mostly male) war veterans during the postwar reconversion was both very real and widespread.

The federal government itself was no small contributor to such discrimination. The 1940 Selective Training and Service Act gave returning servicemen who had quit their jobs to serve the right to have those jobs back provided they applied within forty days of being discharged (Ballard 1983, 45). That step alone gave some four million returning servicemen first dibs on as many jobs. Nor were women helped by the fact that the US Employment Service, which operated a network of government-employment placement offices during and immediately after the war, gave priority to veterans as soon as the war ended, although it must be said that it did so in large part because hiring firms themselves preferred them (Rose 2018, 31). Finally, the federal government itself dispensed with many of its wartime female nonmilitary workers, the number of whom fell from a peak of about 1.1 million to less than half a million by 1947 (US Department of Labor 1953, 30).

With a few (mostly left-wing) exceptions, labor unions were also notoriously chauvinistic. Rather than "accord women an equal place in their works," they tended to look upon them "as interlopers and 'wage cutters' who undermined union standards" (Warne 1945, 203). Consequently, even though more than three million women workers made up 22 percent of trade union membership in 1944—up from just 800,000 when the war started—"most unions unceremoniously discarded their female members at war's end" (Kessler-Harris 1982, 291).

But the prejudice against women workers and in favor of veterans wasn't just the doing of misogynistic bureaucrats and unions. Instead, Colston Warne (1945, 203) explains, it reflected "the mood of the nation," informed by both a desire to reward mostly male war veterans for their sacrifices and an "archaic attitude toward the place of women in industry" that was far from being confined to men alone.

It's also true that millions of women workers were laid off during demobilization and that millions left the labor force, including more than half of the 2.7 million married "Rosies" (after "Rosie the Riveter") who entered it during the war and were especially likely to be sacrificed to make way for returning veterans (Goldin 1991, 750). In all, roughly 5 million women had joined the labor force during the war. Because roughly a quarter million left at various times before the war ended, the net gain between March 1940 and April 1945 was about 4.75 million. Although most working women expressed a desire to keep on working after the war, between then and 1947 the female labor force declined by 3.25 million, of whom only some 520,000 were officially classified as unemployed (US Department of Labor 1953, Tables 2 and 14). Considering the severe discrimination they faced, it's easy to imagine that many if not most of the remaining two million or so left the labor market not because they wanted to but because they understood that employers no longer wanted them, just as Coppola claims.

A Rosier Picture

Yet despite all these indisputable truths, the discouraged women workers story, understood to mean that millions of women left the labor force involuntarily as the armed services demobilized, doesn't bear scrutiny.

To understand why, it helps, first, to appreciate the extraordinary lengths to which the government went to coax extra women *into* the labor force during the war. In mid-1943, the War Manpower Commission concluded that keeping the war industries working at full capacity would take another four million women workers and that, with most single women already working, many married women would have to be lured into the workforce somehow. By appealing to nonworking women's patriotism and (mostly) by offering them extraordinarily high pay, the commission eventually managed to recruit even more new women workers than it intended to (Rupp 1978, chap. 6; Schweitzer 1980). Almost all these recruits only planned to work "for the duration," on the understanding that the end of the war would restore the labor market status quo ante. As the war continued, some—especially the more educated recruits who gained white-collar jobs (Goldin and Olivetti 2013)—changed their minds. But on the whole the Rosies who entered the labor force during the war, married Rosies especially, were far less intent on continuing to work when peace returned than women who had already been working before Pearl Harbor.

It's seldom possible to say for certain whether women who leave the labor force have done so voluntarily or not, and that was especially so before 1967, when the Bureau of Labor Statistics (BLS) first started asking nonworking women, in its monthly Current Population Survey, why they weren't working or seeking work.[1] It so happens, however, that in 1944 and 1945 two separate Labor Department bureaus conducted special surveys that, taken together, come as close to supplying an answer as one could dare to hope.

One of those surveys, by the Woman's Bureau, found that of over thirteen thousand women workers surveyed in ten major "war production centers" during 1944 and early 1945, 25 percent, including most married Rosies, didn't wish to continue working after it. Those who wanted to stay employed, in contrast, were for the most part *not* "those who had been swept into the labor force during its wartime expansion" (US Department of Labor 1946b, 5).

The other survey, conducted by the BLS, was based on interviews of 5,100 women working in the spring of 1945, 3,600 of whom were resurveyed that winter (US Department of Labor 1946a). At the time of the resurvey almost all the War Department's contracts had been terminated, most war factories and shipyards had either permanently shut down or were undergoing reconversion, and more than two million women war workers had been laid off (Ballard 1983, 135–36). Like its Women's Bureau counterpart, the spring BLS survey found that 25 percent of surveyed war industry workers, including, once again, a disproportionate number of married workers, planned to quit working when the war ended. The winter follow-up discovered in turn that 29 percent of those resurveyed had indeed left and that most who did so were married.[2] In contrast, only 5 percent of non–war industry women workers surveyed in the spring were planning to leave the labor force after the war, and precisely that share had in fact left it by October.

If the war industry women surveyed by the Women's Bureau were representative of the 4.6 million women employed in 1945 as "operatives and kindred workers," meaning most semiskilled factory workers, many of whom were then producing munitions, aircraft, ships, and other war matériel, some 1.15 million women operatives were planning to quit their jobs months before any mass layoffs occurred.

In fact, between 1945 and 1947 the number of female factory workers fell by 1.2 million, implying, once again, that just 4 percent were let go who hadn't planned to leave the workforce. Allowing that nearly 14.6 million women were working in non–war-related industries in the spring of 1945 and that 5 percent of those women also planned to leave the labor force when the war ended brings the total *planned* women's labor force reduction to just under 2 million. According to the Office of War Mobilization and Reconversion

(Steelman 1946, 59), between August 1945 and February 1946, total nonfarm employment of women actually fell by 2.21 million, half a million of whom were among those counted as unemployed at the end of that stretch.[3] Assuming that women who had been planning to leave the labor force months before V-J Day did in fact leave voluntarily, these numbers leave no room at all for any discouraged women workers!

Furthermore, quite a few *unplanned* labor market departures were themselves voluntary: the extraordinary number of spur-of-the-moment engagements that took place as soon as troops started coming home caused almost as many formerly working single women to become housewives and mothers. According to Cynthia Harrison (1989, 25), "No one had to force women into marriage and motherhood. The marriage rate, 84.5 per thousand women in 1945, shot up to 120.7 in 1946 and 106.8 in 1947" and "fluctuat[ed] between 78 and 98 per thousand for the next ten years." The first year of the baby boom, 1946, witnessed 1,340,504 first births, a record number (Federal Security Agency 1949, xxiv).[4]

Marc Miller (1980) has looked into the specific case of women workers in Lowell, Massachusetts, where several war-based businesses, including Remington Arms, US Rubber, and the Atlantic Rayon Company's Parachute Division, relied heavily on women workers either newly recruited to the workforce or hired away from textile mills, the town's main employers before the war. What he says of circumstances in Lowell is entirely consistent with our own back-of-the-envelope results. "There seems to have been little complaint," Miller says, "about having men return home and resume the old economic hierarchies. . . . Some Lowell women gladly left their work after their husbands returned and found employment; these women had seen work only as an option 'for the duration.' Others left as the postwar baby boom began. As one woman recalled, she had intended to find work in Lowell after her government office closed, but found herself 'in the family way' and didn't return to work" (58).

Of course, many former war workers who wanted to keep working also found themselves without jobs. But in Lowell at least, other "work existed for most of the women who sought it, albeit at lower wages" (Miller 1980, 59). Although what had been an exceptional demand for female manufacturing workers during the war fell off with demobilization, recent research (Shatnawi and Fishback 2018) concludes that despite that drop, the postwar demand for such workers was considerably higher than it would have been had demand merely reverted to its booming 1920s growth path.

Does this mean that most laid-off women workers weren't victims of discrimination after all? Hardly. First of all, it's possible that at least some of the women who were planning to quit working months before the war ended planned to do so only because they knew that discrimination would make their postwar job prospects extremely dim. It's possible, but it isn't very likely: in general, would-be workers become discouraged *after* losing their jobs, and most do so only after being unemployed for some time. As the Bureau of Employment Security's Olga Halsey (1946, 7) put it in June 1946, "unemployment is the winnowing process by which many ultimate withdrawals from the labor force will be accomplished. . . . Many of those who find they cannot get the type of work they want or for which they are qualified by their wartime experience, at wages which compare favorably with wartime earnings, will give up the effort sooner or later. . . . As the length of unemployment increases, more marginal workers will withdraw." Halsey herself worried that the women's labor force would continue to shrink as more unemployed women workers became discouraged and quit searching for jobs. But that never happened. Instead, the women's labor force started growing again. By 1951 it was back at its wartime peak, which it went on to surpass.

It was mainly women who didn't leave the labor force, most of whom had been working before Pearl Harbor, who turned out to be discrimination's biggest victims. Most of these women needed to keep working to support themselves, if not their dependents. After reviewing numerous Women's Bureau surveys of wartime women workers, Mary-Elizabeth Pidgeon (1952, 71) thought it was probably being "conservative to say that at least half this country's women workers consider themselves responsible for the entire or partial support of others, in addition to self-support."

Women who couldn't afford to quit working suffered not by becoming so discouraged that they quit the labor force but by becoming temporarily (and officially) unemployed at first and then, like some former women war workers in Lowell, by accepting jobs that paid much less and were otherwise less satisfying than their wartime jobs. As Sheila Tobias and Lisa Anderson put it, "Rosie stopped riveting, but she did not stop working" (quoted in Kossoudji and Dresser 1992, 434). More accurately, Rosie didn't stop working unless she no longer had to work.

Happy Days

By the start of 1948, there could no longer be any doubt: the Great Depression wasn't coming back. Instead of collapsing at war's end as many feared it would, combined government and private spending (as measured by nominal GDP) hardly budged between 1945 and 1946. They then started climbing again. Consequently, as we've seen, the unemployment rate ended up being as low as it had been in the latter 1920s, while the consumer price level, far from falling again as many feared it would, rose at alarming rates as soon as controls were lifted, finally stabilizing toward the end of the decade.

Nor was the avoidance of a postwar slump just a temporary result of good luck. A decade later, Brookings economist Bert Hickman (1958, 117) was able to commemorate twelve years of "impressive" growth "unmarked by serious economic contraction."

Missing the Mark

What was behind this remarkable achievement? The proximate cause was a revival of private spending far exceeding what many economists, especially Keynesians, predicted. That revival proved more than sufficient to compensate for a reduction in government spending that was itself greater than most had allowed for.

Consider, for example, a pair of painstaking and influential but otherwise representative forecasts prepared just after V-J Day by Everett Hagen, chief of the Fiscal Policy and Program Planning Division of the Office of War Mobilization and Reconversion. Despite the late date and the fact that Hagen somewhat *overestimated* postwar government spending while underestimating the pace of demobilization, his "more favorable" forecast underestimated

1946 GNP by about 12 percent, mainly by underestimating both consumer spending and private capital formation. Hagen's "less favorable" forecast underestimated 1946 GNP by more than 15.5 percent. Both of Hagen's forecasts put the number of unemployed at 8.1 million during the first quarter of 1946, overestimating it by more than 5.5 million. But while the more favorable forecast had the unemployment level dropping steadily to 5.6 million by mid-1947, the less favorable one had it *increasing* to 9.3 million, an overestimate of almost 7 million (Hagen 1947).

Recalling at the end of that decade Hagen's forecast and others like it, Bureau of the Budget economist Michael Sapir (1949, 278–79) observed that "we forecast deflation, deficiencies of demand, a tendency for prices to fall, sizable unemployment, [and] a rather bearish mood in the business world. Instead, inflationary pressures have been constant and general: prices and wages have risen, incomes are at record levels, sustaining demands far above available supplies; employment, after the first shock on the munitions industries has been high, and in no month since V-J Day has unemployment been more than 2¾ million."

So much for what happened. The $64,000 questions are these: *Why* didn't the reduction in government spending lead to an overall decline in spending and corresponding unemployment? And what caused private spending to grow enough to make up for that decline after having been at low levels for so long?

Guaranteed Stability?

Before we can answer those questions, we must address claims to the effect that private spending wasn't really what kept the postwar economy humming. Some economists instead insist that despite appearances, the federal government was still propping up the US economy in the years that followed the war. According to Alan Sweezy (1972), like some fake perpetual motion machine running on well-hidden batteries, what appeared to be a largely private market economy capable of sustaining itself and even growing was in fact an economy still heavily dependent on government support. Alvin Hansen's concern about chronically deficient private spending was, in other words, correct after all. "What Hansen said," Sweezy writes, "was that we could not get full employment, except in temporary spurts, if government expenditures did not play a larger role in the economy. Since larger meant larger than before the depression, when the federal government's expenditures on goods and services were about 6 percent of GNP, one can hardly prove him wrong by showing we have had full employment with government purchases at several times that percentage" (122–23).

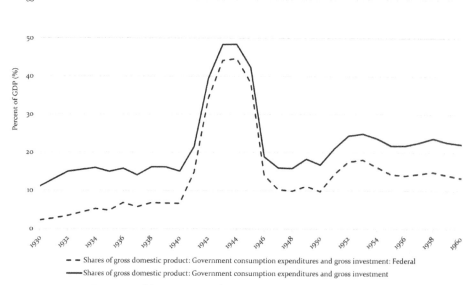

FIGURE 24.1. Percentage of GDP consisting of government expenditures, federal and all levels, 1930–1960 (Data from FRED*, Federal Reserve Bank of St. Louis, https://fred.stlouisfed.org/graph/?g=1pDBN.)

Harold Vatter (1985, 151–52) also attributes the lack of a severe postwar slump to increased government spending. Provided one allows for "large and growing state and local expenditures," he says, "civilian and military [federal government] expenditures . . . were sufficient to maintain a generally high level of employment and to avoid a severe recession."

But a look at government spending on all levels just before and just after the war contradicts both Sweezy's and Vatter's claims. As figure 24.1 shows, instead of rising after the war to "several times" its prewar level, the ratio of such spending to GDP hardly rose at all. The small increase that did take place hardly seems capable of accounting for the difference between depression and prosperity. Furthermore, growth in the government's share of total spending mainly served to offset a corresponding decline in the share consisting of consumer spending, leaving the potentially far more volatile contribution of private investment as capable of causing trouble as ever. "Even if it is assumed that a pronounced curtailment of government spending is not likely to recur for some time to come," Hickman (1958, 129) observes, "it must be recognized that private investment is still sizeable enough to fall as far below its full employment share of GNP as it did after 1929." If the United States avoided an immediate postwar downturn, it wasn't because private investment didn't matter as much as it once did. It was because investment, instead of falling again, not only picked up but *stayed* up.

A more subtle argument holds that the postwar federal government's greater willingness to tolerate deficits caused by downturns, as signaled by the 1946 Employment Act, tamed the business cycle, because even unintentional deficits served as "automatic stabilizers": instead of trying to keep its budget balanced during recessions, the postwar government increased its relief payments while letting its revenues shrink. The greater the government's share of GDP—and the part relief payments played in it—and the more its revenues depended on private earnings, the more effective the resulting automatic deficits became in taming the business cycle (DeLong 1996).

But however important automatic stabilizers may eventually have become, they clearly weren't responsible for the absence of an immediate postwar slump: those stabilizers only come into play when federal revenues decline and relief spending goes up, causing a larger deficit. But nothing of the sort happened after the war. Instead, as we've noted, demobilization led to a sustained postwar *revival* of private spending. As E. Cary Brown (1959, 44) observes, the problem that automatic stabilizers help solve "is not that of raising the sunken hulk of the economy but rather of keeping it on a fairly even keel." And what the US private economy experienced after the war was one *big* uplift.

Nor for that matter is there much evidence that automatic stabilizers have *ever* helped to stabilize the US economy (DeLong 1996, 47). A painstaking study of post-1960 experience by Alisdair McKay and Ricardo Reis (2016, 176) offers no support at all for "the usual arguments about the benefits of [automatic] stabilizers in aggregate demand management." On the contrary, by the end of the 1960–2011 period those authors study, so-called stabilizers were making output and employment *more* volatile than they would have been otherwise.

As for deliberate fiscal policy actions, these have also proven far less helpful in stabilizing the postwar economy than the passage of the 1946 Employment Act has led many to suppose. "Looking back at the budget since World War II," Brad DeLong (1996, 47) says, "it is difficult to argue that on balance 'discretionary' fiscal policy has played *any* stabilizing role" (see also Gordon 1980). Instead of tending to be countercyclical, or at least less cyclical than private spending, postwar federal spending has often been procyclical. Up to 1960 it was also the *least* stable of "all major categories of final domestic demand during the postwar years" (Hickman 1960, 209). A study of the period 1958–1997 concludes that on the whole fiscal policy was "at best negligibly stabilizing" during that time and that fiscal policy "shocks," meaning changes in fiscal policy that weren't systematic responses to other macroeconomic shocks, were "unambiguously destabilizing" (Jones 2002, 712).

Such findings reflect the fact that despite the 1946 Employment Act, instead of reflecting "basically Keynesian behavior," as John Modell (1989, 219) and many others suppose, the ups and downs of federal spending have mainly reflected changes in perceived defense needs. Consequently, instead of limiting "such short-term instability as has occurred," changes in federal spending were often its chief cause (Hickman 1958, 128). On those few occasions when increased government spending has helped to counter downturns, as happened in 1949, it has done so by accident.[1] "If big government is regarded as a structural feature of the economy," Hickman cautions, "the fact that the overwhelming bulk of federal purchases of goods and services is for national security and may therefore shift up or down with changes in the international or military situation must also be accepted" (129).

In short, Hickman (1958, 236) concludes, "it cannot be maintained . . . that the potential range of private autonomous demand had been radically diminished by the growth of federal expenditure." Although the federal government's increased relative importance "augmented economic stability in some respects," it also "diminished it in others," the result being, at best, a wash. It follows that, if the government really did make the postwar economy more stable than the prewar economy, it must have done so not simply by getting bigger or by actively countering fluctuations in private spending but by adopting other beneficial policies.

Pent-Up Demand

Before we look into those other policies, it will pay to take a closer look at the postwar revival of private-sector spending, starting with consumption. Government economists assumed that what had been a simple prewar relation between private disposable income and consumption expenditures would also hold in the immediate postwar period. Instead, as we've seen, postwar consumption spending turned out to be much greater than what they'd forecasted. The government's experts failed to consider what one astute academic economist—Wesleyan's James J. O'Leary (1945, 37)—recognized at the time as "powerful new factors" that had come into play during the war. Of these new factors, the most important by far was the rationing, if not the complete lack, of all sorts of consumer goods. That many goods, and durable goods especially, weren't available during the war was hardly a secret. But government economists assumed that whatever consumers couldn't spend on autos and refrigerators they were instead spending on clothing, liquor, and other nondurables.

To say that the economists were mistaken on this point would be putting it mildly. Far from keeping up with disposable income during the war, consumption as a share of income nose-dived, while the personal savings rate shot up. "Instead of 'spilling-over' into nondurable expenditures," Michael Sapir (1949, 303) writes, money that couldn't be spent on durable goods "flowed into . . . liquid assets such as currency, bank deposits, and federal government securities," including war bonds. The government, for its part, encouraged workers to buy its bonds by appealing to their patriotism and arranging to have the bonds paid for through payroll deductions (Brunet and Hlatshwayo 2022, 29). By D-Day the public was saving almost 30 percent of its posttax income, as compared to less than 5 percent in 1929.[2]

When the war ended, the public, having practiced abstinence for several years, was sitting on more than $150 billion worth of highly liquid assets, with a matching urge to start shopping (Higgs 1999, 607). With many durable goods still hard to come by at first, the public—especially returning veterans (Sapir 1949, 318)—started out by going on a nondurable-goods spending spree. But eventually, as controls were lifted and reconversion made durable goods increasingly available, demand for them also rose enough to keep their producers in the black and to make jobs available for most former defense workers and demobilized military personnel who wanted them.

Yet it wasn't the case, as some economic historians have assumed, that Americans drew down their wartime savings to finance their shopping spree. Instead, as Robert Higgs (1999, 607–9) has pointed out and as James O'Leary predicted would happen, although the public reduced its savings *rate* after the war, it didn't *dissave* at all. "On the whole," Michael Sapir (1949, 613) observes, citing a careful Federal Reserve study, families "did not want to spend their liquid assets in 1946 on such things as automobiles, refrigerators, and consumer goods generally." Instead, they "preferred if possible to buy out of income, or perhaps borrow on short-term."[3] In fact, although they no longer piled up savings as they had during the war, after the war Americans saved at a rate at first equal to and eventually greater than that of the 1930s and even the 1920s. By 1950 the US savings rate was more than twice its pre-Depression level, and it wasn't to fall any lower until the mid-1980s.

The Investment Revival

That Americans were both consuming more and saving more after the war than they had for many years, and were doing so despite huge cutbacks in government spending, could mean only one thing: businesses were doing their part to buoy up the postwar economy.

And so they were. The postwar investment revival, or whatever forces were behind it, was arguably the most important of the "powerful new factors" driving US economic activity after the war. "In current dollars," Higgs (1999, 609) observes, "gross private domestic investment leaped from $10.6 billion in 1945 to $30.6 billion in 1946, $34.0 billion in 1947, and $46.0 billion in 1948. Relative to GNP, that surge pushed the private investment rate from 5.0 percent in 1945 (it had been even lower during the previous two years) to 14.7 percent in 1946 and 1947 and 17.9 percent in 1948. As a standard for comparison, one may note that the investment rate had been nearly 16 percent during the latter half of the 1920s, before hitting the skids during the depression."

Impressive as the upturn of gross investment was, the revival of *net* investment, which is what actually fuels economic growth, was still more so. "Revival" is the right word because, as we've seen, for most of the 1930s and also while the United States was at war, net private investment gave way to private capital consumption. Having plunged deep into negative territory before Roosevelt took office, private net domestic investment recovered somewhat before dropping to zero again during the 1937 downturn. A second recovery began in 1938, only to be halted by America's entry into the war. During the war, net private investment was once again negative: official statistics put it at minus $6.2 billion.[4] Finally, between 1945 and 1946 net private investment leaped from next to nothing to $18.5 million, "an unprecedented amount" (Higgs 2004, 504). After that net investment swayed between two and three times its 1929 level until the 1960s, when it began rising even higher.

A particularly striking change within this larger development was the rise in net private *fixed* investment, that is, private-sector spending on structures, equipment, and production inputs other than raw materials. Fixed investment differs from total private investment in excluding changes to firms' stocks of unsold goods, or inventory investment. Although inventory investment is often deliberate, in which case it's no less a sign of business buoyancy than investment of other sorts, it can also be an unwanted result of falling demand (Khan 2003). Low inventories may, on the other hand, be a sign of recovery.[5] For this reason, the extent of net fixed private investment is an especially reliable indicator of both the progress of economic recovery and investment's contribution to it. To judge by that measure, shown in figure 24.2, recovery made very little progress during the New Deal but took a giant leap just after the war. Even the fillip given to American manufacturers by Europe's mobilization never managed to raise real net private fixed investment much beyond 80 percent of its August 1929 level. In 1947, it was almost *four times* as high. Statistics such as these show that whatever adjectives may accurately describe the stagnation of investment in the 1930s, "secular" isn't one of them.

No less remarkable than the investment recovery itself is the fact that many American businessmen had been preparing for it. Those businessmen

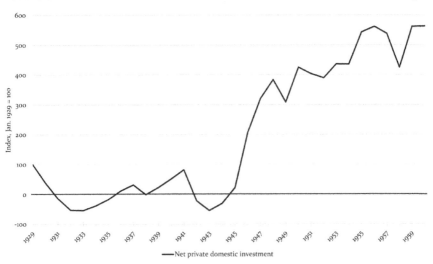

FIGURE 24.2. Net private fixed domestic investment, 1929–1960, index numbers, 1929 = 100. (Data from FRED®, Federal Reserve Bank of St. Louis, https://fred.stlouisfed.org/graph/?g=1pDBO.)

were anticipating a big and enduring postwar jump in consumer spending and doing so just as the administration's economists were fretting about a postwar economic collapse. Instead of taking advantage of high wartime earnings to pay correspondingly high dividends and despite steep taxation of excess corporate profits, many firms used those earnings to build up their reserves. By war's end they'd amassed $25 billion, enough to pay for not just repairs and maintenance deferred during the war but also "substantial facility and equipment expansion" (Ballard 1983, 138; see also Lutz 1945). Just before the war ended, the government estimated that private industry was ready—and, just as importantly, willing—to finance almost 75 percent of the $9 billion in postwar investment then considered essential to achieving full postwar employment (Ballard 1983, 138).

Economists have long understood that "business cycles are mainly about fluctuations in private investment" (Martin 2016; cf. Gordon 1955, 23), that severe downturns inevitably involve a collapse in such investment, and that self-sustaining recoveries after such downturns, with robust real economic growth, are possible only if private investment itself recovers. Expansionary monetary and fiscal policies unaccompanied by such a recovery can equip people with money to offer for goods. But they alone can't deliver the goods.[6] In a very fundamental sense, the postwar revival of private investment was not just a sign that the US economy had recovered. It was the very essence of recovery.

But what was behind it, and why hadn't it happened sooner?

Postwar Monetary Policy

Despite many dire forecasts, the US economy avoided a severe post–World War II depression, and appeared to do so with only modest help from the federal government. Although it drastically reduced its military expenditures as soon as the war ended, the government didn't make up for that reduction with any corresponding increase in public works or other peacetime spending. Nor did it substantially reduce the private sector's tax burden. Yet instead of slumping again, the economy saw its first investment boom since the 1920s.

So much for postwar fiscal policy. But what about monetary policy? Might the postwar economy have been kept humming with the help of generous doses of easy money? Could that have been *all* it really needed to prosper again?

These questions are worth asking for at least two reasons. First, as we've seen, the partial recoveries that took place during the mid and late 1930s were themselves mainly due not to fiscal stimulus but to monetary growth fueled by heavy gold imports. So it's only reasonable to wonder whether monetary expansion was also the key to the US economy's postwar performance. Second, postwar Federal Reserve policy appears to have been exceedingly easy, having mainly consisted of the continuation, up to the famous Treasury Accord of March 4, 1951, of the Fed's wartime commitment to keep interest rates low by propping-up the prices of various Treasury securities (Romero 2013).

Before the Accord

That US monetary policy was easy during World War II no one denies. At first, gold flows remained the main driver of monetary expansion. And, thanks to the "cash-and-carry" policy adopted soon after the war began in

Europe, allowing US merchants to sell war materials to Germany's enemies provided they paid in cash, gold flooded into the United States like never before. In just two years, the US monetary gold stock grew by $5.5 billion. During that same time the Fed's government security holdings hardly budged, and banks hardly borrowed from it. So it was entirely thanks to all that gold that the US monetary base grew by about $3.35 billion, allowing the money stock (currency and commercial bank deposits) in turn to expand by about $13 billion.

Because the Lend-Lease Act of March 1941 allowed countries at war with Germany to get war matériel from us on relatively easy terms, its passage caused the gold inflow to quickly taper off. But once the United States itself went to war, Fed officials determined "to use [the act's] powers to assure at all times an ample supply of funds for financing the war effort" (Richardson 2013). The result was a set of new policies that proved to be an even more potent cause of monetary stimulus than gold imports ever were.

Of those new policies, the most important consisted of the Fed's formal agreement to buy as many three-month Treasury bills as necessary to keep the rate the Treasury paid on them at just three-eighths of 1 percent. The Fed also offered, though informally, to keep the interest rate on twenty-five-year Treasury bonds at 2.5 percent. Once these agreements went into effect during the summer of 1942, instead of pursuing monetary policy in the usual sense, the Fed, in Chairman Eccles's words, "merely executed Treasury decisions" (Meltzer 2003, 579).

As a result of these arrangements, the Fed went on to purchase very large amounts of Treasury securities, expanding the monetary base and total money stock correspondingly. The last grew more than 20 percent in both 1942 and 1943 and by not much less than 15 percent during 1944 and 1945. Thanks to wartime price controls, posted consumer prices only rose by about 11 percent during this same period. No one doubted that they'd increase a lot more once those controls were lifted. Yet the Fed's interest rate pegging went on for several years after the war ended. Its formal agreement to peg the bill rate ended in 1947, causing that rate to initially jump to 1 percent and then rise even more. But rates on longer-term Treasury securities never exceeded their wartime targets until the Treasury Accord went into effect.

It's tempting to suppose therefore that up to the time of the Treasury Accord longer rates remained below their "natural" levels and that, once the war ended, those unnaturally low levels gave an artificial boost to private investment spending, albeit perhaps at the cost of a delayed, if not very severe, late 1940s downturn (Amato 2005).

Not So Easy

But this is another of those temptations that need resisting. For starters, it's worth noting that the same Keynesians who had been so keen on fiscal stimulus saw no corresponding advantage in easy money policies. The view then prevailing among them, Allan Meltzer (2003, 607) observes, "was that monetary policy had, at most, modest effects on output and prices." Consequently, they neither recommended nor promoted a postwar easy money policy. It follows that if the Fed really did pursue such a policy, it must have done so for reasons other than the standard macroeconomic ones widely recognized today.

As we've seen, although he became a Keynesian with no help from John Maynard Keynes, Fed Chair Marriner Eccles's views on the respective roles of fiscal and monetary policy resembled those of most Keynesians of his era: while he had long favored aggressive deficit spending to combat depression, he considered attempts to do the same by resorting to easy money futile. Recall how Eccles's opinion prompted Representative Alan Goldsborough's famous remark comparing easy monetary policy to "pushing on a string" (Taylor 2015). Eccles was also a thoroughgoing inflation hawk who considered an "inflated money supply" the fundamental cause of rising prices. If he allowed the Fed to cooperate with the Treasury during the war, he did so reluctantly, for patriotic reasons, and not without frequently criticizing the Treasury's heavy borrowing.

Of course, neither Eccles's views on monetary stimulus nor those of Keynesians generally ruled out the possibility that monetary policy remained as easy after the war as it had been during it. Fed officials might have chosen to keep money easy for reasons other than a desire to stimulate economic activity. For example, then as now Fed officials worried that rate increases would harm bondholders and worsen the deficit. And the fact remains that rates weren't allowed to rise, except to a very limited extent, until 1950.

But plenty of other evidence suggests that while longer-term interest rates did indeed stay low after the war ended, their low levels were no longer a symptom of easy money. Instead, money growth was subdued throughout the immediate postwar period. How could that be? Friedman and Schwartz (1963, 577) call the modest pace of monetary expansion "the foremost puzzle of the immediate postwar period." But as they themselves recognize, solving the puzzle isn't all that hard: one need only take account of the dramatic postwar change in federal government borrowing. During the war the US government borrowed heavily, and rates were held down despite that borrowing by a combination of substantial Fed purchases of Treasury securities and the government's (apparently credible) commitment to take steps to avoid postwar inflation.[1] After the war, in contrast, rates stayed low with little help from the Fed, because instead of borrowing heavily, the government began paying off its wartime debt. Between the start of 1946 and the end of 1948, the Federal government shed $37 billion of its outstanding interest-bearing debt, reducing it from $227 billion to $190 billion.

During the same period, the Federal Reserve added little to its holdings of federal debt. On the contrary, except during 1947–1948 and the first months of the Korean War, it *reduced* its holdings (Patel 1958, 82). Nor can the two exceptional periods be said to have been ones during which the Fed lapsed back into its wartime easy money ways. During the first period, although the Fed's Treasury bond holdings rose from $1.5 billion to $11 billion, it first offset all but $1 billion of that increase by selling shorter-term securities and then, as an extra check against inflation, raised banks' minimum reserve requirements. When the Fed reentered the bond market during the Korean War, it raised banks' minimum reserve requirements yet again, enough "to reduce potential bank credit expansion by about $12 billion" (1953, 86). In short, the International Monetary Fund's I. G. Patel says, "It would be a mistake to think that the Federal Reserve Banks' open market operations in support of the bond market" during the immediate postwar years "led to any steady monetization of the public debt" (82).

Tight-Money Inflation?

In truth, Allan Meltzer (2003, 631) observes, "the Fed had little enough to do" to keep longer-run interest rates from rising above their wartime targets after the war. Until the Korean War began, its main challenge was keeping them from falling *below* those targets, as they did frequently. Doing that meant selling rather than buying Treasury securities, which, as Patel (1953, 84) notes, was "the reverse of debt monetization." Money growth decelerated accordingly, with annual M1 growth quickly declining from its wartime double-digit levels to less than 6.5 percent in 1946, 5.51 percent in 1947, less than one-half of 1 percent in 1948, and *minus* 1 percent in 1949! Nor did Fed officials mind this: as far as they were concerned, the Fed's principal postwar duty wasn't helping the government pay its bills: it was keeping a lid on inflation.

Even so, inflation was a problem. Although controls had kept the observed rate of consumer price inflation below 2 percent during the last years of the war, once they were relaxed that rate rose quickly, reaching a peak year-on-year value of over 20 percent in March 1946. It's important, however, to distinguish here between the inflation that consisted of prices "catching up" to their equilibrium levels after controls were lifted and the inflation that was due to an ongoing easy money policy. That the inflation of the latter 1940s was mainly of the first sort is suggested by the fact that, after rising quickly to its spring 1947 peak, the inflation rate fell off just as quickly. Although the outbreak of the Korean War led to another burst of inflation, the main cause of that was a wave of "scare buying" by a public convinced that the government was about to start rationing goods again. Consequently, that inflation also tapered off quickly.[2] So, even that burst of inflation can't be blamed on deliberate Fed policy.

Instead, according to most assessments of early postwar Fed policy, to the extent that the Fed was responsible for changes in the behavior of consumer prices, it influenced them not by keeping money too loose but by tightening too much in response to both "catch-up" and "scare buying" inflation. The Fed's response to the period's catch-up inflation almost certainly contributed to the 1949 recession, which witnessed the first outbreak of *deflation* in the United States since the 1930s. So, even though the average inflation rate for the whole 1946–1951 period was a far from trivial 6.5 percent, Alan Meltzer (2003, 582) is right to insist that during this time the Fed "was far from an 'engine of inflation.'"

Net Investment, Naturally

If the Fed wasn't an engine of inflation, might it still have been an "engine of investment"? The combination of low nominal interest rates and high inflation during most of the 1946–1951 period meant that real (inflation-adjusted) interest rates were mostly negative, sharply so during 1946 and 1947. It was during those two years that private net fixed investment took off. As inflation declined afterward, giving way to deflation in 1949 while nominal rates rose, real rates shot up, and investment fell off again. This sounds, some may say, like a classic case of excess money causing an unsustainable investment boom by driving real interest rates below their "natural" levels.

But here again, appearances deceive. Stepping back to take in the larger picture shows that despite the 1949 setback, there was nothing unsustainable about the postwar investment revival. Instead, after that relatively minor setback, net private fixed investment returned to and soon exceeded its previous postwar high. What's more, after the March 1951 Treasury Accord freed interest rates from their former limits, net private investment kept on growing at a modest rate, with only minor interruptions, for almost two decades and did so notwithstanding the fact that rates eventually rose substantially. Since inflation was kept in check during that time, real interest rates rose by roughly the same amount. These developments strongly suggest that the postwar revival of net investment didn't depend on the Fed's ability to keep interest rates low.

$$* * *$$

To conclude, neither fiscal nor monetary stimulus played any substantial part in the postwar investment boom. Postwar fiscal policy had as its chief aim reducing the federal debt and was correspondingly austere. Postwar monetary policy had as its chief aim keeping a lid on inflation and so tended toward overtightening. Despite being essentially conservative, neither policy was so stringent as to have stood in the way of a robust recovery of overall private spending. That was itself a helpful contribution. But if we're to discover the ultimate source of the pronounced and permanent revival of investment that was the real key to a lasting recovery, we must keep looking.

The Great Rapprochement

What finally ended the Great Depression? We've seen that whatever it was, it took place not during the 1930s but sometime between then and the end of World War II, when a remarkable postwar revival occurred instead of the re-newed depression many feared. We've also seen that while postwar fiscal and monetary policies weren't austere to the point of preventing that revival, they alone can't explain it, because they can't explain the reawakening of private business investment from its slumber that lasted for a decade and a half.

Animal Spirits

To get to the bottom of that reawakening, we must recall the part that busi-nessmen's fear of punitive federal government policies played in investment's prewar quiescence. By the mid-1930s, as we've seen, New Deal policies and rhetoric had given businessmen ample reason to be apprehensive about the future. The planners frightened small businesses by treating them as relics of a bygone age and compelling them to abide by codes mainly set by their larger rivals. The trustbusters scared big businesses by threatening to break them up. Neither group put much store in either monetary or fiscal policy, let alone John Maynard Keynes's advice to the effect that a depression was not the right time to be pushing their reforms. This was one of several respects in which, far from having tested Keynesian policies, the New Deal was at loggerheads with Keynes's own advice for achieving economic recovery.

Although it has long been customary to boil that advice down to a call for augmenting total spending ("aggregate demand") through expansionary fiscal or monetary policy, Keynes himself did not leave it at that. Instead, in *The General Theory*'s chapter "The State of Long-Term Expectations," he recognizes a problem distinct from that of deficient demand, one that policy-makers trying to end recessions or depressions must also reckon with. The problem is the "extreme precariousness" of entrepreneurs' assessment of the profits they can expect to gain from their long-term investments. "Most, probably," Keynes says, "of our decisions to do something positive, the full consequences of which will be drawn out over many days to come, can only be taken as a result of animal spirits—of spontaneous urge to action rather than inaction, and not as the outcome of a weighted average of quantitative benefits multiplied by quantitative probabilities. . . . If the animal spirits are dimmed and the spontaneous optimism falters, leaving us to depend on nothing but a mathematical expectation, enterprise will fade and die" (Keynes 1936b, 162).

When Keynes wrote these words, the animal spirits of US industry were as dim as they'd ever been. And enterprise would not really revive until those mercurial sylphs once again cast their spell, making businessmen put aside "the thought of ultimate loss . . . as a healthy man puts aside the expectation of death" (Keynes 1936b, 162). For better or worse, this made economic prosperity "excessively dependent on a political and social atmosphere which is congenial to the average business man. If the fear of a Labour Government or a New Deal depresses enterprise, this need not be the result either of a reasonable calculation or of a plot with political intent;—it is the mere consequence of upsetting the delicate balance of spontaneous optimism. In estimating the prospects of investment, we must have regard, therefore, to the nerves and hysteria and even the digestions and reactions to the weather of those upon whose spontaneous activity it largely depends."

Keynes presumably had such thoughts in mind in February 1938, when he wrote to Franklin Roosevelt, privately this time, to say that if his administration wished to promote recovery, it had to give businessmen reason to be optimistic. That meant being nice to them:

> Businessmen have a different set of delusions from politicians, and need, therefore, different handling. They are . . . easily persuaded to be "patriots," perplexed, bemused, indeed terrified, yet only too anxious to take a cheerful view, vain perhaps but very unsure of themselves, pathetically responsive to a kind word. You could do anything you liked with them, if you would treat them (even the big ones), not as wolves or tigers, but as domestic animals by nature. . . . It is a mistake to think that they are more immoral than politicians. If you work them into the surly, obstinate, terrified mood, of which domestic animals, wrongly handled, are so capable, the nation's burdens will not get carried to market; and in the end public opinion will veer their way. (Keynes 1982 [1938], 7)

As we saw in chapter 18, far from being unique to Keynes, the belief that US businessmen felt discouraged and that they badly needed encouragement if the economy was to fully recover was Depression-era conventional wisdom to which even some New Dealers themselves subscribed. Alexander Sachs, another of Roosevelt's unofficial economic advisers who ran the National Recovery Administration's economic research division, later maintained that entrepreneurship had been "stifled" by the National Recovery Administration and other New Deal programs as well as by policymakers' all-too-evident contempt for capitalists. Businessmen, Sachs said, simply couldn't be expected to invest in such an environment. Getting them to do so meant freeing them "from the crippling controls and hostile atmosphere built up by the Roosevelt Administration" (Rosen 2005, 5). At one point Sachs shared his reflections with Keynes, who affirmed in reply that recovery depended on Roosevelt becoming "reasonably kind to business" (187).

Although Europe's rearmament gave many US businesses a new lease on life, it didn't suffice to dispel businessmen's fears. According to a November 1941 *Fortune* poll, more than 90 percent of business executives still anticipated "some kind of radical restructuring of the nation's economy that would decrease their expected returns from investing in their businesses" (Rosen 2005, 70). Little wonder that private investment remained scanty.

What businessmen didn't know that November was that the confidence they'd lost during the 1930s was about to be restored, with a vengeance. By the end of a year during which the US government did all it could do to "persuade them to be patriots," the animal spirits that had been dimmed for so long glowed brighter than ever.

Reform on Ice

The proximate cause of this dramatic change in businessmen's outlook was, of course, America's entry into World War II. That step was to completely overhaul the government's treatment of businessmen. However, as Alan Brinkley (1995) explains in *The End of Reform*, the stage for this dramatic turnaround was set several years before, by the 1937–1938 collapse. From then on, Brinkley says, the New Deal's reform plans were drowned by a "growing conservative tide in national politics" (139).

When that drowning took place, the New Deal's planners were already out of favor with Roosevelt; and when the European war began, they'd already ceased to be "either numerous or influential" (Brinkley 1995, 40). (Rexford Tugwell, the planners' leader, had left at the end of 1936.) In the meantime, the public had become extremely leery of Roosevelt's Brandeisian-inspired attacks on business, regarding them—much as Keynes and Sachs did—as discouraging recovery. According to an August 1, 1938, report in *Forbes,* "all yardsticks for measuring public sentiment reveal[ed] that President Roosevelt's antibusiness policies are losing their popularity" (Best 1991, 199; see also Polenberg 1975, 254). When Gallup asked around the same time what the government should do to hasten recovery, the favored answer—"Let business alone"—echoed French businessmen's famous reply "Laissez nous faire!" to Louis XIV's comptroller general of finance, Jean-Baptiste Colbert, when he asked how the government might help them.

The results of the 1938 election reflected these opinions. Republican victories, including eighty-one new seats in the House and eight in the Senate and thirteen new governorships, were widely seen as a rejection of the New Deal. Joseph Alsop, already a highly respected journalist, called the vote "a repudiation of precisely the intellectual liberalism for which the New Dealers stand" (quoted in Best 1991, 204). Because many of the Democrats who survived the election were conservative southerners, most of whom never cared for the New Deal, the administration could no longer count on Congress's support for its domestic reform initiatives. "For God's sake," one administration-friendly congressman begged the White House, "don't send us any more controversial legislation!" (Burns 1956, 339). Nor were old initiatives safe: the new Congress quickly pulled the plug on several New Deal programs, including the Commodity Credit Corporation, the Works Progress Administration, and the National Youth Administration. Gary Best calls the June 1938 passage of the Fair Labor Standards Act—a measure that was ultimately "so watered down . . . that it could have little impact on the national economy" (Burns 1956, 344)—the New Deal's "final twitch" (Best 1991, 204).

So much for public opinion. "The only question that remained," Best (1991, 205) says, "was whether Roosevelt and his advisers would accept the verdict and change course." At first, some didn't. Not long after the election, Roosevelt used the occasion of the National Association of Manufacturer's annual convention to take "another of his cracks" at businessmen (Moley 1938). But other New Dealers quickly got the point. By mid-December the *New York Herald Tribune's* Walter Lippmann could already sense a change among some "from a prejudice against business" to a "wish to free business to flourish" (*New York Herald Tribune,* December 13, 1938, cited in Best 1991, 205). Before long, again according to the *Herald Tribune,* a "civil war for the president's mind" was being waged between the administration's die-hard radicals, who wanted Roosevelt to keep up his attacks on business, and its "converted" moderates.

Freed Enterprise

America's involvement in World War II completed this process of regime change. It did so first by causing the Roosevelt administration to renounce its plans for radical economic reform, and then by convincing many that reports of capitalism's decrepitude had been premature.

Even before the United States entered the conflict, World War II had added a fourth R—rearmament—to the New Deal triad of relief, recovery, and reform, and it did not take long for that upstart R to start shoving the original three aside. By putting many formerly unemployed Americans to work, rearmament rendered New Deal relief and recovery efforts otiose, at least temporarily. And conservatives in Congress, if not the New Dealers themselves, were convinced that rearming either Europe or the United States and doing so quickly meant putting New Deal reform efforts on hold. "The conservative bloc forged during the New Deal era," Charlie Witham (2016, 22) observes, "reminded Roosevelt that there would be no question of the nation's defense being provided by anything other than private enterprise: there was no suggestion of nationalizing industries as in Europe. Rather, federal censure of big business was relaxed as corporations were enticed to switch to war production."

It appears as well that after Pearl Harbor Roosevelt no longer needed much convincing. Despite having long vilified American businessmen, he couldn't possibly achieve his ambitious rearmament goals, including fulfilling his promise to get sixty thousand warplanes built in 1942, without their cooperation. He also understood "that businessmen would respond more readily to direction from other businessmen than to orders from what they considered a hostile federal government" (Brinkley 1995, 190; see also Herman 2012, 119).

Businessmen thus came to play important roles in the federal government itself, often as heads of newly established government departments (Witham 2016, 22, 60). Whereas over the course of the New Deal "the economic headquarters of the country had . . . moved from Wall Street to Washington," so that "no major decision could any longer be made in Wall Street without the question being asked, 'What will Washington say to this?'" (Allen 1940, 218), Wall Steet now began taking over Washington. "By mid-1942," Brinkley (1995, 190) observes, "over ten thousand business executives (most of them Republicans) had moved into offices, cubicles, and even converted bathrooms in the hopelessly overcrowded headquarters of the war agencies." At first these businessmen-bureaucrats, many of them "dollar-a-year" men whose real salaries continued to be paid by their old companies, "had to confront New Dealers who opposed their role and suspected their motives" (Herman 2012,

54). But their growing numbers soon "shifted the balance of influence within key departments away from those with low, New Deal assumptions about business toward a more pro-business outlook" (60).

As businessmen filed into Washington, many of the New Deal's heavy hitters filed out. A year after Pearl Harbor, hardly any were left (Brinkley 1995, 145). Of the biggest guns, Harry Hopkins, Henry Wallace, and Harold Ickes alone remained. But businessmen no longer had much reason to fear Hopkins, who tried to patch things up with them after he became secretary of commerce in December 1938.[1] They had even less to fear when he went to London to serve as Roosevelt's personal emissary to Winston Churchill. Wallace, upon becoming vice president, was assigned to various war mobilization boards, where he tried pitting his not so business-friendly mobilization philosophy against Jesse Jones's, and lost. Later, as secretary of commerce, Wallace "made no significant reforms and chose conservative businessmen for his top aids" (Macdonald 1947, 36). Ickes, who had taken "a sadistic delight in needling businessmen" (Cady 1981, 162) and considered handing control of government agencies to them "an affront to Democracy" (Herman 2012, 72), thus found himself isolated and impotent (Brinkley 1995, 145). And his loneliness can only have increased after the 1942 election sent fifty-three former Democratic representatives—eight Senators and forty-five congressmen—packing.

So, what began as a temporary expedient ultimately resulted in a permanent shift in government policy from high-handed interference with business, especially big business, to indulging it.[2] As Brian Waddell (1999, 233) puts it, the war set "the nation on a trajectory of political development very different from that begun during the New Deal. Mobilization . . . shifted political authority and resources from New Dealers to military and corporate personnel . . . and quashed controversial aspects of New Deal interventionism."

Capitalism, After All

As the war dragged on, many New Dealers themselves discovered, in working alongside businessmen, that they "did not always have horns" after all (Brinkley 1995, 173). Nor could the New Dealers deny the war industries' impressive achievements: "No other wartime economy," Arthur Herman (2012, 255) observes, "depended more on free enterprise incentives than America's, and . . . none produced more of everything in quality and quantity, both in military and civilian goods." Although the government let loose the reins on private enterprise and relied, for the most part, on carrots rather than sticks to persuade it to produce war matériel, the United States produced more military supplies than all the other combatants combined and did so with the least sacrifice of consumer goods output, even making allowances for exaggerated wartime output statistics. Even in 1944, when 70 percent of US manufacturing was being devoted to winning the war, more than half of all US businesses, including several major military contractors, were still making consumer goods. In this respect, the United States was the *least* mobilized of all World War II belligerents (335–36).

It's no wonder, then, that many liberals who once considered businessmen their bitter enemies were now ready to bury the hatchet. "The capitalism that had been damned as bankrupt just a few years before," Robert Collins (1981, 81) writes, "was now celebrated for its prodigious feats of production." The war thus "muted liberal hostility to capitalism and the corporate world," diverting liberals' efforts into less confrontational channels (7).

This change of attitude was evident in politicians' rhetoric as well as in actual policies. According to Collins (1981, 80–81), "the attacks on business—both actual and rhetorical—of the late 1930s petered out," giving businessmen "a welcome respite from the tensions of the Depression and the New Deal." "By 1945," Alan Brinkley (1995, 6–7) says, "the critique of modern capitalism that had been so important in the early 1930s . . . was largely gone, or at least so attenuated as to be of little more than rhetorical significance."

Ickes, admittedly, was having none of it. Instead of seeing the US economy's wartime experience as proof that capitalism was alive and kicking, he thought it demonstrated the merits of National Recovery Administration–type corporatist planning. He thus imagined that the war would deal the coup de grâce to the idea that government "should rely upon private enterprise and individual initiative to invent and develop." But hardly anyone else thought so. "What is striking," Mark Wilson (2016, 183–84) says, "is how little traction [Ickes's] perspective had during the reconversion period and longer Cold War era." American policymakers instead drew a conclusion precisely opposite Ickes's, as did businessmen generally. So far as they were concerned, "the fifteen-year debate over the health of U.S. capitalism had . . . been settled in favor of private enterprise" (Witham 2016, 60). Paul Koitsinen (1973, 478) puts it bluntly: "With the conclusion of hostilities, New Deal liberal ideology had been undermined."

Besides appearing to demonstrate the merits of capitalism, the war gave a bad odor to anything that smacked of fascism, including the activist managerial state. Between them, Italy's invasion of Ethiopia, the Spanish Civil War, and the rise and crimes of Hitler forever laid to rest the "cautious admiration for Mussolini" and corporatism that many New Dealers once expressed (Brinkley 1995, 155; see also Whitman 1991). The Cold War in turn put left-wing interventionists on the defensive. As a result of both wars, Alan Brinkley (1995, 155) observes, Americans not only saw "autocracy as the greatest threat to democracy and peace." They also came to see the United States as "admirable above all for *not* being a totalitarian state." And not being a totalitarian state meant rejecting both fascism and socialism in favor of something closer to free enterprise.

Nor was there a lack of support for the genuine free enterprise article. Several postwar antitotalitarian writings, above all Friedrich Hayek's (1944) *The Road to Serfdom,* treated the interventionist state not as a desirable compromise between totalitarianism and laissez-faire but instead as a malignant tumor that threatened to metastasize into full-blown totalitarianism, casting it in the role New Dealers once assigned to large, inadequately regulated corporations. Works such as Hayek's didn't just appeal to conservatives and libertarians. Among American liberals, they reinvigorated "a powerful strain of Jeffersonian anti-statism . . . that had been present all along" (Brinkley 1995, 160). Hayek's book itself also impressed at least one very prominent European liberal. After reading *The Road to Serfdom* on his way to the 1945 Bretton Woods Conference, Keynes wrote to Hayek from a New Jersey hotel, calling it "a grand book" and declaring himself "in agreement with virtually the whole of it; and not only in agreement with it, but in a deeply moved agreement."

Although Keynes and Hayek are usually regarded as poles apart, with Keynes serving as the principal bête noire of capitalism's champions, viewed against the background of the New Deal's more heavy-handed efforts, let alone against that of outright fascism, socialism, and communism, they had much in common. Both men considered themselves liberals, and both preferred capitalism to any sort of totalitarianism. Setting aside a recondite (albeit bitter) dispute about the role of saving on one hand and monetary expansion on the other in either causing or combating business cycles (Kurz 2019; White 2012, 137–41), the difference between them, though far from trivial, was in an important respect one of degree rather than in kind. It's true, of course, that Keynes, in supposing that "those carrying it out" would be "rightly oriented in their own minds and hearts," was far less wary of government planning than Hayek, who believed instead that "the worst get on top" (White 2012, 171–72). But unlike many of his other contemporaries, including die-hard American New Dealers, Keynes was, in the British academic argot of the time, a "Thermostater" rather than a "Gosplanner": he favored having the government contribute to and manage aggregate demand, especially by making up for slack private investment, but he was not keen on all-around government planning (Singh 2009, 371).

Robert Skidelsky (2020, 2) portrays the difference between Hayek and Keynes nicely as one concerning "the nature of the inoculation needed against the collectivist virus. Keynes wanted to inject a limited amount of what they both called 'planning' into the economy to protect the patient from its virulent form. Hayek claimed that Keynes's vaccine was bound to bring on the full-blown disease. Keynes in turn thought that Hayek's intransigent resistance to any encroachment on market allocation was likely to bring on the very evils it claimed to prevent." In truth, both Hayek and Keynes played their part in the postwar capitalist revival, and it is only because that revival took place that they can now be cast, in textbooks, monographs, and humorous videos, as extreme antagonists (Wapshott 2011; Emergent Order 2010).

Spontaneous Optimism

Between them, the war boom and changed political climate swept away most of the concerns that had stood in the way of a revival of business confidence, "allow[ing] businessmen to finally shake off the pessimism of the Depression years" (Witham 2016, 6; see also Hickman 1960, 161). Capitalism now seemed healthier than ever, and "no one wanted to return to the state of uncertainty that dominated the pre-war years" (Witham 2016, 6).

Much as businessmen tended then, and still tend, to be fiscal conservatives, and despite the tendency of many today to deprecate Keynesianism, back in the 1940s Keynesianism was a welcome change from the old New Deal, with its antibusiness rhetoric, micro-interference, sometimes punitive taxes, and continuous, often disconcerting experimentation. It was indeed largely thanks to "the significant effort by elements of the business community . . . to arrange a detente with the New Deal" (Collins 1978, 370) that what Roosevelt called "compensatory fiscal policy" became his administration's preferred (if never actually implemented) means for averting a postwar depression.

Our review in chapter 20 of attempts to test the "regime uncertainty" hypothesis, specifically meaning the claim that New Deal policies and rhetoric discouraged business investment, led to the conclusion that the hypothesis was both hard to prove and hard to dismiss. But that conclusion referred to evidence from the 1930s only. The wartime and postwar record greatly strengthens the case for the regime uncertainty hypothesis. It does so in part by disposing of the rival hypothesis that businessmen had simply run out of profitable new investment opportunities. Writing during the war, H. W. Arndt (1944, 65), who subscribed to the "no more opportunities" thesis, observed that if it was correct, it would be "extremely unlikely that . . . private enterprise unaided by [large-scale] expansionist measures" would bring about a full recovery. But post–New Deal experience mostly supports the regime uncertainty hypothesis by showing how completely the revival of business investment coincided with that of business confidence.

When economists today say that World War II ended the Great Depression, most have in mind the consequences of massive wartime spending, not the government-business détente the war inspired. Yet that détente ultimately mattered more, for it endured, whereas the spending didn't. That détente is what made possible the rallying of animal spirits that was crucial to the postwar investment boom. "Conventional wisdom has it," Gary Best (1991, 222) observes, "that the massive government spending of World War II finally brought a Keynesian recovery from the depression." However, Best continues, the fact that the government *was no longer at war with business,* as it had been during the original New Deal, deserves more credit. "That," Best says, "and not the emphasis on spending alone, is the lesson that needs to be learned."[3]

Yet Another New Deal?

"By 1945," Alan Brinkley (1995, 269) says, "American liberals . . . had reached an accommodation with modern capitalism. . . . They had, in effect, detached liberalism from its earlier emphasis on reform." The new "liberalism was a result of many things: of the failures and unintended consequences of some of the reform efforts of the early 1930s; of the impact of the recession of 1937–38, the frustrations that unexpected crisis had created, and the reassessments it had inspired; of the emergence of a new set of economic ideas—ultimately identified with John Maynard Keynes—that provided an alternative to older, more institutional approaches; of the dramatic economic growth of the 1940s, the experiences of wartime economic mobilization, the resurgence of popular conservatism, and the growing fear of totalitarianism" (266–67).

Postwar liberals were "less inclined to challenge corporate behavior [and] more reconciled to the existing structure of the economy." Nor were they keen on "controlling or punishing 'plutocrats' and 'economic royalists,' an impulse central to the New Deal rhetoric of the mid-1930s. . . . 'Planning' now meant an Olympian manipulation of macroeconomic levers, not direct intervention in the day-to-day affairs of the corporate world" (Brinkley 1995, 7). Keynesian thinking clearly contributed to this change. But such thinking is properly seen not as a continuation of the New Deal but as an *alternative* to it. The (mostly younger) New Dealers who stayed in Washington after Truman became president hoped that his "21-point plan" (Truman 1945b), of which the Full Employment Bill was but one component, would bring about a full-fledged New Deal revival. But with the exception of a few minor provisions, the rest of that plan fared even worse in Congress than the Full Employment Bill itself did. According to Thomas Emerson (1991, 328), the Office of War Mobilization and Reconversion lawyer who led the effort to rally support for the plan, its failure "was devastating to the morale" of surviving New Dealers because it meant that "progressive action on the part of the government was ended for the indefinite future." Consequently, many, including Emerson himself, soon left Washington for good.

Alas, games with names make the straightforward fact that the New Deal had breathed its last before the war ended harder to recognize than it ought to be. Although most of the more influential liberals of the Truman years, including many Keynesians, had little "interest or faith in many of the reform ideas that had once been central to the New Deal," many were nonetheless content to "wrap themselves in [the New Deal's] mantle" (Brinkley 1995, 4, 265). Consequently, their less reform-oriented and "experimentally-minded" (Emerson 1991, 310) brand of liberalism came to be regarded by many historians not as something that supplanted the New Deal but instead as either a continuation of the Second New Deal or a "Third New Deal" with roots in the 1937 downturn (Jeffries 1996). One historian even has the Second New Deal, which most sources say lasted no later than 1938, reaching its "intellectual zenith" during the war (Hamby 1968, 598), as if the Second New Deal hadn't consisted of just the sort of business-intimidating experiments and reforms that the war swept aside and that Keynes himself bewailed!

The thinking of the most prominent US Keynesian supports the view that the turn to Keynesianism represented a departure from rather than a mere twist upon the New Deal. Although Alvin Hansen was nominally a New Dealer, during an interview with him toward the end of 1941, Richard Strout learned that Hansen did "not give a whoop about the New Deal one way or another" (Strout 1941, 888–89): unlike true-blue New Dealers, but like many later Keynesians, Hansen considered the role of government to be a "marginal" one, aimed at "promoting the expansion of private enterprise" through the use of deficit spending to avoid or counter unemployment.

This isn't to say that the New Deal, properly understood, contributed nothing to postwar stability and growth. First and most importantly, New Dealers managed—albeit with plenty of help from Herbert Hoover's men—to put an end to the monetary crisis that had brought an already depressed US economy to its knees. For decades (not forever, alas), early New Deal reforms made bank runs rare while making banking crises appear to be a thing of the past. How long the Great Depression might have lasted had the banking situation not been stabilized is anyone's guess. To the extent that they increased the size of government, New Deal reforms also reduced somewhat the US economy's vulnerability to adverse changes in private investment, if only by sacrificing some long-run growth.

It remains true, nonetheless, that the Great Depression was still going strong when World War II broke out in Europe. Although recovery commenced once the banking crisis was resolved and the dollar's gold anchor was weighed, it did so in fits and starts. Subsequent New Deal policies were mainly responsible for the fits. The partial recovery itself was mainly a result of the "gold rush" begun by devaluation and kept going by Hitler's rise to power and the subsequent, rapidly growing odds of war.

To point these things out isn't to condemn the New Deal root and branch, for as has been emphasized here again and again, economic recovery was not New Dealers' only goal. Those wishing to celebrate the New Deal might do so, first of all, by pointing to any of its many longer-term achievements they consider worthwhile. They can also observe that the New Deal provided jobs to millions of otherwise unemployed Americans while helping many, through mortgage refinancing, to keep their homes and farms. And if those who celebrate the New Deal don't mind letting Hoover appointees share some of the credit, they can claim that by resolving the banking crisis and loosening the dollar's "golden fetters," early New Deal actions ended the Great Contraction, thereby making recovery *possible*. But they cannot say, without contradicting a wealth of evidence, that most subsequent New Deal policies and rhetoric promoted recovery more than they hampered it.

✳ ✳ ✳

The practical lesson to be drawn from our assessment of the New Deal's bearing on recovery ought to be obvious enough. When the next severe downturn occurs, policymakers and other experts will once again cast about for ways out. Relying on conventional wisdom, many will be tempted to seek them among various New Deal undertakings. But if, as has been argued here, many New Deal policies held back recovery, while those that helped most—such as ensuring bank deposits and relaxing gold standard limits on monetary expansion—are as unrepeatable as losing one's virginity, they'd be wiser to treat most of the New Deal episode as a warning about steps best avoided and to look elsewhere for better ones.

Notes

Preface

1. By the same token, I have nothing to say about New Deal securities regulation and the Tennessee Valley Authority (TVA), because the studies of them that I'm aware of are inconclusive as to their bearing on recovery. Concerning the 1933 Securities Act and the 1934 Securities Exchange Act and the challenges involved in assessing their bearing on corporate investment, see Hubbard (1934) and Eiteman (1940). Concerning the TVA, most of its dams and other projects were completed too late for their consequences to have played any part in the pre–World War II recovery (Powell 2003, 141–52); I implicitly consider the more immediate stimulus effects of TVA-related spending in chapter 13 on New Deal fiscal policy. For (unflattering) assessments of the TVA's long-term bearing on regional economic development, see Chandler (1984) and Kitchens (2014).

Chapter One

1. Currer Bell [Charlotte Brontë], *Jane Eyre.*

2. After claiming, reasonably, that Darby's numbers are best for answering the question "did the New Deal help people," Eric Rauchway (2008) goes on to suggest, ludicrously, that no one would choose to refer to the BLS-Lebergott series except to "show[] the New Deal in the worst possible light." In fact, economic historians of all sorts routinely refer to the BLS-Lebergott statistics not because they have it in for the New Deal but because those statistics are useful for answering *other* questions. Brad DeLong (2008) gets this right. "The fact that a huge number of people were on work relief jobs in the late 1930s," he correctly says, "is powerful evidence that the economy-as-we-know-it did not recover from the Great Depression until the 1940s."

3. That this peak occurred in an election month was no coincidence. WPA payments tended to increase substantially in election years even when economic conditions were on the upswing. Concerning the politics of New Deal relief spending; see Wright (1974) and Couch and Shughart (1998) For an account published in November 1938 with specific reference to the WPA, see Sullivan (1938). That serious abuses of relief spending occurred doesn't prove that the Roosevelt administration either condoned or benefited from them. According to Wallis, Fishback, and Kantor (2006, 343), Roosevelt "gained little or nothing from such abuses" and strove to limit them.

4. As Jason Smith (2016) notes, while Eichengreen's chart is meant to illustrate how nations that hastened to abandon the gold standard tended to emerge from the Depression most rapidly, a look beyond the period it covers suggests that the connection is less cut and dried than his chart makes it seem and that the different degrees of recovery had more to do with differences in fiscal policy.

5. Besides the United States, the countries surveyed were Australia, Canada, Czechoslovakia, Denmark, Estonia, France, Germany, Hungary, Italy, Japan, Latvia, the Netherlands, Poland, South Africa, Sweden, Switzerland, and the United Kingdom.

6. Since they're referring to the same statistics mentioned here, it's puzzling to find Eichengreen and Hatton (1988, 11) describing the United States as one of several nations that experienced a "strong recovery" in industrial unemployment, while declaring that in France and several other nations unemployment rose "to persistently higher levels after 1930." Although in some countries unemployment peaked after 1933, in no case did it rise "persistently" afterward. In France it rose to 14.5 percent in 1935 but fell to just 8.1 percent by 1939.

Chapter Two

1. Rauchway (2019) maintains that Hoover's October 21, 1932, Madison Square Garden speech (Hoover 1932a), with its summary and harsh criticism of Roosevelt's supposed plans, proves that Roosevelt must have revealed those plans. In fact, it proves just the opposite: Hoover says clearly in it that the New Deal plan he describes, far from ever being made "clear and explicit" by his opponent, is a conjecture based on indirect evidence including "the legislative acts . . . sponsored and passed in the Democratic-controlled House of Representatives in the last session of Congress" and "the type of leaders who are campaigning for the Democratic ticket." Rauchway's (2019, 202) reference to the "scholarship" upon which Hoover's remarks were based itself hints at this fact: no scholarship is needed to discover something "clear and explicit." Although some of Hoover's conjectures were prescient, many, including the most incendiary ones, had no basis at all in anything Roosevelt actually promised to do during his campaign.

2. Although Roosevelt (1932a) told the crowd at Chicago Stadium that he was "sure that the farmers of this Nation would agree ultimately to such planning of their production as would reduce the surpluses and make it unnecessary in later years to depend on dumping those surpluses abroad in order to support domestic prices," this committed him to nothing beyond welcoming voluntary restraint on farmers' part of the sort Hoover himself considered palatable.

3. Because Warburg, like Morley, parted company with Roosevelt and then became one of his more severe critics, Rauchway (2019, 209) attributes this and other complaints by Warburg to his "tendentious hostility." But Warburg was hardly alone in thinking that by endorsing the platform's "sound currency" plank Roosevelt committed himself to upholding the gold standard.

Chapter Three

1. Alas, the one failure—of the Home Bank of Canada in August 1923—was also Canada's worst ever: when it failed, the Home Bank's assets were worth less than a fifth of the $15.5 million owed its depositors and other creditors. Tens of thousands of Canadians lost their life savings. But the Home Bank was far from being a mere victim of the agriculture slump: instead, its officers ran it into the ground while cooking its books.

2. After holding steady for several years, the index of prices of farm goods fell by about 20 percent following the stock market crash. Although it grew out of a proposal specifically aimed at protecting US farmers, the Smoot-Hawley Tariff Act of 1930 ended up contributing to that decline by reducing the demand for US exports of all kinds. It did this both directly and by causing many countries to retaliate with their own stiff tariffs (Mitchener, O'Rourke, and Wandshneider 2022). Concerning the harm done to banks by the post-1929 decline in the value of bank investments other than loans to farmers, see Temin (1976, 106–7) and White (1984).

3. "Reconstruction Finance Corporation Act," January 22, 1932, FRASER, https://fraser .stlouisfed.org/title/6261.

4. The year 1932 was the last in which Congress convened on the first Monday of December. In 1933 the date was changed to January 3, where it has remained ever since.

5. The near coincidence of Glass turning down the Treasury portfolio with Michigan's bank holiday makes it impossible to say which event contributed more to the subsequent run on gold, for either may have increased the perceived likelihood of devaluation. James Butkiewicz (1999) overlooks this coincidence in arguing that, because the dollar only started to depreciate on major exchanges after Michigan's holiday, it must have been that holiday, rather than doubts about Roosevelt's devotion to the gold standard, that triggered the run on gold. Wigmore (1987), on the other hand, points to the Carter Glass story without mentioning Michigan's bank holiday.

6. According to a painstaking econometric study by Calomiris and Mason (2003b), the panic that took hold among bank depositors in early 1933 was the only one that clearly qualifies as "nationwide." Calomiris and Mason note that their model cannot distinguish a panic stemming from a generalized fear of bank insolvencies from one due to fear of devaluation. It is worth noting, however, that the second most widespread panic they identify is the one that followed Britain's September 1931 suspension of the gold standard, which was itself clearly a run on the dollar.

Chapter Four

1. Refusing to take advantage of its legal right to take up to ninety days to meet depositors' requests, Howard Savings met all the demands upon it, extending its hours until six that evening to do so ("Bank Meets All Calls" 1933). It survived until 1992.

2. The characterization seems, at very least, a willfully perverse one to foist on the man history knows as "the Great Humanitarian." Referring specifically to Hoover's conduct during the banking crisis, Raymond Moley (1966, 210) upholds that traditional view, observing—as if anticipating Rauchway's opposite claim—that "the charge that Hoover was indifferent to human suffering . . . was unfair. It was not because of Hoover's indifference that he failed. It was the ineptitude of so many of his efforts to stem the decline." In a work otherwise as sympathetic to Roosevelt as Rauchway's, Jonathan Alter (2007, 181) levies the charge of cold-bloodedness not at Hoover but at his successor. "It is hard to avoid the conclusion," Alter writes, "that he [Roosevelt] intentionally allowed the economy to sink lower so that he could enter the presidency in a more dramatic fashion."

3. "Emergency Banking Relief Act," March 9, 1933, FRASER, https://fraser.stlouisfed.org /title/1098.

4. In her very thorough study of New Deal banking reforms, Helen M. Burns (1974, 113) goes a step further, declaring that "neither the Emergency Banking Act nor the Banking Act of 1933 was intrinsically related to the New Deal program. One was borne of necessity, the other of compromise. . . . The development of a Roosevelt banking program lay in the future."

5. H.R. 1471, 73rd Congress (1933), 6.

6. For this reason, I believe that so far as the banks that were licensed to reopen at once are concerned, Peter Conti-Brown and Sean H. Vanatta (2021) exaggerate the part examinations played in rendering credible Roosevelt's claim that only "sound" banks would reopen. Other banks did pose a challenge, but the examiners had more time to contend with those, and, as we'll see, many of those the soundness of which remained in doubt were only reopened after they agreed to have their capital augmented by the RFC.

7. The sole exception, Harriman National Bank, went into receivership in October 1933. Joseph Harriman, its chairman and former president, had by then been arraigned for fraud. He was found guilty and sentenced to several years in prison in 1934. Three days later his confidential secretary hurled herself out the window of a Manhattan skyscraper ("Business: Guilty Harriman" 1934).

8. Eventually only 179 of the banks licensed to reopen on March 15 were suspended between then and the end of the year (Board of Governors of the Federal Reserve System 1936, 59).

Chapter Five

1. "Banking Act of 1933," June 16, 1933, FRASER, https://fraser.stlouisfed.org/title/991.

2. To this list we might add a fourth item, noted by Golembe in a subsequent interview (Burstein 1998), namely, that FDIC "insurance" isn't really insurance at all. Unlike genuine insurance policies, it covers depositors for losses regardless of their cause. The FDIC's insurance "fund" is also nothing more than an accounting fiction: instead of being retained and invested by the FDIC, the "premiums" it collects from banks go into the federal government's general coffers. "The government's guarantee of deposit," Golembe explains, "was given the name 'insurance' because that sounded much less radical than 'guarantee.' . . . The problem with calling it 'deposit insurance' which it clearly is not, is that some bankers and most academics began to believe it!"

3. The 1933 Banking Act did away with double liability for national bank shares issued after its passage while leaving this provision in place for outstanding ones. The 1935 Banking Act allowed any bank to exempt all its shareholders from double liability six months after it publicly announced its intent to do so. Most state bank regulators also did away with double liability during the Depression. Jonathan Macey and Geoffrey Miller (1992, 32, 61) argue, compellingly, that double liability was "remarkably effective at protecting bank creditors, including depositors" and "that the nation took a wrong turn" by replacing it with government-administered deposit insurance.

4. In the deposit insurance context, "moral hazard" refers to the tendency of depositors to take advantage of having their deposits insured by placing them with relatively risky banks. "Adverse selection" refers to the tendency of riskier banks to be most likely to lobby for, join, and stay enrolled in deposit insurance schemes.

5. Some Mississippi banks had branches in their head office cities only. Washington allowed branching between 1907 and 1920, when it prohibited the establishment of further branches.

6. Grossman (1994, 674) also finds that "despite anecdotal evidence and the great stress placed on its importance in the literature," the extent of central bank last-resort lending was not an important determinant of banking system stability.

7. Another reason why deposit insurance schemes multiplied during the 1980s and 1990s was the publication of Douglas Diamond and Philip Dybvig's influential 1983 paper, for which they recently won the Bank of Sweden prize, purporting to supply a rigorous, theoretical justification for deposit insurance (Diamond and Dybvig 1983). Because it assumes that banks only make safe

investments while depicting bank runs as random events, the Diamond-Dybvig theory does not allow for moral hazard. Such question-begging assumptions make deposit insurance seem like a no-brainer. Concerning them and other shortcomings of the Diamond and Dybvig theory, see Selgin (2020a, 2020b).

8. Although there is plenty of anecdotal evidence of moral hazard problems in all of the state-sponsored insurance arrangements, Kansas's has been especially well documented. For that case, see Alston, Grove, and Wheelock (1994), Wheelock and Wilson (1994), and Wheelock and Wilson (1995).

9. Whether this achievement was worthwhile is another matter. After comparing the actual costs of deposit insurance with back-of-the-envelope estimates, based on plausible assumptions, of what post–Great Depression bank failures would have cost without it, Eugene White (1998, 119) finds it "hard to escape the conclusion that deposit insurance did not substantially reduce aggregate losses from bank failures and may have raised them."

10. These remarks refer to uninsured banks, which were the only sort on the eve of the Banking Act's passage. Because deposit insurance can make depositors indifferent to the risks their banks take, insured banks may in fact be tempted to take on riskier assets for the sake of attracting depositors through higher interest payments. According to Charles Calomiris and Matthew Jaremski (2019), that is precisely what banks participating in twentieth-century state insurance schemes did until those schemes failed. The ironic implication of this is that by introducing nationwide deposit insurance, the 1933 Banking Act also supplied a rational for Regulation Q that was not present beforehand!

11. The Pecora Commission held hearings between April 1932 and March 1933 as part of its investigation of the causes of the 1929 crash. The commission was named after Ferdinand Pecora, the chief council charged with writing its final report who also presided over the last and most sensational phase of those hearings.

12. Thus Paul Volcker declared, in 1986, that "Congressional hearings on the securities practices of banks *disclosed* that bank affiliates had underwritten and sold unsound and speculative securities, published deliberately misleading prospectuses, manipulated the price of particular securities, misappropriated corporate opportunities to bank officers, [and] engaged in insider lending practices and unsound transactions with affiliates" (Benston 1990, 12, emphasis added).

13. See Moore (1934), Edwards (1942), White (1986), Benston (1990), Kroszner and Rajan (1994), Ang and Richardson (1994), and Puri (1994).

14. That activities prohibited by the Glass-Steagall provisions in 1933 weren't to blame for the preceding banking crisis doesn't necessarily mean that repeal of some of those same provisions played no part in the 2007–2009 crisis. For arguments that it didn't, see McDonald (2016) and Mahoney (2018). For the opposite view, see Wilmarth (2018).

15. Some of the more important contributions to the debate on whether stock prices in the late 1920s were unjustified by fundamentals are, in chronological order, Dominguez, Fair, and Shapiro (1988); White (1990); DeLong and Shleifer (1991); Bierman (1991); Cecchetti (1992); Rappoport and White (1993); and McGrattan and Prescott (2004).

Chapter Six

1. Both Hoover's critics and his champions have tried to correct the record regarding his willingness to resort to government intervention in response to the Depression. For an excellent survey, see Patrick O'Brien and Philip Rosen (1981a, 1981b). Although Steven Horwitz (2011),

in an otherwise excellent contribution to this effort, attributes the phrase "Hoover New Deal" to Murray Rothbard, Rothbard himself (1972, 128n31) borrowed it from Chase National Bank economist Benjamin Anderson.

2. The fons et origo of the myth that the RFC was Hoover's idea appears to be Jesse Jones's 1951 memoir (1951, 14). Despite their opposite party affiliations, Meyer and Jones were friends until 1942, when the *Washington Post*, which Meyer had owned since 1933, published an editorial harshly critical of Jones's handling of the RFC's synthetic rubber program. When the two men ran into each other that evening at the entrance to the Willard Hotel ballroom, where the Alfalfa Club was holding its annual dinner, the confrontation ended in fisticuffs. Meyer, the younger of the two, was sixty-six years old. Asked about the fight the next day, Roosevelt remarked, off the record, that he hoped "there wouldn't be a second round" (Tuttle 1981, 35–36). It was, some say, the grudge Jones held against Meyer ever after that caused him to downplay Meyer's part in the RFC's establishment.

3. In fairness to Hoover and to the bankers behind it, the NCC's failure was not entirely their fault. Instead, the NCC's efforts were frustrated by the Federal Reserve's refusal to loosen its own credit eligibility requirements, as the NCC's organizers had hoped it would do in its dealings with the NCC.

4. Other large RFC loans also raised eyebrows because prominent Republicans were among their recipients' directors. They included loans for more than $26 million that the RFC made to two Cleveland banks whose directors happened to include Charles Dawes's successor, Atlee Pomerene, and Joseph Nutt, the treasurer of the Republican National Committee. Although it may have been a coincidence, the fact is that Republicans commanded the boards of almost every big bank the RFC helped during the Hoover years (Flynn 1933).

5. The importance of the RFC's loans to defunct banks shouldn't be underestimated. Those loans may actually have accomplished more than its loans to open banks. As Lester Chandler (1970, 149) explains, besides allowing depositors at failed banks to be paid quickly, RFC loans helped conservators avoid having to liquidate failed banks' assets in a hurry, which would have meant realizing less on them as well as harming other institutions holding the same assets by depressing their prices. Between March 1933 and October 1937, the RFC authorized more than $875 million of such loans.

6. On the opposite views of New York Fed officials and commercial bankers on one hand, and Chicago Fed officials and commercial bankers on the other, concerning whether the RFC should support insolvent banks, see Mason (2009, 80–82).

7. Title II of the same act—the so-called Bank Conservation Act—substantially increased the ability of closed national banks to take advantage of RFC loans and stock purchases. It did so by allowing the comptroller of the currency to appoint conservators to them while replacing a former rule requiring unanimous (creditor) consent for any reorganization with a rule allowing creditors representing 75 percent or more of a national bank's liabilities or stockholders owning two-thirds of its capital to decide whether to reorganize.

Chapter Seven

1. For Fed circulars, executive orders and proclamations, and various other official documents referred to here pertaining to the banking emergency, see US Department of the Treasury (1933).

2. H.R. 1471, 73rd Congress (1933), 1.

3. Although the Treasury's silver purchases added $1.22 billion to Fed member bank reserves between late 1933 and the end of 1938, most of these purchases resulted not from the Thomas Amendment but instead from the Silver Purchase Act of 1934. In any case, their effect on the money stock was mostly offset by the Treasury's concurrent retirement of $900 million in national bank notes. The Treasury's net contribution to bank reserves was just $320 million—a very small share of the total increase of about $6 billion, most of which was due to gold inflows.

4. Morgenthau became acting secretary of the treasury in November 1933, when William Woodin, who was then gravely ill, took a leave of absence. Morgenthau became treasury secretary in his own right when the dying Woodin resigned on December 31, 1933.

5. Although some experts (e.g., Eichengreen 1995, 342) attribute the summer 1933 "boomlet" to the dollar's depreciation, we'll see later that this spurt of activity was also, and perhaps mostly, a consequence of businessmen's decision to boost production ahead of NRA-inspired increases in the cost of labor and other inputs.

6. In March 1934, Hitler congratulated Roosevelt "for his heroic efforts in the interests of the American people," telling him that his "successful battle against economic distress is being followed by the entire German people with interest and admiration" (Toland 1977, 324).

Chapter Eight

1. Madsen (2001, 327–28) reaches a similar conclusion for both the United States and other countries hard-hit by the Depression. The decline in agricultural prices, he says, had significant macroeconomic effects "because the agricultural sector played an important role in the total economy at the time" and also "because the agricultural decline had spill-over effects to other sectors of the economy." In particular, Madsen finds that the decline in agricultural prices contributed significantly to the general collapse of investment during the Depression's first years (350).

2. According to Eric Rauchway (2018, 78), Roosevelt also "indicated to Hoover the importance of a farm bill, telling the president at their White House meeting on November 22 that if a law incorporating his [and progressing Republicans'] ideas about farm relief could be passed in the lame-duck sitting, then he might be able to avoid calling Congress into a special session on March 4, because the nation's most pressing economic need would already have been addressed." This, of course, was long before anyone had any inkling of the banking crisis that would erupt in the weeks leading to Roosevelt's inauguration.

3. "Agricultural Adjustment Act," May 12, 1933, FRASER, https://fraser.stlouisfed.org/title /6439.

4. The Brookings Institution's conclusion is the flip side of one reached recently by Joshua Hausman, Paul Rhode, and Johannes Wieland (2021, 676). They observe that, because farmers probably "had a higher MPC [marginal propensity to consume] than the agents benefitting from lower farm product prices," the mere redistribution of earnings *away* from farmers at start of the Depression would almost certainly have been contractionary even if it hadn't been a source of banking system distress. The fact that farmers were often heavily indebted to their banks tended, on the other hand, to increase their propensity to consume.

5. Whereas tenant farmers paid their landlords for the right to farm on part of their property and owned the resources they employed to do so, sharecroppers were typically mere farm laborers whose pay consisted of a share (usually one half) of either the proceeds from sales of their crops or the crops themselves.

6. As the term suggests, a "managing" tenant took part in farm management decisions. While Black managing tenants suffered along with ordinary tenants and sharecroppers from AAA-inspired crop reduction, white managing tenants do not appear to have been displaced to any similar extent. Far from going unnoticed at the time, the adverse effect of AAA's cotton program on sharecroppers and many tenants became a national scandal that compelled Chester Davis, the AAA's head, to launch an investigation into them. Despite uncovering abundant evidence of southern landlords' violation of their AAA contracts, the investigation did not lead to any change in the AAA's policies. On the contrary, when the head of its legal division tried in 1935 to have its contracts interpreted and enforced in a manner less prejudicial to tenants and sharecroppers, he and most of his staff were fired. The reason wasn't other New Dealers' indifference to dispossessed farmers' plight. Instead, it was a simple matter of party politics. "The New Deal could function without the socially conscious lawyers," Lawrence J. Nelson (1983, 433) pithily explains, "but it risked paralysis without the support of conservatives in and out of the AAA."

7. Despite agreeing with him, Schultz regretted Davis's decision to emphasize the AAA's failure to promote recovery rather than its contribution to agricultural reform.

8. Hausman, Rhode, and Wieland (2021) credit the redistribution of income toward farmers, to which the dollar's depreciation contributed, for much of the spring 1933 recovery while noting that contemporary press accounts did the same. They find, on the other hand, that the AAA contributed little to recovery during its first months.

9. 7 U.S.C. 601 et seq. (1933), 9.

10. As in the Schechter Poultry case, the Supreme Court's AAA decision rested in part on a strict interpretation of the commerce clause. In this case the court determined that since the output of farms wasn't interstate commerce, Congress lacked any constitutional authority to regulate it. Because the whole purpose of the processing tax was to compensate farmers for producing less, the tax was but a means to an unconstitutional end" (*United States v. Butler*, 1936). The court also held that Congress had unconstitutionally delegated its power to tax to the Department of Agriculture.

Chapter Nine

1. Because "hourly earnings" can change owing to either increased overtime pay or workers shifting from lower to higher wage-rate jobs, they are a less than perfect proxy for hourly wage rates. Unfortunately, the only hourly wage rate index available for the Great Depression period stops in 1935. Up to that point, for what it's worth, the two measures are closely correlated.

2. "National Industrial Recovery Act," June 16, 1933, FRASER, https://fraser.stlouisfed.org/title/1136/item/1511.

3. As John Flynn (1934) points out, Roosevelt's own "planners" had relatively little to do with the drafting of the NIRA. Nor can they be said to have wholeheartedly favored its approach to industrial planning. Rex Tugwell (1932), for one, considered the Chamber of Commerce and Swope proposals on which the NIRA was based half-baked. "It is," he said in an article published just as he was being asked to join Roosevelt's Brain Trust, "a logical impossibility to have a planned economy and to have businesses operating its industries." Although Tugwell believed that the NIRA improved on those proposals by providing for government approval and enforcement of whatever plans businessmen came up with, he felt that it still granted them too much influence.

4. The press was particularly concerned by the licensing provision, which it viewed as a threat to its freedom. For that reason, although newspapers agreed to sign on to the blanket

code, they insisted on having a clause added giving notice that by doing so they weren't waving their constitutional rights (Patch 1933).

5. The NIRA's Section 7(a) affirmed workers' right to bargain collectively and imposes penalties on employers who seek to prevent their doing so, while Section 7(b) allowed the president to give legal sanction to collective bargaining agreements, thus making them enforceable in the courts.

6. "National Labor Relations Act," July 5, 1935, FRASER, https://fraser.stlouisfed.org/title/5568.

7. Although Roosevelt ultimately supported the Wagner Act, James MacGregor Burns (1956, 219) says that he did so only "at the last moment, when it was due to pass away," having done nothing to aid its passage until then. "By coming out for the bill," Burns writes, "Roosevelt could influence some important provisions still open, and he could wangle his way out of what might be called an administration defeat."

8. The departure consists of replacing the usual New Keynesian assumption of "sticky" prices, which has them adjust slowly even though agents are forward-looking, with one that has prices responding sluggishly to actual shocks only.

9. In a vector autoregression model, the observed value of each variable at any given moment is modeled as a linear combination of past values of that variable itself and other variables in the system. In a structural vector autoregression model, restrictions are imposed on the values or signs of some regression coefficients.

Chapter Ten

1. That the Brookings Institution has itself chosen not to make the early studies that secured its good reputation available, online or otherwise, is as regrettable as it is puzzling.

2. After the NRA was declared unconstitutional, Paul Homan (1936, 170), one of the Brookings report's authors, observed, less delicately, that the "mad haste" that followed the agency's establishment led to "so absurdly chaotic a mass of non-administrable rules that the Administration should be profoundly grateful to the Supreme Court for relieving it of its embarrassing offspring."

3. Sherwood Fine (1944, 89) likewise sees the burst of activity that spring and early summer as nothing more than businessmen's attempt to "beat the codes."

Chapter Eleven

1. "Home Owners' Loan Act," June 13, 1933, FRASER, https://fraser.stlouisfed.org/title/850.

2. But see Keehn and Smiley (1977, 475), who draw attention to "the numerous methods that national banks used to grant loans secured by mortgages and real estate" despite the prohibition.

3. Delinquent loans and members' loss of confidence weren't the only reason B&Ls were losing their funding. Another was competition from postal savings banks, deposits at which were implicitly guaranteed by the government. Sebastian Fleitas, Matthew Jaremski, and Steven Sprick Schuster (2023, 16) argue that during the Depression, postal savings banks "stripped funds from B&Ls" and that had it not been for this competition from a government-sponsored rival, they "would have maintained a significantly larger number of investors and may have been able to expand lending during the period" (see also O'Hara and Easley 1979).

4. Although Rose (2011, 1094) claims to "find little support" for the belief "that HOLC officials set out to indirectly recapitalize mortgage lenders" and proposes instead that their goal was "increasing [lenders'] participation," I see no reason for treating these as alternative hypotheses:

whether HOLC officials thought in terms of recapitalizing lenders or not, it was only by offering to do so, at least implicitly, that they succeeded in gaining their cooperation.

5. According to a consistent index constructed by Jonathan Rose (2022, 917) using data from repeat Baltimore home sales, between 1939 and 1945 house prices more than doubled, even surpassing their mid-1920s peak. Rose also finds that the same price data "show no meaningful recovery until the onset of World War II." There is therefore no reason to assume that the HOLC's activities themselves played a part in boosting Baltimore house prices.

6. Thus, Egede et al. (2023, 1534) write that "to determine mortgage worthiness, the HOLC assessed and ranked neighborhoods using racial composition as a central factor. Neighborhoods with a large Black community were flagged as unstable and considered 'hazardous' investments, thereby rendering residents incapable of receiving HOLC loans." Although the conventional story's locus classicus is Kenneth Jackson (1980; see also Jackson 1985, 197–203), Jackson's own telling of it recognizes that the HOLC did not itself discriminate against minorities or poor neighborhoods.

7. The FHA, one of several results of the June 27, 1934, National Housing Act, was the New Deal's other major housing market initiative. Except for discussing its part in institutionalizing redlining, I pass over it because I share the consensus view of economists, succinctly stated by Alexander Field (1992, 794), that its "activity in the 1930s had a comparatively modest immediate or direct influence on the housing industry" and that "like so much of the New Deal, its real significance would be experienced after the war." According to Grebler, Blank, and Winnick (1956, 148), although it's likely that FHA insurance "helped to accelerate the expansion of residential building" before the war, it's also true that much of the construction financed by FHA-insured loans "would probably have occurred without them."

8. Before becoming Roosevelt's second treasury secretary, Morgenthau served as governor of the Farm Credit Administration, a federal agency Roosevelt had created in March to take charge of the Farm Credit System.

9. Because of its mounting cost, Roosevelt tried to stop to the Treasury's interest rate subsidy in 1937 by vetoing legislation extending the 3.5 percent federal land bank mortgage rate until 1944, only to have Congress override his veto ("Senate Overrides" 1937).

Chapter Twelve

1. That the CCC did not contribute to recovery isn't very surprising, given that its avowed aim, like that of the Federal Farm Board, its Hoover-era predecessor, was not so much promoting growth in national income as assuring US farmers their "fair share" of it. Hence, Henry Wallace in his 1936 annual report as secretary of agriculture stated that "even full domestic employment . . . would not remove the need" for those programs and the programs' persistence long after the depression ended (US Department of Agriculture 1940, 21). Yet the "fair share" goal itself was rather dubious because the brief pre–World War I period that served as the basis for arriving at it happened to be one during which farmers were more prosperous than ever. Concerning this see Arant (1941).

2. As Cho (1953, 168) explains, although Jones had to resign his position as RFC chairman upon being made federal loan administrator in 1940, because his authority in the new post "transcended that of [the RFC's] Board of Directors," he continued to dictate the RFC's policies and supervise its activities.

3. Even so, some RFC investments remained outstanding as late as the early 1970s. (I thank Joseph Mason for pointing this out to me.)

Chapter Thirteen

1. To play up this proximate cause isn't to dismiss theories, such as those of Hayek, Robbins, and other Austrian School economists, that treat the Depression as having been, to some extent at least, the unavoidable consequence of a prior "malinvestment boom," where that boom was itself a result of excessively *easy* monetary policy. But while it may be inevitable that such a boom must end with a realignment of relative prices that renders unprofitable many investments undertaken during it, it doesn't follow that the failure of those investments must lead to a general collapse of spending with the damage that entails, much less that such a collapse is a necessary part of the recovery process. As Lester Chandler (1970, 114) points out, the Austrian School economists "never explained persuasively . . . how a general deflation of national money income, employment, and prices would facilitate and expedite correction of maladjustments in specific sectors of the economy."

2. As Alexander Field (2011, 33–34) observes, Brown's downplaying of the contribution of government spending during the 1930s refers only to its modest addition to overall spending. It doesn't follow that public works and other government projects didn't have substantial longer-term supply-side consequences. Field (2011, 19–41; 2003) himself claims that those undertakings were a factor, albeit a relatively minor one, in making the 1930s "the most technologically progressive decade of the [twentieth] century." But while such technological progress increased the US economy's *potential* output, it could not itself close the gap between that potential and reality.

3. Taking account of the fiscal policies of state and local governments only makes the New Deal deficits seem even less adequate. "From a small deficit in 1933," Lester Chandler (1970, 139) observes, "these governmental units shifted to surpluses in all of the following years as their revenues were increased by both the rise of their effective tax rates and the rise of receipts induced by the rise of national income. Thus, the fiscal policies of state and local governments after 1932 were less supportive than they had been in earlier years and made virtually no net contribution to aggregate demand for output."

4. The exceptions occur when Ramey and Zubairy exclude World War II from their sample, in which case they find multipliers as high as 1.6 for certain horizons. In their "Supplementary Appendix" Ramey and Zubairy (2017) report that they obtained "almost identical" results for debt-financed federal spending as those reported in their main study.

5. Jacobson, Leeper, and Preston attribute 27 percent of the innovations to the New Deal–era gold stock to fiscal policy innovations and 60 percent to "exogenous" supply disturbances. However, they also find that unlike fiscal policy–based additions to the gold stock, "exogenous" additions contributed little if anything to upward price level and output movements.

6. Although at one point Jacobson, Leeper, and Preston (2023, 11) allow that Roosevelt "waffled" on fiscal policy, they propose that he only did so to disarm his critics. In fact, as we've seen, Roosevelt's fiscal conservatism was perfectly sincere.

7. According to Ellen McGrattan (2012), the undistributed profits tax and other New Deal taxes on corporate earnings were the chief cause of the steep decline in tangible business investment between 1933 and 1938.

Chapter Fourteen

1. If the silver purchase program did the US economy little good, it proved to be an absolute disaster for China. Until the program began, the fact that China was on a silver standard rather

than a gold standard helped it to steer clear of the worldwide Depression. But by dramatically increasing the price of silver, US silver purchases confronted China with its own severe deflationary crisis. According to Milton Friedman (1982), by forcing China to abandon its silver standard and thereby setting the stage for wartime inflation and postwar hyperinflation, US monetary policies played a part in China's turn to communism.

2. A question arises as to whether, by continuing its open market purchases, the Fed would have jeopardized its ability to maintain the gold standard, if only by raising self-fulfilling fears of devaluation. Chang-Tai Hsieh and Christina Romer (2006) consider the possibility carefully but find no evidence that the public entertained any fear of devaluation. Fed officials likewise appear to have been unconcerned. "The gold standard constraint," Hsieh and Rommer write, "was hardly mentioned in initial or ongoing discussion of the program" (164).

3. "Collateral requirements" is more accurate than "reserve requirements." As Benjamin Anderson (1949, 262) explains, although Federal Reserve notes were issued by the twelve Federal Reserve banks, technically they were obligations of the US government, which in supplying them to those banks "had to receive collateral in exchange."

Chapter Fifteen

1. Although the National Industrial Recovery Act establishing the National Recovery Administration was signed on June 16, 1933, only four industries had approved codes before the President's Reemployment Agreement established a blanket code on August 1. For that reason, I treat the latter date as marking the National Recovery Administration's effective start.

2. Those seeking more formal evidence of the importance of various policies and other developments to be emphasized in the discussion to follow can find it either in specific sources mentioned in the text or in two more general econometric studies by Jason Taylor and Todd Newmann (2013, 2016).

3. According to Eline Poelmans, Jason Taylor, Samuel Raisanen, and Andrew Holt (2022), the partial repeal of Prohibition may also have contributed to the pre-NRA recovery. Within little more than a fortnight after the passage of the March 22 Cullen-Harrison Act, twenty states had legalized beer sales, creating seventy thousand new jobs in April alone, or more than 15 percent of that month's total employment gains.

Chapter Sixteen

1. Several factors contributed to the Fed's limited capacity to offset gold-based reserve growth through open market sales. One was the fact that after mid-1936, member bank excess reserves exceeded the Fed's government security holdings of just over $2.4 billion. Another was that the Fed needed the income generated by those securities to cover its operating expenses.

2. Concerning the determinants of banks' demand for excess reserves, see Frost (1971) and Wilcox (1984).

3. The National Labor Relations Act's lack of clarity regarding the legality of closed shops was corrected by the 1947 Taft-Hartley Act, which made them illegal while also prohibiting mass picketing, wildcat (or "quickie") strikes, and various other former union tactics.

Chapter Seventeen

1. Nor is it only fans of the New Deal who regard it as a Keynesian undertaking. According to Amity Shlaes (2007, 11), "what we now call Keynesianism . . . gave license for perpetual experimentation—at least as Roosevelt and his administration applied it."

2. Note, however, that the conventional distinction between planners and trustbusters summarized here has recently been challenged by Sanjukta Paul (2024). "While some degree of divergence between camps identified by these terms is undeniable," Paul says, "the idea that they map onto a clear conflict of principal on the question of competition or planning is at best greatly exaggerated." Instead "the antitrust tradition of the earlier populist era . . . had always aimed to cultivate dispersed forms of economic coordination while targeting those forms . . . that concentrated economic planning in a few hands."

3. A good example of how scholars have tended to exaggerate Keynes's influence is Jordan Schwarz's (1987, 119) claim that Adolf Berle was "probably the highest ranking official in Washington conversant with Keynes' ideas in 1938." The only support Schwarz offers for this claim is the fact that Berle "advocated increasing America's national wealth through 'pump priming,' a Keynesian term for the effect government expenditures could have in multiplying the national income." In fact William Hard, an American writer, had used the expression "pump priming" to refer to countercyclical government spending as long ago as 1916 (Anderson 1944, 145), and by 1930 this usage was well established. Hoover himself referred to pump priming in making his case for the Reconstruction Finance Corporation. Nor was the notion of a government-spending "multiplier" a Keynesian innovation. Here as well even Hoover anticipated Keynes. According to the final report of the 1921 President's Conference on Unemployment, of which Hoover, that committee's chair, was principal author, "The expenditure of the wages of those *directly* and *indirectly* employed by such expansion [of public works] creates a demand for goods, and the *successive* expenditure of the funds put into circulation initiates an increase of private production, which is greater than, i.e., a *multiple* of, the increased expenditure on public works" (quoted in Anderson 1944, 98).

4. Roosevelt himself appeared to acknowledge making recovery take a back seat to reform in his 1939 message to Congress when he spoke of his administration's having finally "passed the period of internal conflict in the launching of our program of social reform" so that its "full energies may *now* be released to invigorate the processes of recovery *in order to preserve our reforms*" (Roosevelt 1941b, 3:7, emphasis added).

5. Keynes's rejection of much of the thinking behind the National Recovery Administration and Agricultural Adjustment Administration predated the New Deal. In "The Raising of Prices," one of several letters he published in the London *Times* and the *New Statesman* in March 1933 (republished as *The Means to Prosperity*), Keynes (1933b, 17) called "the idea of raising prices of commodities by restricting their supply," with which Neville Chamberlain, then England's chancellor of the exchequer, had then been flirting, "worse than useless." Instead of serving to diminish employment, Keynes said, "it is, rather, a method of distributing more evenly what employment there is, at the cost of somewhat increasing it." According to Elliot Rosen (2005, 80), Roosevelt's longtime friend Viscount Astor (US National Archives n.d.) sent advance copies of Keynes's letters to the White House. Of Roosevelt's reaction to these, assuming he read them, there's no record. In any event, one doubts that Keynes would have been impressed by Raymond Moley's claim that in criticizing the National Recovery Administration he "missed" the fact that

it was "not primarily concerned with increasing production, but with spreading work" ("3 Reply to Keynes on NRA Criticism" 1934).

6. But see Zweig (2011) concerning whether Keynes ever really said that "when the facts change, I change my mind."

7. In *Stable Money: A History of the Movement*, Fisher (1934, 351–52) attributes the failure of the London Economic Conference to the irreconcilable difference between the desire of delegates from several countries, including France and England, to see their currencies' US dollar exchange rates stabilized before taking steps to raise their national price levels, and Roosevelt's desire to reflate the US price level before entering into any agreements to stabilize exchange rates. Roosevelt's preference was, of course, the position Fisher himself urged him to take prior to the conference.

8. Despite its apparent failure in the 1930s, and the many economists who disparaged it then and since, Warren's theory still has its adherents. These include Scott Sumner, who besides defending Warren offers a nice summary of the difference between his and Fisher's thinking (Sumner 2018). Sumner draws here on Sebastian Edwards's (2018) fine account of Roosevelt's gold policy and the economists who influenced it in *American Default*.

Chapter Eighteen

1. If any British economist deserves credit for inspiring these economists' support for fiscal and (in several cases) monetary stimulus, that economist was not John Maynard Keynes but rather Ralph Hawtrey, who influenced several of them either directly or indirectly through Allyn Young, who taught at Harvard between 1920 and 1927. For details, see Laidler (1993).

2. There was nothing inconsistent or hypocritical about Hoover's apparent about-face: his position all along had been that countercyclical public works spending should be provided for by limiting such spending in good times so as to accumulate a "reserve" of unspent funds when depression threatened.

3. Lest this exception should itself be considered a departure from Hooverian austerity, it is only fair to note how, more than a year and a half earlier, Hoover (1931) likewise pledged "that if the time should ever come that the voluntary agencies of the country, together with the local and State governments, are unable to find resources with which to prevent hunger and suffering in my country, I will ask the aid of every resource of the Federal Government because I would no more see starvation amongst our countrymen than would any Senator or Congressman."

4. The standard story is well stated by Thomas Ferguson (1984, 43). "Faced with another steep downturn in 1937," Ferguson writes, "the Roosevelt team confirmed its new economic course. Rejecting proposal to revive the National Recovery Administration (NRA) and again devalue the dollar, it adopted an experimental program of conscious 'pump priming,' which used government spending to prop up the economy in a way that foreshadowed the 'Keynesian' policies of demand management widely adopted by Western economies after 1945."

Chapter Nineteen

1. As Mark Leff (1984, 135) reports, Hugh Johnson recalled Roosevelt "fuming" around this time that "industry had bucked him before, and when they saw him again, they were going to come to him on their hands and knees."

2. One estimate puts the ultimate cost to the public of those failures at $638 million, or just over 24 percent of the face value of the securities involved. But no such estimate could be made

until 1946, when all the failed companies had finally been reorganized. Until then, much greater losses were anticipated.

3. On October 4, 1932, a Chicago grand jury indicted Insull and several codefendants on charges of embezzlement and larceny. During the trial that began later that month, the indictees' chief defense lawyer argued that the government was making them scapegoats for the Depression. The jury apparently agreed: at midnight on November 24, 1934, after deliberating for just five minutes, it found them not guilty on all counts.

4. In fact, that's just what happened. According to Paul Mahoney (2012, 63), the new law's death sentence provision was regarded by traders "as detrimental to both the controlling companies at the top of the utility pyramids and to the controlled companies in the lower tiers of the pyramids." For utilities that were already financially distressed, the "loss of a continuation option" was bound to mean collapsing share values. Whatever sort of justice this entailed, it can hardly be said to have compensated utility shareholders for the harm that utility holding companies are supposed to have done them.

5. For an enthralling account of the battle for control of the nation's utilities, culminating in the passage of the Wheeler-Rayburn Act, see Amity Shlaes (2007).

6. According to Calomiris and Hubbard (1995), only about one-quarter of all firms issued bonds in 1936, with just 10 percent of those that did accounting for 90 percent of the value of bonds issued.

Chapter Twenty

1. Concerning what Dinardo and Hallock mean by "large," for their baseline event "window," consisting of recorded strike periods plus each surrounding month, they report cumulative average abnormal returns in directly affected industries of minus 3.2 percent for strikes resulting in union wins, minus 5.6 percent for strikes involving violence, minus 9.8 percent for recognition strikes, and minus 18.1 percent for industry-wide strikes. The coefficients are all statistically significant at the 5 percent confidence level.

2. In his figure, Mathy transposes the dates of the Anschluss and the Munich Agreement.

Chapter Twenty-One

1. DeLong and Summers refer to the government's share of GNP rather than GDP, but these differ only slightly.

2. Elsewhere Higgs (1992) and Steven Horwitz and Michael McPhillips (2013) ask a more fundamental question concerning the wartime increase in output and the associated drop in unemployment, namely whether, setting the accuracy of wartime statistics aside, these constituted "'economic recovery' in any sense relevant to American households' day-to-day experience" (Horwitz and McPhillips 2013, 343). That Americans continued to endure hardship throughout the war, either in the shape of severe home-front deprivations or as servicemen whose many sufferings included the prospect of either dying early or being permanently disabled, can hardly be gainsaid. Still, the question seems moot, the answer hinging as it ultimately must on whether winning the war was a "public good." The more important question was whether something apart from war and the spending it entailed could keep the US economy from lapsing back into a depression.

3. Concerning the challenge of defining "full employment," see Nourse (1956). Challenged by critics of his 1942 pamphlets to say what that expression meant, Hansen answered that "at 'full

employment' there would be at any one time between 2 and 3 million unemployed" (194). The unemployment rate in 1946 turned out to be slightly lower than the top of that range.

4. "Employment Act of 1946," February 20, 1946, FRASER, https://fraser.stlouisfed.org /title/1099.

5. A noteworthy exception was Federal Reserve chairman Marriner Eccles, who prior to the war had been the Roosevelt administration's most insistent champion of Keynesian countercy-clical policies. The war made inflation Eccles's chief concern: by 1945 he was convinced that to keep inflation at bay after the war the government would have to have its peacetime budget in balance. Inevitably Eccles and Hansen, who was then serving as a special consultant to the Board of Governors, clashed, causing Hansen to quit that August ("Hansen Is Dropped by Reserve Board" 1945). Concerning the progress of Eccles's thinking, see Vernengo (2009).

Chapter Twenty-Two

1. According to Jack Stokes Ballard (1983, 124), aircraft, munitions, and shipbuilding firms alone employed 5.6 million workers in mid-1945, compared to just 700,000 in 1939. After the war, production in each of these industries shrank to levels that hardly higher than those before the war.

2. After 1945 the story gets more complicated. The OPA was scheduled to shut down at the end of June 1946. President Truman vetoed a bill that would have kept a much-weakened version of it going for another year, but he did so only because he had hoped to sign alternative legisla-tion that would keep it open without weakening it as much (Truman 1946). Because that alterna-tive legislation was delayed, the OPA was briefly allowed to expire, with the result that prices that had still been controlled, including those on meat, shot up rapidly. In July, the alternative OPA bill secured Truman's signature, allowing controls on meat prices to be reinstated. But those led to such severe shortages and consumer backlash that Truman had them lifted in October, which was not quickly enough to keep their consequences from costing the Democrats dearly in the midterms (Donovan 1977, 229–38). Finally, on November 9, 1946, Truman shut down the OPA for good, claiming that continued controls "would do the nation's economy more harm than good" (Truman 1946).

So much for the strictly American part of the story. Sadly, what happened in the United States was a comedy compared to concurrent happenings in Europe and elsewhere, where the war and its aftermath led to far more severe food shortages, and US authorities' mishandling of price controls, among other blunders, frustrated their efforts to stave off famine. Concerning this, see Bernstein (1964).

Chapter Twenty-Three

1. Although the BLS had then been producing regular estimates of the number of discour-aged workers for a decade, in 1979, after a close vote, the National Commission on Employment and Unemployment elected not to consider such workers unemployed on the grounds that they showed no "distinctive attachment to the work force" (Finegan 1981, 88).

2. Twenty-nine percent is the value reported in the BLS survey's Table 1. Elsewhere (US Department of Labor 1946b, 5) that survey says that only 28 percent of surveyed women work-ers left the labor force. Because the higher figure is slightly more favorable to the discouraged worker hypothesis, I've chosen to rely on it.

3. The main reason for setting women farmworkers aside is that farm labor is highly seasonal, with its peak in the summer and autumn. Because the survey period ended in February, which is in the low season, including them would have artificially inflated the number of women who left the labor force by adding some 800,000 women to that number who rejoined the labor force several months later. Furthermore, besides women directly hired by farmers, 1.5 million wartime women farmworkers were volunteers serving in the Women's Land Army and other emergency programs set up to recruit replacements for drafted male farmworkers (Prater 2022; Rasmussen 1951). Although practically all of these volunteers left the labor force after the war, there's little reason to suppose that any did so involuntarily, for their jobs paid very little, making a desire to assist the war effort "the primary reason women enrolled for farm work" (Rasmussen 1951, 143).

4. According to John Modell (1989, 170), whether they chose to leave the labor force or not, women who married during the war often put off having children until it ended. Consequently, demobilization led to not only a burst of marriages but also an even larger burst in new family formation. As Hugh Rockoff (1998, 98) notes, the high 1946 birth rate is itself evidence that the US economy wasn't depressed then, for despite postwar euphoria, men and women continued to consider the prospects for economic security and adequate real earnings in deciding whether to have children.

Chapter Twenty-Four

1. Although the federal government's response to the 1949 downturn is often considered a successful application of Keynesian fiscal policy, to even describe it, as Benjamin Caplan (1956, 27) has, as "a limited test with very mixed results," is being generous. As Caplan (a member of that period's Council of Economic Advisers) notes, until well into 1949, the council's chief concern then was not recession but inflation. For that reason Truman, acting on the council's advice, repeatedly pressed an anti-inflationary program on a reluctant Republican-controlled Congress. By the time Truman finally managed in July 1948 to get Congress to agree to impose some anti-inflationary measures, the boom had tapered off. "It was," Caplan says, "a case of locking the barn after the horse was stolen" (37).

From that summer on, the signs of a weakening economy became increasingly evident. Yet the Council of Economic Advisers continued to be concerned about inflation, and Truman kept calling for more measures to counter it. He continued to do so even after the 1949 downturn began (Caplan 1956, 38). Although it's true that expansionary fiscal measures ultimately helped to avoid a more severe downturn, these were mainly the result of steps Congress took a year earlier *despite* Truman's recommendations (and those of the Council of Economic Advisers), including stepped-up defense spending, the Marshall plan, and a $5 billion tax cut, the last of which passed over Truman's veto (37, 41). In short, it appears that deliberate deficit spending informed by Keynesian economics and the 1946 Employment Act played no part at all in the 1949 recovery.

2. It may put the extent of the public's World War II–era saving into perspective to compare it to what the public saved during the 2020–2021 COVID-19 pandemic, when lockdowns, business closings, and the disease itself had effects similar to those of wartime shortages and rationing. Defining "excess saving" as any savings above 7.5 percent of disposable personal income, Gillian Brunet and Sandile Hlatshwayo (2022, 3) determine that the public's excess savings during the pandemic amounted to 6.8 percent of its disposable income. The corresponding figure for World War II was 16.8 percent.

3. Despite wartime credit controls, total consumer credit began to grow rapidly immediately after V-J Day. When controls were finally lifted on November 1, 1947, credit grew still more rapidly (McHugh 1947). One must bear in mind, however, that this growth was from a record-low wartime level and that rapid as it was, incomes also rose rapidly so that it took until 1952 for consumer credit to return to roughly the same percentage of personal income it represented in 1940.

4. Some years ago, Robert J. Gordon (1969) claimed that official statistics "mislaid" $45 billion in wartime private investment by wrongly treating spending on government-owned privately operated plant and equipment as government investment. But as Robert Higgs (2004, 508, 515) notes, most such investment, besides having often been overvalued in the first place and wearing out rapidly from intensive use, "proved to have little or no value after the war." Interestingly, Gordon himself appeared to recognize this when, in discussing research by Ellen R. McGratten and R. Anton Braun some years after his 1969 article appeared, he observed that "much of the GOPO [government-owned privately operated] capital sold to private operators after the war was specifically tailored to wartime use" (Gordon 1993, 257). For evidence that the government's wartime investment contributed little to postwar prosperity, see McLaughlin (1943) and, for the South in particular (where a disproportionate share of that investment went), see Lewis (2007) and Jaworski (2017).

5. Thus, Keynes (1936a, 545) observed that "the increase in inventories in 1929 was probably for the most part designed to meet demand which did not fully materialize; whilst the small further increase in 1930 represented accumulations of unsold stocks." The very low level of inventories at the end of 1933, Keynes concluded, "was an almost certain herald of some measure of recovery. In general an aggregate of net investment which is based on an increase in business inventories beyond normal is clearly precarious."

6. The worst postwar case of a severe downturn marked by a lack of real net private domestic investment occurred in 2009 during the Great Recession, when such investment briefly turned negative (Martin 2016; Higgs 2013). Five years later, it was still only two-thirds of its 2007 peak. Yet poor as this performance was, it pales beside that of net private investment between 1929 and 1946.

Chapter Twenty-Five

1. According to Mark Toma (1992, 639–40), during the war "the Treasury and Fed were implicitly committed to future money growth rates that would be consistent with low long-run inflation and [that the Treasury would] at the same time would restrict the quantity of government bonds that would be covered by the ⅜ percent peg. . . . In fact, the Fed encouraged limits on the weekly issues of new Treasury bills throughout the pegging period, although Treasury pressure sometimes served as a countervailing force."

2. For details, see Binder and Brunet (2022) and sources cited therein.

Chapter Twenty-Six

1. A speech Hopkins gave in February 1934 was taken by *The Economist* as proof that Hopkins understood, even at that early date, "that the administration had been wrong in mixing so much reform with its recovery" (Best 1991, 207).

2. That "big" business benefited disproportionately from this indulgence is clear from the distribution of wartime contracts. "Through 1944," Paul Koistinen (1973, 446) points out, "the

armed services contracted with some 18,539 firms. Consistently, however, 100 corporations received at least two-thirds of the contracts; 30 corporations almost one-half. Subcontracting did
not significantly change the picture since most of it took place among the larger corporations.
Expenditures for research and plants and equipment followed a similar pattern."

   3. Complementing the business-government rapprochement stressed here was a business-
labor rapprochement that also contributed to postwar prosperity. According to David Stebenne
(1996, 140–41), between 1945 and 1950 business and labor leaders "abandon[ed] the pattern of
bitter antagonism" that had prevailed during the 1930s. "Unions," Stebenne says, "gave up trying
to win control over the management of large enterprises" while "pledging to link their wage and
benefit demands to improvements in worker productivity" and while management agreed "to
end its efforts to win back prerogatives lost during the 1930s and 1940s, to stop trying to break
existing unions, to grant fringe benefits that supplemented the state's very limited social welfare system, to support Cold War programs, and to pursue investment and output policies that
would help bring about high levels of unemployment." The postwar business-government rapprochement was particularly crucial to fulfilment of the last part of this business-labor bargain.

References

Aaronson, Daniel, Daniel Hartley, and Bhashkar Mazumder. 2021. "The Effects of the 1930s HOLC 'Redlining' Maps." *American Economic Journal: Economic Policy* 13, no. 4 (November): 355–92.

Ackerman, David M. 1996. *Presidential Emergency Powers: The So-Called "War Powers Act of 1933."* Congressional Research Service Report number 95–753, August 20.

Adelstein, Richard P. 1991. " 'The Nation as an Economic Unit': Keynes, Roosevelt, and the Managerial Ideal." *Journal of American History* 78, no. 1 (June): 160–87.

Aiken, Paul C. 1936. *Administrative Law and Procedure under the NIRA.* Washington, DC: NRA Organization Studies Section.

Akerlof, George A., and Robert J. Shiller. 2009. *Animal Spirits: How Human Psychology Drives the Economy, and Why It Matters for Global Capitalism.* Princeton, NJ: Princeton University Press.

Allen, Frederick Lewis. 1940. *Since Yesterday: The Nineteen-Thirties in America, September 3, 1929–September 3, 1939.* New York: Harper & Brothers.

Allen, William R. 1977. "Irving Fisher, F. D. R., and the Great Depression." *History of Political Economy* 9, no. 4 (Winter): 560–87.

Alston, Lee J. 1983. "Farm Foreclosures in the United States during the Interwar Period." *Journal of Economic History* 43, no. 4 (December): 885–903.

Alston, Lee J., Wayne A. Grove, and David C. Wheelock. 1994. "Why Do Banks Fail? Evidence from the 1920s." *Explorations in Economic History* 31, no. 4 (October): 409–31.

Alter, Jonathan. 2007. *The Defining Moment: FDR's Hundred Days and the Triumph of Hope.* New York: Simon & Schuster.

Amato, Jeffery D. 2005. "The Role of the Natural Rate of Interest in Monetary Policy." BIS Working Papers No. 171, Bank for International Settlements, March.

Amenta, Edwin, Kathleen Dunleavy, and Mary Bernstein. 1994. "Stolen Thunder? Huey Long's 'Share Our Wealth,' Political Mediation, and the Second New Deal." *American Sociological Review* 59, no. 5 (October): 678–702.

Anari, Ali, James Kolari, and Joseph Mason. 2005. "Bank Asset Liquidation and the Propagation of the U.S. Great Depression." *Journal of Money, Credit, and Banking* 37, no. 4 (August): 753–73.

Anderson, Benjamin M. 1924. "Artificial Prices a Menace to Economic Stability: The Farmer's Problem and the Revised McNary-Haugen Bill." *Chase Economic Bulletin* 4, no. 2 (May): 1–17.

Anderson, Benjamin M. 1949. *Economics and the Public Welfare: A Financial and Economic History of the United States, 1914–1946.* New York, London: D. Van Nostrand.

Anderson, Clay J. 1944. "The Development of the Pump-Priming Theory." *Journal of Political Economy* 52, no, 2 (June): 144–59.

Anderson, Richard G. 2010. "The First U.S. Quantitative Easing: The 1930s." *Economic Synopses*, no. 17 (June 30). https://doi.org/10.20955/es.2010.17.

Ang, James S., and Terry Richardson. 1994. "The Underwriting Experience of Commercial Bank Affiliates Prior to the Glass-Steagall Act: A Re-examination of Evidence for Passage of the Act." *Journal of Banking and Finance* 18, no. 2 (January): 351–95.

Anginer, Deniz, and Asli Demirgüç-Kunt. 2018. "Bank Runs and Moral Hazard: A Review of Deposit Insurance." World Bank Group Policy Research Working Paper No. 8589, September.

Arant, Willard D. 1941. *Farm Parity Fallacy.* New York: National Economy League.

Arndt, H. W. 1944. *The Economic Lessons of the Nineteen-Thirties.* Oxford: Oxford University Press.

Arnold, Thurman. 1938. "What Is Monopoly?" *Vital Speeches of the Day* 4, no. 18 (July): 567–70.

Associated Press. 2022. "U.S. Government Checks Constituted 40% of Farmers' Income in 2020: USDA." *MarketWatch*, December 31. https://www.marketwatch.com/story/u-s-government -checks-constituted-40-of-farmers-income-in-2020-usda-01609444429.

Awalt, Francis Gloyd. 1969. "Recollections of the Banking Crisis in 1933." *Business History Review* 43, no. 3 (Autumn): 347–71.

Bachmann, Rüdiger, and Christian Bayer. 2013. "'Wait-and-See' Business Cycles?" *Journal of Monetary Economics* 60, no. 6 (September): 704–19.

Baker, Harlan. 2017. "A Woman to Reckon With: The Vision and Legacy of Frances Perkins." *Democratic Left,* December 8. https://www.dsausa.org/democratic-left/a_woman_to_reckon _with_the_vision_and_legacy_of_frances_perkins/.

Baker, Scott R., Nicholas Bloom, and Steven J. Davis. 2016. "Measuring Economic Policy Uncertainty." *Quarterly Journal of Economics* 131, no. 4 (November): 1593–636.

Bakke, E. Wright. 1940. *The Unemployed Worker: A Study of the Task of Making a Living without a Job.* New Haven, CT: Yale University Press.

Bakker, Gerben, Nicholas Crafts, and Pieter Woltjer. 2016. "Onwards and Upwards: American Productivity Growth during the Great Depression." VoxEU.org (blog), Centre for Economic Policy Research, February 5. https://voxeu.org/article/american-productivity-growth-during-great-depression.

Ballard, James Stokes. 1983. *The Shock of Peace: Military and Economic Mobilization after World War II.* Washington, DC: University Press of America.

"Bank Meets All Calls." 1993. *New York Times*, March 3.

Barber, William J. 1996. *Designs within Disorder: Franklin D. Roosevelt, the Economists, and the Shaping of American Economic Policy, 1933–1945.* Cambridge: Cambridge University Press.

Barnett, Barry J. 2000. "The U.S. Farm Financial Crisis of the 1980s." *Agricultural History* 74, no. 2 (Spring): 366–80.

Beaudry, Paul, and Franck Portier. 2002. "The French Depression of the 1930s." *Review of Economic Dynamics* 5, no. 1 (January): 73–99.

Bellush, Bernard. 1955. *Franking Roosevelt as Governor of New York.* New York: Columbia University Press.

Belongia, Michael T., and R. Alton Gilbert. 1985. "The Farm Credit Crisis: Will It Hurt the Whole Economy?" *Federal Reserve Bank of St. Louis Review* 67 (December): 5–15.

Bendiner, M. R. 1935. "Capital Goods Industries and Recovery." *CQ Researcher*, December 11. https://cqpress.sagepub.com/cqresearcher/report/capital-goods-industries-recovery-cqre srre1935121100.

Benedict, Murray R. 1934. "Some Policy Problems in a Federal Farm Credit Program." *Journal of Farm Economics* 16, no. 1 (January): 45–54.

Benedict, Murray R. 1942. "Farm Finance: Dangers and Opportunities in Wartime." California Agricultural Extension Service Circular 126, October.

Benedict, Murray R. 1953. *Farm Policies of the United States, 1790–1950: A Study of Their Origins and Development.* New York: Twentieth Century Fund.

Benston, George J. 1964. "Interest Payments on Demand Deposits and Bank Investment Behavior." *Journal of Political Economy* 72, no. 5 (October): 431–49.

Benston, George J. 1990. *The Separation of Commercial and Investment Banking: The Glass-Steagall Act Revisited and Reconsidered.* New York: Oxford University Press.

Bernanke, Ben S. 1983a. "Irreversibility, Uncertainty, and Cyclical Investment." *Quarterly Journal of Economics* 98, no. 1 (February): 85–106.

Bernanke, Ben S. 1983b. "Nonmonetary Effects of the Financial Crisis in the Propagation of the Great Depression." *American Economic Review* 73, no. 3 (June): 257–76.

Bernanke, Ben S., Vincent R. Reinhart, and Brian P. Sack. 2004. "Monetary Policy Alternatives at the Zero Bound: An Empirical Assessment." *Brookings Papers on Economic Activity*, no. 2: 1–78.

Bernstein, Barton J. 1964. "The Postwar Famine and Price Control, 1946." *Agricultural History* 38, no. 4 (October): 235–40.

Bernstein, Barton J. 1965. "The Removal of War Production Board Controls on Business, 1944–1946." *Business History Review* 32, no. 2 (Summer): 243–60.

Best, Gary Dean. 1991. *Pride, Prejudice, and Politics: Roosevelt versus Recovery, 1933–1938.* New York: Praeger.

Bierman, Harold. 1991. *The Great Myths of 1929 and the Lessons to Be Learned.* New York: Greenwood.

Binder, Carola Conces, and Gillian Brunet. 2022. "Inflation Expectations and Consumption: Evidence from 1951." *Economic Inquiry* 60, no. 2 (April): 954–74.

Board of Governors of the Federal Reserve System. 1936. "Bank Suspensions, 1892–1935." September 26.

Board of Governors of the Federal Reserve System. 1977. "The Impact of the Payment of Interest on Demand Deposits." January 31.

Board of Governors of the Federal Reserve System. 2014. "Does the Federal Reserve Own or Hold Gold?" FAQs: About the Fed. Last updated December 3, 2014. https://www.federalre serve.gov/faqs/does-the-federal-reserve-own-or-hold-gold.htm.

Bodenhorn, Howard. 2002. *State Banking in Early America: A New Economic History.* New York: Oxford University Press.

Boeckel, Richard M. 1934. "Dollar Depreciation and Devaluation." *CQ Researcher*, January 30. https://cqpress.sagepub.com/cqresearcher/report/dollar-depreciation-devaluation-cqres rre1934013000?tab=Footnotes.

Boeckel, Richard M. 1936. "The Deficit and the Public Debt." *CQ Researcher*, May 2. https:// cqpress.sagepub.com/cqresearcher/report/deficit-public-debt-cqresrre1936050200.

Bordo, Michael, and Arunima Sinha. 2016. "A Lesson from the Great Depression That the Fed Might Have Learned: A Comparison of the 1932 Open Market Purchases with Quantitative Easing." NBER Working Paper No. 22581, National Bureau of Economic Research, Cambridge, MA, August.

Bordo, Michael D., and David C. Wheelock. 2013. "The Promise and Performance of the Federal Reserve as Lender of Last Resort, 1914–1933." In *The Origins, History, and Future of the Federal Reserve: A Return to Jekyll Island,* edited by Michael D. Bordo and William Roberds, 59–98. New York: Cambridge University Press.

Boyle, James E. 1936. "The AAA: An Epitaph." *Atlantic Monthly* 157 (February): 217–25.

Bratter, Herbert M. 1941. "The Committee for the Nation: A Case History in Monetary Propaganda." *Journal of Political Economy* 49, no. 4 (August): 531–53.

Brecher, Michael. 1997. *Strike!* Cambridge, MA: South End.

Breitenlechner, Max, Gabriel P. Mathy, and Johann Scharler. 2021. "Decomposing the U.S. Great Depression: How Important Were Loan Supply Shocks?" *Explorations in Economic History* 79 (January): Article 101379.

Bremer, William W. 1975. "Along the 'American Way': The New Deal's Work Relief Programs for the Unemployed." *Journal of American History* 62, no. 3 (December): 636–52.

Brinkley, Alan. 1993. "The Antimonopoly Ideal and the Liberal State: The Case of Thurman Arnold." *Journal of American History* 80, no. 2 (September): 557–79.

Brinkley, Alan. 1995. *The End of Reform: New Deal Liberalism in Recession and War.* New York: Vintage Books.

Brinkley, Alan. 2002. "The New Deal Experiments." In *The Achievement of American Liberalism: The New Deal and Its Legacies,* edited by William Chafe, 1–20. New York: Columbia University Press.

Brody, David. 1975. "The New Deal and World War II." In *The New Deal: The National Level,* edited by John Braeman, Robert H. Bremner, and David Brody, 267–309. Columbus: Ohio State University Press.

Browder, Robert Paul, and Thomas G. Smith. 1986. *Independent: A Biography of Lewis W. Douglas.* New York: Knopf.

Brown, E. Cary. 1956. "Fiscal Policy in the 'Thirties: A Reappraisal." *American Economic Review* 46, no. 5 (December): 857–79.

Brown, E. Cary. 1959. "The Policy Acceptance in the United States of Reliance on Automatic Stabilizers." *Journal of Finance* 14, no. 1 (March): 40–51.

Brown, William Adams, Jr. 1940. *The International Gold Standard Reinterpreted, 1914–1934.* New York: National Bureau of Economic Research.

Brunet, Gillian, and Sandile Hlatshwayo. 2022. "War, Pandemic, and Household Saving: The COVID-19 Pandemic through the Lens of WWII." Unpublished working paper, April 8.

Bryan, Dan. 2012. "The Great (Farm) Depression of the 1920s." American History USA. Last updated March 6, 2012. https://www.americanhistoryusa.com/great-farm-depression-1920s/.

"Budget for 1934 Nearly Balanced, 'Hard Boiled Basis' Used." 1933. *New York Times,* May 4.

Bundt, Thomas P., Thomas F. Cosimano, and John A. Halloran. 1992. "DIDMCA and Bank Market Risk: Theory and Evidence." *Journal of Banking & Finance* 16, no. 6 (December): 1179–93.

Burns, Helen M. 1974. *The American Banking Community and New Deal Banking Reforms, 1933–1935.* Westport, CT: Greenwood.

Burns, James MacGregor. 1956. *Roosevelt: The Lion and the Fox.* New York: Harcourt, Brace & World.

Burstein, Melvin L. 1998. "Interview with Carter H. Golembe." Federal Reserve Bank of Minneapolis, June 1, 1998. https://www.minneapolisfed.org/article/1998/interview-with-carter-h-golembe.

"Business: Guilty Harriman." 1934. *Time*, July 2.

Butkiewicz, James L. 1995. "The Impact of a Lender of Last Resort during the Great Depression: The Case of the Reconstruction Finance Corporation." *Explorations in Economic History* 32, no. 2 (April): 197–216.

Butkiewicz, James L. 1999. "The Reconstruction Finance Corporation, the Gold Standard, and the Banking Panic of 1933." *Southern Economic Journal* 66, no. 2 (October): 271–93.

Cady, Darrel. 1981. "The Historical Record : A Bibliographical Essay." In *Economics and the Truman Administration*, edited by Francis H. Heller, 143–70. Lawrence: Regents Press of Kansas.

Calomiris, Charles W. 1990. "Is Deposit Insurance Necessary? A Historical Perspective." *Journal of Economic History* 50, no. 2 (June): 283–95.

Calomiris, Charles W., and R. Glenn Hubbard. 1995. "Internal Finance and Investment: Evidence from the Undistributed Profits Tax of 1936–37." *Journal of Business* 68, no. 4 (October): 443–82.

Calomiris, Charles W., and Matthew Jaremski. 2019. "Stealing Deposits: Deposit Insurance, Risk-Taking, and the Removal of Market Discipline in Early 20th-Century Banks." *Journal of Finance* 79, no. 2 (April): 711–54.

Calomiris, Charles W., and Joseph R. Mason. 1997. "Contagion and Bank Failures during the Great Depression: The June 1932 Chicago Banking Panic." *American Economic Review* 87, no. 5 (December): 863–83.

Calomiris, Charles W., and Joseph R. Mason. 2003a. "Consequences of Bank Distress during the Great Depression." *American Economic Review* 93, no. 3 (June): 937–47.

Calomiris, Charles W., and Joseph R. Mason. 2003b. "Fundamentals, Panics, and Bank Distress during the Depression." *American Economic Review* 93, no. 5 (December): 1615–47.

Calomiris, Charles W., Joseph R. Mason, Marc Weidenmier, and Katherine Bobroff. 2013. "The Effects of Reconstruction Finance Corporation Assistance on Michigan's Banks' Survival in the 1930s." *Explorations in Economic History* 50, no. 4 (October): 526–47.

Calomiris, Charles W., Joseph R. Mason, and David Wheelock. 2023. "Did Doubling Reserve Requirements Cause the 1937–38 Recession? New Evidence on the Impact of Reserve Requirements on Bank Reserve Demand and Lending." Federal Reserve Bank of St. Louis Economic Research Working Paper No. 2022–011C, August 15.

Caperaa, Philippe, and Louis Eeckhoudt. 1977. "Interest-Bearing Demand Deposits and Bank Portfolio Behavior: Comment." *Southern Economic Journal* 44, no. 2 (October): 395–98.

Caplan, Benjamin. 1956. "A Case Study: The 1948–1949 Recession." In *Policies to Combat Depression*, edited by Universities-National Bureau Committee for Economic Research, 27–58. New York: National Bureau of Economic Research.

Carlson, Marc A., and David C. Wheelock. 2014. "Navigating Constraints: The Evolution of Federal Reserve Monetary Policy, 1935–59." Finance and Economics Discussion Paper No. 2014-44, Federal Reserve Board, Washington, DC, June.

Carosso, Vincent P. 1949. "The Waltham Watch Company: A Case History." *Bulletin of the Business Historical Society* 23, no. 4 (December): 165–87.

Carrozzo, Peter M. 2008. "A New Deal for the American Mortgage: The Home Owners' Loan Corporation, the National Housing Act and the Birth of the National Mortgage Market." *University of Miami Business Law Review* 17, no. 1 (Winter): 1–46.

Carter, Zachary D. 2020. *The Price of Peace: Money, Democracy, and the Life of John Maynard Keynes.* New York: Random House.

Case, H. C. M. 1960. "Farm Debt during the Early 1930s." *Agricultural History* 34, no, 4 (October): 173–81.

Cecchetti, Stephen G. 1992. "The Stock Market Crash of 1929." In *The New Palgrave Dictionary of Money and Finance*, Vol. 3, edited by Peter Newman, Murray Milgate, and John Eatwell, 573–76. London: Macmillan.

Chandler, Lester V. 1970. *America's Greatest Depression, 1929–1941.* New York: Harper & Row.

Chandler, William U. 1984. *The Myth of the TVA: Conservation and Development in the Tennessee Valley, 1933–1983.* Cambridge, MA: Ballinger.

Chase, Stuart. 1932. *A New Deal.* New York: Macmillan.

Cho, Hyo. 1953. "The Evolution of the Functions of the Reconstruction Finance Corporation: A Study of the Growth and Death of a Federal Lending Agency." PhD diss., Ohio State University.

"Cite Past in Reserve Move." 1932. *New York Times*, April 16.

Clague, Ewan, and Saya S. Schwartz. 1935. "Real Jobs–Or Relief?" *Survey Graphic* 24, no. 6 (June): 293–95.

Clavin, Patricia. 2002. "Explaining the Failure of the London World Economic Conference." In *The Interwar Depression in an International Context*, edited by Harold James, 77–97. Munich: Oldenbourg.

Cochrane, John H. 2013. "More New-Keynesian Paradoxes." The Grumpy Economist (blog), January 19. https://johnhcochrane.blogspot.com/2013/01/more-new-keynesian-paradoxes.html.

Cochrane, John H. 2017. "The New-Keynesian Liquidity Trap." *Journal of Monetary Economics* 92 (December): 47–63.

Cohen, Adam. 2009. *Nothing to Fear: FDR's Inner Circle and the Hundred Days That Created Modern America.* New York: Penguin.

Cohen-Setton, Jérémie, Joshua K. Hausman, and Johannes F. Wieland. 2017. "Supply-Side Policies in the Depression: Evidence from France." *Journal of Money, Credit and Banking* 49, nos. 2–3 (March–April): 273–317.

Cole, Harold L., and Lee E. Ohanian. 2004. "New Deal Policies and the Persistence of the Great Depression: A General Equilibrium Analysis." *Journal of Political Economy* 112, no. 4 (August): 779–816.

Collins, Robert M. 1978. "Positive Business Responses to the New Deal: The Roots of the Committee for Economic Development, 1933–1942." *Business History Review* 52, no. 3 (Autumn): 369–91.

Collins, Robert M. 1981. *The Business Response to Keynes, 1929–1964.* New York: Columbia University Press.

Commercial and Financial Chronicle. 1933. Vol. 136, no. 3537 (April 8). https://fraser.stlouisfed.org/title/commercial-financial-chronicle-1339/april-8-1933-517121.

Commercial and Financial Chronicle. 1935a. Vol. 140, no. 3630 (January 19). https://fraser.stlouisfed.org/title/commercial-financial-chronicle-1339/january-19-1935-517161

Commercial and Financial Chronicle. 1935b. Vol. 141, no. 3677 (December 14). https://fraser.stlouisfed.org/title/commercial-financial-chronicle-1339/december-14-1935-517182.

Conti-Brown, Peter. 2016. *The Power and Independence of the Federal Reserve.* Princeton, NJ: Princeton University Press.

Conti-Brown, Peter, and Sean H. Vanatta. 2021. "The Logic and Legitimacy of Bank Supervision: The Case of the Bank Holiday of 1933." *Business History Review* 95, no. 1 (Spring): 87–120.

Coppola, Frances. 2022. "The Great Unemployment Fudge." Coppola Comment (blog), May 13. https://www.coppolacomment.com/2022/05/the-great-unemployment-fudge.html.

Couch, Jim, II, and William F. Shughart. 1998. *The Political Economy of the New Deal*. Cheltenham, UK: Edward Elgar.

Courtemanche, Charles, and Kenneth Snowden. 2011. "Repairing a Mortgage Crisis: HOLC Lending and Its Impact on Local Housing Markets." *Journal of Economic History* 71, no. 2 (June): 307–37.

Cox, Albert H. 1966. "Regulation of Interest Rates on Bank Deposits." *Michigan Business Studies* 17, no. 4. Ann Arbor: University of Michigan Graduate School of Business Administration, Bureau of Business Research.

Cox, Albert H. 1967. "Regulation of Interest on Deposits: An Historical Review." *Journal of Finance* 22, no. 2 (December): 274–96.

Cox, Garfield V. 1936. "Some Distinguishing Characteristics of the Current Recovery." *American Economic Review* 26, no. 1 (March): 1–10.

Crawford, Arthur Whipple. 1940. *Monetary Management under the New Deal: The Evolution of a Managed Currency System—Its Problems and Results*. Washington, DC: American Council on Public Affairs.

Critchlow, Donald T. 1984. "Robert S. Brookings: The Man, the Vision and the Institution." *Review of Politics* 46, no. 4 (October): 561–81.

Crowther, Don Q. 1938. "Analysis of Strikes in 1937." *Monthly Labor Review* 46, no. 5 (May): 1186–205.

Crum, W. L., R. A. Gordon, and Dorothy Wescott. 1938. "Review of the First Quarter of 1938." *Review of Economics and Statistics* 20, no. 2 (May): 89–96.

Currie, Lauchlin. 1938. "Causes of the Recession." Unpublished memorandum. Marriner S. Eccles Papers, box 63, folder 11, item 9. FRASER, Federal Reserve Bank of St. Louis. https://fraser.stlouisfed.org/archival/1343/item/464079.

Daglish, Toby, and Lyndon Moore. 2018. "Railroad Bailouts in the Great Depression." Working paper, September 6. https://pseweb.eu/ydepot/seance/512888_DM2_1_Tables.pdf.

Daniels, Roger. 2015. *Franklin D. Roosevelt: Road to the New Deal, 1882–1939*. Chicago: University of Illinois Press.

Darby, Michael R. 1976. "Three-and-a-Half Million U.S. Employees Have Been Mislaid: Or, an Explanation of Unemployment, 1934–1941." *Journal of Political Economy* 84, no. 1 (February): 1–16.

Davis, Chester C. 1936. "The Agricultural Adjustment Act and National Recovery." *Journal of Farm Economics* 18, no. 2 (May): 229–41.

Davis, J. Ronnie. 1968. "Chicago Economists, Deficit Budgets, and the Early 1930s." *American Economic Review* 58, no. 3, part 1 (June): 476–81.

Davis, Joseph S. 1935. "AAA as a Force in Recovery." *Journal of Farm Economics* 17, no. 1 (February): 1–14.

"Dawes Bank Loan by RFC Attacked." 1932. *New York Times*, August 30.

Dayen, Dale. 2014. "Farm Bill 2014: It's Even Worse Than the Old Farm Bill." *New Republic*, February 4.

DeLong, J. Bradford. 1996. "Keynesianism, Pennsylvania Avenue Style: Some Economic Consequences of the Employment Act of 1946." *Journal of Economic Perspectives* 10, no. 3 (Summer): 41–53.

DeLong, J. Bradford. 2008. "Eric Rauchway vs. Alex Tabarrok on New Deal Unemployment." Grasping Reality (blog), November 9. https://www.bradford-delong.com/2008/11/eric-rauchway-v.html.

DeLong, J. Bradford, and Andrew Shleifer. 1991. "The Stock Market Bubble of 1929: Evidence from Closed-End Mutual Funds." *Journal of Economic History* 51, no. 3 (September): 675–700.

DeLong, J. Bradford, and Lawrence H. Summers. 1988. "How Does Macroeconomic Policy Affect Output?" *Brookings Papers on Economic Activity*, no. 2: 433–94.

Demirgüç-Kunt, Asli, and Enrica Detragiache. 2002. "Does Deposit Insurance Increase Banking System Stability? An Empirical Investigation." *Journal of Monetary Economics* 49, no. 7 (October): 1373–406.

Demirgüç-Kunt, Asli, Edward J. Kane, and Luc Laeven. 2008. "Determinants of Deposit-Insurance Adoption and Design." *Journal of Financial Intermediation* 17, no. 3 (July): 407–38.

Democratic National Convention. 1932. "1932 Democratic Party Platform: June 27, 1932." The American Presidency Project. https://www.presidency.ucsb.edu/node/273214.

Depew, Briggs, Price V. Fishback, and Paul W. Rhode. 2013. "New Deal or No Deal in the Cotton South: The Effect of the AAA on the Agricultural Labor Structure." *Explorations in Economic History* 50, no. 4 (October): 466–86.

Diamond, Douglas W., and Philip H. Dybvig. 1983. "Bank Runs, Deposit Insurance, and Liquidity." *Journal of Political Economy* 91, no. 3 (June): 401–19.

Dinardo, John, and Kevin F. Hallock. 2002. "'When Unions Mattered': Assessing the Impact of Strikes on Financial Markets, 1925–1937." *Industrial and Labor Relations Review* 55, no. 2 (January): 219–33.

Dixit, Avinash K., and Robert S. Pindyck. 1994. *Investment under Uncertainty.* Princeton, NJ: Princeton University Press.

Dominguez, Kathryn, Ray C. Fair, and Matthew D. Shapiro. 1988. "Forecasting the Depression: Harvard versus Yale." *American Economic Review* 78, no. 4 (September): 595–612.

Donovan, Robert J. 1977. *Conflict and Crisis: The Presidency of Harry S. Truman, 1945–1948.* New York: Norton.

Drake, Paul W. 1989. *The Money Doctor in the Andes: The Kemmerer Missions, 1923–1933.* Durham, NC: Duke University Press.

Ebersole, J. Franklin. 1933. "One Year of the Reconstruction Finance Corporation." *Quarterly Journal of Economics* 47, no. 3 (May): 464–92.

Eccles, Marriner S. 1935. "Memorandum on Gold Inflow and Expected Deflation," October 22. Marriner S. Eccles Papers, box 49, folder 1, item 4. University of Utah. https://fraser .stlouisfed.org/archival-collection/marriner-s-eccles-papers-1343/memorandum-gold -inflow-expected-deflation-464196.

Eccles, Marriner S. 1936a. "Comments on the Fiscal and Monetary Policies of the Roosevelt Administration," June 18. Marriner S. Eccles Papers, box 75, folder 8, item 1. University of Utah. https://fraser.stlouisfed.org/archival-collection/marriner-s-eccles-papers-1343/comments -fiscal-monetary-policies-roosevelt-administration-460042.

Eccles, Marriner S. 1936b. "Memorandum to Secretary Morgenthau," April 25. Marriner S. Eccles Papers, box 49, folder 2, item 2. University of Utah. https://fraser.stlouisfed.org/archi val-collection/marriner-s-eccles-papers-1343/memorandum-secretary-morgenthau -460413.

Eccles, Marriner S. 1939. "Radio Address: Under the auspices of the National Radio Forum, Conducted by the Washington Evening Star, broadcast Over the National Broadcasting Company Network." January 23. https://fraser.stlouisfed.org/title/446/item/7658.

Edwards, Chris. 2018. "Agricultural Subsidies." Cato Institute. Last updated April 16, 2018. https://www.downsizinggovernment.org/agriculture/subsidies.

Edwards, George W. 1942. "The Myth of the Security Affiliate." *Journal of the American Statistical Association* 37, no. 218 (June): 225–32.

Edwards, Sebastian. 2017. "Gold, the Brains Trust, and Roosevelt." *History of Political Economy* 49, no. 1 (March): 1–30.

Edwards, Sebastian. 2018. *American Default: The Untold Story of FDR, the Supreme Court, and the Battle over Gold.* Princeton, NJ: Princeton University Press.

Egede, Leonard E., Rebekah J. Walker, Jennifer A. Campbell, Sebastian Linde, Laura C. Hawks, and Kaylin M. Burgess. 2023. "Modern Day Consequences of Historic Redlining: Finding a Path Forward." *Journal of General Internal Medicine* 38, no. 6 (May): 1534–37.

Eggertsson, Gauti B. 2008. "Great Expectations and the End of the Depression." *American Economic Review* 96, no. 4 (September): 1476–516.

Eggertsson, Gauti B. 2012. "Was the New Deal Contractionary?" *American Economic Review* 102, no. 1 (February): 524–55.

Eggertsson, Gauti B., and Benjamin Pugsley. 2006. "The Mistake of 1937: A General Equilibrium Analysis." *Monetary and Economic Studies* 25, S1 (December): 157–208.

Eichengreen, Barry. 1992a. *Golden Fetters: The Gold Standard and the Great Depression, 1919–1939.* New York: Oxford University Press.

Eichengreen, Barry. 1992b. "The Origins and Nature of the Great Slump Revisited." *Economic History Review* 45, no. 2 (May): 213–39.

Eichengreen, Barry, and T. J. Hatton. 1988. "Interwar Unemployment in International Perspective: An Overview." In *Interwar Unemployment in International Perspective,* edited by Barry Eichengreen and T. J. Hatton, 1–59. Dordrecht: Springer.

Eichengreen, Barry, and Jeffrey Sachs. 1985. "Exchange Rates and Economic Recovery in the 1930s." *Journal of Economic History* 45 (4) (December): 925–46.

Eichengreen, Barry, and Marc Uzan. 1993. "The 1933 World Economic Conference as an Instance of Failed International Cooperation." In *Double-Edged Diplomacy: International Bargaining and Domestic Politics,* edited by Peter B. Evans, Harold K. Jacobson, and Robert D. Putnam, 171–205. Berkeley: University of California Press.

Einzig, Paul. 1933. *The Sterling-Dollar-Franc Tangle.* London: Macmillan.

Eiteman, Wilford J. 1940. "Security Regulation and the Volume of New Issues." *Southern Economic Journal* 7, no. 1 (July): 27–36.

Emergent Order. 2010. "Fear the Boom and Bust: Keynes vs. Hayek." YouTube (video), January 24. https://www.youtube.com/watch?v=d0nERTFo-Sk

Emerson, Thomas I. 1991. *Young Lawyer for the New Deal: An Insider's Memoir of the Roosevelt Years.* Savage, MD: Rowman and Littlefield.

Epstein, Gerald, and Thomas Ferguson. 1984. "Monetary Policy, Loan Liquidation, and Industrial Conflict: The Federal Reserve and the Open Market Operations of 1932." *Journal of Economic History* 44, no. 4 (December): 957–83.

Eskin, Leonard. 1946. "The Labor Force in the First Year of Peace." *Monthly Labor Review* 63, no. 5 (November): 669–80.

Ezekiel, Mordecai, and T. W. Schultz. 1935. "[AAA as a Force in Recovery]: Discussion." *Journal of Farm Economics* 17, no. 1 (February): 14–19.

Faber, Jacob W. 2020. "We Built This: Consequences of New Deal Intervention in America's Racial Geography." *American Sociological Review* 85, no. 5 (October): 739–75.

Fackler, James S., and Randall E. Parker. 2005. "Was Debt Deflation Operative during the Great Depression?" *Economic Inquiry* 43, no. 1 (January): 67–78.

Farmer, Roger E. A. 2021. "The Importance of Beliefs in Shaping Macroeconomic Outcomes." *Oxford Review of Economic Policy* 36, no. 3 (Autumn): 675–711.

Fausold, Martin L. 1977. "President Hoover's Farm Policies 1929–1933." *Agricultural History* 51, no. 2 (April): 362–77.

"Federal Agencies under New Set-up." 1993. *New York Times*, July 3.

Federal Deposit Insurance Corporation. 1934. *Annual Report*. Washington, DC: Federal Deposit Insurance Corporation.

Federal Deposit Insurance Corporation. 1997. *History of the Eighties: Lessons for the Future*, Vol. 1, *An Examination of the Banking Crises of the 1980s and Early 1990s*. Washington, DC: Federal Deposit Insurance Corporation.

Federal Security Agency. 1949. *Vital Statistics of the United States, 1947: Part II, Natality and Mortality Data for the United States Tabulated by Place of Residence*. Washington, DC: US Government Printing Office.

Feinstein, Charles H., and Katherine Watson. 1995. "Private International Capital Flows in Europe in the Inter-War Period." In *Banking, Currency, and Finance between the Wars*, edited by Charles H. Feinstein, 94–130. Oxford, UK: Clarendon.

Fenberg, Steven. 2011. *Unprecedented Power: Jesse Jones, Capitalism, and the Common Good*. College Station: Texas A&M University Press.

Ferguson, Thomas, 1984. "From Normalcy to New Deal: Industrial Structure, Party Competition, and American Public Policy in the Great Depression." *Industrial Organization* 38, no. 1 (Winter): 41–94.

Field, Alexander J. 1992. "Uncontrolled Land Development and the Duration of the Depression in the United States." *Journal of Economic History* 52, no. 4 (December): 785–805.

Field, Alexander J. 2003. "The Most Technologically Progressive Decade of the Century." *American Economic Review* 93, no. 4 (September): 1399–413.

Field, Alexander J. 2008. "The Impact of the Second World War on US Productivity Growth." *Economic History Review* 61, no. 3 (August): 672–94.

Field, Alexander J. 2011. *A Great Leap Forward: 1930s Depression and U.S. Economic Growth*. New Haven, CT: Yale University Press.

Field, Alexander J. 2013. "Economic Growth and Recovery in the United States: 1919–1941." In *The Great Depression of the 1930s: Lessons for Today*, edited by Nicholas Crafts and Peter Fearon, 358–94. Oxford: Oxford University Press.

Field, Gregory B. 1990. "'Electricity for All': The Electric Home and Farm Authority and the Politics of Mass Consumption, 1932–1935." *Business History Review* 64, no. 1 (Spring): 32–60.

Fine, Sherwood M. 1944. *Public Spending and Postwar Economic Policy*. New York: Columbia University Press.

Finegan, T. Aldrich. 1981. "Discouraged Workers and Economic Fluctuations." *Industrial and Labor Relations Review* 35, no. 1 (October): 88–102.

Fiorito, Luca, and Sebastano Nerozzi. 2009. "Jacob Viner's Reminiscences from the New Deal (February 11, 1953)." *Research in the History of Economic Thought and Methodology* 27, part 1: 75–136.

Fishback, Price. 2010. "US Monetary and Fiscal Policy in the 1930s." *Oxford Review of Economic Policy* 26, no. 3 (Autumn): 385–413.

Fishback, Price. 2017. "How Successful Was the New Deal? The Microeconomic Impact of New Deal Spending and Lending Policies in the 1930s." *American Economic Review* 55, no. 4 (December): 1435–85.

Fishback, Price V., Alfonso Flores-Lagunes, William C. Horrace, Shawn Kantor, and Jaret Treber. 2011. "The Influence of the Home Owners' Loan Corporation on Housing Markets during the 1930s." *Review of Financial Studies* 24, no. 6 (June): 1782–813.

Fishback, Price V., Jonathan Rose, and Kenneth Snowden. 2013. *Well Worth Saving: How the New Deal Safeguarded Home Ownership*. Chicago: University of Chicago Press.

Fishback, Price V., Jonathan Rose, Kenneth A. Snowden, and Thomas Storrs. 2024. "New Evidence on Redlining by Federal Housing Programs in the 1930s." *Journal of Urban Economics* 141: 103462. https://doi.org/10.1016/j.jue.2022.103462.

Fishback, Price V., William C. Horrace, and Shawn Kantor. 2005. "Did New Deal Grant Programs Stimulate Local Economies? A Study of Federal Grants and Retail Sales during the Great Depression." *Journal of Economic History* 65, no. 1 (March): 36–71.

Fishback, Price V., Shawn Kantor, and Todd C. Neumann. 2004. "New Deal Work Relief and Private Wages." Unpublished working paper, February 12.

Fishback, Price, and Valentina Kachanovskaya. 2015. "The Multiplier for Federal Spending in the States during the Great Depression." *Journal of Economic History* 75, no. 1 (March): 125–62.

Fisher, Irving. 1933. "The Debt-Deflation Theory of Great Depressions." *Econometrica* 1, no. 4 (October): 337–57.

Fisher, Irving. 1934. *Stable Money: A History of the Movement*. New York: Adelphi.

Fitzgerald, Kate. 1995. "Sears, Ward's Take Different Paths in the Burgeoning Postwar Years, a Gamble Pays Off for the 'General.'" *Ad Age*, July 31.

Fleck, Robert K. 1999. "The Marginal Effect of New Deal Relief Work on County-Level Unemployment Statistics." *Journal of Economic History* 59, no. 3 (September): 659–87.

Fleitas, Sebastian, Matthew Jaremski, and Steven Sprick Schuster. 2023. "The U.S. Postal Savings System and the Collapse of Building and Loan Associations during the Great Depression." *Southern Economic Journal* 89, no. 1 (April): 1196–215.

Flynn, John T. 1933. "Inside the R.F.C.: An Adventure in Secrecy." *Harper's Magazine* 166 (January): 161–99.

Flynn, John T. 1934. "Whose Child Is the NRA?" *Harper's Magazine* 169 (September): 385–94.

Folsom, Burton, Jr. 2008. *New Deal or Raw Deal? How FDR's Economic Legacy Has Damaged America*. New York: Threshold Editions.

Foster, William Trufant, and Waddill Catchings. 1927. *Business without a Buyer*. New York: Houghton Mifflin.

Freidel, Frank. 1956. *Franklin D. Roosevelt: The Triumph*. Boston: Little, Brown.

Freidel, Frank, ed. 1964. *The New Deal and the American People*. Englewood Cliffs, NJ: Prentice Hall.

Freidel, Frank. 1969. "The New Deal in Historical Perspective." In *The New Deal: Analysis and Interpretation*, edited by Alonzo L. Hamby, 12–31. New York: Weybright and Talley.

Freidel, Frank. 1973. *Franklin D. Roosevelt: Launching the New Deal*. Boston: Little, Brown.

Friedman, Milton. 1992. "Franklin D. Roosevelt, Silver, and China." *Journal of Political Economy* 100, no. 1 (February): 62–83.

Friedman, Milton, and Anna J. Schwartz. 1963. *A Monetary History of the United States, 1867–1960*. Princeton, NJ: Princeton University Press and National Bureau of Economic Research.

Friedman, Milton, and Anna J. Schwartz. 1982. *Monetary Trends in the United States and United Kingdom: Their Relation to Income, Prices, and Interest Rates, 1867–1975*. Chicago: University of Chicago Press and National Bureau of Economic Research.

Frost, Peter A. 1971. "Banks' Demand for Excess Reserves." *Journal of Political Economy* 79, no. 4 (July–August): 805–25.

Fuller, Robert Lynn. 2009. *Drifting toward Mayhem: The Bank Crisis in the United States, 1930–1933*. Raleigh, NC: Lulu.com.

Fuller, Robert Lynn. 2014. *Phantom of Fear: The Banking Panic of 1933*. Jefferson, NC: McFarland.

Future Hindsight. n.d. "How Keynes Influenced FDR's New Deal." https://www.futurehindsight.com/blog/how-keynes-influenced-fdrs-new-deal.

Galbraith, John Kenneth. 1984. "Keynes, Roosevelt, and the Complementary Revolutions." *Challenge* 26, no. 6 (January–February): 4–8.

Galenson, Walter, and Arnol Zellner. 1957. "International Comparison of Unemployment Rates." In *The Measurement and Behavior of Unemployment*, edited by Universities–National Bureau Committee for Economic Research, 439–584. Princeton, NJ: Princeton University Press.

Gambs, Carl M. 1975. "Interest-Bearing Demand Deposits and Bank Portfolio Behavior." *Southern Economic Journal* 42, no. 1 (July): 79–82.

Ganzel, Bill. 2003. "Farming in the 1930s." Wessels Living History Farm. https://livinghistoryfarm.org/farming-in-the-1930s/making-money/a-new-deal/.

Garrett, Garet. 2023 [1938]. "For Five Years, There Has Been No American System." In *New Deal Rebels*, edited by Amity Shlaes, 223–38. Great Barrington, MA: American Institute for Economic Research.

Gates, Sarah Jane. 2017. "More Lives Than a Cat: A State and Federal History of Bank Deposit Insurance in the United States, 1829–1933." PhD diss., University of North Carolina at Greensboro.

Gay, Edwin F. 1931. "The Gold Problem." *Foreign Affairs* 9, no. 2 (January): 195–203.

Gleason, Alan H. 1959. "Foster and Catchings: A Reappraisal." *Journal of Political Economy* 67, no. 2 (April): 156–72.

Glock, Judge. 2019. "The 'Riefler-Keynes' Doctrine and Federal Reserve Policy in the Great Depression." *History of Political Economy* 51, no. 2 (April): 297–327.

Glock, Judge. 2021. *The Dead Pledge: The Origins of the Mortgage Market and Federal Bailouts, 1913–1939*. New York: Columbia University Press.

Goldin, Claudia. 1991. "The Role of World War II in the Rise of Women's Employment." *American Economic Review* 81, no. 4 (September): 741–56.

Goldin, Claudia, and Claudia Olivetti. 2013. "Shocking Labor Supply: A Reassessment of the Role of World War II on Women's Labor Supply." *American Economic Review* 103, no. 3 (May): 257–62.

Goldmon, Camille. 2017. " 'Refusing to Be Dispossessed' " African American Land Retention in the U.S. South from Reconstruction to World War II." MA thesis, University of Arkansas.

Goldstein, Judith. 1989. "The Impact of Ideas on Trade Policy: The Origins of U.S. Agricultural and Manufacturing Policies." *International Organization* 43, no. 1 (Winter): 31–71.

Golembe, Carter H. 1960. "The Deposit Insurance Legislation of 1933: An Examination of Its Antecedents and Its Purposes." *Political Science Quarterly* 75, no. 2 (June): 181–200.

Golembe, Carter H., and Clark Warburton. 1958. *Insurance of Bank Obligations in Six States during the Period 1829–1866*. Washington, DC: Federal Deposit Insurance Corporation. https://fraser.stlouisfed.org/title/830.

Gordon, Robert A. 1955. "Investment Behavior and Business Cycles." *Review of Economics and Statistics* 37, no. 1 (February): 23–34.

Gordon, Robert J. 1969. "$45 Billion of U.S. Private Investment Has Been Mislaid." *American Economic Review* 59, no. 3 (June): 221–38.

Gordon, Robert J. 1980. "A Consistent Characterization of a Near-Century of Price Behavior." *American Economic Review* 70, no. 2 (May): 243–49.

Gordon, Robert J. 1993. "[The Macroeconomics of War and Peace]: Discussion." *NBER Macroeconomics Annual* 8: 257–58.

Gordon, Robert J., and Robert Krenn. 2010. "The End of the Great Depression 1939–41: Policy Contributions and Fiscal Multipliers." NBER Working Paper No. 16380. National Bureau of Economic Research, Cambridge, MA, September.

Grebenyuk, P. S. 2019. "The Gold Factor and Soviet Gold Industry during the Stalin Epoch." *History* 64, no. 3 (October): 890–912.

Grebler, Leo, David M. Blank, and Louis Winnick. 1956. *Capital Formation in Residential Real Estate: Trends and Prospects.* Princeton, NJ: Princeton University Press.

Gressley, Gene M. 1964. "Thurman Arnold, Antitrust, and the New Deal." *Business History Review* 38, no. 2 (Summer): 214–31.

Grossman, Richard S. 1994. "The Shoe That Didn't Drop: Explaining Banking Stability during the Great Depression." *Journal of Economic History* 54, no. 3 (September): 654–82.

Grossman, Richard S., and Christopher M. Meissner. 2010. "International Aspects of the Great Depression and the Crisis of 2007: Similarities, Differences, and Lessons." *Oxford Review of Economic Policy* 26, no. 3 (Autumn): 318–38.

Gulen, Huseyin, and Mihai Ion. 2016. "Policy Uncertainty and Corporate Investment." *Review of Financial Studies* 29, no. 3 (March): 523–64.

Gutwillig, Jacob H. 2014. "Glass versus Steagall: The Fight over Federalism and American Banking: Note." *Virginia Law Review* 100, no. 4 (May): 771–815.

Hagen, Everett E. 1947. "Forecasting Gross National Product and Employment during the Transition Period: An Example of the 'Nation's Budget' Method." In *Studies in Income and Wealth,* edited by Conference on Research in Income and Wealth, 94–109. New York: National Bureau of Economic Research.

Halsey, Olga S. 1946. "Women Workers and Unemployment Insurance since VJ-Day." *Social Security Bulletin* 9, no. 6 (June): 3–10, 48.

Hamby, Alonzo L. 1968. "Sixty Million Jobs and the People's Revolution: The Liberals, the New Deal, and World War II." *The Historian* 30, no. 4 (August): 578–98.

Hamilton, David E. 1985. "The Causes of the Banking Panic of 1930: Another View." *Journal of Southern History* 51, no. 4 (November): 581–608.

Hanes, Christopher. 2013. "Monetary Policy Alternatives at the Zero Bound: Lessons from the 1930s U.S." Working Paper, Department of Economics, State University of New York at Binghamton, February.

Hanes, Christopher. 2019. "Quantitative Easing in the 1930s." *Journal of Money, Credit and Banking* 51, no. 5 (August): 1169–207.

Hanes, Christopher. 2020. "Explaining Anomalous Wage Inflation in the 1930s United States." *Journal of Economic History* 80, no. 4 (December): 1031–70.

Hanes, Richard C., and Sharon M. Hanes, eds. 2002. *Historic Events for Students: The Great Depression.* Farmington Hills, MI: Thomson-Gale.

Hansen, Alvin H. 1939a. "Economic Progress and Declining Population Growth." *American Economic Review* 29, no. 1 (March): 1–15.

Hansen, Alvin H. 1939b. "Memorandum on the Present Social Security Program and the Problem of Whether It Constitutes a Drag on Recovery." In *Diaries of Henry Morgenthau, Jr.,* Book 185, 281–83. Franklin D. Roosevelt Presidential Library and Museum. https://fraser.stlouisfed.org/archival/6880.

Hansen, Alvin H. 1941. *Fiscal Policy and Business Cycles.* New York: Norton.

Hansen, Alvin H. 1943. *After the War—Full Employment*. Washington, DC: National Resources Planning Board.

Hansen, Alvin H. 1963. "Was Fiscal Policy in the Thirties a Failure?" *Review of Economics and Statistics* 45, no. 3 (August): 320–23.

"Hansen Is Dropped by Reserve Board." 1945. *New York Times*, August 15.

Hardy, Charles O., and Jacob Viner. 1935. *Report on the Availability of Bank Credit in the Seventh Federal Reserve District: Submitted to the Secretary of the Treasury*. Washington, DC: US Government Printing Office.

Harris, Max. 2019. "Glut of Gold: The Tripartite Agreement and the Gold Scare of 1937." Unpublished manuscript, May 28.

Harrison, Cynthia. 1982. *On Account of Sex: The Politics of Women's Issues, 1945–1968*. Berkeley: University of Chicago Press.

Harrison, Sharon G., and Mark Weder. 2006. "Did Sunspot Forces Cause the Great Depression?" *Journal of Monetary Economics* 53, no. 7 (October): 1327–39.

Harriss, C. Lowell. 1951. *History and Policies of the Home Owners' Loan Corporation*. New York: National Bureau of Economic Research.

Harrod, Roy. 1951. *The Life of John Maynard Keynes*. New York: Norton.

Hausman, Joshua K. 2016. "What Was Bad for General Motors Was Bad for America: The Automobile Industry and the 1937/38 Recession." *Journal of Economic History* 76, no. 2 (June): 427–77.

Hausman, Joshua K., Paul W. Rhode, and Johannes F. Wieland. 2019. "Recovery from the Great Depression: The Farm Channel in Spring 1933." *American Economic Review* 109, no. 2 (February): 427–72.

Hausman, Joshua K., Paul W. Rhode, and Johannes F. Wieland. 2021. "Farm Product Prices, Redistribution, and the Early U.S. Great Depression." *Journal of Economic History* 81, no. 3 (December): 649–87.

Hawley, Ellis W. 1966. *The New Deal and the Problem of Monopoly: A Study in Economic Ambivalence*. Princeton, NJ: Princeton University Press.

Hayek, Friedrich H. 1944. *The Road to Serfdom*. London: Routledge.

Hemmings Contributor. 2018. "What Killed Kaiser-Frazer." *American City Business Journals*. Last updated September 24. https://www.hemmings.com/stories/article/what-killed-kaiser-frazer.

Henderson, David R. 2010. "The U.S. Postwar Miracle." Mercatus Center Working Paper No. 10–67, November.

Henderson, David R. 2013. "Galbraith and the Southern Sharecroppers." Econlog (blog), August 16. https://www.econlib.org/archives/2013/08/galbraith_and_t.html.

Henderson, Leon. 1944. "Enterprise in Postwar America." In *Postwar Goals and Economic Reconstruction*, edited by Arnold J. Zurcher and Richmond page, 1–18. New York: New York University.

Herman, Arthur. 2012. *Freedom's Forge: How American Business Produced Victory in World War II*. New York: Random House.

Hickman, Bert G. 1958. "Postwar Cyclical Experience and Economic Stability." *American Economic Review* 48, no. 2 (May): 117–34.

Hickman, Bert G. 1960. *Growth and Stability of the Postwar Economy*. Washington, DC: Brookings Institution.

Higgs, Robert. 1992. "Wartime Prosperity? A Reassessment of the U.S. Economy in the 1940s." *Journal of Economic History* 52, no. 1 (March): 41–60.

Higgs, Robert. 1997. "Regime Uncertainty: Why the Great Depression Lasted So Long and Why Prosperity Resumed after the War." *Independent Review* 1, no. 4 (Spring): 561–90.

Higgs, Robert. 1999. "From Central Planning to the Market: The American Transition, 1945–1947." *Journal of Economic History* 59, no. 3 (September): 600–623.

Higgs, Robert. 2004. "Wartime Socialization of Investment: A Reassessment of U.S. Capital Formation in the 1940s." *Journal of Economic History* 64, no. 2 (June): 500–520.

Higgs, Robert. 2009. "A Revealing Window on the U.S. Economy in Depression and War: Hours Worked, 1929–1950." *Independent Review* 14, no. 1 (Summer): 151–60.

Higgs, Robert. 2013. "The Sluggish Recovery of Real Net Domestic Private Business Investment." *Independent Review* 18, no. 2 (Fall): 313–15.

Hill, Julie Anderson. 2010. "Bailouts and Credit Cycles: Fannie, Freddie, and the Farm Credit System." *Wisconsin Law Review* 1: 1–77.

Hillier, Amy E. 2003. "Redlining and the Home Owners' Loan Corporation." *Journal of Urban History* 29, no. 4 (May): 394–420.

Hinchey, Mary E. 1965. "The Frustration of the New Deal Revival, 1944–1946." PhD diss., University of Missouri.

"Hoarders in Fright Turn In $30,000,000." 1933. *New York Times*, March 10.

Hoffpauir, Jennifer. 2009. "The Environmental Impact of Commodity Subsides: NEPA and the Farm Bill." *Fordham Environmental Law Review* 20, no. 1 (January): 233–65.

Hoffsommer, Harold. 1935. "The AAA and the Cropper." *Social Forces* 13, no. 4 (May): 494–502.

Hofstadter, Richard. 1960. "The Right Man for the Biggest Job." *New York Times Magazine*, no. 109, April 3, 121–22.

Hogler, Raymond L. 2005. "The Historical Misconception of Right to Work Laws in the United States: Senator Robert Wagner, Legal Policy, and the Decline of American Unions." *Hofstra Labor and Employment Law Journal* 23, no. 1 (Fall): 101–52.

Homan, Paul T. 1936. "The Pattern of the New Deal." *Political Science Quarterly* 51, no. 2 (June): 161–84.

Hoover, Herbert. 1931a. "The President's News Conference: February 3." The American Presidency Project. https://www.presidency.ucsb.edu/node/207018.

Hoover, Herbert. 1931b. "Statement on Financial and Economic Problems: October 7." The American Presidency Project. https://www.presidency.ucsb.edu/node/207812.

Hoover, Herbert. 1932a. "Campaign Speech at Madison Square Garden: October 31." The American Presidency Project. https://www.presidency.ucsb.edu/node/208073.

Hoover, Herbert. 1932b. "Statement about the Emergency Relief and Construction Legislation, July 6, 1932." Courtesy of the National Archives. https://history.iowa.gov/sites/default/files/primary-sources/pdfs/history-education-pss-hoover-emergency-source.pdf.

Hoover, Herbert. 1932c. "Statement about Signing the Emergency Relief and Construction Act of 1932: July 17, 1932." The American Presidency Project. https://www.presidency.ucsb.edu/node/207221.

Hoover, Herbert. 1951. *The Memoirs of Herbert Hoover*, Vol. 3, *The Great Depression*. New York: Macmillan.

Hopkins, Harry L. 1936. *Spending to Save: The Complete Story of Relief*. New York: Norton.

Horowitz, David A. 1993. "Senator Borah's Crusade to Save Small Business from the New Deal." *The Historian* 55, no. 4 (Summer): 693–708.

Horwitz, Steven. 2011. "Herbert Hoover: The Father of the New Deal." Cato Institute Brief Paper Series No. 122, Cato Institute, Washington, DC, September.

Horwitz, Steve G., and Michael J. McPhillips. 2013. "The Reality of the Wartime Economy: More Historical Evidence on Whether World War II Ended the Great Depression." *Independent Review* 17, no. 3 (Winter): 325–47.

Howard, Donald S. 1943. *The WPA and Federal Relief Policy.* New York: Russell Sage Foundation.

Howenstine, E. Jay, Jr. 1946. "Public Works Policy in the Twenties." *Social Research* 13, no. 4 (December): 479–500.

Hoyt, Homer. 1939. *The Structure and Growth of Residential Neighborhoods in American Cities.* Washington, DC: Federal Housing Administration.

Hsieh, Chang-Tai, and Christina D. Romer. 2006. "Was the Federal Reserve Constrained by the Gold Standard during the Great Depression? Evidence from the 1932 Open Market Purchase Program." *Journal of Economic History* 66, no. 1 (March): 140–76.

Hubbard, Joseph B. 1934. "Security Flotations and the Securities Act." *Review of Economics and Statistics* 16, no. 9 (September): 189–92.

Hughes, Jonathan. 1986. *The Vital Few: The Entrepreneur and American Economic Progress.* New York: Oxford University Press.

Irwin, Douglas. 2012. "Gold Sterilization and the Recession of 1937–1938." *Financial History Review* 19, no. 3 (December): 249–67.

Jackson, Kenneth T. 1980. "Race, Ethnicity, and Real Estate Appraisal: The Home Owners Loan Corporation and the Federal Housing Administration." *Journal of Urban History* 6, no. 4 (August): 419–52.

Jackson, Kenneth T. 1985. *Crabgrass Frontier: The Suburbanization of the United States.* New York: Oxford University Press.

Jacobson, Margaret M., Eric M. Leeper, and Bruce Preston. 2023. "Recovery of 1933." NBER Working Paper No. 25629, National Bureau of Economic Research, Cambridge, MA, April.

Jalil, Andrew J., and Gisela Rua. 2016. "Inflation Expectations and Recovery in Spring 1933." *Explorations in Economic History* 62 (October): 26–50.

Jalil, Andrew J., and Gisela Rua. 2017. "Inflation Expectations in the U.S. in Fall 1933." *Research in Economic History* 33: 139–69.

Jabaily, Robert. 2013. "Bank Holiday of 1933." Federal Reserve History. Last updated November 22, 2013. https://www.federalreservehistory.org/essays/bank-holiday-of-1933.

Jaremski, Matthew, and David Wheelock. 2020. "Banking on the Boom, Tripped by the Bust: Banks and the World War I Agricultural Price Shock." *Journal of Money, Credit and Banking* 52, no. 7 (October): 1719–54.

Jaremski, Matthew, and Gabriel Mathy. 2018. "How Was the Quantitative Easing Program of the 1930s Unwound?" *Explorations in Economic History* 69 (July): 27–49.

Jaworski, Taylor. 2017. "World War II and the Industrialization of the American South." *Journal of Economic History* 77, no. 4 (December): 1048–82.

Jeffries, John W. 1996. "A 'Third New Deal'? Liberal Policy and the American State, 1937–1945." *Journal of Policy History* 8, no. 4 (October): 387–409.

Jensen, Richard J. 1989. "The Causes and Cures of Unemployment in the Great Depression." *Journal of Interdisciplinary History* 19, no. 4 (Spring): 553–83.

Ji, Yangyang. 2021. "The Effect of New Deal Policies Revisited." *CESifo Economic Studies* 67, no. 2 (June): 238–49.

Johnson, D. Gale. 1954. *Agricultural Price Policy and International Trade.* Essays in International Finance No. 19. Princeton, NJ: Princeton University Press.

Jones, Byrd L. 1972. "The Role of Keynesians in Wartime Policy and Postwar Planning, 1940–1946." *American Economic Review* 62, nos. 1–2 (March): 125–33.

Jones, Jesse H. 1939. *Reconstruction Finance Corporation Seven-Year Report to the President and the Congress of the United States, February 2, 1932 to February 2, 1939.* Washington, DC: Reconstruction Finance Corporation.

Jones, Jesse H. 1951. *Fifty Billion Dollars: My Thirteen Years with the RFC (1932–1945).* New York: Macmillan.

Jones, John Bailey. 2002. "Has Fiscal Policy Helped Stabilize the Postwar U.S. Economy?" *Journal of Monetary Economics* 49, no. 4 (May): 709–46.

Josephson, Rhea. 1933. "The National Industrial Recovery Act—Its Permanent Feature." *St. John's Law Review* 8, no. 1 (December): 201–4.

Kane, Edward J. 1992. "The Savings and Loan Insurance Mess." *Society* 29, no. 3 (March): 4–10.

Kazakévich, Vladimir D. 1938. "Public Works in Two Depressions." *Science & Society* 2, no. 4 (Fall): 471–88.

Keehn, Richard H., and Gene Smiley. 1977. "Mortgage Lending by National Banks." *Business History Review* 51, no. 4 (Winter): 474–91.

Keeton, William R. 1984. "Deposit Insurance and the Deregulation of Deposit Rates." Federal Reserve Bank of Kansas City *Economic Review* (April): 28–46.

Keller, Morton. 1999. "The New Deal: A New Look." *Polity* 31, no. 4 (Summer): 657–63.

Kennedy, David. 1999. *Freedom from Fear: The American People in Depression and War, 1929–1945.* New York: Oxford University Press.

Kennedy, David. 2011. "F.D.R.: Budget Hawk." *New York Times,* July 29. https://www.nytimes.com/roomfordebate/2011/07/20/presidents-and-their-debts-fdr-to-bush/fdr-budget-hawk.

Kennedy, Susan Estabrook. 1973. *The Banking Crisis of 1933.* Lexington: University Press of Kentucky.

Kesselman, Jonathan A., and N. E. Savin. 1978. "Three-and-a-Half Million Workers Were Never Lost." *Economic Inquiry* 16, no. 2 (April): 205–25.

Kessler-Harris, Alice. 1982. *Out to Work: A History of Wage-Earning Women in the United States.* Oxford: Oxford University Press.

Keynes, John Maynard. 1923. *A Tract on Monetary Reform.* London: Macmillan.

Keynes, John Maynard. 1930. *A Treatise on Money.* 2 vols. London: Macmillan.

Keynes, John Maynard. 1933a. "From Keynes to Roosevelt: Our Recovery Plan Assayed." *New York Times,* December 31.

Keynes, John Maynard. 1933b. *The Means to Prosperity.* London: Macmillan.

Keynes, John Maynard. 1934. "Sees Need for $400,000,000 Monthly to Speed Recovery." *New York Times,* June 10, 1 and 6.

Keynes, John Maynard. 1936a. "Fluctuations in Net Investment in the United States." *Economic Journal* 46, no. 183 (September): 540–47.

Keynes, John Maynard. 1936b. *The General Theory of Employment, Interest and Money.* London: Macmillan.

Keynes, John Maynard. 1936c. "The Supply of Gold." *Economic Journal* 46, no. 183 (September): 412–18.

Keynes, John Maynard. 1982 [1938]. "Letter of February 1 to Franklin Delano Roosevelt." In *The Collected Writings of John Maynard Keynes,* Vol. 21, *Activities, 1931–1939,* edited by Donald Moggridge. London: Macmillan.

Keyserling, Leon H., Robert R. Nathan, and Lauchlin B. Currie. 1972. "Discussion." *American Economic Review* 62, nos. 1–2 (March): 134–41.

Khan, Aubhik. 2003. "The Role of Inventories in the Business Cycle." Federal Reserve Bank of Philadelphia *Business Review*, Q3, 38–46.

Kiley, Michael. 2016. "Policy Paradoxes in the New-Keynesian Model." *Review of Economic Dynamics* 21 (July): 1–15.

Kimmel, Lewis H. 1939. *The Availability of Bank Credit, 1933–1938.* New York: National Industrial Conference Board.

King, Willford I. 1935. "Some Results of Government Attempts to Foster Recovery." *Journal of Farm Economics* 17, no. 2 (May): 240–49.

Kitchens, Carl. 2014. "The Role of Publicly Provided Electricity in Economic Development: The Experience of the Tennessee Valley Authority, 1929–1955." *Journal of Economic History* 74, no. 2 (June): 389–419.

Klein, Maury. 2001. "The Stock Market Crash of 1929: A Review Article." *Business History Review* 75, no. 2 (Summer): 325–51.

Klemme, Ernest M. 1939. "Industrial Loan Operations of the Reconstruction Finance Corporation and the Federal Reserve Banks." *Journal of Business of the University of Chicago* 12, no. 4 (October): 365–85.

Knerr, Douglas. 2015. *Suburban Steel: The Magnificent Failure of the Lustron Corporation.* Columbus: Ohio State University Press.

Koistinen, Paul A. C. 1973. "Mobilizing the World War II Economy: Labor and the Industrial-Military Alliance." *Pacific Historical Review* 42, no. 4 (November): 443–78.

Kosmerick, Todd. 2017. "World War I and Agriculture." Special Collections, NC State University Libraries. Last updated August 18, 2017. https://www.lib.ncsu.edu/news/special-collections/world-war-i-and-agriculture.

Kossoudji, Sherrie A., and Laura J. Dresser. 1992. "Working Class Rosies: Women Industrial Workers during World War II." *Journal of Economic History* 52, no. 2 (June): 431–46.

Kurz, Heinz D. 2019. "The Keynes-Sraffa-Hayek Controversy." In *The Elgar Companion to John Maynard Keynes,* edited by Robert Diamon and Harald Hagemann, 275–82. Cheltenham, UK: Edward Elgar.

Krock, Arthur. 1933. "Washington Sifts Ideas." *New York Times*, March 8.

Krock, Arthur. 1965. "Reminiscences." *Centennial Review* 9, no. 2 (Spring): 222–52.

Krooss, Herman E. 1970. *Executive Opinion: What Business Leaders Said and Thought on Economic Issues, 1920s–1960s.* Garden City, NY: Doubleday.

Kroszner, Randall S., and Raghuram G. Rajan. 1994. "Is the Glass-Steagall Act Justified? A Study of the U.S. Experience with Universal Banking Before 1933." *American Economic Review* 84, no. 4 (September): 810–32.

Laidler, David. 1993. "Hawtrey, Harvard, and the Origins of the Chicago Tradition." *Journal of Political Economy* 101, no. 6 (December): 1068–103.

League of Nations. 1932. *Report of the Gold Delegation of the Financial Committee.* Geneva: League of Nations.

League of Nations. 1939. *World Economic Survey, 1938–1939.* Geneva: League of Nations.

Lebergott, Stanley. 1948. "Labor Force, Employment, and Unemployment, 1929–39: Estimating Methods." *Monthly Labor Review* 67, no. 1 (July): 50–53.

Lee, Bradford A. 1982. "The New Deal Reconsidered." *Wilson Quarterly* 6, no. 2 (Spring): 62–76.

Leff, Mark H. 1984. *The Limits of Symbolic Reform: The New Deal and Taxation, 1933–1939.* Cambridge: Cambridge University Press.

Lehmann, Fritz. 1940. "The Gold Problem." *Social Research* 7, no. 2 (May): 125–50.

Lent, George E. 1948. *The Impact of the Undistributed Profits Tax, 1936–1937.* New York: Columbia University Press.

Lescohier, Don D. 1935. *History of Labor in the United States, 1896–1932,* Vol. 3, *Working Conditions.* New York: Macmillan.

Leuchtenburg, William E. 1963. *Franklin D. Roosevelt and the New Deal, 1932–1940.* New York: Harper & Row.

Levinson, Marc. 2016. *An Extraordinary Time: The End of the Postwar Boom and the Return of the Ordinary Economy.* New York: Basic Books.

Lewandrowski, Jan, James Tobey, and Zena Cook. 1997. "The Interface between Agricultural Assistance and the Environment: Chemical Fertilizer Consumption and Area Expansion." *Land Economics* 73, no. 3 (August): 404–27.

Lewis, Robert. 2007. "World War II Manufacturing and the Postwar Southern Economy." *Journal of Southern History* 73, no. 4 (November): 837–66.

Lindley, Ernest Kidder. 1934. *The Roosevelt Revolution: First Phase.* London: Victor Gollancz.

Lindley, Ernest Kidder. 1937. *Half Way with Roosevelt.* New York: Viking.

Lowenstein, Asher. 2011. "The 'Speculative Orgy' of Commercial Banks: Intentions and Impact of the Glass-Steagall Act." Bachelor's thesis, Baruch College.

Lutz, Friedrich A. 1945. "The Interest Rate and Investment in a Dynamic Economy." *American Economic Review* 35, no. 5 (December): 811–30.

Lyon, Leverett S., Paul T. Homan, Lewis L. Lorman, George Terborgh, Charles L. Dearing, and Leon C. Marshall. 1935. *The National Recovery Administration: An Analysis and Appraisal.* Washington, DC: Brookings Institution.

Lyons, Eugene. 1948. *Our Unknown Ex-President: A Portrait of Herbert Hoover.* Garden City, NY: Doubleday.

Macdonald, Dwight. 1947. "Henry Wallace." *Politics* (March–April): 33–44.

Macey, Jonathan R., and Geoffrey P. Miller. 1992. "Double Liability of Bank Shareholders: History and Implications." *Wake Forest Law Review* 27, no. 1 (Spring): 31–62.

Madsen, Jakob B. 2001. "Agricultural Crises and the International Transmission of the Great Depression." *Journal of Economic History* 61, no. 2 (June): 327–65.

Mahoney, Paul G. 2012. "The Public Utility Pyramids." *Journal of Legal Studies* 41, no. 1 (January): 37–66.

Mahoney, Paul G. 2018. "Deregulation and the Subprime Crisis." *Virginia Law Review* 104, no. 2 (April): 235–300.

Martin, Fernando M. 2016. "Private Investment and the Great Recession." Federal Reserve Bank of St. Louis *Economic Synopses* 1, January 8.

Martin, George. 1976. *Madam Secretary: Frances Perkins.* Boston: Houghton Mifflin.

Mason, David L. 2004. *From Buildings and Loans to Bailouts: A History of the American Savings and Loan Industry, 1813–1995.* Cambridge: Cambridge University Press.

Mason, Joseph R. 2000. "Reconstruction Finance Corporation Assistance to Financial Intermediaries and Commercial & Industrial Enterprise in the U.S., 1932–1937." Unpublished working paper, January 17.

Mason, Joseph R. 2001. "Do Lender of Last Resort Policies Matter? The Effects of Reconstruction Finance Corporation Assistance to Banks during the Great Depression." *Journal of Financial Services Research* 20, no. 1 (September): 77–95.

Mason, Joseph R. 2003. "The Political Economy of Reconstruction Finance Corporation Assistance during the Great Depression." *Explorations in Economic History* 40, no. 2 (April): 101–21.

Mason, Joseph R. 2009. "The Evolution of the Reconstruction Finance Corporation as a Lender of Last Resort in the Great Depression." In *Bailouts: Public Money, Private Profit,* edited by Robert E. Wright, 70–107. New York: Columbia University Press.

Mason, Joseph R., and Daniel Schiffman. 2002. "Too-Big-to-Fail, Government Bailouts, and Managerial Incentives: The Case of Reconstruction Finance Corporation Assistance to the Railroad Industry during the Great Depression." Working Paper, Drexel University and Bar Ilan University, October.

Mathy, Gabriel P. 2016. "Stock Volatility, Return Jumps and Uncertainty Shocks during the Great Depression." *Financial History Review* 23, no. 2: 165–92.

Mathy, Gabriel P. 2018. "Hysteresis and Persistent Long-Term Unemployment: The American Beveridge Curve of the Great Depression and World War II." *Cliometrica* 12, no. 1 (January): 127–52.

May, Dean L. 1976. "Sources of Marriner S. Eccles's Economic Thought." *Journal of Mormon History* 3: 85–99.

Mayer, Thomas, and Monojit Chatterji. 1985. "Political Shocks and Investment: Some Evidence from the 1930s." *Journal of Economic History* 45, no. 4 (December): 913–24.

McCoy, Patricia A. 2008. "The Moral Hazard Implications of Deposit Insurance: Theory and Evidence." In *Current Developments in Monetary and Financial Law,* Vol. 5, 417–41. Washington, DC: International Monetary Fund.

McDonald, Oonagh. 2016. "The Repeal of the Glass-Steagall Act: Myth and Reality." Cato Institute *Policy Analysis* No. 84, November 16.

McElvaine, Robert S. 1993. *The Great Depression: America, 1929-1941.* New York: Times Books.

McGrattan, Ellen R. 2012. "Capital Taxation during the U.S. Great Depression." *Quarterly Journal of Economics* 127, no. 3 (August): 1515–50.

McGrattan, Ellen R., and Edward C. Prescott. 2004. "The 1929 Stock Market: Irving Fisher Was Right." *International Economic Review* 45, no. 4 (November): 991–1009.

McHugh, Laughlin F. 1947. "Consumer Credit in the Postwar Period." *Survey of Current Business* 27, no. 11 (November): 11–24.

McKay, Alisdair, and Ricardo Reis. 2016. "The Role of Automatic Stabilizers in the U.S. Business Cycle." *Econometrica* 84, no. 1 (January): 141–94.

McLaughlin, Glenn E. 1943. "Wartime Expansion in Industrial Capacities." *American Economic Review* 33, no. 1, part 2 (March): 108–18.

Meltzer, Allan H. 2003. *A History of the Federal Reserve,* Vol. 1, *1913-1951.* Chicago: University of Chicago Press.

Miller, Marc. 1980. "Working Women and World War II." *New England Quarterly* 53, no. 1 (March): 42–61.

Miscamble, Wilson D. 1982. "Thurman Arnold Goes to Washington: A Look at Antitrust Policy in the Later New Deal." *Business History Review* 56, no. 1 (Spring): 1–15.

"Missouri Pacific Put in Bankruptcy." 1933. *New York Times,* April 1.

Misukiewicz, Claude. 2015. "Lewis L. Lorwin and 'The Promise of Planning': Class, Collectivism, and Empire in U.S. Economic Planning Debates, 1931-1941." MA thesis, Georgia State University.

Mitchell, Broadus. 1947. *Depression Decade: From New Era through New Deal, 1929-1941.* Armonk, NY: M. E. Sharpe.

Mitchener, Kris, Kevin Hjortshøj O'Rourke, and Kirsten Wandshneider. 2022. "The Smoot-Hawley Trade War." *Economic Journal* 132 (October): 2500–33.

Mitchener, Kris James, and Gary Richardson. 2020. "Contagion of Fear." NBER Working Paper No. 26859, National Bureau of Economic Research, Cambridge, MA, March.

Modell, John. 1989. *Into One's Own: From Youth to Adulthood in the United States, 1920–1975.* Berkely: University of California Press.

Moley, Raymond. 1938. "The State of the Union." *Newsweek*, December 12.

Moley, Raymond. 1939. *After Seven Years.* New York: Harper & Brothers.

Moley, Raymond. 1948. "Reappraising Hoover." *Newsweek*, June 14.

Moley, Raymond. 1966. *The First New Deal.* New York: Harcourt, Brace & World.

Moore, Geoffrey H. 1983. *Business Cycles, Inflation, and Forecasting.* 2nd ed. Cambridge, MA: Ballinger and National Bureau of Economic Research.

Moore, Terris. 1934. "Security Affiliate versus Private Investment Banker: A Study in Security Origination." *Harvard Business Review* 12 (July): 478–574.

Moreno, Paul. 2002. "An Ambivalent Legacy: Black Americans and the Political Economy of the New Deal." *Independent Review* 6, no. 4 (Spring): 513–39.

Musgrave, Richard A. 1987–1988. "U.S. Fiscal Policy, Keynes, and Keynesian Economics." *Journal of Post Keynesian Economics* 10, no. 2 (Winter): 171–82.

Myers, William Starr, and Walter H. Newton. 1936. *The Hoover Administration: A Documented Narrative.* New York: Scribner.

Myrdal, Gunnar. 1944. *An American Dilemma: The Negro Problem and Modern Democracy.* New York: Harper & Row.

National Transportation Committee. 1933. *The American Transportation Problem.* Washington, DC: Brookings Institution.

Neely, Michelle Clark. 1994. "Going Interstate: A New Dawn for U.S. Banking." Federal Reserve Bank of St. Louis *Regional Economist* (July): 5–9.

Nelson, Lawrence J. 1983. "The Art of the Possible: Another Look at the 'Purge' of the AAA in 1935." *Agricultural History* 57, no. 4 (October): 416–35.

Nerozzi, Sebastiano. 2011. "From the Great Depression to Bretton Woods: Jacob Viner and International Monetary Stabilization (1930–1945)." *European Journal of the History of Economic Thought* 18, no. 1 (February): 55–84.

Nettels, Curtis. 1934. "Frederick Jackson Turner and the New Deal." *Wisconsin Magazine of History* 17, no. 3 (March): 257–65.

Newton, John. 2022. "What's in the New COVID-19 Relief Package for Agriculture?" American Farm Bureau Federation, December 22. https://www.fb.org/market-intel/whats-in-the-new-covid-19-relief-package-for-agriculture.

Norton, Hugh S. 1977. *The Employment Act and the Council of Economic Advisers, 1946–1976.* Columbia: University of South Carolina Press.

Nourse, Edwin G. 1956. "Defining Our Employment Goal under the 1946 Act." *Review of Economics and Statistics* 38, no. 2 (May): 193–204.

Nourse, Edwin G., Joseph S. Davis, and John D. Black. 1937. *Three Years of the Agricultural Adjustment Administration.* Washington, DC: Brookings Institution.

Noyes, Charles E. 1940. "Government Farm Loans." *CQ Researcher*, May 27. https://cqpress.sagepub.com/cqresearcher/report/government-farm-loans-cqresrre1940052700.

O'Brien, Anthony Patrick, and Paul B. Trescott. 1992. "The Failure of the Bank of United States, 1930: Note." *Journal of Money, Credit and Banking* 24, no. 3 (August): 384–99.

O'Brien, Patrick, and Philip T. Rosen. 1981a. "Hoover and the Historians: The Resurrection of a President, Part I." *Annals of Iowa* 46, no. 1 (Summer): 25–42.

O'Brien, Patrick, and Philip T. Rosen. 1981b. "Hoover and the Historians.: The Resurrection of a President, Part II." *Annals of Iowa* 46, no. 2 (Fall): 83–99.

Ogburn, William F., and A. J. Jaffe. 1936. "Business Conditions in Presidential Election Years." *American Political Science Review* 30, no. 2 (April): 269–75.

O'Hara, Maureen, and David Easley. 1979. "The Postal Savings System in the Depression." *Journal of Economic History* 39, no. 3 (September): 741–53.

O'Leary, James J. 1945. "Consumption as a Factor in Postwar Employment." *American Economic Review* 35, no. 2 (May): 37–55.

Olson, James Stuart. 1972. "The End of Voluntarism: Herbert Hoover and the National Credit Corporation." *Annals of Iowa* 41, no. 6 (Fall): 1104–13.

Olson, James Stuart. 1975. "Rehearsal for Disaster: Hoover, the R.F.C., and the Banking Crisis in Nevada, 1932–1933." *Western Historical Quarterly* 6, no. 2 (April): 149–61,

Olson, James Stuart. 1982. *Saving Capitalism: The Reconstruction Finance Corporation and the New Deal, 1933–1940*. Princeton, NJ: Princeton University Press.

Olson, John Maurice Clifton, Jr. 1966. "An Analysis of Fiscal Policy during the Truman Administration (1945–1953)." PhD diss., University of Southern California.

"135 Banks Reopen Here; Rush to Put Money Back Shows Restored Faith as Holiday Ends." 1933. *New York Times*, March 14.

Paarlberg, Don. 1983. "Effects of New Deal Farm Programs on the Agricultural Agenda a Half Century Later and Prospect for the Future." *American Journal of Agricultural Economics* 65, no. 5 (December): 1163–67.

Park, Haelim, and Patrick Van Horn. 2015. "Did the Reserve Requirement Increases of 1936–37 Reduce Bank Lending? Evidence from a Quasi-Experiment." *Journal of Money, Credit and Banking* 47, no. 5 (August): 791–818.

Patch, Buel W. 1933. "Press Freedom under the Recovery Program." *CQ Researcher*, November 4. https://cqpress.sagepub.com/cqresearcher/report/press-freedom-under-recovery-program-cqresrre1933110400.

Patch, Buel W. 1936. "Unemployment and Recovery." *CQ Researcher*, May 19. https://cqpress.sagepub.com/cqresearcher/report/unemployment-recovery-cqresrre1936051900.

Patch, Buel W. 1939. "Closed Banks and Banking Reform." *CQ Researcher*, August 12. https://cqpress.sagepub.com/cqresearcher/report/closed-banks-banking-reform-cqresrre1933081200.

Patel, I. G. 1953. "Monetary Policy in Postwar Years." *IMF Staff Papers* 3, no. 1 (April): 69–131.

Paul, Sanjukta. 2024. "The First New Deal: Planning, Market Coordination, and the National Industrial Recovery Act of 1933." Phenomenal World, March 28. https://www.phenomenalworld.org/analysis/the-first-new-deal/.

Peach, William Nelson. 1941. *The Security Affiliates of National Banks*. Baltimore: Johns Hopkins University Press.

Pearson, F. A., W. I. Myers, and A. R. Gans. 1957. "Warren as Presidential Advisor." *Farm Economics*, no. 211 (Winter): 5598–676.

Peppers, Larry C. 1973. "Full Employment Surplus Analysis and Structural Change: The 1930s." *Explorations in Economic History* 10, no. 2 (Winter): 197–210.

Perkins, Frances. 1946. *The Roosevelt I Knew*. New York: Viking.

Perry, Nathan, and M. Vernengo. 2014. "What Ended the Great Depression? Re-evaluating the Role of Fiscal Policy." *Cambridge Journal of Economics* 38, no. 2 (March): 349–67.

Phillips, Ronnie J. 1997. "The Chicago Plan and the Reserve Requirement Increase of 1936–37." *History of Economic Ideas* 5, no. 2: 53–67.

Pidgeon, Mary Elizabeth. 1952. *Women Workers and Their Dependents.* Women's Bureau Bulletin No. 239. Washington, DC: US Government Printing Office.

Pindyck, Robert S. 1991. "Irreversibility, Uncertainty, and Investment." *Journal of Economic Literature* 29, no. 3 (September): 1110–48.

Poelmans, Eline, Jason E. Taylor, Samue Raisanen, and Andrew C. Holt. 2022. "Estimates of Employment Gains Attributable to Beer Legalization in Spring 1933." *Explorations in Economic History* 84 (April): 1–20.

Polenberg, Richard. 1975. "The Decline of the New Deal, 1939–1940." In *The New Deal: The National Level,* edited by John Braeman, Robert H. Bremner, and David Brody, 246–66. Columbus: Ohio State University Press.

Posner, Richard. 1970. "A Statistical Study of Antitrust Enforcement." *Journal of Law and Economics* 13, no. 2 (October): 365–419.

Powel, Jim. 2003. *FDR's Folly: How Roosevelt and His New Deal Prolonged the Great Depression.* New York: Three Rivers.

Prater, Lisa Foust. 2022. "Wartime Farm Women Fought from Home." *Successful Farming,* March 15. https://www.agriculture.com/family/women-in-agriculture/wartime-farm-women-fought -from-home.

"The Presidency: Revolving Rabbit." 1939. *Time,* July 3.

"The Presidency: Signings." 1933. *Time,* June 26.

"President Pushes Extension of NRA with Full Power." 1935. *New York Times,* March 23.

Preston, Howard. 1936. "Our Farm Credit System." *Journal of Farm Economics* 18, no. 4 (November): 673–84.

Price, David A., and John R. Walter. 2019. "It's a Wonderful Loan: A Short History of Building and Loan Associations." Federal Reserve Bank of Richmond *Economic Brief* No. 19-01, January.

"Price Controls under N.R.A." 1934. *CQ Researcher,* March 19. https://cqpress.sagepub.com /cqresearcher/report/price-controls-under-nra-cqresrre1934031900.

Puri, Manju. 1994. "The Long-Term Default Performance of Bank Underwritten Security Issues." *Journal of Banking & Finance* 18, no 2 (January): 397–418.

Putney, Bryant. 1936. "Politics and Business in 1936." *CQ Researcher,* January 4. https://cqpress .sagepub.com/cqresearcher/report/politics-business-1936-cqresrre1936010400.

Rafti, Jonian. 2015. "Roosevelt's Recession: A Historical and Econometric Examination of the Roots of the 1937 Recession." *Inquiries Journal* 7, no. 6: 1–8.

Rajan, Raghuram, and Rodney Ramcharan. 2015. "The Anatomy of a Credit Crisis: The Boom and Bust of Farm Prices in the United States in the 1920s." *American Economic Review* 105, no. 4 (April): 1439–77.

Ramey, Valerie A. 2011. "Identifying Government Spending Shocks: It's All in the Timing." *Quarterly Journal of Economics* 126, no. 1 (February): 1–50.

Ramey, Valerie A., and Sarah Zubairy. 2015. "The US Fiscal Multiplier: Historical Evidence." VoxEU.org (blog), Center for Economic Policy Research, January 23. https://voxeu.org /article/us-fiscal-multiplier-historical-evidence.

Ramey, Valerie A., and Sarah Zubairy. 2017. "Supplementary Appendix to Government Spending Multipliers in Good Times and in Bad: Evidence from U.S. Historical Data." Unpublished manuscript. https://econweb.ucsd.edu/~vramey/research/RZ_Supplementary_Appendix.pdf.

Ramey, Valerie A., and Sarah Zubairy. 2018. "Government Spending Multipliers in Good Times and in Bad: Evidence from US Historical Data." *Journal of Political Economy* 126, no. 2 (April): 850–901.

Rampell, Catherine. 2009. " 'Great Recession': A Brief Etymology." *New York Times,* March 11.

Rappoport, Peter, and Eugene N. White. 1993. "Was There a Bubble in the 1929 Stock Market?" *Journal of Economic History* 53, no 3 (September): 549–74.

Rasmussen, Wayne D. 1951. *A History of the Emergency Farm Labor Supply Program, 1943–1947.* US Department of Agriculture, Bureau of Agricultural Economics Agricultural Monograph No. 13. Washington, DC: US Government Printing Office.

Rauchway, Eric. 2008. "(Very) Short Reading List: Unemployment in the 1930s." The Edge of the American West (blog), Chronicle of Higher Education, October 10. https://www.chronicle.com/blognetwork/edgeofthewest/very-short-reading-list-unemployment-in-the-1930s.

Rauchway, Eric. 2013. " 'The Queer Personality and Floating Mind': What Did Keynes Say to and about Roosevelt?" Crooked Timber (blog). https://crookedtimber.org/2013/06/17/the-queer-personality-and-floating-mind-what-did-keynes-say-to-and-about-roosevelt-2/.

Rauchway, Eric. 2014. "Going off Gold and the Basis for Bretton Woods." Berkeley Economic History Seminar, March 31. https://eml.berkeley.edu/~webfac/eichengreen/e211_sp14/rauchway_econ 211_3-31-14.pdf.

Rauchway, Eric. 2015. *The Money Makers: How Roosevelt and Keynes Ended the Depression, Defeated Fascism, and Secured a Prosperous Peace.* New York: Basic Books.

Rauchway, Eric. 2018. *Winter War: Hoover, Roosevelt, and the First Clash over the New Deal.* New York: Basic Books.

Rauchway, Eric. 2019. "The New Deal Was on the Ballot in 1932." *Modern American History* 2, no. 2 (July): 201–13.

Reeves, William D. 1968. "The Politics of Public Works, 1933–1935." PhD diss., Tulane University.

Renshaw, Patrick. 1999. "Was There a Keynesian Economy in the USA between 1933 and 1945?" *Journal of Contemporary History* 34, no. 3 (July): 337–64.

Republican Party Platforms. 1932. "Republican Party Platform of 1932." The American Presidency Project, https://www.presidency.ucsb.edu/node/273383.

Richardson, Gary. 2013. "The Federal Reserve's Role during WWII." *Federal Reserve History.* Federal Reserve Bank of St. Louis, November 22. https://www.federalreservehistory.org /essays/feds-role-during-wwii.

Richardson, Gary, and Patrick Van Horn. 2018. "In the Eye of a Storm: Manhattan's Money Center Banks during the International Financial Crisis of 1931." *Explorations in Economic History* 68 (April): 71–94.

Richardson, Gary, Alejandro Komai, and Michael Gou. 2013. "Banking Act of 1935." *Federal Reserve History,* Federal Reserve Bank of St. Louis. https://www.federalreservehistory.org /essays/banking-act-of-1935.

Rockoff, Hugh. 1998. "The United States: From Ploughshares to Swords." In *The Economics of World War II,* edited by Mark Harrison, 81–121. Cambridge: Cambridge University Press.

Rockoff, Hugh. 2020. "Off to a Good Start: The NBER and the Measurement of National Income." NBER Working Paper No. 26895, National Bureau of Economic Research, Cambridge, MA, March.

Romasco, Alberto. 1983. *The Politics of Recovery: Roosevelt's New Deal.* New York: Oxford University Press.

Romer, Christina D. 1990. "The Great Crash and the Onset of the Great Depression." *Quarterly Journal of Economics* 105, no. 3 (August): 597–624.

Romer, Christina D. 1992. "What Ended the Great Depression?" *Journal of Economic History* 52, no. 4 (December): 757–84.

Romer, Christina D. 1999. "Why Did Prices Rise in the 1930s?" *Journal of Economic History* 59, no. 1 (March): 167–99.

Romer, Christina D. 2009. "From Recession to Recovery: The Economic Crisis, the Policy Response, and the Challenges We Face Going Forward." Testimony before the Joint Economic Committee, October 22. https://obamawhitehouse.archives.gov/administration/eop/cea/From RecessionToRecovery.

Romero, Jessie. 2013. "The Treasury-Fed Accord." Federal Reserve History, November 22. https://www.federalreservehistory.org/essays/treasury-fed-accord.

Roos, Charles F. 1937. *NRA Economic Planning.* Cowles Commission for Research in Economics Monograph No. 2. Bloomington, IN: Principia.

Roose, Kenneth D. 1948. "The Recession of 1937–38." *Journal of Political Economy* 56, no. 3 (June): 239–48.

Roose, Kenneth D. 1951. "The Role of Net Government Contribution to Income in the Recession and Revival of 1937–38." *Journal of Finance* 6, no. 1 (March): 1–18.

Roose, Kenneth D. 1954. *The Economics of Recession and Revival: An Interpretation of 1937–38.* New Haven, CT: Yale University Press.

Roosevelt, Franklin D. 1932a. "Address Accepting the Presidential Nomination at the Democratic National Convention in Chicago: July 2." The American Presidency Project. https://www.presidency.ucsb.edu/node/275484.

Roosevelt, Franklin D. 1932b. "Campaign Address in Topeka, Kansas on the Farm Problem: September 14." The American Presidency Project. https://www.presidency.ucsb.edu/node/289318.

Roosevelt, Franklin D. 1932c. "Campaign Address on Progressive Government at the Commonwealth Club in San Francisco, California: September 23." The American Presidency Project. https://www.presidency.ucsb.edu/node/289312.

Roosevelt, Franklin D. 1933. *Looking Forward.* New York: John Day.

Roosevelt, Franklin D. 1937. "Annual Message to Congress: January 6." The American Presidency Project. https://www.presidency.ucsb.edu/node/209043.

Roosevelt, Franklin D. 1938. *Public Papers and Addresses of Franklin D. Roosevelt.* 5 vols. (1928–1936). New York: Random House.

Roosevelt, Franklin. 1941a. "Annual Message to Congress on the State of the Union: January 6." The American Presidency Project. https://www.presidency.ucsb.edu/node/209473.

Roosevelt, Franklin. 1941b. *Public Papers and Addresses of Franklin D. Roosevelt.* 4 vols. (1937–1940). New York: Macmillan.

Roosevelt, Franklin D. 1950. *Public Papers and Addresses of Franklin D. Roosevelt.* 4 vols. (1941–1945). New York: Harper & Bros.

Rose, Jonathan D. 2010. "Hoover's Truce: Wage Rigidity in the Onset of the Great Depression." *Journal of Economic History* 70, no. 4 (December): 843–70.

Rose, Jonathan D. 2011. "The Incredible HOLC? Mortgage Relief during the Great Depression." *Journal of Money, Credit and Banking* 43, no. 6 (September): 1073–107.

Rose, Jonathan D. 2013. "A Primer on Farm Mortgage Debt Relief Programs during the 1930s." Unpublished working paper, April 22.

Rose, Jonathan D. 2014. "The Prolonged Resolution of Troubled Real Estate Lenders during the 1930s." In *Housing and Mortgage Markets in Historical Perspective,* edited by Eugene N. White, Kenneth Snowden, and Price Fishback, 245–84. Chicago: University of Chicago Press and National Bureau of Economic Research.

Rose, Jonathan D. 2022. "Reassessing the Magnitude of Housing Price Declines and the Use of Leverage in the Depressions of the 1890s and 1930s." *Real Estate Economics* 50, no. 4 (Winter): 907–30.

Rose, Nancy Ellen. 1994. *Put to Work: Relief Programs in the Great Depression.* New York: Monthly Review Press.

Rosen, Elliot A. 2005. *Roosevelt, the Great Depression, and the Economics of Recovery.* Charlottesville: University of Virginia Press.

Rothbard, Murray N. 1972. "Herbert Hoover and the Myth of Laissez-Faire." In *A New History of Leviathan: Essays on the Rise of the American Corporate State,* edited by Ronald Radosh and Murray N. Rothbard, 111–45. New York: E. P. Dutton.

Rozwenc, Edwin C. 1949. *The New Deal: Revolution or Evolution?* Boston: D. C. Heath.

Rupp, Leila J. 1978. *Mobilizing Women for War: German and American Propaganda, 1939–1945.* Princeton, NJ: Princeton University Press.

Rust, Owen. 2021. "We're All Keynesians Now: The Economic Effects of the Great Depression." The Collector (blog). https://www.thecollector.com/economic-effects-of-the-great -depression/

Rutterford, Janette, and Dimitris P. Sotiropoulos. 2017. "The Rise of the Small Investor in the US and the UK, 1895 to 1970." *Enterprise & Society* 18, no. 3 (September): 485–535.

Sagalyn, Lynne Beyer. 1980. "Housing on the Installment Plan: An Economic and Institutional Analysis of Contract Buying in Chicago." PhD diss., Massachusetts Institute of Technology.

Saloutos, Theodore. 1974. "New Deal Agricultural Policy: An Evaluation." *Journal of Economic History* 61, no. 2 (September): 394–416.

Samuelson, Paul A. 1943. "Full Employment after the War." In *Postwar Economic Problems,* edited Seymour E. Harris, 27–54. New York: McGraw Hill.

Samuelson, Paul A. 1944. "Unemployment Ahead." *New Republic,* September 11.

Santoni, G. J. 1986. "The Employment Act of 1946: Some History Notes." Federal Reserve Bank of St. Louis *Review,* November: 5–16.

Sapir, Michael. 1949. "Review of Economic Forecasts for the Transition Period." In *Studies in Income and Wealth,* Vol. 11, prepared by the Conference on Research in Income and Wealth, 275–368. New York: National Bureau of Economic Research.

Sargent, James E. 1973. "Oral History, Franklin D. Roosevelt, and the New Deal: Some Recollections of Adolf A. Berle, Jr., Lewis W. Douglas, and Raymond Moley." *Oral History Review* 1: 92–109.

Saulnier, Raymond J., Harold G. Halcrow, and Neil H. Jacoby. 1958. *Federal Lending and Loan Insurance.* Princeton, NJ: Princeton University Press.

Saunders, Charles B., Jr. 1966. *The Brookings Institution: A Fifty-Year History.* Washington, DC: Brookings Institution.

Schiffman, Daniel A. 2003. "Shattered Rails, Ruined Credit: Financial Fragility and Railroad Operations in the Great Depression." *Journal of Economic History* 63, no. 3 (September): 802–25.

Schlesinger, Arthur M., Jr. 1958. *The Age of Roosevelt,* Vol. 2, *The Coming of the New Deal.* Boston: Houghton Mifflin.

Schlesinger, Arthur M., Jr. 1960. *The Age of Roosevelt,* Vol. 3, *The Politics of Upheaval.* Boston: Houghton Mifflin.

Schultz, T. W. 1935. "AAA as a Force in Recovery: Discussion by T. W. Schultz." *American Journal of Agricultural Economics* 17, no. 1 (February): 17–19.

Schumpeter, Joseph A. 1939. *Business Cycles: A Theoretical, Historical, and Statistical Analysis of the Capitalist Process.* New York: McGraw Hill.

Schumpeter, Joseph A. 1942. *Capitalism, Socialism, and Democracy.* New York: Harper & Brothers.

Schumpeter, Joseph A. 1951. *Ten Great Economists from Marx to Keynes.* New York: Oxford University Press.

Schwartz, Anna J. 1997. "From Obscurity to Notoriety: A Biography of the Exchange Stabilization Fund." *Journal of Money, Credit and Banking* 29, no. 2 (May): 135–53.

Schwarz, Jordan A. 1987. *Liberal: Adolf A. Berle and the Vision of an American Era.* New York: Free Press.

Schweitzer, Mary M. 1980. "World War II and Female Labor Force Participation Rates." *Journal of Economic History.* 40, no. 1 (March): 89–95.

Selgin, George. 2000. "The Suppression of State Banknotes: A Reconsideration." *Economic Inquiry* 38 no. 4 (October): 600–615.

Selgin, George. 2020a. "Modeling the Legend, or, the Trouble with Diamond and Dybvig: Part I." Alt-M (blog), December 17, 2020. https://www.cato.org/blog/modeling-legend-or-trouble -diamond-dybvig-part-i.

Selgin, George. 2020b. "Modeling the Legend, or, the Trouble with Diamond and Dybvig: Part II." Alt-M (blog), December 18, 2020. https://www.cato.org/blog/modeling-legend-or-trouble -diamond-dybvig-part-ii.

Selgin, George. 2021. "An Unnecessary Evil: How Canada Ended up Insuring Bank Deposits." Alt-M (blog), November 15, 2021. https://www.cato.org/blog/unnecessary-evil-how -canada-ended-insuring-bank-deposits.

"Senate Overrides Farm Loan Veto." 1937. *New York Times*, July 23.

Shatnawi, Dina, and Price Fishback. 2018. "The Impact of World War II on the Demand for Female Workers in Manufacturing." *Journal of Economic History* 78, no. 2 (June): 539–74.

Shepherd, Geoffrey. 1942. "Stabilization Operations of the Commodity Credit Corporation." *Journal of Farm Economics* 24, no. 3 (August): 589–610.

Shipbuilding History. n.d. "Emergency Shipbuilders." http://shipbuildinghistory.com/ship yards/emergencylarge.htm.

Shlaes, Amity. 2007. *The Forgotten Man: A New History of the Great Depression.* New York: HarperCollins.

Short, Eugenie Dudding, and Gerald P. O'Driscoll. 1983. "Deposit Insurance in a Deregulated Financial Environment: The Case for Reform." Federal Reserve Bank of Dallas Research Paper No. 8305, Federal Reserve Bank of Dallas, TX, October.

Silber, William L. 2009. "Why Did FDR's Bank Holiday Succeed?" Federal Reserve Bank of New York *Economic Policy Review* 15, no. 1 (July): 19–30.

Singh, Ajit. 2009. "Better to Be Rough and Relevant Than to be Precise and Irrelevant: Reddaway's Legacy to Economics." *Cambridge Journal of Economics* 33, no. 3 (May): 363–79.

Skidelsky, Robert. 2001. *John Maynard Keynes*, Vol. 3, *Fighting for Freedom, 1937–1946.* New York: Viking Penguin.

Skidelsky, Robert. 2020. "Keynes v Hayek: The Four Buts . . ." In *From the Past to the Future: Ideas and Actions for a Free Society.* Stanford, CA: Hoover Institution. https://www.hoover.org /sites/default/files/mps_skidelsky.pdf.

Slichter, Gertrude Almy. 1956. "Franklin D. Roosevelt and the Farm Problem, 1929–1932." *Mississippi Valley Historical Review* 43, no. 2 (September): 238–58.

Slichter, Sumner H. 1932. "Should the Budget Be Balanced?" *New Republic*, April 20.

Slichter, Sumner H. 1938. "The Downturn of 1937." *Review of Economics and Statistics* 20, no. 3 (August): 97–110.

Smiley, Gene. 1983. "Recent Unemployment Rate Estimates for the 1920s and 1930s." *Journal of Economic History* 43, no. 2 (June): 487–93.

Smiley, Gene. 2002. *Rethinking the Great Depression.* Chicago: Ivan R. Dee.

Smiley, Gene, and Richard H. Keehn. 1988. "Margin Purchases, Brokers' Loans and the Bull Market of the Twenties." *Business and Economic History* 17: 129–42.

Smith, Jason. 2016. "About that Graph . . ." Information Transfer Economics (blog), June 25. https://informationtransfereconomics.blogspot.com/2016/06/about-that-graph.html.

Smith, Noah. 2020. "FDR's New Deal Worked. We Need Another One." *Bloomberg,* May 15. https://www.bloomberg.com/view/articles/2020-05-15/u-s-economy-needs-another-new -deal-for-coronavirus-depression.

Snyder, Robert E. 1975. "Huey Long and the Presidential Election of 1936." *Journal of the Louisiana Historical Association* 16, no. 2 (Spring): 117–43.

Sobel, Robert. 1968. *The Great Bull Market: Wall Street in the 1920s.* New York: Norton.

Sobel, Robert. 1998. *Coolidge: An American Enigma.* Washington, DC: Regnery.

Spero, Herbert. 1939. *Reconstruction Finance Corporation Loans to the Railroads, 1932–1937.* New York: Bankers Publishing.

Spielmans, John V. 1941. "Strikes under the Wagner Act." *Journal of Political Economy* 49, no. 5 (October): 722–31.

Sprinkel, Beryl Wayne. 1952. "Economic Consequences of the Operations of the Reconstruction Finance Corporation." *Journal of Business of the University of Chicago* 25, no. 4 (October): 211–24.

Stanton, Bernard F. 2007. *George F. Warren: Farm Economist.* Ithaca, NY: Cornell University Press.

Stebenne, David L. 1996. "The Postwar 'New Deal.'" *International Labor and Working Class History* 50 (Fall): 140–47.

Steelman, John R. 1946. *The Second Year of Peace: Eighth Report to the President, the Senate, and the House, by the Director of War Mobilization and Reconversion.* Washington, DC: US Government Printing Office.

Steil, Benn. 2024. *The World That Wasn't: Henry Wallace and the Fate of the American Century.* New York: Avid Reader.

Stein, Herbert. 1966. "Pre-Revolutionary Fiscal Policy: The Regime of Herbert Hoover." *Journal of Law and Economics* 9 (October): 189–223.

Stein, Herbert. 1990. *The Fiscal Revolution in America.* Washington, DC: AEI.

Steindl, Frank G. 2007. "What Ended the Great Depression? It was Not World War II." *Independent Review* 12, no. 2 (Fall): 179–97.

Sternshen, Bernard. 1964. *Rexford Tugwell and the New Deal.* New Brunswick, NJ: Rutgers University Press.

Stokey, Nancy L. 2016. "Wait-and-See: Investment Options under Policy Uncertainty." *Review of Economic Dynamics* 21 (July): 246–65.

Strout, Richard Lee. 1941. "Hansen of Harvard." *New Republic* 105 (December 29): 888–90.

Sullivan, Lawrence. 1938. "Relief and the Election." *The Atlantic,* November 1938.

Sumner, Scott. 2001. "Roosevelt, Warren, and the Gold Buying Program of 1933." *Research in Economic History* 20 (November): 135–72.

Sumner, Scott. 2010. "What Evils Can Result from an Election! (1932, pt. 3 of 5)." TheMoneyIllusion (blog), March 23. https://www.themoneyillusion.com/what-evils-can-result-from -an-election-1932-pt-3-of-5/.

Sumner, Scott. 2015. *The Midas Paradox: Financial Markets, Government Policy Shocks, and the Great Depression.* Oakland, CA: Independent Institute.

Sumner, Scott. 2018. "Irving Fisher and George Warren." TheMoneyIllusion (blog), June 7. https://www.themoneyillusion.com/irving-fisher-and-george-warren/.

Sunbury, Ben. 1990. *The Fall of the Farm Credit Empire.* Ames: Iowa University Press.

Sundquist, James L., Bertram R. Gross, Leon H. Keyserling, and Walter S. Salant. 1981. "The Employment Act of 1946." In *Economics and the Truman Administration,* edited by Francis H. Heller, 97–109. Lawrence: Regents Press of Kansas.

Sweezy, Alan R. 1972. "The Keynesians and Government Policy, 1933–1939." *American Economic Review* 62, no. 2 (May): 116–24.

"Taxpayers Revolt: Democrats Admit Loss of Former Enthusiastic Backers of New Deal." 1938. *New York Times,* November 10.

Taylor, Jason E. 2011. "Work-Sharing during the Great Depression: Did the 'President's Reemployment Agreement' Promote Reemployment?" *Economica* 78, no. 309 (January): 133–58.

Taylor, Jason E. 2019. *Deconstructing the Monolith: The Microeconomics of the National Recovery Act.* Chicago: University of Chicago Press.

Taylor, Jason E., and Todd C. Neumann. 2013. "The Effect of Institutional Regime Change within the New Deal on Industrial Output and Labor Markets." *Explorations in Economic History* 50, no. 4 (October): 582–98.

Taylor, Jason E., and Todd C. Neumann. 2016. "Recovery Spring, Faltering Fall: March to November 1933." *Explorations in Economic History* 61, no. 3 (July): 54–67.

Taylor, Jason, and George Selgin. 1999. "By Our Bootstraps: Origins and Effects of the High-Wage Doctrine and the Minimum Wage." *Journal of Labor Research* 20, no. 4 (December): 447–62.

Taylor, Jason E., and Richard K. Vedder. 2010. "Stimulus by Spending Cuts: Lessons from 1946." Cato Institute *Policy Report* 32, no. 3 (May–June): 1–7.

Taylor, Timothy. 2015. "Pushing on a String: An Origin Story." Conversable Economist (blog), July 30. https://conversableeconomist.blogspot.com/2015/07/pushing-on-string-origin-story.html.

Telser, Lester G. 2001. "Higher Member Bank Reserve Ratios in 1936 and 1937 Did Not Cause the Relapse into Depression." *Journal of Post Keynesian Economics* 24, no. 2 (Winter): 205–16.

Temin, Peter. 1976. *Did Monetary Forces Cause the Great Depression?* New York: Norton.

Temin, Peter. 1996. "The Great Depression." In *The Cambridge Economic History of the United States,* Vol. 3, *The Twentieth Century,* edited by Stanley L. Engerman and Robert L. Gallman, 301–28. Cambridge: Cambridge University Press.

Temin, Peter, and Barrie A. Wigmore. 1990. "The End of One Big Deflation." *Explorations in Economic History* 27, no. 4 (October): 483–502.

"Text of du Pont's Address before Industrialists." 1937. *New York Times,* December 8.

"Text of the Roosevelt-Howard Letters." 1935. *New York Times,* September 7.

Thies, Clifford F., and Daniel A. Gerlowski. 1989. "Deposit Insurance: A History of Failure." *Cato Journal* 8, no. 3 (Winter): 677–93.

Thomas, Norman. 1938. *Socialism on the Defensive.* New York: Harper & Brothers.

Thorndike, Joseph J. 2009. "'The Unfair Advantage of the Few': The New Deal Origins of 'Soak the Rich' Taxation." In *The New Fiscal Sociology: Taxation in Comparative and Historical Perspective,* edited by Isaac William Martin, Ajay K. Mehrotra, and Monica Prasad, 29–47. Cambridge: Cambridge University Press.

Thorndike, Joseph J. 2010. "The Fiscal Revolution and Taxation: The Rise of Compensatory Taxation, 1929–1938." *Law and Contemporary Problems* 73, no. 1 (Winter): 95–122.

"3 Reply to Keynes on NRA Criticism." 1934. *New York Times*, January 1.

Timberlake, Richard H., Jr. 2007. "Gold Standards and the Real Bills Doctrine in U.S. Monetary Policy." *Independent Review* 1 no. 3 (Winter): 325–54.

Titcomb, James. 2015. "How the Bank of England Abandoned the Gold Standard," *The Telegraph*, January 7. https://www.telegraph.co.uk/finance/commodities/11330611/How-the-Bank-of -England-abandoned-the-gold-standard.html.

Toland, John. 1977. *Adolf Hitler*. London: Book Club Associates.

Toma, Mark. 1992. "Interest Rate Controls: The United States in the 1940s." *Journal of Economic History* 52, no. 3 (September): 631–50.

Traflet, Janice M. 2013. *A Nation of Small Shareholders: Marketing Wall Street after World War II*. Baltimore: Johns Hopkins University Press.

Truman, Harry S. 1945a. Letter to Ganson Purcell, Chairman of the SEC, 17 May 1945. Files of Chairmen Ganson Purcell and James J. Caffrey, and Commissioners Robert H. O'Brien and Robert K. McConnaughey, 1939–1948, box 50, Records of the Securities and Exchange Commission, RG 266, National Archives, College Park, MD.

Truman, Harry S. 1945b. "Special Message to the Congress Presenting a 21-Point Program for the Reconversion Period: September 6." The American Presidency Project. https://www .presidency.ucsb.edu/node/230568.

Truman, Harry S. 1946. "Veto of the Price Control Bill: June 29." The American Presidency Project. https://www.presidency.ucsb.edu/node/232234.

Tugwell, Rexford G. 1932. "The Principle of Planning and the Institution of Laissez Faire." *American Economic Review* 22, no. 1 (March): 75–92.

Tugwell, Rexford G. 1956. Review of James MacGregor Burns, "Roosevelt: The Lion and the Fox." *Chicago Sun-Times*, August 12.

Tugwell, Rexford G. 1957. *The Democratic Roosevelt*. Garden City, NY: Doubleday.

Tugwell, Rexford G. 1965. "Transition: Hoover to Roosevelt, 1932-1933." *Centennial Review* 9, no. 2 (Spring): 160–91.

Tugwell, Rexford G. 1968. *The Brain Trust*. New York: Viking.

Tugwell, Rexford G. 1970. "Roosevelt and Frankfurter: An Essay Review." *Political Science Quarterly* 85, no. 1 (March): 99–114.

Tuttle, William M., Jr. 1981. "The Birth of an Industry: The Synthetic Rubber 'Mess' in World War II." *Technology and Culture* 22, no. 1 (January): 35–67.

US Bureau of Demobilization. 1947. *Industrial Mobilization for War: History of the War Production Board and Predecessor Agencies: 1940–1945*. Washington, DC: US Government Printing Office.

US Department of Agriculture. 1940. *Report of the Secretary of Agriculture*. Washington, DC: US Government Printing Office.

US Department of Agriculture. 2024. "Farm Sector Income & Finances: Farm Sector Income Forecast." Economic Research Service, February 7.

US Department of Labor. 1936. *Analysis of Strikes and Lockouts in 1934 and Analysis for September 1935*. Washington, DC: US Government Printing Office.

US Department of Labor. 1940. "Economic Status of WPA Workers Dismissed under 1939 Relief Act." *Monthly Labor Review* 50, no 3 (March): 622–27.

US Department of Labor. 1946a. *Women Workers in Ten War Production Areas and Their Postwar Employment Plans*. Bulletin No. 209. Washington, DC: US Government Printing Office.

US Department of Labor. 1946b. *Workers' Experiences during First Phase of Reconversion*. Bulletin No. 876. Washington, DC: US Government Printing Office.

US Department of Labor. 1953. *Women as Workers: A Statistical Guide.* Washington, DC: US Government Printing Office.

US Department of the Treasury. 1932. *Annual Report of the Secretary of the Treasury on the State of the Finances for Fiscal Year ended June 30, 1932.* Washington, DC: US Government Printing Office.

US Department of the Treasury. 1933. *Documents and Statements Pertaining to the Banking Emergency.* Washington, DC: US Government Printing Office.

US Federal Housing Administration. 1935. *Underwriting Manual: Underwriting and Valuation Procedure under Title II of the National Housing Act.* Washington, DC: US Government Printing Office.

US Government Accountability Office. 2022. *Coronavirus Food Assistance Program: USDA Should Conduct More Rigorous Reviews of Payments to Producers.* GAO-22-104397. https://www.gao.gov/products/gao-22-104397.

US House. 1929. *Agricultural Relief: Hearings before the Committee on Agriculture.* Committee on Agriculture, 71st Cong., 1–3 sess., March 27. https://books.google.com/books?id=yOccAAA AMAAJ&pg=PP5#v=onepage&q&f=false

US House. 1933. *Banking Act of 1933: Report (To Accompany H.R. 5661).* Committee on Banking and Currency, 73rd Cong., 1st sess., H. Rep. no. 150.

US House. 1935. *Banking Act of 1935: Hearings Before the Committee on Banking and Currency on H.R. 5357.* Committee on Banking and Currency, 74th Cong., 1st sess., February 21–April 8.

US House. 1939. *Investigation of Concentration of Economic Power: Economic Prologue.* Temporary National Economic Committee, December 1–3, 1938.

US National Archives. n.d. "Vincent Astor: Millionaire, Philanthropist, Spy, and Friend of President Roosevelt." Google Arts & Culture. https://artsandculture.google.com/story/vincent-astor-u-s-national-archives/EgVxQyhXXB8A8A?hl=en.

US Senate. 1937. "Reorganization of the Federal Judiciary: Adverse Report." Committee on the Judiciary, 75th Cong., 1st sess., June 7.

US Senate. 1938. *Unemployment and Relief: Hearings before a Special Committee to Investigate Unemployment and Relief on S. Res. 36.* Special Committee to Investigate Unemployment and Relief, 75th Cong., 3rd sess., January 4–22.

US Senate. 1941a. *Devaluation of the Dollar and Stabilization Fund: Hearings before the Committee on Currency and Banking.* Committee on Currency and Banking, 77th Cong., 1st sess., June 13–19.

US Senate. 1941b. *Final Report and Recommendation of the Temporary National Economic Committee.* 77th Cong., 1st sess., Senate Doc. No. 35.

US Senate. 1945. *Administration of Certain Lending Agencies of the Federal Government.* Hearings before the Committee on Commerce on S.375. 79th Cong., 1st sess., January 24 and 25 (statement of Hon. Jesse H. Jones, Secretary of Commerce and federal loan administrator).

US Senate. 1950. *Study of Reconstruction Finance Corporation.* Hearings before a Subcommittee of the Committee on Banking and Currency. 81st Cong., 1st and 2nd sess. (multiple volumes).

US Senate. 1951. *Study of Reconstruction Finance Corporation. Interim Report.* Committee on Banking and Currency, 82nd Cong., 1st Session, S. Rep. 76.

Vatter, Harold G. 1985. *The U.S. Economy in World War II.* New York: Columbia University Press.

Vedder, Richard K., and Lowell E. Gallaway. 1991. "The Great Depression of 1946." *Review of Austrian Economics* 5, no. 2 (September): 3–31.

Velde, François. 2009. "The Recession of 1937—A Cautionary Tale." Federal Reserve Bank of Chicago. *Economic Perspectives* 33 (4th quarter): 16–37.

Vernengo, Matías. 2009. "A Hands-off Central Banker? Marriner S. Eccles and the Federal Reserve, 1934–51." In *American Power and Policy*, edited by Robert Leeson, 69–90. London: Palgrave Macmillan.

Vernon, J. R. 1994. "World War II Fiscal Policies and the End of the Great Depression." *Journal of Economic History* 54, no. 4 (December): 850–68.

Vox. 2022. "Why People Thought Steel Houses Were a Good Idea." YouTube. https://www.you tube.com/watch?v=jnxjRXwC1no.

Waddell, Brian. 1999. "Corporate Influence and World War II: Resolving the New Deal Political Stalemate." *Journal of Policy History* 11, no. 3 (July): 223–56.

Wallace, Henry A. 1934. *New Frontiers*, New York: Reynal & Hitchcock.

Wallace, Henry A. 1945. *Sixty Million Jobs*. New York: Reynal and Hitchcock, Simon and Schuster.

Waller, Spencer Weber. 2004. "The Antitrust Legacy of Thurman Arnold." *St. John's Law Review* 78: 569–614.

Wallis, John Joseph, and Daniel K. Benjamin. 1981. "Public Relief and Private Employment in the Great Depression." *Journal of Economic History* 41, no. 1 (March): 97–102.

Wallis, John J., Price V. Fishback, and Shawn E. Kantor. 2006. "Politics, Relief, and Reform: Roosevelt's Efforts to Control Corruption and Political Manipulation during the New Deal." In *Corruption and Reform: Lessons from America's Economic History*, edited by Edward L. Glaeser and Claudia Goldin, 343–72. Chicago: University of Chicago Press.

Wapshott, Nicholas. 2011. *Keynes Hayek: The Clash That Defined Modern Economics*. New York: Norton.

Warburg, James P. 1934. *The Money Muddle*. London: Routledge.

Warburg, James P. 1935. *Hell Bent for Election*. New York: Doubleday.

Warne, Colston E. 1945. "The Reconversion of Women." *Current History* 8, no. 43 (March): 200–206.

Warren, George F., and Frank A. Pearson. 1935. *Gold and Prices*. New York: Wiley.

Wasem, Ruth E. 2013. *Tackling Unemployment: The Legislative Dynamics of the Employment Act of 1946*. Kalamazoo, MI: W.E. Upjohn Institute for Employment Research.

Weiman, David. 2011. "Imagining a World without the New Deal," *Washington Post*, August 12.

Weinstein, Michael M. 1980. *Recovery and Redistribution under the NIRA*. Amsterdam: North-Holland.

Wheelock, David C. 1995. "Regulation, Market Structure and the Bank Failures of the Great Depression." Federal Reserve Bank of St. Louis *Review* 77, no. 2 (March–April): 27–38.

Wheelock, David C. 2008. "The Federal Response to Home Mortgage Distress: Lessons from the Great Depression." Federal Reserve Bank of St. Louis *Review* 90, no. 31 (May–June, part 1): 133–48.

Wheelock, David C., and Paul W. Wilson. 1994. "Can Deposit Insurance Increase the Risk of Bank Failure? Some Historical Evidence." Federal Reserve Bank of St. Louis *Review* 76, no. 3 (May/June): 57–71.

Wheelock, David C., and Paul W. Wilson. 1995. "Explaining Bank Failures: Deposit Insurance, Regulation, and Efficiency." *Review of Economics and Statistics* 77, no. 4 (November): 689–700.

White, Ahmed. 2010. "The Depression Era Sit-Down Strikes and the Limits of Liberal Labor Law." *Seton Hall Law Review* 40, no. 1: 1–81.

White, Eugene Nelson. 1983. *The Regulation and Reform of the American Banking System, 1900–1929*. Princeton, NJ: Princeton University Press.

White, Eugene Nelson. 1984. "A Reinterpretation of the Banking Crisis of 1933." *Journal of Economic History* 44, no. 1 (March): 119–38.

White, Eugene Nelson. 1986. "Before the Glass-Steagall Act: An Analysis of the Investment Banking Activities of National Banks." *Explorations in Economic History* 23, no. 1 (January): 33–55.

White, Eugene Nelson. 1990. "The Stock Market Boom and Crash of 1929 Revisited." *Journal of Economic Perspectives* 4, no. 2 (Spring): 67–83.

White, Eugene Nelson. 1998. "The Legacy of Deposit Insurance: The Growth, Spread, and Cost of Insuring Financial Intermediaries." In *The Defining Moment: The Great Depression and the American Economy in the Twentieth Century*, edited by Michael D. Bordo, Claudia Goldin, and Eugene N. White, 87–122. Chicago: University of Chicago Press and National Bureau of Economic Research.

White, Eugene Nelson. 2014. "Lessons from the Great American Real Estate Boom and Bust of the 1920s." In *Housing and Mortgage Markets in Historical Perspective*, edited by Eugene N. White, Kenneth Snowden, and Price Fishback, 115–58. Chicago: University of Chicago Press and National Bureau of Economic Research.

White, Lawrence H. 2012. *The Clash of Economic Ideas: The Great Policy Debates and Experiments of the Last Hundred Years*. New York: Cambridge University Press.

The White House. 1933. "Press Conference #1." FRANKLIN: Access to the FDR Library's Digital Collection, March 8. http://www.fdrlibrary.marist.edu/_resources/images/pc/pc0183.pdf

The White House. 1947. Council of Economic Advisers. *Economic Report of the President, Transmitted to the Congress January 8, 1947*. Washington, DC: US Government Printing Office.

The White House. 2006. Council of Economic Advisers. *Economic Report of the President: Transmitted to the Congress February 13, 2006*. Washington, DC: US Government Printing Office.

Whitman, James Q. 1991. "Of Corporatism, Fascism, and the First New Deal." *American Journal of Comparative Law* 39, no. 4 (Autumn): 747–78.

Wicker, Elmus. 1971. "Roosevelt's 1933 Monetary Experiment." *Journal of American History* 57, no. 4 (March): 864–79.

Wicker, Elmus. 1980. "A Reconsideration of the Causes of the Banking Panic of 1930." *Journal of Economic History* 40, no. 3 (September): 571–83.

Widmar, David. 2019. "Farm-Level Implication of MFP Payments." Agricultural Economic Insights (blog), November 10. https://aei.ag/2019/11/10/farm-level-implication-of-mfp-payments/.

Wieland, Johannes F. 2019. "Are Negative Supply Shocks Expansionary at the Zero Lower Bound?" *Journal of Political Economy* 127, no. 3 (April): 973–1007.

Wigmore, Barrie A. 1987. "Was the Bank Holiday of 1933 Caused by a Run on the Dollar?" *Journal of Economic History* 47, no. 3 (September): 739–55.

Wilcox, James A. 1984. "Excess Reserves in the Great Depression." NBER Working Paper No. 1374. National Bureau of Economic Research, Cambridge, MA, June.

Williams, John C. 2003. "The Natural Rate of Interest." Federal Reserve Bank of San Francisco *Economics Letter* 32 (October): 1–3.

Williams, John H. 1931. "The Gold Problem." *Proceedings of the Academy of Political Science* 14, no. 3 (June): 111–17.

Williams, John H. 1942. "The Implications of Fiscal Policy for Monetary Policy and the Banking System." *American Economic Review* 32, no. 1 (March): 234–49.

Wilmarth, Arthur E., Jr. 2018. "Was Glass-Steagall's Demise Both Inevitable and Unimportant?" The CLS Blue Sky Blog, September 18. https://clsbluesky.law.columbia.edu/2018/09/18/was -glass-steagalls-demise-both-inevitable-and-unimportant/#_ftnref4.

Wilson, Joan Hoff. 1977. "Hoover's Agricultural Policies, 1921–1928." *Agricultural History* 51, no. 2 (April): 335–61.

Wilson, Mark R. 2016. *Destructive Creation: American Business and the Winning of World War II.* Philadelphia: University of Pennsylvania Press.

Wilson, William H. 1966. "The Two New Deals: A Valid Concept?" *The Historian* 28, no. 2 (February): 268–88.

Witham, Charlie. 2016. *Post-War Business Planners in the United States, 1939–48: The Rise of the Corporate Moderates.* London: Bloomsbury.

Withers, Hartley. 1914. *Poverty and Waste.* New York: E. P. Dutton.

Woytinsky, Wladimir S. 1942. *Three Aspects of Labor Dynamics.* Washington, DC: Social Science Research Council Committee on Social Security.

Wright, Gavin. 1974. "The Political Economy of New Deal Spending: An Econometric Analysis." *Review of Economics and Statistics* 56, no. 1 (February): 30–38.

Wright, Robert. 2001. "Clinton's One Big Idea." *New York Times*, January 16.

Young, James T. 1935. Review of *The National Recovery Administration: An Analysis and Appraisal,* by Leverett S. Lyon et al. *American Political Science Review* 29, no. 5 (October): 881–83.

Zelizer, Julian E. 2000. "The Forgotten Legacy of the New Deal: Fiscal Conservatism and the Roosevelt Administration, 1933–1938." *Presidential Studies Quarterly* 30, no. 2 (June): 331–58.

Zweig, Jason. 2011. "Keynes: He Didn't Say Half of What He Said. Or Did He?" *Wall Street Journal*, February 11.

Index

Page numbers followed by "f" or "t" refer to figures or tables, respectively.